FEEL ALIVE II

UNLOCK

your infinite

POWER

RALPH SMART

One of the hallmarks of Ralph Smart books is the depth of diving deep within yourself to unlock your true power and fly.

Published by Infinite Waters

ISBN: 978-1-0369-0836-2

First published by Ralph Smart Ltd. 2025

Typeset by Ralph Smart

Printed and bound in United Kingdom by Lightning Source Ltd.

Being free is your birthright!

www.ralphsmart.com

Dedicated to

Mama Catherine and the Infinite Waters Deep Divers

May your lives be filled with blessings

Yours sincerely

Ralph

"I was very pleased with the session and the insight that was given. My concerns were listened to and I felt like I was talking to a best friend. I would recommend a consultation to anyone because of the authentic and genuine advice that was given to help me be happier and worry less about my problems."

Erica Suter, Client

"I love watching Ralph's videos on Youtube and I was given the gift of a private consultation with him over Skype. I couldn't have asked for a greater gift than this, for the session was like watching the same Ralph on Youtube, but times 100 because of the personal interaction.Thank you Ralph!

"Kevin Eftekhari, Client

"Many thanks to Infinite Waters, AKA Ralph Smart, for providing me with his invaluable insight, which I found to be extraordinarily helpful on my journey toward personal growth & self discovery. It was so wonderful seeing him on Skype! He's truly as genuine as he comes across on YouTube."

Janine Blunt, Client

"This man was sent by the universe to guide many souls who are in the search for enlightenment, freedom and inner self love. He is a universal enlightened soul who has the ability to connect, change and touch many hearts with his intelligent and spiritual approach. Keep up the mission! Infinite Love!"

Tamara Scott, Client

"My session with Ralph was insightful, simple to the point, and pleasant. His competency in relating and understanding people is vast, he will listen and put you at ease. He is the real deal!"

Mamoni K, Client

"I'm glad, I have decided to take the counselling session with Ralph — it helped me broaden my perspective and gave me very practical things to do to maintain that positive attitude."

Philip Smirnov, Client

"The impact Ralph had on me in our 1-to-1 session was absolutely incredible. He showed me the clear path to my biggest goals, without judgement. His words are powerfully precise and cut through a lot of the noise that I was hearing previously.. Straight up, he's an awesome guy."

Rafael Eliassen, Client

"With gratitude I honor the deep wisdom I've been given along the path. I honor each lesson, no matter how difficult, for it brought me here. I celebrate this moment and I allow the feeling of gratitude to bathe my cells."

Vincent Lauren, Client

"It was an amazing session, I struggled at the start thinking if I should get coaching and Ralph really helped me open up, when I've been feeling stuck for so long. Like a energy ball of positivity, I remembered who I was. Honouring myself and being honest with my emotions."

Karen Jones, Client

"I found my session with Ralph to be an absolutely valuable experience. I was really being listened to and understood. I was going through one of the toughest and scariest experiences of my life in the past two weeks, and in a time of great fear, I felt undeniable positivity in his presence."

Patrick Kim, Client

By the same author

Feel Alive By Ralph Smart

Tryathon The Love Of A Galaxy

The Book Of 1111 Infinite Quotes

FEEL ALIVE II

UNLOCK

your infinite

POWER

RALPH SMART

Table of Contents

1	The 3D/5D Split Has Begun	19
2	Never Feel Alone In Your Truth	27
3	Dealing With Other People's Perspectives	33
4	12 Lies People Accept As Truth	41
5	12 Life Lessons People Learn Too Late	47
6	30 Life Lessons Learnt In 30 Years	55
7	Become A Ghost, Delete Social Media	67
8	Sacrifice And Get Disciplined	73
9	Delete Friends, Find Yourself	79
10	For People Who Don't Fit In Anywhere	85
11	Why You're Alone	91
12	Find Yourself When You're Lost, Alone & Unmotivated	97
13	5 Powerful Ways Twinflames Recognise Each Other	103
14	10 Secrets Soul Mates Won't Tell You	107

Table of Contents

15   10 Things To Remember If Your Partner Ends Your Relationship   115

16   How To Decide To Let Someone Go   123

17   How To Spot Your True Soul Mate   129

18   How To Tell if Someone's Meant To Be In Your Life   135

19   Accept Yourself Before It's Too Late   141

20   Stop Chasing Love And Relationships   148

21   5 Ways To Get Rid Of Anxiety   150

22   Be Brave, Lose The Fear, Go For It   156

23   How To Accept Yourself 100%   162

24   How To Get A Tranquil Mind   170

25   How To Let Go Of The Past   174

26   How To Let Go Of What's Weighing Your Heart Down   180

27   How To Completely Heal Your Body And Mind   190

28   How To Achieve Supreme Confidence   198

Table of Contents

29 Stop Being Nice, How To Gain Respect — 204

30 Why People Try To Bring You Down — 210

31 Alkaline Drinks To Flush Out Toxins And Mucus — 216

32 Alkaline Foods To Flush Out Toxins And Mucus — 220

33 10 Secrets Marijuana Smokers Won't Tell You — 224

34 How To Stop Feeding Your Fears — 230

35 How To Stop Living In The Past — 235

36 Stop People, Situations Destroying Your Peace Of Mind — 241

37 How To Stop Procrastinating — 248

38 How To Not Take Things Personally, And Care Less — 254

39 Stop Resistance, Move Forward: 10 Breakthrough Secrets — 260

40 Why I Stopped Watching Porn — 268

41 7 Signs Your Manifestation Is Near — 272

42 8 Life Changing Affirmations For Wealth, Success, & Happiness — 278

Table of Contents

43	12 Secrets To Attract Anything With Your Mind	284
44	How To Manifest Breakthroughs And Make Good Things Come	294
45	The 'Thank You' Secret	300
46	How To Manifest 33 Magic	304
47	How To Manifest Magic Money	308
48	How To Manifest Money	314
49	How To Successfully Manifest Your Dreams And Goals	322
50	How To Move Out Of A Scarcity Mind	330
51	How To Attract A Water Relationship	336
52	How To Attract Someone You Want	344
53	The 7 Hermetic Principles	352
54	9 Passive Income Ideas, How I Make $28K Per Week	360
55	How To Think And Grow Rich	368
56	How I Quit My 9-5, And Replaced It With Freedom	376

Table of Contents

57 Stop Chasing Money And Financial Freedom 382

58 10 Reasons You Should Never Open Your Third Eye 390

59 10 Signs You're Highly Awake 398

60 How To Lucid Dream 406

61 The Dark Side Of Being Highly Awake 412

62 The Nine Types Of Chosen Ones 418

63 8 Messages From The Universe You Shouldn't Ignore 426

64 10 Signs The Universe Is Telling You Something Important 434

65 10 Warning Signs From Universe You're On The Wrong Path 442

66 12 Signs You're Doing Better Than You Think 448

67 10 Smart Ways To Find Your True Purpose 456

68 How To Let Go And Trust The Universe 464

69 How To Receive Messages From The Universe 470

70 Shadow Work 101 480

Table of Contents

71   How To Stop Thinking About Someone You Love   490

Introduction

Meet Ralph Smart – YouTube Sensation with over Two Million Subscribers

Ralph Smart- If you haven't heard the name before, you've been missing out on something big-something that millions have discovered before you. And as you start your Smart journey today,undoubtedly you'll tap into a phenomenon that has the potential to take your world and consciousness to the next level. Ralph Smart has been helping millions of people around the world become the better version of themselves since 2008. One of the UK's most talented YouTubers with over 2m followers and counting, Ralph has been featured in numerous major publications. A dedicated self-improvement content creator, Smart started his mission to save and change lives by posting one motivational video per day and has remained committed to the challenge since. In these videos millions of people are finding the road map to true happiness, personal fulfilment and overall wellness.

A YouTube Star, Leading the Charge in Personal Development

His YouTube Channel, Infinite Waters (Diving Deep) is a reservoir of knowledge into which many have dipped into and drank their fill. As a result, Ralph Smart's name has become a buzz word in conversations in the virtual and physical spheres. His inspiration is so powerful that it has reached far into the corners of the earth. A recipient of YouTube's major gold award, this Ralph has truly mastered the art of converting knowledge and talent into an impressively successful movement. With millions of viewers and subscribers, Ralph Smart stands out as YouTube's most popular motivational coach. His YouTube channel has been ranked in the top five in categories such as motivation, yoga and personal development. Of course, his popularity is a clear indicator of the depth of his expertise. His channel has attracted two million subscribers and his videos have views ranging from thousands to millions. His videos explore topics and issues that affect individuals from all levels of society and the testimonials seen in the comment sections reveal that his advice is yielding positive results. These include topics related to relationships, mental health and motivation. In addition to self-improvement videos, he also has a collection of calming music videos on his channels.

Ralph Smart- Leading Authority

It is no wonder that Smart has been able to appeal to so many followers. He has amassed an depth knowledge in the fields of psychology and criminology, two disciplines that focus on human thinking and behaviour. His formal training in the field started when he entered Westminster University at a remarkably early age of 17. Smart then engaged in deep exploration of the human condition. His tenacity and determination paid off when he graduated with BA (honours) in Criminology and Psychology at the age of 20. This expansive knowledge coupled with his oratorical expertise have been masterfully combined by Smart to create unique content that appeal to a wide audience. His content collection is impressive with over 100 videos posted to YouTube, and of course, this collection is continuously expanding as Smart channels his energy toward attaining his main objective-helping millions of people around the world to discover and become their best selves.

The Road Ahead for Ralph Smart

Without a doubt, Ralph Smart has stamped an indelible print on the virtual road as one of YouTube's most successful influencers. He has coached, encouraged and inspired his way into the hearts of millions worldwide who are now reaping the benefits of his remarkable expertise. With a rapidly growing reputation that has already crossed gender, race and geographic boundaries, this exceptional influencer is poised to multiply his impact over time, reaching millions more with his life-changing message of self-improvement.

Chapter One

The 3D/5D Split Has Begun

I hope you're getting your butt into the heart of nature these days because this is where it's at. Nature is where the party happens. We're in 5D out here. The 3D, 5D split has begun. And it's important to avoid distractions during this pivotal time. So, how do you avoid distractions and stay focused on your purpose? Have you noticed there's a massive split that's happened in the world between the 3D and the 5D?

Now the 3D deals with limitation, fear, and lack. And the 5D, well, it's a little Samba baby. It deals with love, freedom. And with this split happening, we're gonna talk about something that's affecting a lot of people. And that is how to avoid distractions in the matrix and stay focused on your purpose. A lot of people say, gosh, Ralph, you're so consistent. You're so focused on your purpose,

Right now, we are living in a whole new world and this is not Aladdin. We're living in a world where some people are truly waking up to who they really are and what this world is. And they're freeing themselves from all of these chains of society. And they're becoming their greatest version. And they're letting go of society's expectations, congratulations, and they're following their dreams.

At the same time, the 3D seeks to distract you away from your true purpose every single second. Bread and circuses surround us, sports and entertainment surround us.

Celebrity gossip surrounds us, and it's hard to stay focused out here in the sea of distractions. If you are someone who's dealing with a whole load of distractions right now, if you are someone who is finding it hard to stay in your true purpose, remind yourself of this, deep divers, remind yourself of this, that energy flows where attention goes. I said energy flows where attention goes.

If you wanna live in the 5D with a cat down the road, where love reigns supreme, where you can become your greatest version, you have to realize this, that energy, your energy flows where your attention goes. So remind yourself that they call it paying attention for a reason because anytime you pay attention, you are making an energetic cash transaction. There's a reason why they call money currency.

It's all energy, it's all energy. So what you pay attention to, you are actually giving your energy to. So make sure whatever you pay attention to in this world, in the matrix, that you have a ROI – a return on investment.

Look, I pay attention to everything that helps me grow, that helps me become my greatest version because it's worth it. You know why? Because I get my return on investment. But sometimes, deep divers, you're watching something, maybe a music video, maybe someone on the news, and you're like, oh my gosh, my whole energy feels depleted right now. They've just stolen your energy.

So you've paid them something, that's your attention, but you haven't gotten anything back in return. That's not smart. And that's what distracts you from your true path and purpose. So to avoid these distractions and stay focused on your purpose, say, I'm only going to share my energy and allow my energy to flow where I receive energy back. It's got to be reciprocal because energy flows where attention goes. I'm only going to pay attention to what is helping me become my greatest version. I'm going to do away with conversations no longer helping me evolve.

I'm going to do away with people who are keeping me in an arrested state of development, in the 3D, full of fear. Ain't nobody got time for that, not even the cat down the road. Deep divers, we're all about the 5D. You've got to remind yourself if what they're talking about is not helping you evolve, it's a distraction.

You've got to let go of entertaining anything that's not helping you grow as a human being. That's what helped me along my journey to avoid distractions and stay focused on my purpose. Stop entertaining gossip, drama.

If it's not helping you build your empire of greatness, ain't nobody got time for that. What if I told you, anything that's not helping you grow doesn't love you? Anything that's not helping you grow, evolve, become your greatest version, doesn't love you. Those gossip sites like TMZ, they don't love you.

They just want to distract you. And you've got to be self-disciplined to say, you know what? I'm going to choose because it's a choice. I'm going to choose to do what's right for me. I'm going to choose to make sure I'm no longer allowing myself to be tempted by lower vibrations and lower frequencies.

So, deep divers, the 3D, 5D split has begun how to avoid distractions and stay focused on your purpose. The three monkeys, see no evil, hear no evil, speak no evil, right? You have to remind yourself, deep divers, you're not only consuming through your mouth, you are consuming through all of your senses.

Don't just be concerned, seven day vegan challenge about stuffing a whole bunch of goji berries in your mouth. Also be concerned also about your mental diet. What are you feeding your mind? What are you listening to? That's also part of your diet.

What are you looking at? Are those images going to benefit you in your journey to become your greatest version? Or are they going to destroy you? So the three monkeys have that in the back of your mind. See no evil, hear no evil, speak no evil. And this is how to avoid distractions and stay focused on your purpose.

Now, what is evil? E-V-I-L. Evil is when you live in reverse. L-I-V-E, E-V-I-L, get it? We get distracted from our true purpose when we are living in reverse, when we are doing what the creator said not for us to do. So we've got to be firm with ourselves and say, you know what, I don't want to live in reverse.

It's so easy to get seduced out here in the matrix, but not everything that glitters is gold. Remind yourself, this whole system is a trap designed to take you away from who you really are. You've got to focus on yourself.

Do you watch the news regularly? No, because it's full of fear. Ain't nobody got time for that. The only time I watch the news is just to see what they're not saying. And... I say to myself, I am the news. Gaia is the real news.

People say, gosh, Ralph, how come you're always focused on your purpose, on your mission? And I tell them it's because I place myself in the right environment that reminds me what I'm here to do. It reminds me of the job at hand.

It reminds me I'm a multi-dimensional being having a human experience and I woke up like this all magical and fly, woo! Your environment governs who you eventually become. Your environment either brings you back into the greater part of who you really are or it takes you further away from who you really are. Ever gone into a neighbourhood and all of your dreams and visions are out of the window? You got no hope anymore? That environment did that to you.

When I'm out there in the heart of nature... in Gaia, just breathing in that good ass prana – I'm in the perfect place to manifest anything I desire.

A plant can only grow with sunlight and water in the right environment. You are a human plant. You are a human plant. To avoid distractions and stay focused on your true purpose, I realize you must place yourself in the right environment because once you do, you can grow to your full potential.

Are you focusing too much on the elections? The elections, the elections. Who are you voting for? Democrat, Republican? Well, I'm voting for myself. Vote for yourself every single day. Don't get caught up in the circus out there. It's all designed to distract you.

Deep divers, look, how I actually stay focused on my true purpose every single day and avoid distractions is to make sure I've got the right people in my ears. The cat down the road. I've got the right energy in my ears. I've got the right words in my ears.

What if I told you a lot of people walking around with headphones can't even hear themselves? Take off your headphones and listen to yourself, listen to your intuition. That's how to avoid distractions. What if I told you there are certain songs designed to keep you at a low frequency and vibration designed by the manipulators of the matrix? What if I told you that you have to make sure you have the right sound frequencies in your ears to avoid distractions and stay focused on your purpose? So I've got my mentor in my ear. I've got my mom in my ear who's also a mentor. I've got the cat down the road in my ear.

I've got the sounds of the birds, bees, leaves and trees in my ear. And this helps me to stay focused on my true purpose. Look, a lot of people let themselves go. Don't allow yourself to let yourself go. Because you've got to take care of yourself. Brush your teeth and all of that.

Yeah, you've got to do that. Many people get distracted because they just let themselves go. They drink too much and they forget that it has consequences. It's called a hangover. You can't be at your best the next day. Don't allow yourself to get in that position.

Stay focused and realize that you don't want to tempt yourself because there are so many temptations in this matrix. Say, actually, I'm going to restrict my screen time. Let me remind you, there's no wifi in the heart of nature, but I swear there's a better connection.

TikTok was designed to distract you. Now, if you do use it, make sure you've got a timer to say, I'm only going to use this for five seconds, then you've got to leave. You've got to leave and get your ass in the heart of nature because that's going to remind you who you really are so you can become your greatest version and be in your true purpose.

Check your screen time. It should be below one hour every single day. And this is how to avoid distractions and stay focused on your true purpose. Do you know how much time people spend on their mobile phone? It's over seven hours in the US and six hours across the world. That's a whole lot of time, a whole lot of distractions. At the same time, you've got to remind yourself there is a solution.

Switch it off. Switch it off and get the real connection. Remember who you really are. Remember, meaning put yourself back together. Remember, meaning go back to the membership of your true sovereignty. Meaning, come back to source energy. Come back to core frequency.

This is how to avoid distractions and stay focused on your true purpose. A lot of people get distracted. You know why? Because they forget about who they really are. They forget about why they came here. They forget about their true mission and purpose. They get lost in the source. Yeah, and this matrix claims so many souls. Right now, the 3D, 5D split has begun. There's a battle for the hearts and minds of the people.

There are inorganic ones who want to trick you, who want to deceive you, who want to distract you to steal your energy. And you have to say, you know what? I'm going to make it to the fifth dimension and I'm going to make sure I don't fall into their traps. I'm going to stay focused on my purpose because you know why? Listen, this is where I want my future self to be.

This is where I want my future self to live. This is how to avoid distractions and stay focused on your true purpose. Many years ago, I planted the seeds that my future self is now thanking me for.

Woo! So, imagine right now where you want your future self to be and how you want your future self to live. How you want your future self to live. Surely you want to wake up with a whole bunch of blueberries in your mouth on a beach somewhere in Costa Rica, living your best life, living it up.

Well, make sure you don't distract yourself right now because what you do now will influence who you will become tomorrow.

So make the most of every single second right now. Remind yourself, you don't need everything. You don't need carpets, do you? No. You don't need brick walls, do you? No. So why do you consume all that information? Sometimes you have to have a filter to say, actually, I'm not going to wake up with bad news on my phone. Turn off your phone. This is how to avoid distractions and stay focused on your purpose.

As soon as you wake up, don't reach for the phone. Say, you know what, I'm going to go for a jog. This is what will help you move back into true focus on your purpose.

It will release all of those beautiful endorphins and focus and discipline your mind. A lot of people don't realize the phone is a trap. As soon as you wake up, if you reach for that, of course you're going to be distracted. You're looking at everyone else's life, but you're not actually living.

So anything that you see, it must help you become your greatest version. And remind yourself, deep divers, that distractions will cease to exist. The moment you move into your true purpose and are grateful to be there, every single day I say, hey, I've won the lottery.

Do you think I'm going to waste it? Do you think I'm going to allow myself to be distracted? No, because I know if I do, it's going to take a long time to get back here because we're in the 5D, baby. Oh, we're in the 5D, doing a little Samba, baby. So don't rest on your laurels. That's how to not get distracted. Don't rest on your laurels. Like I told you, live life like you're on the run. Remind yourself, a lack of focus is the death of all potential.

So, remind yourself, the 3D, 5D split has begun and there are a lot of distractions in the 3D matrix. And to move to the 5D, you're going to have to avoid distractions and stay focused on your purpose.

2   Never Feel Alone In Your Truth

With each step, realize we are never alone unless we abandon ourselves, embrace the power of being alone and rise higher...

How do you make sure you never feel alone and stand strong in your truth? Someone wrote to me, they're like, Ralph, as I'm transitioning from the 3D to the 5D, sometimes I wake up and I'm like, oh my gosh, I'm all alone. Is this natural? Is this normal?

Now, truth be told, as you are transitioning from the 3D to the 5D, you are going to feel alone, very alone. Not even the cat down the road is going to be by your side. You're going to be all alone, really alone. And I'm here to tell you, it's not a bad thing. No, no, it's not a bad thing.

There's a power in being alone. You see, you've been told that being alone is a bad thing from society. If you are alone, oh my gosh, you've got no friends. No, being alone is beautiful. It's magnificent. You feel empowered. I spend a lot of time alone. But there's a difference between being alone and feeling alone, okay? There's a difference between being alone and feeling alone

I embrace being alone. And guess what? I never, ever feel alone. How come, Ralph? Look, I realized this – that we're actually all connected. Everything is like this in the universe. Our ego tricks us into believing in the idea of separation. The truth is you can never actually be alone even if you tried. Now, the art is to embrace being alone because that's how you find your true power.

That's how you find yourself. And in this 3D, 5D split, let's face it, a lot of people are becoming awake and aware of this matrix of how fake society is. And they're like, you know what? I'm going to take a trip to Thailand by myself and find myself. And then you find out you're all alone. Now, don't panic. Embrace the gift of being alone and remind yourself you don't have to feel alone. You know why? Because everything is connected. That's right. Everything is connected.

Many times in life, we find ourselves around people we no longer vibe with. We no longer gel with. I'm an alien. I'm an illegal alien. You're an alien, deep divers, right? I get it. I've been there. And that's okay. You're not antisocial. You just don't like being around fake people. And you have to honor your true authenticity. This is how to never feel alone and stand strong in the midst of this 3D, 5D split that's happening. Your consciousness is growing.

You're starting to see the world in a whole different way. And you want to take people with you. Your mom, your dad, your brother, your sister, even a cat down the road somewhere. But you can't. Because how you see the world is different from how the crowd sees the world. And to never feel alone and stand strong, remind yourself that the crowd is the matrix. The crowd is lost. They're going in the wrong direction. Allow yourself the freedom to not follow the crowd because the crowd is lost.

Follow your one true heart. Stop trying to keep up with the Jones. Stop trying to keep up with the trends and the popular things to do in society. You're not missing out. They're missing you. But it's going to take time to really trust yourself to say, actually, it's okay to be alone. Remind yourself, Deep Divers, during this 3D, 5D split, some people get it. Some people don't. When you have graduated, you can no longer go back to kindergarten. And when you have graduated, you might find yourself alone for a period of time. But once again, even the feeling of being alone is only temporary.

I felt alone, along my early journey because I was raising the frequency, raising the vibration. I was ready to get away from that concrete jungle, okay? I was in the city of London. I was ready to get out. And that's what I did. I went to Brazil. I went to Cape Verde Islands. I went all around the world, Ethiopia, right? Traveled to over 30 countries. And I needed this. I needed to be free and be alone. And guess what? I met a lot of people along the way.

I thought I was going alone. I came back with like 150 friends from all around the world. Isn't that something? Isn't that beautiful? So sometimes when you remind yourself how the universe works, we are never alone. The universe always sends someone. We are never alone. The universe always sends someone. Let me repeat that one more time. If you are feeling alone right now, look up.

Because the universe has sent that person into your life for a reason to remind you we are never alone because the universe will always send someone, okay? Sometimes you hear these stories – someone traveling around the world all alone, a solo trip. And then as soon as they land, they meet someone in the hotel, in a restaurant, in the bar. And now they're best friends all of a sudden.

Like how come? It's like the universe arranged that divine meeting. Ah, yes, the universe is going to make sure you have the right people in your life when you need them the most. Remind yourself that it's okay to spend time alone. Our society discourages it. It doesn't want people connecting with themselves.

I told you, turn your phone off. You know, a lot of people think their phone is their friend. No, you know who your real friend is? Hug yourself right now. You are your greatest friend. Switch the phone off. There's no Wi-Fi out in nature, but I swear there's a better connection. Hug yourself right now and say, there's a better connection. Get your ass into the heart of nature and spend time with yourself. That me-time, you need this to become your greatest version.

The more time you spend with yourself, the more you get to gnōthi sauton, right? That means know thyself. The oracle would say, know thyself in the temple of Apollo, right? In ancient Egypt, it would say, know thyself on every temple. You can only know yourself, when you spend time with yourself and realize that you're not a loner.

No, you're actually becoming your greatest version because you're getting to know who you really are, your light and your dark. It's acceptance. It's self-love. It's evolution.

Do not, I repeat, do not abandon yourself. Many days I felt alone and the universe said, Ralph, do not abandon yourself. Do not abandon yourself. Do not abandon yourself. I took the universe's advice, and I never abandoned myself. I realized that we are never alone unless we abandon ourselves. Self-care is needed. Make sure you don't let yourself go.

Look after yourself. Cultivate that self-love, that self-appreciation and realize you're doing better than you think. A lot of people feel alone in this world. You know why? Because they are mentally unkind to themselves. They say, hey, I'm not good enough. I should have done better. They trash talk themselves and beat themselves up. The cat down the road is like, just stop that right now. Start being mentally kinder to yourself.

What happens when you no longer believe in what you were told as a child? What happens when you're outgrowing the very society that you were born into? Sometimes you might feel like an outlaw, an outcast, a fringe dweller, and you've got to wear that with a badge of honor. I had to realize, the times I felt like I didn't fit into this world, that was a blessing.

You know why? Because I realized I was here to create a new one. And you are custom-made, you're not regular.

Realize it's okay to leave the crowd. And it's okay to be who you really are. And to say, you know what? I don't want to fit in just to get along, to go along. No, I'm going to stand in my truth unapologetically.

I'm going to say things which are really going to shake people. If they can't handle it, too bad. I'm going to speak my truth even if I lose friends. They weren't my friends anyway. I'm going to sing my song. With this 3D, 5D split, learn from Ralph Smart that when you have the courage to speak your truth, even if your voice shakes, you're going to hear the choir.

I said, you know what? I want to speak my truth to the whole world. Then a cat down the road pulled up. I'm like, wow, I got one subscriber, fantastic. And I started to sing my song. Then I heard other people singing it. I heard a gigantic choir, right? Raising the frequency.

I thought I was alone. Then I realized that actually… There were so many people out. There were so many people like me out there in the world. So it takes courage and bravery to start speaking your truth and being brave. And once you do, I guarantee you, you will never feel alone.

Once again, I can be alone. But my oh my, I never feel alone because I know I've got family all around the world. I've got a soul tribe in every single country on this planet. And so do you. But you're going to have to start singing your song. You're going to have to start singing your song and living your truth unapologetically.

Are you going to hide behind someone? Are you going to hide in the closet? Are you going to lock your doors and become a recluse? No, you are going to be who you are 100% without apology. And this is how to never feel alone. Because you have taken the first step in embracing the totality of who you are.

Yes, people may not be around you now, but I guarantee you, if you continue to live your truth, you're going to inspire other people and they are going to be a part of your family. You've got a family outside of your family, okay?

Look, one of the laws of power I love is do not isolate yourself. Do not isolate yourself. There are so many people out there, who have so much knowledge they could share with the world. So many gifts and talents, but they hide it away. They're like, who would want to know that? Who am I anyway? I'm just an insignificant me. Nothing could be further from the truth.

So you have to start reminding yourself, do not isolate yourself. When I realized I had a gift, I said, you know what? I'm going to share it with the world. I was in my back garden, a beautiful Afro.

My mom was looking out of the window like, who is that? What is my son doing? I'm like, breathing in that good ass prana, baby. Like, I swear, people must've thought I was crazy. I didn't care. You know why? Because I embraced myself. I didn't feel alone. I realized that I'm going to create a community and that community is in the millions.

Infinite Waters. Have you heard of it? Yeah, you are part of it. You are a part of it, right? So I had to learn, Ralph, don't isolate yourself. Share with the world. Reach out. Reach out to people, okay? Nobody is born on an island. I need people like you need people. We all need people. Even the cat down the road needs people, okay?

Remind yourself that the wilderness is necessary. When you take a look at Buddha, you always see Buddha alone, right? Jesus Christ, always spent some time alone in the wilderness.

These great masters and sages spent time alone to really find out who they are and activate their dormant powers. So many people are sleeping giants in this society and they never actually activate their powers. You know why? Because they never spend time alone to figure out how it works.

And I had to spend time alone to meditate. I had to go in the wilderness for 40 days and 40 nights, and I came out a true master, okay? So I want you to realize that it's okay to go hiking alone. It's okay to travel alone.

It's okay to go to the cinema alone. It's okay to watch a movie alone. It's okay to go for a walk with a cat down the road alone. Because you're gonna find yourself. Most people in this world never find themselves. And a prerequisite to finding yourself is going into the wilderness and being alone, okay? Hearing your inner voice.

Allow yourself to be custom-made. You didn't come here to fit in. You know why? Because you were born custom-made. Also allow yourself to outgrow people. Sometimes you outgrow your circles, right? You outgrow the people you used to hang around. You know why? Because you're going to the next level of consciousness. Your awareness is expanding. You can no longer act like you don't know what's happening in the world. Your eyes are awake. Congratulations. You're waking up to the matrix.

A lot of people still don't get it. They're hypnotized, under a trance. And you're like, ain't nobody got time for that. And the moment you say that, you're going to find yourself alone. But you have to stand strong and remind yourself there are other people out there just like you and you have to reach out to them. That's what I did and now we've got infinite waters.

You're also going to have to allow yourself to be a pioneer. To boldly go where no man or woman or cat down the road or beautiful butterflies have gone before. And the universe is asking you to be a pioneer. Show the world what they have never seen before. When we talk of how to never feel alone and stand strong, embrace being a pioneer.

I had to do that. I had to say, okay, I'm going to be a pioneer. A lot of people say, "Ralph, gosh, I was watching you when I was 15. I'm now 25. I've got two children. I'm like, wow, they watch you too, Ralph." And they're like, they've got children. I'm like, really? I had to be a pioneer and to never feel alone. Take that request from the universe to be a pioneer.

Show the world what they've never seen before, do it. Allow yourself to be truly unique without apologizing for it.

Remind yourself that being unique means you are in your true power, okay? Your uniqueness is what makes you great. And remind yourself it's okay to be alone, but you never have to feel alone. You know why? Because everything is connected. We're all connected.

Chapter Three

Dealing With Other People's Values And Perspectives

Someone wrote to me, a beautiful soul, they said, Ralph, I know you know the true values of life. How can I deal with people with different values to myself and different perspectives? I watch you every single day, Ralph. I love you.

I love you too. And, look, as I said, the 3D/5D split has begun. We all know that we're not all the same because we have different beliefs, different thoughts, different ways of seeing this whole thing.

I told you, there is a massive split happening between 3D and 5D. And this is the reason why you might know someone, you might be married to them, maybe a best friend, a family member who thinks totally differently than how you think. They've got different values, different perspectives, different perspectives.

Life isn't easy sometimes because we are around people who have different values to ourselves. They see the world differently to us. And sometimes you're actually living with this person.

You might be married to them. Could be a mom, your dad, your brother, your sister, even a random stranger or best friend, even the cat down the road, right? Can't we all just get along? No, we can't. Because you see, sometimes there's a clash of ideologies, a clash of beliefs, a clash of values, a clash of perspectives. And this is the reason why life can be very hard for some people. So how did I deal with it coming up?.

Let me reiterate, there is a massive split happening on the planet. I told you, you've got the vaccinated versus the people who aren't vaccinated. You've got people who are like, hey, I'm pro-trans. You've got people who are like, no, I'm not for these trans people and the LGBT community and all of that stuff. There's a massive split happening right now.

You've got people who say, I love ChatGPT. It helps me with my homework. And you've got some people who say, I hate artificial intelligence. I prefer cats and humans.

You've got some people who are like, hey, I wanna really level up and become my greatest version. And then you've got some people who are like, no, I just wanna stay where I've always been in my comfort zone. I don't wanna do any leveling up, right?

So the split has already begun. And sometimes, when you are working on yourself and you're with someone else who's not really there with you, not really working on themselves, they don't share the same enthusiasm, the same passion, it can be tough because it's not just anyone. Sometimes it can be someone that you look up to, your mom, your dad, your best friend. Sometimes we outgrow people.

We outgrow situations. We outgrow where we once were. First and foremost, you have to accept yourself, you have to accept yourself unapologetically. You have .to accept yourself to the point where you're like, hey, this is me, take it or leave me alone. They're leaving you alone right now. You gotta say that.

You've gotta remind yourself, you're not here to kiss ass. You're not here to people please. I always tell you deep divers, I'm not here to tell you what you wanna hear. I'm here to tell you what you need to hear. Now, you can respectfully, respectfully disagree.

Okay, you've gotta remind yourself deep divers, there are over 8 billion people on this planet. Each and every one of us has a different way of seeing this whole thing that's happening on this planet. And that's okay. Respect other people's perspectives, their values, but don't allow it to interfere with yours.

As you are awakening, as you are finding out who you really are, as you are finding out that you've been lied to, you've been lied to in this matrix, you might find that other people around you are still fast asleep, still drinking the Jim Jones

Kool-Aid and now it's tricky. Because you know that being free is your birthright and they're like, hey, just shut up and be quiet and get to work in the matrix. And you're like, no, I wanna be free. So you're gonna have to realize that you're gonna have to let go of these people. You're gonna have to also realize not everyone you lose is a loss. And you're also gonna have to realize not everyone wakes up at the same time. When I was first starting Infinite Waters, I was way ahead of my time.

I was talking about concepts and ideas that nobody was talking about. I had people giving me the fluoride stare like, huh, huh? But I kept going. You know why? Because this was my truth.

I had to honor it. I'm like, hey, I don't care if you've got different perspectives than me. If you have different values than me, this is my truth. And guess what? Fast forward like 10 years, these people who doubted me, who are against me, they're like, Ralph, gosh, I'm so proud of you. Can we hang out? And I'm like, no. You're gonna have to remind yourself, life is not about pleasing people.

Life is about being honorable, respecting yourself, staying loyal to yourself. People always talk about loyalty. What about loyalty to yourself? Learn how to be loyal to yourself. Learn every single day. It is all about realizing you can't please everyone.

And certain people that are close to you, you're gonna have to disappoint them. They're gonna have to find out who you really are and they're gonna have to respect it. You see, we respect people when they stand up for what they want and know what they want and are not ashamed of what they want.

We respect people who have found out who they really are. And you have to remind yourself, it's not about other people's values and perspectives, it's about you standing on your square and saying, these are my values, this is what I stand for, this is me. And sometimes you're gonna have to have that blunt conversation with a loved one to say, hey, look, this is me. If you don't like it, too bad. I don't even like your lifestyle that much, but I'm not trying to change you. I'm allowing you space to live how you wanna live.

So you've gotta allow me space to live how I wanna live. You've gotta remind yourself, find a community. I've got the Infinite Waters community. It is the best community in the world. We've got the cat down the road in the community. We've got butterflies floating around in the community.

There's no place I'd rather be than in this community. I've got a whole support network. When I first started coming up, there were many people who said, gosh, Ralph, I don't see it the way you see it. And I'm like, that's cool. But someone out there does. And they are my support network. So I'm not alone. We are never alone unless we abandon ourselves. Don't think you're alone.

You have a tribe out there who sees the world just as you. You have a tribe out there who shares the same values as you. You have a tribe out there who has a similar perspective as you.

Honor this tribe because they are your foundation that you stand upon. Oh my gosh. So when I started to grow and my values and my perspective started to inspire other people, the same people who had different values and perspectives than me were like, oh my gosh, maybe I should listen to Ralph Smart because it seems millions of other people are.

You see, you don't have to convince people to have the same values as you. What are my values, by the way? Being free is your birthright. Live life to the full. The universe reveals its secrets to people who dare to follow their hearts. Follow your heart. Let love guide you and not fear.

Simple values, family, love, relationships. Put that first, put God first, put the universe first. And remind yourself, remind yourself to be humble because just as it's given, it can be taken away. Simple values, right? You've got to remind yourself, you're not here to convince people to think like how you think. You are here to show people why the way you live is working for you. You're not here to convince people to say, hey, be like me, have the same values.

Seven day vegan challenge. I've been plant-based for over 18 years. I've got meat eaters watching my channel. I've got people who eat octopus and they eat whales. They eat all kinds of things, right? Even carpets. That's cool. Do what you want to do. I'm just sharing with you what's helped me along my journey.

And in turn, it's inspired a lot of other people. Shout out to Odd1sOut who said, there's this guy who always says seven day vegan challenge. That video has over 30 million views.

So just by me living my truth and holding my values dear to me and not bowing down or changing, it has inspired other people to take a look at my values, my perspectives. So you've got to remind yourself, this is what happens when instead of convincing people, all you do is show them, show them your life. Be an example of the life you're living.

This is how to deal with people with other values and other perspectives. Be an example. I don't go around telling people, hey, wake up from the matrix, wake up from the matrix. No, I just tell them, hey, I've manifested a YouTube gold award, number one bestselling book, Feel Alive by Ralph Smart on Amazon. They're like, oh, let me listen to this guy. You know why? Because it's a success.

We're drawn to that. You've got to remind yourself many times when we talk about this massive split that's happening, some people are awake and aware, some people are fast asleep. You're going to have to realize nothing is personal.

Even your mom or your dad might be telling you, hey, don't live that lifestyle. Because no matter how old you are, you're still a child in their eyes, right? Doesn't matter if you're 50 years old, you're still a little boy, a little girl.

Look, you're going to have to remind yourself there's something called the generation gap. Your mom, your dad, they were born in a different time period. Life has changed. Life has changed. Things have moved on. It's a whole new world right now. So you've got to remind yourself it's not personal. It's just that that's how they were raised. So when you remind yourself that everyone has a different programming in this matrix, like when you tell your children, hey, don't do that, don't do that. That's coming from your insecurities and your fears, but it's a whole new world.

They have to make up their own mind. You see people who love you... those people will always respect your values and your perspectives, even if they're values and perspectives are different than your own. People who love you always want the best for you. So take that into consideration.

Many people, they're like, hey, if you don't have the same values as me, if you don't see the world the same as me, I don't like you anymore. No, you didn't like me to begin with. You have to get away from these people.

You have to remind yourself that energy is contagious. If you are around a lot of fearful people long enough, you start becoming fearful yourself. You've got to remind yourself, you're going to the next level. You're outgrowing your circle because you know something, you have new information, you have different values right now.

You want more from life. You don't want to be another brick in the wall. You don't want to be another cog in the wheel. You want something more, something greater. You've awakened, awakened to your true purpose.

And a lot of people are just rolling out of bed saying, what? Don't feel ashamed. Don't feel guilty. Embrace who you are unapologetically. If they can't deal with it, too bad. You've got to remind yourself every single day, every single day to protect your energy. This is how to deal with people with different values, perspectives, because there's a massive split happening between 3D and 5D.

Some people, they don't mind living in fear every single day, waking up to bad news. Some people want more. They want to vibrate in love.

They want to do a little Samba, baby. They want to raise the frequency. They want to travel the world and see the beauty of Gaia. And some people are just stuck in their comfort zone. And that's the reason why it's up to you to place yourself in the right environment so that you can blossom and grow. Remind yourself, deep divers, every single day to protect your energy.

Protect your energy. Protect your energy. I've got a shield around me at all times. This is the way to deal with other people's perspectives and values that aren't in alignment to your own. Protect your energy. There are people who don't care about any human beings and that's the way they live.

And then there are people who have compassion, empathy. You want to surround yourself with people like that. Surround yourself with people who are on the same mission as yourself.

Why oh why do we take advice from people who aren't even taking their own advice? Doesn't make sense. You gotta stop doing that. Because you see, if you are 5D, you don't ask the 3D person for advice. You know why? Because you're on another level. You ask someone else who's at the same level as you for advice.

You're so real, Ralph! I know, I know. So you've got to remind yourself that there's levels to this life experience. You've got to remind yourself it's not personal.

You know, you can respectfully still love that person but keep your distance. You live your life, I'm going to live my life. We can still keep peace from a distance. Don't think you're here to be everyone's personal savior and get everyone to like you. That's a recipe for disaster. I told you, people who people-please are the most unhappy people. You know why? Because they find out in the end, even if you do what they want, they still want more. They're never satisfied.

So therefore, you have to start honoring your feelings. You must know what you want. You must know who you are. You must realize in life, as you change, your circle changes. As you change your thoughts, the people now change in your life who are in alignment with the same thought frequency and vibration as yourself.

If you are all about nature, you want to surround yourself with people who are all about nature. If you are all about being free in your eyes or waking up to how crooked this matrix is, you want a support team that sees the world as you do. Otherwise, you're going to be in a comfortable prison around people who aren't doing any good for you.

The split has already begun. It's up to you to make the choice today where you stand. It's up to you to realize you can't serve two masters. You cannot serve two masters. You're going to have to choose respectfully who you are and say, okay, these are my values. These are my principles. These are my morals. This is my perspective of how I see reality. I'm standing by it.

You can stand by yours. You want to focus on people who are where you are. Give your energy to that instead of trying to get people on board with where you are.

I don't spend a second trying to convince people about the matrix and how to wake up and be free. You know why? Because I'm the living embodiment of it. So all I've got to do is open my mouth and say, peace, infinite waters.

People are going to listen all around the world. I'm an example of what I'm talking about. And that actually helps more people to adopt similar values and perspectives to my own. Like being free is your birthright. You're going to have to remind yourself. Life is all about letting go of what is not serving you and making space for what inspires you.

4   12 Lies People Accept As Facts

The unexamind life is not worth living. - Socrates

So I often talk about my journey in becoming my greatest version. There were lots of lies I believed were true. And if we don't question our belief system, we go on to create a lot of hassle for ourselves. Here are the 12 lies I used to tell myself:

1.   I have to struggle to make it

So the first lie I would tell myself was that I had to grind blood, sweat and tears, that I had to struggle to make it. And what I realized along my journey was that actually, when I started to relax more, go out into nature, meditate, my production level was going through the roof. I became more productive. I was a friendlier person to be around because I wasn't so stressed all the time.

So in slowing down, it actually helped me to speed up and avoid burnout.

2.   I must win

The second lie I'd tell myself was that I must win. How many of us tell ourselves that every single day, I have to win, I have to reach the finish line.

But wait a minute, wait a minute. If you think you have to win, that means you need competition. You see, this whole concept of winning and losing is part of the duality. But really, there is no winning and there is no losing. There is only the experience, the process. Because if you're in a race, who's by the left? Who's by the right? So it means that you're caught up in competition.

When I realized that I had to surrender to my uniqueness and just really create my own lane, it was a wonderful truth to wake up to.

3.   I am not good enough

The third lie I was living was that I was not good enough. I used to always think, no, no, let me do it again. Nope, not good enough. Because it's not that other people are judging us, we are judging ourselves. We are our own hardest critics.

So the moment I said, what have I got to lose? It's all an illusion anyway, so who cares? It was liberating, and saved a lot of hassle.

4.   My mistakes define me

The fourth lie I used to tell myself was that mistakes define me. A lot of us, we walk around and we wanna appear like we have the perfect life.

I pray that people I see on Facebook are as happy as they pretend to be. Because many times, we think we have to have it all together. We have to be flawless. And any little mistake we make, we're very judgmental towards ourselves. If we did something in the past, we blame ourselves for it. We carry a lot of guilt, a lot of shame, a lot of heavy backpacks on our back.

So what I said to myself was that, okay, any mistake I make is only a stepping stone towards my greatness. I don't have mistakes. I just have learning experiences, curves that go a bit like this, a bit like that.

5.   There is no time

Number five is that there is no time, thinking like, uh-oh, the clock has gone out. We're rushing, we're just always going somewhere, always thinking we don't have enough time. But where? Where are we going? We never end up getting there anyway.

We just need to go somewhere.

So I always used to say to myself, okay, I don't have enough time. I don't have enough time to do what I want. I don't have enough time to call you, I'm sorry. I don't have enough time. Then I said, wait a minute. Actually, I do have enough time. We say we don't have enough time because once again, it allows us, it helps justify where we are.

Oh, I'm busy. What a beautiful excuse. I had to lose my 'busyness' and create time, realize time was an illusion and that we have literally all the time in the world. We can meet up with anyone. It's only a matter of priorities.

6.   Money is real

Number six is that money is real. Now, I talk of money being energy, but this paper money we have is fiat currency. It's not backed by anything. In essence, it's debt notes.

So for a long time, I thought, gosh, I'm stacking up all of this money and I realized the real money was the energy within me. So I don't worship money. I let money work for me and that's why life has become more rich.

7.   They have a better life than me.

No, no. They're doing fabulous. No, no. They are 10 times better than me. A lot of the times we feel other people are well off, better off, doing spectacular, while we on the other hand, we're suffering, we're striving, we're getting left behind.

Talking to so many different people, traveling to different countries, I realized that everybody is going through something. Sometimes you see people smiling at the bus stop. You don't know what they're going through.

So what I realized is that it helps when you're not envious, when you don't look over the fence. Focus on planting your own vision and realizing that you have so much to be grateful for. I'm thankful every single day because it didn't have to happen, but it did. Oh yeah, it did. Oh yeah, it did.

8.   There is a limit to my greatness.

A lot of us, we say, okay, I've reached the peak. I've reached the pinnacle, let me stop now. No, there is no limit. When you're building up that momentum, that's the time you've got to keep on going because you're on a roll. Yeah.

9.   Food is food.

Oh yeah, a big lie I used to tell myself is that food is food. I can eat anything. And because of that mentality, I suffered in a big way.

When you're not conscious of the kind of food you eat, you have to know that it's gonna affect your mental, emotional, and spiritual health. So just taking care of myself, the food I'm eating, lots of plant-based foods, blueberries, strawberries, lots of kale and watercress. You realize the truth that food is not just food. There's levels to this stuff. Oh yeah.

10.   I'm not famous, I'm a nobody.

If I don't make it to the top, where is the top anyway? I realized along my journey that I talk about becoming your greatest version. This has become very popular right now. And I'm connecting with millions of people out there.

At the same time, I haven't changed. And it was never a desire to be famous for the sake of being famous.

A lot of us, we say, I wanna be famous. I wanna be a star. I realized that I was a star way before the fame, and the chains, and the diamonds. Is that a song? No, it's not.

We are all stars. So I don't have to strive to become something. I already am. I am.

11.   You have to become serious when speaking about something serious.

No, you don't. Where is your sense of humor? What helped me along my journey was just loosening up because the more tension we have, we take the fun out of everything. And for me, a great catalyst for creativity is to become playful. That's what's helped me become my greatest version. And every day just seems like a party. Yeah, it's Neverland!

12.   There is only one path, one way.

We speak about oneness, but along my journey, I've realized that whenever I'm sharing with someone, I'm not here to tell you what to do.

I'm here to share with you what's helped me along my journey. That's why I always say, what's helped me along my journey, you get the picture. If you are looking at someone else's life, reading their autobiography and hoping that your life becomes like them, you might be in for a rude awakening because life has something in store for you that is going to be completely different from someone else.

You are irreplaceable. You couldn't live the life I'm living even if you wanted to. I couldn't live the life you're living even if I wanted to.

Why? Because we are all here for a different mission, purpose and we have to follow our calling by being in tune with our heart space. So everybody is on a different path. The plan is to meet at the crossroads.

When you accept people going on their path and you go on your path, there are no problems. That's what we call freedom. So there you have it. Those were the beautiful awakenings I awakened to.

Chapter Five

12 Life Lessons People Learn Too Late

Part of me becoming my greatest version was to realize that, gosh, I wish I knew that sooner. And there are life lessons that people often forget about. There are life lessons that people often learn too late. Well, this chapter is gonna help you out because it's gonna give you something to think about... to really think about.

The best days of your life are coming. Trust it. I repeat, the best days of your life are coming. Trust that, okay? Because it's about to get real good for you. If you're ready, just say thank you. So, we're gonna talk about 12 life lessons people often learn too late. Here they are:

1. Everything is temporary.

Everything is gonna fade away. Oh no, Ralph! Well, it's not all bad because when you realize that everything is temporary, but only the love in your heart will remain, it can put a smile on your face to realize that actually even your worst moments, hard experiences, stressful situations will eventually pass.

Four words, this too shall pass. Everything is fleeting, transient, and forever changing. So that's the good news. And we can also remind ourselves that it all goes back in the box, okay? It doesn't matter how expensive your car is, the house you live in, because the truth is everyone's gonna die. Oh my gosh, don't worry about it, but don't worry about it, because our spirit lives forever. Oh yeah, exactly.

But remind yourself that a lot of people, they learn this life lesson way too late... That everything is temporary. They think that their possessions are gonna stay with them forever. No, that iPhone is gonna break down. It's gonna get destroyed, water inside of it. The car is gonna get a flat tire, okay? Even your house, the roof needs changing.

Everything is gonna fade away. But what we have to learn from this is that that's why we have to make the most of life. That's why we have to cherish people we love.

Call them right now, say, hey, I love you, mom. I love you, cat down the road. But realize, because so many people walk around full of ego, full of greed, not realizing it all goes back in the box.

Just like Monopoly, it all goes back in the box. And this has really helped me become my greatest version.

2.   That there is no perfect moment.

Oh no, no. There is only... now. If not now, when? Like why are people waiting for the perfect moment? Look, what helped me along my journey was to stop waiting for Fridays and stop waiting for summers and stop waiting for someone to fall in love with me because those things will happen. But in the meantime, enjoy right now.

We have to learn this every single day to stop waiting for the perfect moment. Stop waiting for the perfect time to do something because the truth is there is only now. And this has really transformed my entire life. I just do it. Just do it. I just do it.

A lot of people are waiting. They're like, Ralph, next year, I'm gonna do this. I'm like, wait a second. You only have right now, get a move on.

3.   The sacrifices you make today will pay dividends in the future.

The sacrifices that you make today will bring you a marvelous tomorrow. The sacrifices you make today, once again, will pay dividends in the future. And this is huge. We've got to remind ourselves that a lot of people, they don't learn this. They learn it way too late that you're gonna have to sacrifice today for a better tomorrow. And this has changed my entire life. I told you, sweat it out, grind it out because tomorrow you will be smiling in the Caribbean with a whole bunch of grapes in your mouth, doing a little Samba baby, raising the frequency. The sacrifices today that you make will give you a more amazing future.

4.   Your most important relationship is with you, yourself.

Your most important relationship is not with your partner, not with the cat down the road, not with your neighbor; it's with yourself! Like there are so many people who learn this way too late. Well, now you know that your most important relationship is with you, and once you learn how to form a better relationship with yourself, you will have a better life. You got so many people out there who are trying to form relationships outside of themselves, forgetting about the one with themself.

And this really transformed my entire life to say actually, just form a better relationship with yourself, Ralph, accept yourself, love yourself. And it's gonna do wonders.

5.   Your health matters

That green juice is not too expensive. The green juice is not too expensive. The green juice is not too expensive. No superfood is too expensive compared to your health... because your health matters.

So sometimes I see people deep dive a seven day vegan challenge who are like, oh my gosh, those blueberries are so expensive. I'm like, no, your health is far more valuable than that. $10, $20, so what? Have you seen the price of treating serious medical conditions? Hundreds of thousands of dollars? So when it comes to eating to live, I always say that no superfoods are too expensive.

Put that money up for that green juice. Put that money up for that acai bowl because your health matters.

6.   Your comfort zone is poison

That's right, deep divers, your comfort zone is poison. It's a trap, it's a prison.

Get out now. That's what the cat down the road is saying, it's a trap. I know it's comfortable sitting down, watching the TV, but it's actually a slow poison. And a lot of people learn this way too late. They don't learn this in time and they get trapped in their comfort zones. So what's helped me every single day is to realize that growth happens in discomfort.

I'm always in the heart of nature, okay? And I'm realizing I'm moving out of my comfort zone every single day. I'm traveling, going to new places, seeing new faces. So great things happen or life happens outside of your comfort zone, okay?

7.   Nothing worth having comes easy.

Behind every successful life, beautiful life, there is a struggle you don't know about. So this really helped me along my journey to realize that if you want it, Ralph, you're gonna have to do the work. Nothing worth having comes easy, okay? Realize that every single day.

8.   Fall in love with someone who loves you for who you are and not what you have.

Mm, that's right, I said fall in love, or rise in love, with someone who loves you for who you are, not what you have. Ladies, fellas, okay? So many times people hook up with each other but the other person only wants to take from you.

A lot of people learn this way too late. They're like, oh my gosh, I thought they loved me. No, they just loved your backside. I thought they loved me. No, they just loved your bank account. So when you learn to choose someone who loves you for who you are and not what you have, great things happen in your life, okay?

9.   Don't allow one second to ruin 24 hours, a whole day of your life.

Have you noticed when people are faced with testing situations? Sometimes that brief moment can actually ruin their whole entire day. They're fed up in a bad mood for the whole day. I'm like, wait a second, wait a second.

Learn that actually, you don't have to allow one second of disharmony to interfere with 24 hours of peace. I'm not gonna allow one second to have power over my 24 hours of the day.

Yes, things happen. Life is not easy. Even the cat down the road knows that, but we can always choose how we respond. We can't choose what happens to us sometimes in life, but we can always choose how we respond. When your life is crazy, it's hectic, it happens to me all the time.

I'm saying, okay, let me breathe and not react to the situation. If you can learn that you can choose to respond, take a deep breath, breathing in that good ass prana, and how you respond to that situation literally has the power to change the entire situation itself.

So when you are faced with stressful times, don't allow that one second one second to ruin your entire day. Say, you know what? I'm gonna do what Ralph Smart does. What does Ralph Smart do? Woo, breathe in that good ass prana, baby.

.   10.   Your family is forever.

It doesn't matter if you like them or dislike them, hate them or love them. Your family, you can't choose the family you were born into. So I always say, make peace with your family. Make peace with your family, even if you have to love them from a distance. I love you, bye. Make peace with your family. You know why? Because people come and go in your life.

Friends, they will come and go, but your family will always be there, right? Because you can't control who's in your family, right? So always make peace, always, always choose to make peace with your family or honor your family, right?

Honor your family because as we're growing up, we forget that actually, our parents are growing older, right? And I've got a great relationship with my mom, with my family. And I always say, gosh, it's such a blessing to have that. And we should really honor our family, honor our parents. And I know a lot of you may not have good relationships with your family members, and that's cool.

But once again, make peace with them and then move forward. But remind yourself that family is important. Family is very important. And I always say, what matters in life is family. And a lot of people, they learn that way too late. They cuss their family out. The cat down the road is like, don't say that, don't do that.

11.   Failure is a prerequisite for growth.

Mistakes are prerequisites for growth. Don't be afraid of failure. You know, a lot of people, they're afraid of failure. So guess what happens? They never try. Because if you try to do something epic, you're going to fail. Oh, you're going to fail miserably.

You're going to fall flat on your face like, oh my gosh, I'm eating the concrete right now. Yes. You've got to remind yourself, there are no such things as mistakes. There are no such things as mistakes, only stepping stones to help us become our greatest versions.

Remind yourself that failure is needed to get to the next level. Because even failure can teach you something. It shows you that you're trying. It shows you that that's not the way to do it, but here is the way to do it. It leads you to the right direction.

So what a lot of people learn too late is that actually I shouldn't be afraid of failure. I should welcome failure because that means I'm trying and it shows me how not to do something so I can actually learn how to do it.

12.   The journey does not get easier.

We just get stronger. Life is pretty hard. Okay, from the moment you're born, there's a lot of shit to deal with. There's no manual about how to live life. No, you gotta figure this thing out and it's okay if you haven't figured it out. It's okay, you're human.

And the journey does not get easier, but we do. As we progress through life, we do get stronger and we will get to the top of that mountain peak and become our greatest version because that's what we came here to do.

So remind yourself, like Bruce Lee said, don't pray for an easy life. Pray for the strength to overcome a difficult one because it's inevitable. Life is gonna be difficult. And the journey is not gonna get any easier.

But guess what? You, you, yes, you will be the one who gets stronger and overcome any adversity. When I say I'm blessed, I don't mean with materialistic possessions. I mean that things that were sent my way to destroy me, those things didn't even touch my soul because I realized that I'm getting stronger. I can deal with this, woo! And so can you.

6   30 Lessons I Learnt In 30 Years

Life never stops teaching, so I will never stop learning.

Huh? You're in your 30s, Ralph? A lot of people think I'm 18. Some people say I'm 20. Some people say it feels like I'm 10. Because I'm eating those strawberries. I feel fantastic, right?

So, I'm gonna share with you 30 lessons I've learned in 30 years. Now, I get over a thousand questions every single day.

So hopefully this covers one of them, okay? And I don't really talk a lot about me, I'm always helping people, how to this, how to that, but this is really, really gonna help you even more in terms of becoming your greatest version. What's the first lesson?

    1.   Love the skin you're in.

Yes, love the skin you're in... It even rhymes! Growing up, I didn't love the skin I was in and I met people time and time again saying things like, Ralph, I wanna get a tan. I wanna be darker. Some people are like to me, Ralph, I wanna be lighter. You've got people all around the planet trying to bleach their skin.

And what really took me to the next level was loving the skin I was in. Okay, and how did this happen for me? I started to realize the reason why so many people are miserable on the planet is because they don't love the skin they're in, right? We all came from a woman called Lucy in Ethiopia.

Over time, so much manipulation has made people hate the skin they're in. Race being the great illusion, the greatest illusion ever created, okay? There is no such thing as race. If we wanna get scientific, we're talking about carbon, which all life is based on. Just look at the soil, okay? Then you'll understand, overstand, and understand what I'm talking about.

What's the second lesson I've learned in 30 years?

2.   Love yourself 100%.

That is probably the greatest secret in the universe. And it's not as easy as saying, I love myself. No, you've gotta actually prove it by, once again, asking yourself, am I doing what I love every single day? I used to wake up and really dread getting out of bed.

Now I absolutely love it. I'm up before the cat down the road. That's a great achievement, okay? Love yourself 100%, baby.

What's number three?

3.   Accept yourself 100%.

Accept yourself when nobody else does, because the people who really accept themselves, even if they're a bunch of weirdos, yeah, those people are the ones who go super far in life.

Certain people, you might think they're amazing, they're beautiful, they're wonderful. They don't accept themselves, so they don't see it. So once you accept yourself, great things happen.

4.   Care for yourself. Don't let yourself go.

I let myself go along my early journey. Sometimes we just wake up. I did brush my teeth, so that's good. But sometimes I was neglecting myself for a period of time because I was just struggling. I was in the daily grind, okay?

So I learned that self-care is the best care. Care for yourself. Don't neglect yourself. The fifth lesson I learned is this.

5.   See yourself with unconditional positive regard at all times. I know your past is pretty shady. Don't worry about it.

I know you have done a lot of bad things in your life, right? It's okay. Every day you are being reborn. So that's how I look at myself and say, it's okay.

Whatever I do, even if I trip up, I'm always gonna see myself with unconditional positive regard like the great psychologist, Carl Rogers said, right? That's a secret in essence for becoming your greatest version.

6.   Food is huge

Now, number six, this is food time, right? Food lessons. Seven-day vegan challenge is blowing up real crazy. I've learned that eating a plant-based diet literally improves your mental, emotional, and physical health. Before I became a vegan over 12 years ago, I couldn't even run like six miles without feeling tired. Now I run like 12 and I've still got energy. I've got more energy than ever, okay? Food literally changes our DNA. You can eat to live or you can eat to die. It's your choice, right? Food is huge.

That's why a lot of people, as soon as they jump on the seven-day vegan challenge, they're like, Ralph, my third eye is opening. Ralph, I feel so young. Ralph! Yeah, I know, I know. They are getting your age wrong, right? You look like half your age. It's the strawberries, baby.

7.   Don't force others to be like you

Number seven, the seventh lesson. Now, I've been a vegan, yes, over 12 years. This channel has a lot of subscribers. I'm connecting with millions of people and a lot of people message me saying they are enjoying the seven-day vegan challenge.

.And I'm not forceful about it, right? I'm not saying be a vegan or if you're not a vegan, you're a bad person. No, no, no. I'm just living by example to say this is what it's done for me. Being vegan made me rich. By showing compassion for all life, respecting all life. I love the cat down the road. I definitely love the dog down the road, right? So, you don't have to always push that vegan message in people's faces. Just be an example of it, okay?

8.   Let yourself go sometimes

Number eight is that it's okay to eat junk food sometimes. I just eat vegan junk food. Like sometimes you might find me with some vegan donuts.

Sometimes you might find me eating a lot of brownies, right, full of cacao, tryptophan. I'm feeling fantastic, right? Antioxidants going, right? Fruits are nature's candy, right? So I still eat junk food. It's just a different kind, okay? A lot of vegans like Puritans.

They're like, I must only drink cold pressed juice and do this. It's gonna be hard, right? Let yourself go sometimes. Don't worry, I won't judge you.

9.   Do your research

Number nine, now, when it comes to food, it's hard, hard. When I was first becoming a vegan, nobody was supporting me. In fact, people were saying, where are you gonna get your protein? You're losing weight. And yeah, I lost a lot of weight because I was in transition. So I get it.

Like I always tell people, if you are on that plant-based diet, right, give it three years before you can really say, okay, I'm on the plant-based diet right now because your body is gonna go through a lot of changes. But in the end, those people will be asking you for advice. So for me, my advice, a lesson I learned was just do as much research as possible to say, okay, this is really what I wanna eat, okay?

10.   Dr Sebi

I learned a lot growing up from a man called Dr. Sebi, the father of medicine, for me, a genius, right? And this channel has a lot of subscribers, so go and Google him right now, and look up Dr Sebi. He really shook me to the core when he was talking about how our body is electrical, we've gotta eat electrical plant-based foods.

And ever since I switched over, I have insane energy levels, right? Just by eating carbon-based, plant-based foods, right? And the benefits are huge, right? A lot of people are having unnecessary surgery, going to the doctor, spending a lot, huge medical bills, and I'm just stuffing like grapes in my mouth, and it feels fantastic.

11.   How people treat you is how they feel about themselves.

I get it, I've been treated pretty shitty by some people, but I get it, it's not that personal. Ain't got nothing to do with me. Their life is a reflection of how they are treating me.

So if someone right now in your life is treating you terribly, chances are they don't even love themselves. Don't worry about it.

12.   Your real friends are happy when you're happy.

And sad when you're sad, okay? Honor your real friends, okay? You will always know because they're gonna be really rooting for you, and when you fall off, they're gonna be there to help you up, okay?

13.   Real friends are rare.

That's right, really, really rare, okay? They're so rare, you may not even have any. I've got about like three real, real, real, real friends, right? Those are the friends who I could trust, okay? And over time, you're gonna meet a lot of people.

All of a sudden, you got people at your doorstep. Who are these people? Nobody knows, but are they real? Have you put them through the friendship test? That's what I'm talking about. Would they pick you up from the airport at two o'clock in the morning? Maybe, maybe not.

Of course they won't. They're too busy in La La Land, right? So real friends are super rare, and for me, I always spend time, I always have a lot of love for my real friends. Thank you so much.

And the deep divers out there, you're my real friends.

14.   When you're rich and famous, you get friends from nowhere.

What? When you win the lottery, you get friends from nowhere. When you are a YouTube superstar, you get friends from nowhere. Where did you all come from? Nobody knows. Cheese, right? That's what happens, right? You got to be aware of phony people in your life who are only there to enjoy the fruits of your labor.

When you're blowing up, let's just say you've got your own business, you're doing good for yourself, you are going to get a lot of people who want to taste some of that success too. So once again, that's why you've got to be very selective in the company you keep and ask yourself, were they around when I was just starting out? Or are they only here because right now life is so fantastic, okay?

15. How you treat other people says a lot about you.

Now, I'm no saint, sometimes I've been really harsh, hard, and I've been very sensitive at times, of course, I'm a Pisces, right? But sometimes I've had to check myself and say, Ralph, no, no, no, don't do that. And I've realized how I was treating this person was because it said a lot about me, of what I was going through at the time, right?

So I had to pull back and say, come on, let's change this around, right? And that's what you've got to do, right? How you treat someone, if you are being very mean to someone right now, chances are you are mean to yourself, right? I'm always treating people, a lot of people right now with so much love. A lot of people think I'm their partner.

No, no, no, no, no, no, no, no. Cat down the road is, right? That's because I love myself. I've got so much love to give, it's unbelievable. How you treat people says a lot about who you are, okay?

16. It's okay if you don't know your purpose.

Goodness gracious, I don't, I didn't know my purpose for a long time. And I was, I was in, I was graduating.

I was smiling with my mom like, yeah, I just graduated. I don't know what to do with my life. Oh my gosh, right? Driving in the car, still don't know what to do. That's okay. It's a natural process.

17. It's not as complicated as it seems.

If you don't know your life purpose, what makes you smile? Yeah, yeah, yeah, do that. That is your life purpose. You've just forgotten.

You think you need a master's, a PhD. No, you don't. These are just man-made constructions, right? To take you out of when you're crazy dancing around.

That is actually your purpose, okay?

18.   You've got to visualize to materialize.

Now, I remember along my early journey, I went into the garden and I said, I looked up to the sky and said, this is going to be my future. Because I just love being in nature so much.

Then I was recording day after day, just recording. And I was like, I got no money in my bank account. But it felt good. And that's what I'm still doing. And it feels fantastic. I just got a lot of money in my bank account, right? That's what happens after time.

You start to enjoy the fruits of your labor. And it's never been about that. It's just been about realizing you've got to follow your dream. You've got to visualize to materialize, okay? You've got to visualize to materialize.

19.   When it comes to your life purpose, a lot of people are going to come around you who are going to distract you from your purpose.

And a lot of these sometimes people are family and friends. Oh my gosh, yes. Those closest to you, those closest to you will always try and steer you away sometimes from your true life purpose.

I had people around me who were saying, Ralph, what you're doing is a waste of time. Just go and get a regular job. Well, I was already in a regular job, thank you. And it didn't feel good.

.I was tired of the nine-to-five. I wanted to wake up with a bunch of grapes in my mouth. They were like, huh? That's what we're doing. They ain't laughing now, are they?

20.   When we talk of our life purpose, thinking is not enough.

You've got to step into radical action. You've got to ask yourself, what am I doing every single day that's moving me closer towards my dream and passion? I'm up every single day and I'm just sharing, I'm creating, right?

I've created a lifestyle for myself where I just have to talk and I will live in infinite abundance, right? It's a smart way of living when you get paid off your signature, which is your voice. If you are an artist, you get paid off your hand, right? Your brush, we are all.artists. We've just forgotten where our paintbrush went.

21. There is so much we don't know about this planet.

Yeah, a great lesson I learned is to realize how much I don't know. I am still learning. I'm still studying, right? I've just gotten back into skating, like I skate every single day, but I also like riding a lot of bikes now and I really wanna build my own road bike, right? Cause I'm so inspired by cycling right now.

Okay, it's fun. I'm learning, I'm watching videos, okay? This, this, this, and it's so interesting, right? I'm learning also there are other life forms on other planets. I'm learning how humanity has been manipulated, separated through race, religion, politics, once again, gender, all of these divisions, which has created this mess, which we are once, we're fixing once again, okay? But I'm always realizing there is still so much I don't know, so I've got to learn, learn, learn, study, study, study yourself first.

22. The power of intention.

What I've realized is that everything you see around you in this man-made world is created from an idea from someone's head, okay?

Someone said, I want that building over there. It's a human design. Things don't get here by accident, they get here by intention. Okay, so I've just realized the power of intention. If I want something, I've gotta put my intention for that to manifest, okay? It's not just gonna magically happen.

You've gotta actually do it, okay?

23. Most people go through life without questioning their existence.

I did for a long time. And the greatest lesson I had was that I was doing that every single day and my life wasn't going anywhere. And the moment I started to question myself and say, who am I? Question number one, what did I come here to do? What is my purpose? Those three questions helped me become my greatest version and helped me to wake up with loads of strawberries in my mouth, okay? Those three questions, right? You have a higher purpose.

24. It's pointless to hold onto a grudge.

Like, I have a very light heart, but there was a time when I was almost seeing myself say, okay, maybe it makes more sense to hold onto a grudge. Then I realized, wait a minute. It doesn't make sense, right? Because once again, it's gonna prevent you from becoming your greatest version. Like, I'm so free. My heart is so light, right? The ancient Egyptian said, your heart should be as light as a feather.

Right, and my heart is as light as a feather. If you are holding onto a grudge right now, let it go, let it go. Okay, you let it go, fantastic.

25. You don't have to be perfect.

Like, I've learned that in fact, being silly is fantastic sometimes. Don't take yourself so seriously. You aren't here to be a masterpiece. You are a whole work in progress. So for me, any video I make is always fun. Well, first of all, there is no script. I don't even know what I'm gonna say next.

Cranberries, neither did you, right? That's why it's so fun. Because it is improvisation. It is so organic, it is so pure. A lot of us try to be holier than thou. There are no saints here, right? We are just works in progress. I make mistakes all the time.

At the same time, I learn from them, and that's fine. But don't expect yourself to be this perfect being, to have the perfect body, the perfect partner, the perfect bank account. There is no such thing as perfection.

It's all about how it works for you. One person's heaven is another person's hell, and vice versa.

26. Find someone who loves you for who you are.

Not for how much money you have, not for what you can do for them, but who really is very reciprocal with you, okay? And that's what I've learned along my journey.

I feel the genuine love when I've seen someone in relationships, someone is just there because they just love your soul rather than just your body, right? I see women who spend tons and tons and tons of time trying to get that booty in shape. Baby, it looks fantastic. At the same time, that's all the man is going to want from you, just the booty.

But when it comes to your soul, he doesn't want to know about you. He doesn't even want to know your name, right? So you've got to think and realize that your inner essence is far more important than just your booty. Trust me, okay?

27. The best things in life aren't things.

As a psychologist, as a criminologist, as an infinite being, I realized this, that I studied the life of billionaires, people like Bill Gates and said, okay, why is it that Bill Gates doesn't talk about how many cars he's got? Why is it that people with no money always brag about how many cars they've got? What's the secret? You see, sometimes when you have a lot, you've got to realize that all of it is going to disappear anyway.

You can't take it with you. So the best things in life are intangible. They can't be seen. They are ideas. There are things which change people's lives for the better, not just how many cars you've got. Like when I make videos, I always realize, I know that people watch my videos from two years ago, a year ago, three years ago, because they hold infinite value.

So ask yourself today, what am I creating that is going to last forever, right?

28. Invest in yourself.

A great lesson I learned is that you've got to invest in yourself. Invest in yourself. I've spent like over 100,000 easily just on creative tools, over 100,000 cameras, laptops over time, but guess what? I've got all of that back with a cherry on the top, right? Invest, invest in your dream, right? You've got singers who pay sometimes 80,000 just for singing lessons.

You think they're crazy. No, they're not, because this is what they came here to do. When it comes to your life purpose, you want to go on that course you want to go, if it's too expensive, just find a way to pay for it because you are worth it, right? Invest in your own future.

Put that money up. Seven day vegan challenge, buy amazing food to eat. Trust me, you're worth it.

29. Crazy weird people have the most fun.

It's not about fitting in. That's the big lesson I learned in 30 years, right? You don't have to fit in.

In fact, you didn't come here to fit in and be another brick on the wall. You came here to stand out and you can only do that when you are original. When you have signatures, slow motion this side, you've got to stand out, right? If someone says you're weird, that's a compliment.

That probably means you hit the jackpot, okay? Be weird, which in other words is just being authentic. Just be authentic. Once you are authentic, the right people will find you.

30. Get on with it.

When I say get on with it, what I've learned is that don't be a perfectionist. Like there's a reason why I don't put jump cuts in videos. Like I stopped doing that a while ago, a long time ago, like a year or two ago, right? Because I just found that this whole thing is a joke, right? It's a joke in a beautiful way.

Life can't be captured. Once you take a picture, that moment is already over. Life is the infinite flow of movement and nobody knows how much time they've got on the planet.

So once again, like they say, it's written in the stars. I know that I did what I came here to do and that's why I'm in the after party. Have fun every single day. Do what makes you happy every single day and connect with people. Connect with people who remind you who you are every single day.

Connect with people who love you like you love them every single day. And then have a beautiful day.

Chapter Seven

Become A Ghost,
Delete Social Media

Look, become a ghost, delete social media and focus on yourself, this really is the secret recipe to becoming your greatest version.

My mentor told me that Ralph, when you make it inspiring millions of people, you have to share with the world the blueprint of how you did it, how you got there. So that's what I'm here to do.

I know what you're thinking... you're thinking, but Ralph, you're on social media! I know, but let me finish... what I really mean is, delete social media that lacks mental nutrition. Social media that doesn't help you grow as a human being. That kind of social media has got to go. I love social media because let's face it, YouTube is amazing when you use it the right way, right? All of these apps can be used in a beneficial way.

But the problem is a lot of people use these apps like Tik Tok and Instagram, and even Facebook to distract themselves from becoming their greatest version. So I always say delete social media that's not doing anything for you.

During that time that you spent on Instagram faking it to the world – like six hours – you could have actually written the first chapter of your new book and I'm going to buy it. That's an idea for you right there, for you to do in that same time. Just imagine what you could have done productively in those six hours.

So always remind yourself... like people, I do it too... We all waste time some-times following social media that lacks mental nutrition, that doesn't actually help us grow and become our greatest version.

Like I'm on Tik Tok, but I post a video there and then I'm out. I post and then I ghost. I'm like the road runner beep beep. I'm gone because I haven't got time to just waste, like watching things which aren't serving me. Now YouTube, I'm going to watch a video if it can help me. Absolutely. But so many times people spend time on social media like Instagram and all of these apps for external validation. You've mastered the selfie now master thyself.

Social media is like what the world is turned into right now because the truth is YouTube, Instagram, Facebook, they are the new MSNBC, Fox News, BBC, but it's how you use social media. Every single day, make sure you're deleting social media that is toxic for your evolution. Okay?

Embrace social media like infinite waters... I'm biased, but social media that can really help you grow. Okay? That has edutainment. Okay. And all of that stuff, information, get the right information.

Look, Rocky three, it says there is no tomorrow. And I love that, right? There is no tomorrow. And that's what's really helped me become my greatest version to remind myself.

There is no tomorrow. There is only now. So, so many people, the trouble is they think they have time just to be scrolling. No, doom scrolling is going to keep you trapped from becoming your greatest version. So I always say this, spend three minutes on trash every single day on social media that distracts you and then get to business. A lot of people, what happens? They stunt on the gram. They flex on Tik TOK. I'm like, okay.

You're acting like you've made it. They're like, yeah, I made it. What have you made though? You haven't even made your bed!

Look, remind yourself that you can fake it to people you don't know. And you might even fool some people you don't know, but guess what? You can never fool yourself or the cat down the road because the cat down the road knows who you really are deep divers. So what really helped me along my journey, was to realize that this Ralph don't fake it till you make it, just make it because time is your most valuable asset and there is no tomorrow.

You've got work to do. I want to see all of you manifest real big. Okay. And invite me to your summer party. Can I get an invitation? I'm just going to come and do a little samba baby. Of course I'm invited, right? I'm going to invite you.

See, what happens to so many people…They buy things they don't need with money. They don't have to impress people they don't like… that's fight club, right? And that's what happens on social media.

Every single day, you have people pretending and faking it. And all of that is actually in the way of you becoming your greatest version. You know why? Because the secret recipe to becoming your greatest version is learning to live authentically. And that means to say, that actually I'm not going to fake it on Instagram. I'm just going to go out there and be in my purpose every single day. We ain't got time to start stunting or flexing.

Okay. Deep divers. Look, become a ghost, delete social media, and focus on yourself.

. Now let's talk about becoming a ghost. Become like Casper, the friendly ghost deep divers. If it's not helping you evolve, it's a distraction. How many times deep divers have you got into a crowd and you're like, actually, I don't want to be here. I don't need to be here. It's distracting me from my greatness. Yes.

So you have to learn how to be a ghost. People are going to be like, where did Michelle go? Where did Tom go? You disappeared, right? You're nowhere to be seen. You know why? Because you've got work to do.

You know why? Because if it's not helping me grow, it's a distraction. If this conversation is not going to improve my life, what are we talking about? I don't want to know what's up. I don't want to hang out unless we can talk about becoming our greatest version and fly like the birds in the sky.

What really helped me was to remind myself that you have to lose yourself to find yourself. When I think back to say, okay, starting infinite waters, my platform, which is inspiring millions of people, I had to become a ghost. I had to stop hanging around certain people, lose the crowd and really find myself and really focus in and tap into my greatness.

If I was always in the same circles and crowds, there would be no infinite waters, no cat down the road. And we wouldn't want that. Would we know deep divers?

So learn to remind yourself that life requires sacrifice.

Everybody wants to go to heaven. Nobody wants to die. Sometimes you're going to have to become a ghost, disappear for a few months and work on that dream, then come back. And everyone's going to be like, oh my gosh. Oh my gosh. Oh my gosh.

. Exactly. Total transformation. Okay.

I always tell you, we're in a world where there is a sea of distraction every single day. The moment you wake up, you are being distracted on purpose, the media, news stories, chaos, mayhem, anarchy, and you have to focus on yourself.

It's a circus out there. It's a circus, a crazy ass circus. You don't want any part in it, do you? No, you want to focus on yourself because this is the gateway to becoming your greatest version. So how does Ralph smart focus on himself? Once again, there's no wifi out here, but I swear there's a better connection. Focus on yourself means switching your iPhone off, your Android off.

And actually going within where there's a better connection. Look, don't wake up with your phone, wake up having an inner body experience, meditate, sit with your emotions, journal about your feelings. These are all ways to focus on yourself.

It amazes me, so many people in this world are so consumed about what's happening with this celebrity and that celebrity, and they forget about themselves. They neglect themselves.

And you have to remind yourself the secret recipe to becoming your greatest version is to check in. Don't just check out, check out what's going on over there and there and there. Check in.

Okay. Have an appointment with yourself. Say, how am I feeling today? What is my dream today? What do I want to manifest today? Get to know yourself, get to know your core needs and who you want to be in life.

Look, celebrities... you are the celebrity. Stop being so obsessed with what that celebrity is wearing. If that celebrity is not talking about becoming your greatest version, they're a distraction.

I know it's crazy what's happening in Israel and Gaza. It's terrible. What's going on in the Congo, what's going on with Russia and Ukraine is terrible. But at the same time, focus on yourself so you can make a change in the world because we must be the change we wish to see in the world. Remind yourself, the more you focus on yourself, the more you can become your greatest version.

Am I eating to live…(seven-day vegan challenge)? Am I exercising enough? Am I really doing my utmost best to put my best foot forward and make my dream happen this year? That's what it means to focus on yourself. Okay. The only person you should be trying to become better than is who you were yesterday.

Focus on yourself. Forget about what they're doing, what they're doing over there. Focus on yourself. I have no time for comparison. You know why? Because comparison is the greatest thief of your peace of mind. Focus on yourself and run your own race.

8   Sacrifice And Get Disciplined

Everybody wants to go to Heaven but nobody wants to die.

Now, we're gonna talk about becoming a ghost, sacrificing, and getting self-disciplined. You know, Ralph Smart had to become a ghost.

I had to sacrifice, I had to get self-disciplined, and now I'm becoming my greatest version. Do you have a hard time figuring out like how on earth you're gonna manifest that life you want? Well, you've come to the right place because I'm gonna give you the tools to make it possible. Let's make today Manifestation Monday!

So, let's start with the importance of becoming a ghost.

Have you noticed that a lot of people in society are afraid to be alone? I don't wanna be alone, but what if I told you that being alone is a secret gateway to becoming your greatest version? Let me explain. When you spend time with yourself, you can actually discover your true purpose.

You can actually discover your core needs. You can actually get to know yourself. You can actually put up with yourself. You can actually trust yourself. You can actually accept yourself. You can actually love yourself. You can do so much. You can find out who you really are, what you're meant to do. You find yourself.

When you are alone, you know thyself. And this will help you become your greatest version. I had to become a ghost along my early journey.

People were like, Ralph, let's hang out in the club. I'm like, no, I gotta work on this dream. I gotta work on this vision. They're like, Ralph, you're letting the team down. I said, okay, okay. I was prepared to do that because I realized that I had to become a ghost. I had to realize that actually, I had to take a trip into the wilderness. You see, once upon a time, I was a city guy, deep divers. I would always be in the concrete jungle.

Then I realized, I said, where did the cat down the road go? The cat down the road led me to the heart of nature, deep divers. And I realized that nature is so beautiful. That's why I'm in the heart of nature every single day, often alone with a cat down the road. And this has helped me become my greatest version. I'm here meditating. I'm getting present.

I'm raising the frequency. I'm getting into alignment with who I really am. Tuning my mental, emotional, and spiritual and physical body.

Look, I'm encouraging you to become a ghost. Your friends wanna be like, oh my gosh, where did she go? Where did he go? You did the magical disappearing act. Congratulations.

You see, the aborigines and many indigenous cultures had something called a rites of passage. Many indigenous cultures all around the world, Native Americans, all over Africa, they had something called a rites of passage. And when a boy was transitioning to a man, he would have to take a trip into the wilderness alone and spend time alone to become a warrior and find himself. But that actually helped him become his greatest version.

So remind yourself to become a ghost today. If you've always been in a busy environment, go on a silent retreat.

Beware of distractions masquerading as friends in disguise. There are a lot of people who tell you, I'm your friend. But actually they are your biggest distraction taking you away from where you should be and where you're meant to be. You have some people in your life right now who are actually holding you back from your greatness.

Some people are doing that intentionally because they see what you are gonna become. They come around you when you're working. They say, hey, let's just distract ourselves.

Let's just get high and drink. Beware of distractions masquerading as friends in disguise. Become a ghost.

Sometimes you have to let certain people go so you can breathe, so you can find yourself, so you can achieve, so you can go to the next level of your greatness. Because every new level of your life demands a new version of you.

If you are in a circle that feels nothing like a circle, there's no support here. There's no love here. There's no camaraderie here.

You don't have a circle. You have a cage. If you look around right now, deep divers, at your circle and you don't find one tiny grain of inspiration, you don't have a circle, you have a cage.

You have to become a ghost. You have to realize you have to remove yourself. Remove yourself from circles which are actually squares. Square prisons... Remove yourself from circles that don't empower you. This is what's helped me along my journey.

I roll solo. I don't want no trouble. Yes, I have beautiful friends and I've got a whole community here, you wonderful, beautiful people who are really like my extended family.

But a lot of the times I've realized that it's okay to be alone because actually we're never actually alone unless we abandon ourselves. Deep divers, become a ghost. Sacrifice and get self-disciplined.

So sacrifice. A lot of people are afraid of that word. I don't want to sacrifice, Ralph. Well, what if I told you to become your greatest version, to manifest the life that you want? Sacrifice is a prerequisite. It's needed. You know why? Because a lot of people talk about heaven. I want to live a heavenly life. I want to be in heaven right now.

Everybody wants to go to heaven, but nobody's willing to die. Everybody wants to experience the good life, but nobody wants to do the work for it. Everybody wants to hang out at the finish line, but nobody wants to run the race. What's going on? I had to learn sacrifice. I had to learn how to turn down invitations.

I had to learn how to cancel appointments because I realized they weren't in my best interests. And I had to let go of what I thought was going to be good for me to replace it with what the universe actually knew was good for my soul. Sacrifice today, the quick pleasure, the dopamine hit.

Sacrifice that and replace it with long lasting satisfaction. Sacrifice the instant gratification and work on yourself. Because in the end, you will be smiling.

Do something today your future self will thank you for. Do something today your future self will praise you for. Do something today your future self will congratulate you for.

I'm so happy my younger self was doing something that my future self will thank me for. That's why I'm happy and I'm here today. Sacrifice requires fasting.

Seven day vegan challenge. I've been plant-based for over 18 years. And that's why I look 21. I am fasting, I am intermittent fasting, doing intermittent fasting. Then I say to the cat down the road, pass me a whole bunch of grapes, stuff them in my mouth and I feel fantastic. But deep divers, I'm fasting.

But fasting is not only with food, fasting is with habits that aren't serving you. And once you learn the art of fasting from habits no longer serving you, to make space for what actually inspires you, you will be on the way to manifesting your best life and becoming your greatest version.

Now we're living in a whole new world. There is TikTok, which is like huge right now. I'm on TikTok. But I've learned that you have to sacrifice vanity and replace it with actually working on yourself and pursuing your true goals. So everything I do on TikTok is about becoming your greatest version. I have no desire to kind of impress people on TikTok or even pose for the gram and say, hey, I made it, look at me.

You know, a lot of people are doing that. They're faking it on the gram and TikTok, like they're living a life they're actually not. And that's the reason why they're not becoming their greatest version.

I made it. Like ET said, what have you made? You haven't even made your bed. Yeah, you want to pretend to these people out there you don't even know that you're living this marvelous life and you're only fooling yourself.

Don't fake it 'till you make it. Don't fake it 'till you make it, just make it. And that means sometimes switching off your phone and saying, you know what? Right now I'm going to work on myself.

I'm going to focus on my dreams. I'm going to focus on my goals. I'm going to focus on my aspirations.And this is how you become your greatest version. Great work requires silence and focus.

People say, Ralph, you're very disciplined. How did I learn the art of self-discipline? I realized that, okay, I have to control my focus. Who is controlling your focus today? Is it the media? Are they saying, hey, look here and you look there? No, you want to control your own focus and you want to realize whatever you focus on grows.

So focus on what it is you want to manifest today. This is what's going to lead you to becoming your greatest version. What is it I want to do today? What is my goal today? Wake up with an agenda.

I woke up today and I said, okay, I'm going to get my butt into nature, inspire. Wake up with a plan. Don't call it a dream. Have a plan. Get self-disciplined. Be consistent, persevere, realize it's a marathon. Shout out to Nipsey Hussle.

It's a marathon. Life is a marathon. It's not a quick sprint. It's a marathon and it never ends. You see, the truth is, the journey does not get easier. We just get stronger. We just get stronger and stronger through this self-discipline, which means controlling our focus, which means avoiding distractions, temptations, anything that's designed to take us out of who we really are.

Self-discipline is about realizing you've got to be patient. Great things take time. A lot of people, you know, the concentration span is so short right now on the planet.

That's why YouTube has YouTube Shorts. I've uploaded a few short videos, like 10 seconds, 20 seconds, because I know a lot of people haven't got the discipline to listen for more than five minutes, not you, but a lot of people out there, right? Self-discipline requires focus, laser sharp focus. Remind yourself that Rome wasn't built in a day.

Everything you do is putting one brick on top of the other, on top of the other, on top of the other, right? And that's how you build the house. Realize you don't have to do everything in one day. All you have to do is a little bit every day.

It doesn't matter how fast you go, so long as you go. The great story of the tortoise and the hare, okay? They have a race, and the hare should win. It is miles ahead of the tortoise, but it says, you know, just before the finish line, I'm going to take a nap and it falls asleep. And then the tortoise is going so slow, one quick step at a time, and then it actually wins the race. This is a lesson that it's not about how fast you go. It's about just going, following your heart's desires, knowing that it can happen for you.

.It will happen for you. It must happen for you because you are willing this into existence. Self-discipline is all about you realizing where you want to be.

What kind of a life do you want to have for your children? Have something to work towards. Have a vision board. Write down your dream life and do everything every day to work towards that.

Don't allow a second to go by without you paying attention to what it is you're here to do. I always say, live life like you're on the run, okay? Live life like you're on the run because you want to work like there's fire up your backside. Buddha said, the trouble is you think you have time.

A lot of people say, Ralph, I'm going to work on my dreams next year. I'm like, wait a second, there is only now. There is only now: if not now, when? And this is going to help you to stop procrastinating, so you can truly become your greatest version.

9   Delete Friends, Find Yourself

It's Better To Be Alone Than In A Lost Crowd.

A lot of you have seen me throughout the years. You're like, oh my gosh, Ralph, you're still here? Inspiring millions? Looking 18? Oh, you're so kind. It's been a long, a long time coming. And I'm still here, because it's a marathon. But you've seen me, right? You've seen me with a beautiful Afro. Had the Jackson 5 Afro. You saw me in my backyard saying, peace, infinite waters. Fast forward, I'm still here, living my best life, becoming my greatest version.

So I'm proof for you that it is possible for you. Let me tell you this. There's a recipe to becoming your greatest version.

I can't even begin to tell you how much my life has changed since I've been inspiring millions of people. In a phenomenal way, I'm grateful every single day. And I always want to remind you, to give thanks, because when you are grateful, you will attract more things to be grateful for. Now, delete all of your friends. What, Ralph? Why? I love my friends.

Hey, just hang on a minute and read on.

So many people we call friends are not actually our real friends, they are distractions. Big distractions. I know because I had a lot of friends, but I realized that they were distractions.

Because I say this, if you're not helping me evolve, you're a distraction. Beware, in the words of Ralph Smart, beware of distractions masquerading as friends in disguise. What if I told you, a lot of people you call friends are actually your biggest distractions, holding you back from where you need to be.

Some people around you, you don't even realize that's the reason why you're not at this gold level, this diamond level, because energy is contagious. And you wanna replace your friends with real friends. How about that? With partners, with genuine, sincere people, with people who make you feel like sunshine, with people who enrich, key word, enrich your life, with people who help you grow mentally, emotionally, spiritually, physically.

Look, I've got 5,000 friends on Facebook, I don't know any one of them. I know a few, right? But it's so easy just to say, oh, that's my friend, but how have they helped you evolve? And this is a recipe to becoming your greatest version. It's a recipe to becoming your greatest version because I realized that as I was leveling up, I was having fewer people in my life.

Now, that's a great paradox because sometimes when you say, I know this person, that person, this person, not every one of them really has your best interests at hand. Some people are envious of you, they're jealous of you, they're not doing anything with their life, they wanna bring you down, crabs in a barrel, ain't nobody got time for that. But then I said, okay, let me get a few good friends, real friends, and they helped me, I helped them.

So it's quality over quantity, the recipe to becoming your greatest version, become a ghost. I'm afraid to be alone, Ralph. We are never alone unless we abandon ourselves. I wrote a number one best-selling book and another one. First one, Tryathon — The Love of a Galaxy.

The second one, Feel Alive by Ralph Smart is a number one best-selling book. I had to learn how to put glue on my seat and sit down when I was writing those best-selling books. Another best-selling book, Book of 1111 Quotes, and now of course, this one you're reading right now, the one, the only, Feel Alive Part II!

I had to hold back because I'm so excited. But I'm just reminding you when you go within, when you distance yourself from the crowd because the crowd is the matrix, you can find your true superpowers. There's a reason why spiritual masters went into the wilderness for 30 days and 30 nights to find out who they really were.

That's when greatness is gonna come. When you say, you know what? Let me get to know who I truly am.

Let me spend some time meditating, doing a little samba baby, because you are gonna tap into your superhuman abilities. Become a ghost. People are gonna be like, oh my gosh, haven't seen Sarah in a long time.

Haven't seen Richard in a long time. That's because you're busy building your empire and one day they're gonna see you just like they see me right now. Everybody's hitting me up on the phone like, Ralph, can we hang out? Because they know I'm doing big things.

But I had to become a ghost, I had to disappear. And sometimes you have to disappear to become your greatest version. Sometimes you have to detach from what is not serving you to make space for what inspires you.

Sometimes you have to say, I'm sorry to your friends. I can't go to the club today. Why? Because I'm too busy working on my dream and vision. Delete your friends, become a ghost and find yourself the recipe to becoming your greatest version. Find yourself, know thyself... this was written on the temples of ancient Egypt. Know thyself... and in ancient Greece as well.

If you don't know who you are, someone else will decide for you and they'll give you a job to do. And that's not you. And that's why a lot of people are unhappy.

I was there, I was getting some money, but it wasn't my purpose and there's a big difference. Now I'm in my purpose and that's the reason why I'm living my best life. I'm becoming my greatest version.

.The moment I followed my purpose, I became rich, realizing I create happiness. Let me keep it going. If you get a job, you go to work, you come home, you complain about it, what kind of a life are you living? A one that has a lack of gratitude.

And I told you, anytime you do not have gratitude, you will never be manifesting. But anytime you do have gratitude to say, yes, thank you universe for this life I'm living. I love Mondays, I love Tuesdays, I love Wednesdays, I love Thursdays, I love Fridays, I love Saturdays and I love Sundays.

I love every single second of my life because I'm living my best life. Woo! Deep divers, you see the recipe to becoming your greatest version works like this. Every single day, ask yourself, how am I evolving where I am right now? This job, how is it helping me grow as a human being? If it's not, leave.

How are these people in my life helping me evolve as a human being? If they're not, drop them. In the words of Steve Harvey, if you don't like being uncomfortable, do not pursue success. I heard that and I'm like, that's a slow motion, Steve.

Right, you're gonna have to be uncomfortable as well. That's a secret recipe for becoming your greatest version. You wanna put yourself in the danger zone.

You wanna be uncomfortable because without being uncomfortable, there is no growth. Do something that challenges you every single day. That's how you know you're going to the next level.

You see the recipe for becoming your greatest version is learning that it's a marathon. It's not a quick sprint. Everybody wants to hang out at the finish line.

Only the cat down the road wants to run the race, right? Nobody wants to run the race. They all wanna chill out and party at the finish line. Well, it's gonna take working over 10,000 hours. It's going to take investing in your dream. I had to buy cameras, $3,000, $4,000. Lenses, $1,000, 1,000 euros. Why? 1,000 pounds. Why? Because I had to invest. If you don't invest in your dream, you won't get anything back.

You won't get anything back. But in the long run, it's a great investment because now your whole entire life will change. So ask yourself, how am I investing in my dream? How am I sacrificing for the greater good? Sometimes you have to give up something good to get something even better. Stay consistent. Your vision is manifesting. I'm proof that it's possible.

And I'm always gonna be here. I've had to turn down deals. People have contacted me. Ralph, I wanna buy Infinite Waters. Someone gave me a deal of millions. I said, no. Because I know the value this channel provides. I could sell it, get about 20 million. But I'm like, nah, I don't wanna do that. I wasn't born yesterday. I know that this channel is gonna keep on growing. 'Till infinity. But when I get these kinds of offers, I'm like, oh, oh, other people see this value too. And that's only because I see the value of what Infinite Waters Ralph Smart is delivering to millions of people.

When you put value on what you do, this is the recipe to becoming your greatest version. Know your worth, know your value. And for me to do this work, I need the fuel.

Seven-day vegan challenge. I need to be taking care of my health. That's why I look 18. It's because I'm drinking those smoothies. That green juice smoothie, chlorella, spirulina. I'm good to go. Health is wealth. So the recipe to becoming your greatest version is to remind yourself, that it's a marathon. You're gonna fail and it's okay.

You're gonna be uncomfortable. And that's okay. But you're gonna live to see another day. And you have to realize you are not finished yet. Tear up this bullshit excuse you keep giving yourself of why you can't be there or live the life you want. I said, it is happening for me. The universe said, your wish is my command, Ralph.

10   For People Who Don't Fit In

You never came here to fit in, you're custom made darling!

I used to think that I was alone until I started to share with the world. Then I'm like, wait a minute, I'm not alone anymore. This chapter is dedicated to people who feel like they don't fit in anywhere. To outsiders, outcasts, people who don't get along with anybody, people who are distant from their family, even though they live in the same house. It's dedicated to you because I've been there, done that, got the t-shirt. I felt alone for most of my life.

I'm like, oh my gosh, nobody gets me, nobody knows where I'm coming from. Do you know that in many countries, the worst form of torture is keeping someone in isolation, solitary confinement? That is torture. And there are so many people who feel like they are in solitary confinement.

In fact, just before I wrote this, before I got here, there's a woman who always passes by. Then she's like, oh my gosh, I've seen your videos. So we got talking. Then she's like, I feel so alone. I'm normally hyper-social, meeting with friends. And with this whole lockdown, I feel totally abandoned, alone. My whole way of life is gone. I don't know what to do. And I don't like to wear face masks. So I'm the odd one out. What's happening?

Let me tell you. You are going through a metamorphosis. That's what's happening. You're raising the frequency. You're raising the vibration. I had to learn how to be alone. I had to get comfortable in my own skin. If you are alone, if you feel alone, if you don't fit in anywhere, you've come to the right place because my entire life, I grew up feeling like an outcast, an outlaw, a fringe dweller.

I didn't fit in anywhere. Now don't get it twisted. I'm a very likable person, but I never felt comfortable in any circle. I felt like a misfit. And I started to realize it was because I had a different way of seeing the world. You see, I realized this. If you feel like you don't fit in in this world, that's because you came here to create a new one. The universe had big plans for me.

Now, when I look back in hindsight, I realize why I felt alone. Because a lot of people around me at that time growing up, they didn't share the same values as me. What I held important to me, they didn't care about.

Now there were so many people who were forced to be alone with the whole lockdown. And I want to remind you, we are never, ever, ever, ever, ever alone. The universe always sends someone. Huh? Explain Ralph. Let me explain then. You see, I almost gave up on the world.

I'm like, I'm dealing with people who just don't get it. And this is why a lot of people feel alone. Even though there are billions of people on the planet, many of us find it hard to connect with someone on a deeper level.

The reason why you feel alone is because you have depth. You no longer have time for shallow conversations, meaningless friendships, pointless interactions. Because for you, it's all about substance, depth, intimacy… intimacy, which means into me see. And that's why a lot of people feel alone because they don't want to fake it anymore. They don't want to pretend anymore. They're getting tired of pretending.

I would rather be alone than follow a crowd in the wrong direction. And that was me growing up, always standing in my truth, but sometimes standing alone. But like I said, in the beginning of this chapter, I thought I was alone until I started to share with the world. And there are millions of deep divers out there. You see, if we go back in history, it took people to stand in their truth, to be alone, to give us all of these wonderful technologies we have today. All of these wonderful technologies we have right now.

The Wright brothers who created, built, invented the airplane that we fly in today. They built the first one out of spruce wood. They were alone without an idea. Nobody else thought of that. At the same time, we owe it to them for the aviation industry. So sometimes you've got to realize that being alone can be a blessing in disguise because it helps you to know yourself.

Do you know how many people are with people they don't like because they're afraid to be alone? So guess what? They can't think for themselves. Guess what? They have more anxiety. Guess what? They don't love themselves. Guess what? They don't even know who they are. I had to come to nature, learn how to be alone. And by the way, there's a difference between being alone and being lonely. Let me explain. Go on then, Ralph. Okay, chill.

You see, being lonely is different from being alone. When you are lonely, it means you are separate from the whole. And that is the real torture. But being alone is something totally different. When you are alone, it means you are still connected to the whole but you are honoring your uniqueness. You have chosen to be the lion and roar in a world full of sheep.

You have chosen to keep it real with yourself in a world where everybody wants to follow. You have chosen to speak up and say actually what's happening on the planet is utterly ridiculous. In a world where a lot of people are just going along to get along. Congratulations because the reward is coming for you. It came for me. Being alone was the best thing that happened to me.

What? I said being alone was the best thing that happened to me because it helped me to love myself. I realized that a lot of my friends, they didn't want to be in those circles with other people but they were afraid to get to know who they really were. I wasn't.

I said, let me just meditate. Let me find out who I really am. Then I saw it was so beautiful. I've got a whole universe inside of me. If you feel like you don't fit in, it's because you came here to stand out. You have to be different to make a difference. And listen to this. I'm the chosen one. What? I said I'm the chosen one.

That's why a lot of people don't fit into this matrix because it wasn't designed for you. You came here to do greater things. You came here to do greater things than just be a slave to society and you know that. That's why your family doesn't get you. Your friends don't get you because you see the world in a different way than them. They are in the fear frequency.

You are in the love frequency. They want to be controlled. You want to be free and that's why it's hard for a lot of people right now to fit into society because this society was not meant for you. You are a chosen one. You are an old soul in a young body. You're ahead of your time. Congratulations. So I had to learn this and my oh my did it pay off. I want to remind you of this.

.When you spend time alone, one thing happens. You're forced to face yourself.

You're forced to face your shadow.

You're forced to face your fears, your anxiety and therefore you become your greatest version. When you are always distracting yourself, I said this, the human being is on the run from itself. Always trying to get away from yourself. You're actually more lost. I had to be alone to find myself. I had to be alone to become confident. Confidence emanates from the Latin confidere, which means to trust.

I trust myself. I do a little samba and a backflip as well. If you don't fit in, I'm here to remind you there is hope. I told you I thought I was alone until I started to share with the world. There are millions like me. I had to realize that I could only find those other deep divers by putting myself out there.

If you feel like you don't fit in anywhere, I'm urging you to start sharing your story. I'm urging you to start sharing with the world and in turn you will meet your reflections. You will find your tribe.

You thought there was nobody like you. No, there are millions of people like you who see the world like you, who have the same interests and values as you, but you've got to be there so they can see you. You've got to put yourself out there.

You've got to speak up baby so I can see you and then you will find your tribe. It happened to me. I told you I almost gave up on the world, but I'm like wait a minute. I'm just going to share my truth with the world. Whoever listens, we're going to become best friends. Then the cat down the road appeared.

If you feel like you don't fit in anywhere, it's because you're sane and you no longer want to be around fake boring people. You no longer want to be in a society which kills life. You no longer want to be in a society which kills creativity. You want to be free from the matrix. You want to be unplugged and there are so many people all around us who are just satisfied with living a mediocre life.

You can't accept that because you know you came here to be free and the path to freedom, the path to freedom can sometimes be lonely. The path to freedom can sometimes feel like you're all alone, but you're never ever ever ever alone. The universe always sends someone. The universe reveals its secrets to those who dare to follow their hearts. 7 day vegan challenge. It wasn't popular for me to go plant-based.

I grew up in a household of meat eaters. Yes, my sister ate fish predominantly, but most of the people around me were eating steak, beef, chicken, everything. But I said I want to be alone to follow my plant-based journey and guess what? The same people who were judging me back then because I was alone in that journey are now asking for advice.

What? Because they see what I've become through this lifestyle. They see my whole life getting better and better, me living in more abundance. You see first they laugh at you, then they copy you, then they want to be you.

If you are alone, if you don't fit in anywhere, if you feel like an outcast, I'm here to remind you that in actuality it is a blessing in disguise. Let me explain. It means you are a premium cloth. What? You are a premium cloth. You're cut from a different cloth. You're high fabric. It means you are exclusive content. It means you are the original, not the copy. And the original is always worth more than the copy.

In a world full of clones, choose to be yourself. There are so many people who don't fit in anywhere who feel like it's a curse when in actuality you will be the one that will help other people stand in their power. It only takes one person to change the world.

If you go back in history, all the people who changed the world stood alone. Then other people got inspired by them. And that's the gift you have. Don't cry because you're alone. I told you being alone only means that you are still connected to the whole. At the same time, you are honoring your uniqueness. So honor your uniqueness today because that's your power.

Chapter Eleven

Why You're Alone

We are never alone until we abandon ourselves. Look, I meet a lot of people who say, Ralph, I feel alone. I don't fit in. I've got no friends. And for me, I thought that was bad until I realized sometimes it's a blessing in disguise. You see, deep divers growing up, I was alone a lot. But I realized it was because I had a very low tolerance for BS.

Now, if you are alone a lot, if you don't fit into this world, if you realize this is all a matrix, it's all a setup, I'm here to tell you you're not alone. You see, that's the great paradox of being alone. You are actually not alone. There are millions of people who are exactly like you. And all you've got to do is wait on your tribe. You see, not everyone's gonna make it.

Not everyone can go. I want you to look at a pyramid. You see, at the base, you have the masses. As you rise higher up the pyramid, the smaller the ratio, right? The smaller the ratio. And it gets narrower. And also, the air gets purer. You can... You can really breathe. No pollution up there. But you won't find a lot of people up there because not everyone makes it up there. In other words, not everyone makes it on the greatest journey ever, which is the journey within.

You see, we were born alone. And we are gonna leave this matrix alone. But I want to remind you, deep divers. If you feel like you don't fit into this matrix, it's because you came here to create a whole new world. You came here to create a whole new world. You came here to be a pioneer. You came here to be a trendsetter. You came here to stand in your truth. You see, when you stand in your truth right now on the planet, you might find yourself alone.

All of your so-called friends, your family members, they are hypnotized by the mass media, hypnotized in the matrix. But you can think for yourself and that's why you're alone. Because you're not willing to sacrifice your integrity. You're not willing to sacrifice who you really are. Just to people, please. Ain't nobody got time for that.

You see, that's why you're alone and don't fit in and have zero friends because you have values which you stick by. And the truth is, deep divers, there's a big difference between being alone and being isolated.

You see, when you are alone, like I am a lot, I am connected to the whole. I realize everything is interconnected. When you are isolated, you are disconnected from the whole. Separation. No, we are all interconnected. And when you are alone, you have this beautiful epiphany, like I have all the time that I have.

But the greatest journey is going within. You start to realize everything you were told in this matrix is a complete lie. Everything out there is an illusion. And the only real world is the world within yourself. You see, if you are alone right now and don't fit in, I'm here to remind you, I was there. But it was because I came here to create a whole new world.

You see, the great paradox is that if you go back in ancient times, all the great masters, they were always alone. How come they had thousands of disciples? Because when you remember, key word, remember, when you put yourself back together, when you know thyself, you become a monumental inspiration to millions of people.

It's called rites of passage. I spend a lot of time alone in the forest. I spend a lot of time alone on the beach, just meditating, just going within, just breathing in that good-ass prana, baby.

And therefore, I'm able to share with you day in, day out, because I'm recharging. You see, right now, you're going to have to learn how to protect your energy. Right now, you're going to have to learn how to protect your energy. Right now, you're going to have to realize it's better to be alone than follow a crowd going in the wrong direction. A lot of these people are lost. You're hanging around. And you know that if you follow them, it's only going to lead to a dead end. And that's why you choose to be alone. It's not that you're a loner.

.No, you could be around so many people, but right now, you want to work on yourself. Right now, you want to work on yourself. Right now, you want to get to know yourself. And that is commendable.

Look, every single day, we have to realize we have many lives. The cat down the road has nine lives. Okay, we have many lives, deep divers. And being alone, I liken it to shedding your skin. You see, everything we are taught in this matrix is all.about going outside of ourselves.

When you realize you have it all within you, oh baby, you free yourself. And that's the gift that comes with learning how to be alone, learning how to sit with your emotions. You see, most people, they are afraid to be alone.

Most people are afraid to be alone so they end up in a relationship which hurts them in the long run because they settle. People who are alone never settle. They are choosing to stand in their truth, choosing to stand in their authenticity.

I love people, but I'm not going to be around people who are leading me to my lower nature. I'm going to be around people who are leading me to my higher nature. You see, if you don't fit into this matrix, congratulations, it's because you're the chosen one.

Yeah, they called you the black sheep of your family. You are the only one in your family who thinks for themselves, who stopped drinking the Kool-Aid, who is choosing to breathe when everyone else is masked up. You are the only one in your family who has discernment, the ability to judge well, the ability to judge well.

And that's why you might find yourself alone because you've gone to the next level. You are leveling up. You see, you are outgrowing the box they put you in. And that's why you might find yourself being alone. Your third eye is opening. You are decalcifying your pineal gland. Right now, you are aware that this is all a stage. This is all an illusion. But people around you, sometimes they don't get you.

They're like, huh, what are you talking about? Just be quiet, eat the popcorn and watch the TV. And you know that, hey, I don't want to get programmed. So you choose to be alone. And I'm here to tell you, your tribe is waiting. I spent a lot of time alone and I still do. I still do.

But how come I'm inspiring millions of people because I'm reconnecting with myself. I'm protecting my energy. I'm here to remind you, you have the greatest rewards if you are learning how to sit with your emotions, if you are learning how to be alone in a world full of clones, in a world where they want you to be something you're not.

.   That is honorable. That is beautiful because it's the people who are alone who are the pioneers, who are the people that inspire people far and wide because they have gone on the greatest journey ever, which is the journey within.

Look, you laugh at me because I'm different. I laugh at you because you're all the same. I can't tell who's who from who's who, right? When you are alone, you find your power. You step into your true uniqueness. You step into your true superpowers. Because I've spent and I'm spending a lot of time alone, I'm not afraid. I'm not afraid of being who I am.

I accept myself. I love myself 100%. The amount of people, and this is the great paradox, the amount of people who don't love themselves but they're around other people because they've never taken time just to be alone with themselves, just to reconnect with themselves, just to give themselves a big hug.

The amount of people who spend so much time on the gram, on TikTok just trying to win other people's approval but they're still unhappy inside, the amount of people who are chasing fame but they're still unhappy. I'm happy, because it's all within me. I'm complete.

I'm whole. So why you're alone, don't fit in and have zero friends is because you know who you are. You are standing in your truth.

You are not willing to compromise your integrity. You're not afraid to stand even when everyone is going against you because you're that strong and I'm here to congratulate you because you are the chosen one. Ever been around someone's 7-Day Vegan Challenge? And you're eating a delicious acai bowl and they're just talking and talking and talking and you're like, let me just enjoy this, right? Many times we choose to be alone just to eat in peace.

Many times we choose to be alone as well just to be silent. In a world that's so noisy, there is no greater beauty than listening to the wind.

I get all my downloads when I'm alone because I'm sun gazing, I'm listening to the wind, I'm listening to the birds. I'm tuning in to tune all of that out. You see, a lot of people, they don't know how to be alone. They don't know how to put down the phone and now you're turning into a cyborg. Take a break from your phone. Take a break from your smartphone.

.Say, hey, I'm gonna turn it off. I guarantee you, you will have a better connection with yourself. Stop comparing yourself to other people on social media. Stop living a fake life. Stop being afraid to live your authentic truth. See, the greatest minds learn how to be alone and they inspire the most people.

I want to remind you, we are never alone. The universe always sends someone. When you learn how to reconnect to the truth of who you are, you will naturally attract your reflections.

How come I'm attracting so many beautiful Deep Divers into my life? Because I learned how to be alone! I found my truth. Right now is the time you find yours. Remind yourself, like Socrates said, the unexamined life is not worth living.

That means the examined life is worth living. When you are alone, you can reflect, you can be more introspective. You can get more clarity on who you are, on where you need to be, on what you need to do.

If you feel like you don't fit into this world, that's because you came here to create a new one. You are a pioneer. Take time to protect your energy. Take time just to spend time with yourself. Recharge your batteries. Have a beautiful day.

Chapter Twelve

How To Find Yourself When You're Lost, Alone Or Unmotivated

If you feel lost in your life right now, if you feel all alone in your life right now, you have come to the right place. Because a lot of people are lost in the world, let's face it. And a lot of people feel alone in the world, let's face it.

Now, do you feel lost in your life right now? Do you feel alone in your life right now? Be honest. Look, the cat down the road is honest. The cat down the road always feels alone and lost. How to find yourself when you feel lost and unmotivated? I got a great question that came to me.

Someone asked me, Ralph, how can I cope with feeling lost and feeling all alone? And I'm like, I've got to talk about this because all the lonely people, right? Where do they all come from? All the lonely people, where do they all belong? Don't make me sing the Beatles right now. There are a lot of lonely people on planet earth and we have to do something about this.

Hey, I've been there. I've been alone. I've been lost. I felt lonely before, but then I found myself. Let me share with you what's helped me along my journey. How I found myself again when I was feeling lost and unmotivated. How to cope with feeling lost and alone in the world.

It's a big old world, isn't it? And when you feel all alone, it's like, oh my gosh, I can't take this. Like in this massive world of over 7 billion people and I've got no friends. I've got no one to lean on. Not even the cat down the road is around. It's a hard pill to swallow deep divers. I've been there.

When I used to wake up feeling like, oh my gosh, it's me against the world. Shout out to Tupac. Right? I used to seriously wake up with that feeling. I've been lost. I've been like a loose leaf, but I want you to remind yourself of this today. I want you to remind yourself of this today, deep divers.

Everybody you see on planet earth was once lost before they found their path. Everybody you see who is living their purpose right now was once lost before they found their path.

Ralph smart was lost before he began to inspire millions of people. I'm talking from personal experience, deep divers. I used to wake up feeling like, oh my gosh, I don't know what I'm doing here. I don't know where I'm going. Somebody help me. And I just heard my echo. Oh yeah. It was a sad, a sad affair. Then I realized this beauty.

When I was lost, I realized that it's not a bad thing after all. You see, when you are lost and alone, that is a confirmation from the universe that you are in the process of letting go. What?That's right. All you're doing is letting go.

You see, the reason why I was lost was because I refused to be in the crowd. The crowd is the matrix. So when I didn't want to follow the crowd, I'm like, I want to follow myself. I was alone and lost. I'm like, anybody coming with me? No, no, no, no, no. Started to break down. Right. But I realized that it was because I was letting go of what was not serving me. That's why I felt lost.

Like if you are unplugging from this matrix in the beginning, initially you're going to feel lost, confused. Like, oh my gosh, because it's new to you. When I said, I just want to inspire the world. I felt lost in the beginning. Look at my early videos. I didn't have a clue what I was doing. And I still don't know what I'm doing. All I know deep divers is that I'm having a whole lot of fun.

Check this out. Define yourself when you feel lost and unmotivated. To cope with feeling lost and alone. Realize that it's all about the emotions you are creating. I'm creating a lot of positive emotions when I'm in nature. I don't even know where I am right now. I don't even know where I am right now. I'm in the middle of the woods in a, in a, in a mysterious place. Right. But it feels good. So I don't feel lost. I feel like I'm creating a lot of positive energy.

I don't feel lost because, wait a minute, I can hear some birds up there. I've got a beautiful tree behind me. We are never alone. The universe always sends someone. And someone could be in the form of a tree.

Trees are alive, in case you didn't know, right? Birds are alive, right? Nature is alive. You see, we can't be alone even if we tried because everything in this universe is connected. So if you feel lost right now in your life and alone, realize that you aren't alone. We are all in this together. Everybody is connected.

Why do I feel lost then, Ralph? You feel lost because you feel like you have to deal with this all by yourself. And you don't. You can come to nature and just start talking. Start talking aloud. Say, nature, I feel lost. Is anybody out there? And some birds are going to tweet back at you. At least they tweeted, be grateful for goodness sakes.

When I was alone, and lost, it was actually when I just finished university. And that's a real paradox, right? I had just graduated and I felt lost, like, what am I supposed to do? I've just spent so much money.

. I've got a student loan to pay back. And I still don't know what to do with my life, right? I realized that when I was lost in that period of my life, it was because I didn't know who I was. In other words, I was studying for the wrong exam. Then I learned I've got to study for the right exam. In other words, I've got to know thyself.

In ancient Kemet, or Egypt, on every temple, it said, know thyself. Deep divers, the moment I began to know who I was, a multi-dimensional being having a human experience who loves to cat down the road. Oh, baby. I never ever felt lost again because I felt whole within myself. I felt complete within myself. When I'm meditating out here, I can feel the universe right now. I feel at one with the universe. Lost? No.

I feel whole. Sometimes you have to lose yourself to find yourself. If you feel lost right now in your life and alone, with no purpose, no friends, no direction, you feel confused, you feel like a waste. That's good. I was there, deep divers. But I realized I had to go through that experience to find out who I truly was. You see, most people you see running around, they're actually lost.

So what are they doing instead, Ralph? Killing time, working in jobs which aren't serving them. They're there because they don't want to face what we call the existential vacuum or the existential crisis. Have you heard of the existential crisis? This is where you wake up one day and think, oh my gosh, I'm alive and everything is fleeting and everything is changing and everything is transitioning.

Babies are born, people die. Oh my gosh, it's called life. Welcome to planet Earth. It's a lot to take in. All of us feel lost, deep divers. I'm here to tell you, everybody you see has felt lost at some point in their life when they really are faced with the existential crisis.

Like when I'm in nature, along my early journey, I would be like, oh my gosh, we are so insignificant. And Anne is small, but we are all so small. When you go swimming in the ocean, look up and think, I'm like a grain of sand in the universe. . That's the existential crisis. Of course you're going to feel lost, but don't worry about it. Happens to the cat down the road all the time.

How to find yourself when you feel lost and unmotivated? Go for a walk, come out into nature and meet Ralph Smart on the beach or in the forest. How to cope when you feel lost, deep divers. And all alone, phone a friend. No, this is not one who wants to be a millionaire, but you can still phone a friend. And if you learn that you can reach out to other people, you can express your feelings to other people, you will never ever feel alone or lost again.

You don't have to go through this all alone. There is somebody who's going to listen to you. No, there isn't, Ralph. The cat down the road will. Okay. You see, you see, I used to think I'm all alone, I'm lost, but I was refusing to phone a friend.

And many times we think we have to suffer in silence. You don't have to do that. Start going out, start socializing, go to Ralph's Smart 7-Day Vegan Challenge parties and stuff a whole bunch of grapes in your mouth full of resveratrols, good for your heart health and a coconut full of lauric acid.

Realize that when you feel lost, when you are having this breakdown, it's actually a breakthrough. I was lost so I can be found. It's the contrast. Only through contrast can we discover who we truly are. You need to be lost to find yourself. It's the rite of passage.

So realize something better is coming for you. A better view is coming for you. A new perspective is coming for you. When you feel lost, realize it's not the end. It's only the beginning. And something new on the horizon is coming your way. There is something new on the horizon coming your way. A new horizon is coming your way.

You see, this feeling of being lost and alone. Let's take a look at the current day matrix. Most people are on Instagram, on these social media apps, comparing their body to someone else's. Trying to impress people you don't know. Selling your soul for a few silver coins and a coffee. Goodness gracious, is this what the world has come to? Everybody just wants to be liked.

I know. But that's why so many people are lost. Because your value always has to be internal. I can never be lost again. Why? Because I'm so comfortable in my own skin. I love the being I'm becoming. Therefore, I'm not in competition with anybody else. I'm in a league of my own. That's why I never feel lost. And I never feel alone. I never feel alone, deep divers.

Because I embrace my flaws. If you are someone who feels alone and lost, allow yourself to feel alone. And allow yourself to get lost. Like really get lost. Like get shipwrecked. Right? Get shipwrecked.

Go to Thailand, get shipwrecked. And when you realize that when you can allow yourself to feel lost, when you can allow yourself to feel alone, what is going to happen? You're going to start panicking, right? You're going to be full of anxiety. But after time, give it some time. Then you're going to start embracing yourself for the first time. And you will no longer feel lost or alone.

Ever wondered why the great sages and masters, people like Buddha, were always seen alone? Alone, meditating, because they're like, I've got to get away from those people. Because they realize too that the crowd is the matrix.

Do you know how beautiful it is to be alone? I love being alone. Why? Because I can actually hear my one true voice. So if you feel lost and alone, if you feel alone, start seeing the benefits of being alone, that you can hear yourself.

You become more intuitive. You can now love yourself without judging yourself and comparing yourself to other people. If you feel lost today, if you feel lost today, deep divers, realize this today. We all start from somewhere. We've all got to learn. Somehow, someway, we're like, oh my gosh, I got to learn. We all start from somewhere. And there is no shame in feeling lost. There is no shame in not knowing which way to go.

What you have to do, deep divers, when you feel lost and alone, surrender, because you are going through the metamorphosis from the caterpillar to the butterfly. You are transforming into something so beautiful, so magnificent, but you have to die to be born again. Deep divers, how? Define yourself when you're lost and unmotivated.

It's just a phase, deep divers. It won't last forever. Trust me. I used to wake up thinking, will anything ever work out for me? Then I released resistance. I said, okay, universe, whatever happens, happens. And all of a sudden, things started to fall into place. So don't panic about being lost. Don't worry about being alone, because you are never alone, even if you want it to be alone.

. Just focus on loving who you are. Focus on feeling good within yourself. And I guarantee you, you will never feel lost or alone. Just remind yourself, never allow your current state to be your final destination. And once you realize that, well, you'll just say, feels so good to be alive, baby.

Chapter Thirteen

5 Powerful Ways Twin Flames Recognise Each Other

So it's time to talk about twin flames. Have you been dreaming of your twin flame? Is that them, Ralph? Is that them over there? It's like twin flame this and twin flame that. What are some of the ways someone can know if they've met their true twin flame or not?

Now, love is all you need. Love is the elixir of life. Love is the greatest healing force on the planet. However, in so many of our lives, it can remain elusive. Unless your twin flame is right in front of you. And you're like, Ralph, I'm sure that's my twin flame.

So how do we know we are in the presence of our twin flame? How do twin flames recognize each other? Now, what is a twin flame? This is your perfect mirror. Ever met someone who's like, you're like, that's me. Just in a female body. Or that's me just in a male body. It is your perfect mirror. And when you meet your twin flame.

1.   Vibes

The first powerful way twin flames recognize each other is from the vibes. Twin flames recognize each other by their energy, by their vibes, not by their appearances.

Twin flames don't recognize each other because they've got a suit on and they're looking pretty fly. No, they recognize each other from vibes. And if you are in the presence of your twin flame... you have to start going on the journey within to really feel this person from your heart space. And that's how twin flames always recognize each other. The heart already knows what the mind can only dream of.

Twin flames recognize each other from their completion level. The only one that can complete ourselves, is ourselves, but check this out, your twin flame is your reflection, your perfect mirror. In other words, they are another you. In a different time and space. That's why the more complete you become, the more whole you become within yourself, the more you will say, actually, yes, that's my twin flame. Because you have this sense of oneness.

And I know from personal experience. A lot of other people who found their twin flame. They're like, Ralph, yes, I knew she was my twin flame. I knew he was my twin flame from the deep sense of oneness. There is no separation. And that's why in the presence of your twin flame, the ego dissolves. And it's the vibes. In a society where so many of us, we invest in how we look. That's cool.

But twin flames don't actually recognize each other by how they look. They recognize each other by how they make each other feel. It's the vibes and the vibes never lie.

2.   Familiarity

Have you ever met someone? You're like, Ralph, I swear, I know this person. From somewhere. From a past life.

Yes. Twin flames recognize each other from a deep familiarity. From a past life. It's like such a strong bond and such a strong love that you're like, how is this even possible? Because you didn't cultivate this love in this incarnation. You've been traveling and cultivating the love for centuries.

For thousands of years. And that's why sometimes you can see twin flames together. And the love they have is so powerful. That nothing can get in the way. And that's only because they've been incarnating with each other from many past lives. And they're like in this time, in this lifetime, for the next life, we're going to be together again.

We're going to make a pact. They make a pact. They're reborn and they find each other again. That's how twin flames recognize each other. They have what I call the Trinity. Not only a physical connection. They also have a mental connection. They have an emotional connection.

Even more so, they have a heart space connection. They share the same heart. That's how twin flames recognize each other. They share the same heart. Your happiness is their happiness. Your sadness is also their sadness. Because once again, you are one in the same. It's a twin flame. So, also, both of you are each other's best friends, lovers, therapists. Nobody can draw out of you what your twin flame can.

They can draw so much out of you. And that's how twin flames recognize each other. Because they are going to help you grow like nobody else can. They can be silly with you, but also serious with you. They can take you to places nobody else can. And that's how twin flames recognize each other.

3.   Vulnerability

You can tell them anything. You don't have secrets with a twin flame. Because check this out, twin flames recognize each other because they can't hide from each other. They know what each other is feeling right now because once again, they share the same heart. They know when you're lying. They know when you're sad. They know when you're happy. That's how twin flames recognize each other.

They can read you like a book. They know it. They can read your mood. You see, most people you are in a relationship with, sometimes if it's not your twin flame, they don't know when you're sad. They don't know when you're happy. Your twin flame will always know. And you are very vulnerable with your twin flame. You are very authentic with your twin flame. That's how twin flames recognize each other. There is no pretending. There is no I'm better than you. No, there is only mutual love and mutual respect.

Twin flames know that they can recognize each other by the level of surrender. If you can surrender with someone 100%, chances are that's your twin flame. That's very, very rare to do in this society where everybody is ego-based.

Twin flames recognize each other because they can surrender. They can be fully in their heart space without the ego and tell someone their secrets without the fear of feeling ashamed, without feeling guilty, without feeling like they're going to be judged. No, twin flames accept each other 100%.

4.   Food

You're eating similar foods. I realized my twin flame wakes up with a bunch of grapes in her mouth just like me. Both of you share the same food values. If you are vegan, your twin flame is also going to be a vegan. They also have compassion towards animals just like you. So always say, are we eating the same? If you are, that's how twin flames recognize each other.

5.   One of you is always the runner

This always happens in the twin flame relationship. And it's always this resistance and acceptance. But forces will always bring you back together because no matter how far you are apart, twin flames always know, the heart always knows, this is my twin flame because somehow, some way, you always gravitate back towards each other because that is your true twin flame.

Yo! Twin flames be like, I'm running away from my twin flame. Actually, I'm running away from myself. You always get drawn back together if that's your true twin flame.

Chapter Fourteen

10 Secrets Soul Mates Won't Tell You

What is the secret to finding the one? Like a lot of us, we dream of finding this perfect person. But, wait a minute. Are you perfect yourself? So, let me share with you what's helped me along my journey. Because I've been in so many different relationships that I know what feels right and what doesn't.

And I've realized and learned a lot about relationships and when it comes to meeting someone who complements your energy. Right? And someone who definitely doesn't. So, let's start with the first secret soulmates won't tell you.

1.   Look for your soul mate.

Instead of searching for your soulmate, start looking for your soulmate. You see, soulmates won't tell you that it wasn't always peaches and vegan cream. Like they had to get married to themselves first before they could find their other whole. Now, most of us in relationships, if you are looking for the perfect partner. What happens? We're always looking for someone outside of ourselves and we're like half full.

Waiting for someone to complete us. And that was me along my early journey until I realized instead of looking and searching for my soulmate, I had to look for my soulmate. But once you have found your soulmate, you know your soulmate from their energy, not from their words.

That's what helped me along my journey because you see, a lot of people, they talk the good talk. But for me, I can recognize a soulmate from the glance. You know it when you see it. When I talk about soulmates, I'm talking about people helping us evolve — because that's what soulmates are essentially.

We have many different soulmates because we are meeting people at different times to learn different lessons to help us evolve even more. Okay, so when we talk of this complete harmony with someone else, you know it by the way they make you feel.

Okay, by the glance, when people say love at first sight. Okay, this is a secret soulmates won't tell you. When they saw a picture or when they first met that person, they were instantly attracted to that person on all levels. Not just physically, but mentally, spiritually and emotionally.

2.   That they are in a water relationship.

Okay, you've got the water relationship. Then you've got the Coca-Cola relationship. Now I've been in a lot of Coca-Cola relationships. That is the toxic relationship. That is the relationship which is full of arguments. Ever been around someone and you can't stop arguing like you can't stop arguing with them. Yeah, that's a Coca-Cola relationship. It's not good for you.

Water relationships are transparent. Okay, a key ingredient of a soulmate relationship is transparency. In essence, they are your reflection. The water relationship is always giving. It is always pure. The Coca-Cola relationship is contaminated. It's not good for your health.

Okay, that's why a lot of people who are in soulmate relationships, their health starts to improve. They start to get that baby glow. You're like, why are you glowing? Oh my gosh, because you don't even want to know what happened last night.

Or maybe you do because it's so exciting, right? You can't even imagine what we did last night, right?

3.   They are honest with you

Many times we think people who have found the one or their perfect partner, their soulmate, whatever name you want to call it, we think it's all like a fairy tale.

No, absolutely not. I've been in relationships where nobody told me the truth. And when I meet soulmates, people who are at the exact same frequency as myself. Okay, because we don't just have one soulmate, we have many soulmates all over the planet. Probably one in every single country. Okay, so what I realized was that they are honest with you.

It is someone who is 100% honest with you. And a soulmate is very rare. It's like a diamond. Okay, one in a million. Well, actually, diamonds aren't that rare. We'll come to that later. Anyway, they are honest with you. Like they will tell you to just take that off right now. They will tell you what they really feel, even though you're like, well, that's your opinion. But they will tell you how they feel.

They don't have a filter when it comes to even expressing their love to you. They are very vulnerable. They'll tell you what happened to them in their childhood when their parents took away their cookies and they started to cry for like five hours. They'll tell you intimate stories. Like you can be really silly around a soulmate. That's how you know, right? And that's a secret soulmates won't tell you.

If you are around a person and you're always tense and tight, they are definitely not your soulmate. If there is an awkward silence too, no, they aren't your soulmate. So soulmates, they can observe the silence together. That is total honesty. Observing total silence. It's not awkward. It's just fantastic.

4.   You have to go through different people first before you find them

This is something they won't tell you. That many times in a relationship, you have to go through different people first, before you get to me. Right? They realize that no relationship they've been in was a waste because every single relationship led them to that person. Now, a lot of the times we can't forgive ourselves for being with someone. We say, oh my gosh, I can't believe I allowed myself to be with this person.

Right? But, hey. Soulmates won't tell you they are so grateful for every single person they've been in a relationship with because it's led them up to this person. Like, how amazing is that? So soulmates realize that every relationship is actually helping your evolution.

5.   Food and love go together

What's the fifth secret soulmates won't tell you? 7 day vegan challenge. Now, a lot of soulmates won't tell you this. That we have soul food. But then we have soul food. Right? When it comes to food and love. Soulmates know this. That, yes, food and love go together. Absolutely. Absolutely. Absolutely. But they realize that they share a common respect for each other's eating habits. Now, I'll give you a story.

I used to date a woman in Ethiopia. And it was a great relationship. I even went there. That's why I always talk about Ethiopia. And that was at the time I was becoming a vegan. And I was giving her information.

Okay, become a vegan. But she didn't want to hear it. She was like, yeah, maybe. But she was eating a lot of ketchup, right? A lot of junk food. And I'm like, hmm, is this soul satisfying? So soulmates respect each other's eating habits. But at the same time, they work together to eat better together to inspire each other. So when I was in another relationship with someone who had a more compatible eating lifestyle to me, because they were also vegan, it was amazing. It was like a huge, huge inspiration.

Okay, and soulmates will tell you that they have very similar eating habits. If you are vegan, they are vegan. Okay, if you eat this, they eat that. Not all cases are like this, mind you. But the majority. Why? Because you see a soulmate connection is a reflection.

So that's why people always ask me, Ralph, I'm doing the 7 Day Vegan Challenge, and now my relationship is going a bit haywire. I'm not surprised. Because once again, food and love go together. Like once I started to eat more living foods with live enzymes, I wanted to meet someone who shared the same love I have for stuffing strawberries in my mouth and the same love I have for all of these animals.

6.   They are top priority

Okay, what's number six? What's the sixth secret that soulmates won't tell you? Now, a lot of people say I'm busy, and that used to be me along my journey. Like a lot of my early relationships weren't the best.

.Why? Because I was so busy. Like relationships were not my priority. Work was. And a lot of people right now are on that hamster. You're on that wheel, right? You're a hamster on that wheel. Like you're going around really fast. You're a work addict. Ain't nobody got time for relationships. Relationships aren't your top priority.

Now, soulmates, people who have found the one who have great relationships, relationships are a top priority. In fact, they even come ahead of work. Because soulmates, they realized they got the money, right? They got the top job, but they still weren't happy. But they realized for their next level of evolution, they had to be with their other whole to go to the next level. And that's what I realized because when I was just working all the time, I had no time for even the person I was with.

Afterwards, I'm like, gosh, was it really worth it? Because when you meet someone, you are meeting another universe. Do you know how precious and valuable that is? So right now and along my journey, like relationships, great connections, these are the top priority, right? Even more so than work.

But soulmates will tell you that the reason why their connection is the top priority is because they are working together on a similar mission. That's the big secret. Like I've been diving deep. You better be able to dive deep with me, baby. You better. You better.

7.   You that your vibe attracts your tribe.

Now you probably heard this saying, but you have to be in the right place at the right time and have the right frequency. Now, a lot of the times our soulmates are passing into our lives and we don't even know it.

Why? Because once again, we are preoccupied with other things, therefore allowing ourselves to become disturbed. So I realized that, okay, I get it. In relationships, as we change, the types of people we meet also changes.

So check this out. When I was eating a lot of meat, yeah, I did meet a soulmate at that time. We got along great because she liked a lot of meat too.

But then once I became a vegan, I was on a whole different frequency, so that relationship now was incompatible with me, right? So it just wasn't going to happen. So as we change, as your vibe changes, as your energetic frequency changes, the people you attract into your life now change. So if you meet someone who's on the same frequency as yourself, that's a soulmate.

The greatest relationships have the highest levels of resonance. Your vibe attracts your tribe.

8.   Ego can destroy the relationship

. You're still reading those fairy tales, right? What is it, Ralph? Look, ego, a three-letter word, just a tiny three-letter word. That can destroy a relationship. Oh my gosh, that's right. Happened to me along my journey, right? There was a time where we've all been in ego. And I've realized that as my ego is dissolving, ego is not negative, by the way. You actually need the ego to help you become your greatest version. But a lot of us, we let our ego take over to the point where it actually affects our relationships. I talk about men of purpose, women of purpose. A lot of men, women write to me saying, gosh, my boyfriend, my husband, he's never got time for me.

He's always working and this and that. And same thing. Guys write to me saying their girlfriend, their wife is always busy doing other things and stuff. Ego sometimes creates separation. That's why soulmates always work on very similar missions. So they are around each other a lot to have quality time.

Ego, that three-letter word that can destroy a relationship. How does this happen? A lot of people say, well, I'm earning millions of dollars. So that means that I'm better than you in the relationship because I am providing for you.

Like a lot of guys think they can just impress women with money. Women don't care about money. What they do care about is if you're good in bed. Don't worry about it. Look, when you realize this secret that the ego sometimes can get in the way. Let's be honest. But soulmates have allowed their ego to dissolve. So they become one.

Okay, and that is why when you are with your soulmate, you know, because you're not trying to prove anything to them like show off like, okay, I got this. I got that. You don't have to do that. Because like both of you know, you're just really silly anyway. Like they've seen you in your pajamas like dancing around to sweet dreams. Right? You can't hide from them.

They've seen you in your most vulnerable moments, in your most silly moments, in your most beautiful moments. And that is why you are their complement.

9.   It's a heart connection

A lot of us, we have mind connections. Okay, where do you work? Great. I work over there. I cough a lot too. Oh, you cough? Oh, that's great. These are mind connections, by the way.

Right? Mind connection is like status. Okay, you live in Beverly Hills. So do I. Oh, you live in Mayfair. Oh, so do I. Like these are mind connections, right? It's all about what I can get from this person. The heart-based connection is what soulmates have. I will give you an example.

. Growing up, I was more geared towards lust than love. What's the difference between lust and love? Oh my gosh, he's got a great body. Yeah. Or a lot of women say, oh my gosh, he's so tall and dark and handsome, right? I love his shoulders. They don't obviously tell you that, but that's what they're thinking. Why? How do I know this? Because they tell me that.

Look, right? That's beautiful because once again, we're here to reproduce, baby. Let's not get that confused. But at the same time, love is about what you can give to the person. Lust is what you want to take away. So what helped me along my journey was to say, okay, I know this is a soulmate relationship because I want to give more than I want to take. A lot of people are like, gosh, I just can't wait to get in bed with this person because you want to take away.

See, soulmate relationship is like, I can't wait to share this information with this person. I can't wait to help them become their greatest version. I can't wait to help them evolve and for them to help me evolve. That's soulmate, right? That's a secret they won't tell you. They're in their heart, not just in their mind.

10.   When they are around each other, they create a lot of sympathetic vibrations.

What am I talking about? The science of sympathetic vibrations is that it is when vibrations are moving towards each other.

Now, a lot of us, we don't even realize how powerful this is. When vibrations are moving towards each other. You see, in relationships, like I've been with people where I'm trying to get away from this person, even though we're together. It's a hassle. That's not a soulmate. That's not the one because you're trying to get away.

Sympathetic vibrations, you're trying to always move towards each other. Like you're driving to see someone. You're driving to the airport. You're moving together. Right? As soon as you finish work, you're going to meet them. You're moving together.

By being in each other's presence, you now both become better. Now, a lot of Coca-Cola relationships, when you both are together, the frequency decreases. You both feel worse afterwards.

Soulmates won't tell you that when they are both together, the frequency increases. They are better together. Each person becomes better. They're happier. They're glowing more. Mentally, emotionally, physically, spiritually, whatever you want to call it. They are reborn. Just by being with their reflection. So, there you have it.

Chapter Fifthteen

10 Things To Remember If Your Partner Ends Your Relationship

I woke up to this message from someone saying that their girlfriend ended it. And they are devastated, they're heartbroken, they're crushed. Okay? And they're like, she said she just wants some space. What does that mean, Ralph? And they wrote, I'm still in love with her. I want to be happy again. Like, how do I get over this? And this is something that a lot of people go through.

So let me share with you what's helped me along my journey. What I've remembered when these kinds of things happen. Along my early journey, it happened to me. I was in a relationship with someone and they just ended it. And I'm like, oh my gosh, will I ever survive this? And then I woke up the next day in one piece. Let's get scientific.

1.   Life is about change

Let's talk about the science of our heart. A lot of people might tell you, snap out of it. It doesn't help, does it? No, it doesn't help. Columbia university showed that heartbreak is very real. In fact, so real. Okay. Because they did functional magnetic resonance imaging. They studied college students' brains... and what did they find out? When they were shown a picture of their ex, oh my gosh, not you again.

What happened? Their brain lit up just like it would if they were exposed to actual physical pain. Heart math shows that our heart is 60 times greater electrically than our brain and 5,000 times stronger magnetically than our brain.

So our heart is super powerful. So what is the first thing to remember when your partner ends your relationship out of nowhere? Life is full of surprises. Sometimes, good things fall apart so that better things can fall together.

Life is about change. And the reason why sometimes moving on, moving forward can be very difficult is because we don't like to change. Like you like your bed. What if I came into your room and took your bed out of your room? Where did it go? That's kind of like how this is. So allow yourself this period to really get sad, get mad, pull your hair out, and then realize that it's not doing much if I'm getting mad about it, but I can look forward and I can realize that sometimes you might think it's a loss, but in the long run, you might meet someone even better that can help you become your greatest version.

It's all about the experience. Be glad. Be glad that it happened in the first place, right? Out of all of these billions of people, out of all of these billions of people, be glad that it even happened, that you met them.

You met them, right? It didn't have to happen, but it did. What looks as if it's coming apart could actually be coming together, right? What looks like it's coming apart could actually look like it's coming together from a different perspective. Change your perspective. Get a different view, and you're going to start to see that better things are going to come for you.

2. The problem could be our ego

What I've seen along my journey is that your ego is hurting. Not that they ended it for you. You say you're heartbroken. That's not the problem. It's sometimes our ego.

Our ego is our defense mechanism. As soon as something changes, our ego comes out and say, wait a minute, wait a minute. Do you know who I am? You can't do this to me. Hold me back. Somebody, right? Your ego is like your protection. So a lot of us, we are groomed growing up to always pamper our ego. And then when someone leaves us, it's like a blow to the ego. So the more you live in your heart, you start to realize this: that we don't own anybody to begin with. It's an illusion.

Ownership of someone is an illusion. They are choosing to be with you. So once you move more into your heart space, as opposed to the ego, you will be able to move forward, smiling. Maybe not smiling yet, but you will eventually, right?

. 3. Heartbreak could also mean a breakthrough

What I realized along my early journey, when I had a heartbreak when I was younger, is that sometimes a heartbreak can actually be a breakthrough because it actually slows things down. You actually start to say, oh my gosh, that was a really great person.

Maybe I took them for granted. What could I have done differently? Okay. So you get a breakthrough to say, okay, wait a minute. I was really lazy. Or wait a minute. I gave them so much and I didn't get anything back.

So it's no loss there. But it's definitely a time for contemplation. It's a time for reminiscing, being thankful for the good old times and saying, yippee, that you don't have to pick up their dirty laundry anymore.

4. Stop blaming yourself if it didn't work out.

If it was meant to work out, it would have. And that's what I always remind myself along my journey. It's not that it's written in the stars. It's just that if it's supposed to work out, it will.

The whole universe will make it happen. Sometimes the universe is actually doing us a favor by not bringing us together in certain situations for long periods of time. Because once again, we are all here with different people to learn different lessons at different times.

So when you realize that, wait a minute, this is, it's okay. I'm not going to blame myself that it didn't work out. Sometimes things are beyond your control because there is your journey. And then there is the other person's journey. You see the water relationship is where there is a hundred percent resonance. A lot of times in life, people are just coming into our life and they're leaving. It's nothing personal, but just remind yourself that if it was a true connection, then you can still be connected. Whether it's a great friendship or what have you. Okay.

A lot of people are like, Ralph, you can't be friends with someone that you're not going out with. Well, it takes a lot of maturity to do that.

5. Don't externalize your power

Seven day vegan challenge. Don't put all your almond milk in one jar. Don't put all your nuts in one basket. And a lot of us, we do that. Okay. Sometimes we idolize people. We externalize our power. We put other people on a pedestal. I always say, meet me at eye level. I'm not better than you. And I'm not less than you, right?

That's the healthy relationship. Some relationships, what happens is that we put all our eggs in one basket. Sometimes we're even with people for the wrong reasons. Okay. You're like, okay, what can I get from them? Not putting all your eggs in one basket works like this. Yes.

They give you a great deal of happiness. Cause you're like, I don't know how to be happy again. So obviously this person has made you incredibly happy. And that's the beauty of the relationship. At the same time, you've got to realize happiness starts with yourself. If you don't build yourself up, if you don't fill your own cup, what happens if someone else's cup that you have become so dependent on disappears? You're in big trouble, right?

So I started to learn that I've got to fill my own cup because you can't rely on people all the time... sometimes, but not all the time. So you've got to start learning how to find your inner happiness by loving yourself a hundred percent.

6. Focus on all the other connections that are going well in your life right now.

All the other relationships that are going well right now. Maybe you've got a friend that you've been ignoring for the last week. Maybe it's time to give them a call. Right? You see, there is always love around us. Like I've got so much support.

It's mind-boggling. So I'm always realizing it's not that sometimes everything feels like it's crumbling. It's only because where you're looking, you see, you are looking at the lack. You're looking at, oh, my girlfriend left me. That's all you're focusing on, but it's not serving you. Therefore, it's not doing you any favors.

You want to start focusing on the people around you who love you, who are there for you, who care for you, and who will pick up your dirty laundry. No, no, nobody's going to pick up your dirty laundry. Not even the cat down the road. So sorry about that. But focus on people who actually are there for you. Those are the people, once again, who deserve your attention right now. Because the other person doesn't want to hear. They're like, ain't nobody got time for that. Because that's what you said.

You're like, they don't even care, Ralph. I said, I love her and she doesn't even care. Right? It's not personal. Just realize that there is someone better out there for you.

7. This is the time where you have to love yourself a little bit more.

No, no, no. A whole lot more. Because that person who you depended on for so long to love you isn't there. They don't want to know about what you're doing, how you feel about them.

They don't care. Why, Ralph? Nobody knows. Right? So when I've been through this situation in my teenage years, what happened to me was I realized that at the time I didn't really love myself. So I always look for love on the outside. I always look for another person to love me and to validate me and to give me confidence. So when they left, I was really insecure.

I was very nervous, feeling like naked almost. Put some clothes on for goodness sakes, Ralph. So I started to realize, I've got to love myself. And how do you love yourself right now? Go to the place where you find your greatest power. For me, it's skating. It's being on the beach, just sipping a beautiful mango juice. Right? What is it for you? Where do you find your greatest power? What are you passionate about? That is how to start building up the self-love again, which gives you the self-respect, right? Which will help you move forward and then see someone who is in greater resonance with you.

8. Stop trying to substitute.

Stop trying to substitute, right? Your loss, right? It happens all the time. A lot of the times we're in a relationship and it doesn't work out. So immediately we go with someone else just because we don't want to be alone. I would rather be single and happy than with someone else and lying to myself, right? So be careful you don't just substitute, right? You don't just quickly go with someone to fill a void of emptiness because you don't want to be alone.

Take time to heal, especially after a relationship. That's the time where you need to actually go for a massage, something like that, just scratch your back for you, right? But don't just go with anyone because you're like, I don't want to be alone or I'm going to prove that other person wrong. So I'm going to sleep with all of these people.

.You don't have to do that, right? It's got to be real. It's got to be true to yourself.

9. It's never over.

Why do I say it's never over? Because I've realized that even in my own life, sometimes I've thought it was the end of a relationship and then we came back together. And you hear these stories, right? Read memoirs and autobiographies and you hear these stories. Yeah, we didn't talk to each other for like five years and then, wait a minute, you got eight children together.

You're married, living in the Caribbean, drinking coconut juice together, drinking coconut juice every single day together. So you don't really know how this whole story is going to end. You see, what you are focusing on is just a small, tiny piece of your story, which is always changing anyway.

We're so quick to draw conclusions from temporary situations and that's the problem why you might be hurting right now. Realize that you aren't in control and neither are they. When something is supposed to be with you, it will always find its way.

It might take a month, it might take a year, but it will find its way. So realize that, hey, I don't know how this whole story is going to end, but if I'm meant to be with her, I will. Or ladies, if I'm meant to be with him, whatever it is, I will be with him, whatever it is. But don't just think that you know everything. Don't just say, oh, it's over, because you don't know if it's over or not. You might wake up one day and change your mind.

They might change their mind and you both might actually realize what a great connection you have, okay? We're all learning along our journey. We're all evolving. No one's perfect around here.

10. You are worthy

. This is the time where you're probably feeling terrible about yourself. Once again, heartbreak is very real, okay? And therefore, to pick yourself back up, to move forward with strength, mentally and emotionally, you've got to start realizing you are worthy, okay? Every single day, I'm in beautiful high spirits because I realized I am worthy. I'm inspiring millions of people, right? So I always feel worthy.

But more so, I inspire myself. Start inspiring yourself. Don't inspire me. Do something that will make you proud of who you are. And that will help you move through any situation and stay elevated. And then you will see this secret, that the greatest relationship takes place within yourself first. And the more you are in alignment with your true life purpose, you will naturally attract everything you need. And you will end up with someone who has your greatest interests at hand.

Chapter Sixteen

How To Decide To Let Someone Go

How to let someone go when you know there's more... is that you today? Confronted with that big choice, that decision you've got to make. Should I let someone go? I don't need them, bye. When you know there's more, but there could be more.

Okay, let me share with you what's helped me along my journey. I've been in that situation and I'm gonna share with you some secrets I learned. One of the hardest decisions you will ever have to make is choosing whether or not to let someone go or to stay because you know there's more. A lot of us on the planet, we live in the ego mind. And I was for a long time until I realized that you never wanna make a decision when you're in the ego or when you're angry or when you are feeling overwhelmed.

Clarity comes in the heart space. This is sexology, water, fire, hot, cold, yin, yang. Let's start with this. You gotta look at the overall value level they bring to you. What have they ever brought to you that is of value? Okay?

Because once you are in your ego mind, you will say, no, I don't need this person. They don't bring me anything. But in the heart space, you can actually have more clarity to say, have they bought me anything of value? You don't have to like a person to respect someone. But a lot of us have a very hard exterior emanating from our ego mind which says that I am gonna overlook everything about this person because of one experience, one moment, forgetting all the value they have brought you.

So if you know in your heart space, this person, this someone has bought you some value, there's more. If not, there probably isn't more. You see, in our society, a lot of us, we are living a very fast paced lifestyle. That means the majority of our lives are about absolutes. I either like this person or I don't. They are either in my life or they're not. And that is the rigid ego mind.

You see the water relationship and the water mindset is about flexibility. Time and time again, we see how people don't talk to each other for years then say, oh my gosh, I really regret it because I was just so in my ego and we were just arguing over a peanut. Oh my gosh, right? But the ego will always separate you. Only the heart can bring you together.

So meditate on the overall value. And I always have realized along my journey to decide to let go of someone when you know there's more.

Ask yourself, what was the food chemistry like? People really reveal themselves over a meal. Epic mealtime. Like what was that like? How were your conversations over a meal? Sometimes we feel really awkward eating with someone. That says a lot. There's more when you just feel so much euphoria, so elated, so joyful over a beautiful brown rice, avocado salad, and you're just talking nonstop. There's more, right? But if there is zero chemistry over food, you gotta put a question mark because food brings people together.

I look at it like this. When you are making this decision, this choice, you have to ask yourself this, was I only with them for one reason or were they only with me for one reason? You see, many times we can talk of relationships, friendships, interactions, even meeting strangers, and we're only with them for one reason.

Sometimes they've got a nice backside, a nice booty. Sometimes they've got a lot of money. Sometimes they're rich. Or sometimes we can use them to get somewhere else or sometimes we actually, hello, genuinely like them and genuinely care, okay? But if someone is just with you for one reason, sometimes it's just because of your backside, right? Then that's a surface shallow relationship, a

I talk of the emotional expansion range. Now, this is where we are going to dive deep. You're going to start to realize that there are people who we're cool with, we get on with, but we can't really be ourselves, right? And we're like, I never have an argument with them, Ralph.

Yeah, that's because your emotional expansion range with them is very short. There are people who argue a lot, but they have a very wide emotional expansion range, meaning there's more because they have more depth to them. It's easy to say, hi, hi, how are you, to someone for nine years because you've never really been through anything, right? People who have been through a lot will always have a wider emotional expansion range, meaning sometimes they might say stuff to each other they don't mean.

Sometimes they might be in the ego. It doesn't mean you just have to let go of that person. There still could be more, right? Because your emotional expansion range is showing you, it's an indicator that you actually care about this person because you have deeper feelings for this person.

Okay, so you have to have a lot of clarity to say, okay, am I just in my feelings right now, right? Yeah, this person really works me up, but there's more because I can really express a whole range of emotions with this person. I can actually be myself. I can actually tell them how annoyed I am, how pissed off I am, and how much I love them at the end of the day, right? It happens.

Relationships are like a house, right? If a light bulb goes off, you don't buy a new house. You just replace the light bulb. Buy a new one. You fix it. You don't throw everything out, you don't throw the baby out with the bathwater, right? Goodness gracious, right? So there's also the expression range.

And this is, once again, where you have to have a lot of clarity in the heart space. Can you really talk to this person about anything? Could you do that once upon a time? Then there's more. You see, many times we might be with someone and they're great and they're cool, but we really can't spill the beans. We can't allow ourselves to become vulnerable. If you allowed yourself to become vulnerable with someone, if you shared, then there was a realness level there. There's more. It doesn't mean both of you are gonna get married. Not at all. But there is a deep appreciation both of you have or had.

That's why you allowed each other to become vulnerable with each other, right? There are people who we just can't be vulnerable with. Even though we're cool with them, we just, we don't wanna do that. But there are people who literally open us up, right? There's more.

If someone has opened you up, there is more. Now, it swings in roundabouts because a lot of us, we aren't in our heart space throughout the day. Okay, we go to .work, we get shouted at and things happen and everything sometimes falls on our head, including apples and stuff like that. And then we take it out on someone else. That's why you need clarity. You need meditation to really say, okay, I can really express myself with this person.

If you are in a situation where you can't, you're like really closed all the time, you have a filter, you have to think a lot before what you wanna say, then could be that you need to let this person go. You've gotta see the expression level. You've also gotta realize this, that many times you've gotta be mature about it.

I'm still friends with high school girlfriends, right? When I was 16 years old. We're still cool. Because as you mature, as you evolve, you realize the bigger picture. Life is short. You can still be friends with someone, even if it didn't work out, if you both were in your heart space to begin with, if you can both move out of the way of your massive egos and say, actually, there is still some value here, some substance here. There is still something more.

We can both grow and help each other. Doesn't mean we have to get married, right? How many of you are still friends with your exes? How many of you put your hand up right now? Fantastic, right? How many of you say, I'm never gonna talk to this person again? Are you always thinking about them? Right, a few out there, good gosh, right? Ego, separation, heart space, unity. Maturity.

Maturity is also when someone hurts you, okay? Sometimes the people we hang around could even hurt us, right? But you are still able to see things from their perspective. You are now having the bird's eye view and say, okay, I get it. Maybe this person is young. Maybe this person hasn't really had the same experiences I've had, but I get it. No one's perfect. Okay, so a lot of times it's on us to say, okay, I'm deciding, should I let this person go or should I stay a bit longer? Because I know there's more.

When you have the bigger picture, the clarity will come and say, okay, I get it. I know there's more. It's just that I know what this person is going through. And that's okay too. When you realize that you are around someone in any period of your life that takes you to places you've never been before, there's more. To decide to let go of someone when you know there's more, just ask yourself that question.

Have they taken me to places where I've never been before? No, they haven't, Ralph. Then it's time to let that person go. But if they have and you know it, but you're denying it, you are suppressing your emotions or even repressing them, acting like you don't even know what happened, right? You've got to get real with yourself and say, actually, this person did take me to places I've never been before.

There's more. You've got to find out what that more is. And you can only do that when you both come back into the heart space and become mature about the situations, but more so learn how to honor your feelings.

Chapter Seventeen

How To Spot Your True Soul Mate

Have you ever met a random person in the most peculiar place and you're like, oh my gosh, I swear I know you from somewhere. Then they're like, no, you don't. Then you're like, yes, I do. Then they're like, no, you don't. Then you're like, yes, I really do though. Then you realize actually you don't.

But you're like, wait a minute, this feels so good. It feels so right. Like I know you. And then both of you have to part your ways and you're like, no. Yeah, you just met your soulmate. How does it feel? Amazing, Ralph. I just wish it would last a bit longer.

So, have you been looking high and low for your soulmate? You're like, Ralph, where are they? I was doing an Instagram live and a beautiful lady called in. She's like, Ralph, I love your videos. But how can I find my true soulmate? Like, how can I know it's them?

Right now, a lot of people are afraid of even touching anybody. I'm here to tell you, let love guide you, not fear, okay? You're going to be okay. You're going to be all right. Okay?

I always say love is what you need. And right now, a lot of people are in quarantine right now on the planet. A lot of people are fearful and we have to remind ourselves, the only hope we all have right now is to embrace the love vibration.

Now let's talk about soulmates. How did I find my soulmate or soulmates? Okay.

Instead of searching for your soulmate, start searching for your own soulmate. You see, a lot of people are searching for the perfect person without being the perfect person themselves. In ancient Egypt or Kemet, on every temple it said, know thyself. Even the Oracle in the matrix told Neo to know thyself. Okay.

When I started to know who I truly was, then I found my soulmate, my soul. Okay. It has to start with you because the greatest relationship you can have is with yourself. Start finding your own soul. Take off your shoes, come and meet me in nature and place your souls on mother nature. This is called grounding, earthing. Now you are connected with who you really are and now you have found your true soul.

So it starts with that. And once you feel whole within yourself, you will now see your reflection. You will now see your soulmate.

Now, how I actually spotted my true soulmate was to realize there is a big difference between love and lust. You see, love wants to give and lust wants to take. Every single day, if you want to find your soulmate, to know it's them, say, can I give to this person without counting the cost? Do I just want to enrich this person's life? That's how to know you found your true soulmate. When you just want to give to someone, when you want to be someone else's upgrade. When you want to be someone else's upgrade, when you want to help them in their life every single day.

Now you have lust. Okay. A lot of people in this matrix don't actually love, they lust. Okay. Lust is how to know that is not your soulmate. If you see someone's body and you're like, oh my gosh, look at her body. Look at his body. That's cool. That's natural. Even the cat down the road does that. But there's always something deeper than physical connections.

Physical connections are so common, but a mental connection, a spiritual connection, an emotional connection, deep divers, a heart connection is extremely rare. If you have a heart connection with someone, that's how you know you have found your true soulmate.

If you have a spiritual connection with someone, that's how you know you have found your true soulmate. If you have a lustful connection to someone, that's not your soulmate because now you want to take advantage of someone else. Realize this.

If the heart is in it, that's the soulmate. If the heart is not in it, that's not the soulmate. If the ego is there, that is not the soulmate interaction. Anytime you're with someone and it's just ego, pure ego, that is not the soulmate interaction. When the ego is non-existent, that is the soulmate connection because now there is no other. In other words, both of you are becoming one.

Anytime you are with someone and you feel more of yourself, you can do a little samba, baby. You're not embarrassed to speak your heart and mind. You can be vulnerable with them. That's how you know, key word, you can be vulnerable with them. That's how you know you have spotted your soulmate. Don't let them escape. You see, it starts like this.

Deep familiarity. Anytime you click with someone, instantly you get on your vibe together. That's how you know, deep divers, you have found your true soulmate. The bond is instant. It's like you've known them your entire life. Deep divers like, oh my gosh, I've known you forever.

That's how you know, deep divers, that is your soulmate. But anytime you're with someone even for a long time and you still don't even know who they are, you're like, who the hell are you? You don't feel any connection whatsoever, mentally, emotionally, physically, spiritually. That's not your soulmate.

Now your soulmate doesn't even have to be in your age range. They could be way older than you, but you feel this heart connection with this being. It could even be an animal. It could even be the cat down the road, deep divers. How to know, deep divers, you have found your one true or many soulmates? It starts like this.

If you are always arguing with someone, that's not a soulmate interaction. However, if you never ever hardly argue with someone, that special someone, that's your soulmate. Because the soulmate connection is free of arguing. It comprises listening, being heard, and being seen. It's when two people have learned the art of holding the space, deep divers. How to know, deep divers, you have found your true soulmate.

If you can close your eyes and feel them like they're actually here, that's how you know it's the soulmate connection. If you close your eyes and you're like, actually, I don't want to feel this, that's not the soulmate connection. It's all about how you feel and how they feel when both of you connect.

I actually spotted my soulmate, when there was just this mutual respect, appreciation. Key word, appreciation. Both of you appreciate each other. Both of you realize how fortunate you are to be in each other's presence, deep divers. Oh, baby. But anytime you are with someone, they treat you like a doormat. They look down on you. They place themselves on a pedestal and you're like way below them. That's not the soulmate connection.

In the soulmate connection, everybody is equal. Let me repeat that. In the soulmate connection, everybody is equal.

Now, to know that this is your soulmate, what's helped me along my journey, plain and simple, there is something called gaslighting. That's when someone says, hey, you're crazy. It's all in your head. You're making this all up. You're like, no, I'm not. That actually happened.

Gaslighting is a form of manipulation. To know it's a soulmate connection, there is no gaslighting whatsoever. They understand and overstand where you are coming from.

Seven-day vegan challenge! I hope everybody is boosting their immune system with a delicious turmeric smoothie, some cinnamon inside, some chia seeds, and a complete source of protein on top. Now, if you are sharing this with someone else, that's the soulmate connection because the soulmate connection is about sharing and we share food together. That's the soulmate connection. But if you don't want to share your food with me, it's not the soulmate connection. I'm awfully sorry.

So, the soulmate connection is always centered around giving, sharing. It's reciprocal. Reciprocity is the soulmate connection. You scratch my back and I scratch yours. Oh my gosh, your back is so hairy. I'll have to skip that. Actually, I won't because you're my soulmate. I've got love for you.

Another way to know it's the soulmate connection. If both of you can learn from each other, okay? If both of you can learn from each other, grow together, help each other evolve, that's the soulmate connection.

Key word, evolve. If both of you are helping each other evolve, that's the soulmate connection. But if both of you are a distraction to each other, tearing each other apart, that's not the soulmate connection. So, evolution is the keyword to know if it's the soulmate connection or not. If they make you better, if they make you a better human being, if your life has changed since you have been around them, you get inspired, you're smiling more, you're full of energy, and they're doing the same, that's the soulmate connection.

To know is the soulmate, the one and only soulmate, there's effort. When you are with someone and they prioritize you, they make you a priority, deep divers, they make you feel loved, they make you feel cared for, they make you feel needed, they make you feel wanted, that's the soulmate connection. You cannot buy that in a shop. But if they don't make you feel loved, wanted, or needed, they just look down on you like you're a nobody, that's not the soulmate connection.

Okay? So, we have to remind ourselves, the soulmate connection will always make us feel like we are at home with that person. We can be ourselves. We don't have to pretend. We don't have to try hard. They accept us. Key word, accept.

That's how you know it's the soulmate connection. They accept our past because it wasn't glamorous, oh no, it wasn't, but they accept it. That's the soulmate connection.

Chapter Eighteen

How To Tell If Someone's Meant To Be In Your Life

As a psychologist, as a counselor, and as someone who meets a lot of people, I'm gonna share with you how I know certain people are meant to be in my life.

How do we know, right? People just show up in our lives, and we're like, who the hell are you? Okay, so along my early journey, people always ask me what helped me become my greatest version. And it works like this. To go to the next level in anything, in a relationship, at work, you've always gotta surround yourself with a person who is on a higher level than you, or where you aspire to be.

Okay, but you see, a lot of us, we are surrounding ourselves with people who are keeping us at the same level. And it's not their fault, we've gotta take responsibility. We are attracting that into our lives because we have lessons to learn. But for me, becoming your greatest version is all about going to the next level. So I'm gonna share with you five secrets.

1.   Same values

So I'm a vegan, I love plant-based foods, I love animals. If you don't like that, stop reading this, Please stop. Okay, now a lot of people have left. The right people are supposed to be reading this chapter. Thank you. You've gotta be able to be willing to stand up for what you believe in. You see, I'm very open with what I talk about. I'm very honest about what I talk about.

That's why people watch me every single day. And I'm just talking, right? But the numbers don't lie. Same values is where you go to an event like VegFest in Orange County, when I went and I'm talking to these amazing people with strawberries in their mouth and I've got strawberries in my mouth. We're not really having much of a conversation, are we? But it's really fun, okay? Because we're sharing the same values. We have mutual appreciation and mutual respect for one another. That's how I know they're meant to be in my life.

In becoming your greatest version, you've gotta learn this simple secret. The people who are supposed to be in your life are trying to get to you. The people who aren't supposed to be in your life are trying to run away from you.

I know if I meet someone, if it's gonna work or if it's not gonna work, how do I know that? Because I just ask them questions. I say, what do you eat? And then they tell me and I'm like, okay, best friends or not.

Or they say I don't like animals. Then it's gonna be hard to communicate. Some people say, I love this song, I love that song. So we're finding a common bond through a common understanding and understanding our common bonds, right? But you see, a lot of us don't share the same values as other people, so we wonder why there's no relationship and there's no unity in connection.

And that's what happened to me along my early journey. I was trying to force people to stay in my life. No, they were trying to get away from me because they weren't supposed to be there. The people who are in your life will always find themselves coming back to you. They will come back to you. They will run back to you.

In fact, they will give you a big hug and tackle you down to the ground. Those are the people who are supposed to be in your life. Surround yourself with people who are on the same mission as you. That's what I did from the early days of Infinite Waters. That's why we're growing. That's why we're thriving.

That's why life is beautiful. Because I'm only focusing and I'm only working with people who are on the same mission as me. That's all I'm interested in.

2.	Reciprocity

A lot of the time we do things for people and they don't reciprocate. I just bought you ginger tea. You didn't even say thanks. Don't worry about it.

It's okay, it's okay, it's okay. It's okay, okay? Ever been around someone who is just a user? Like you drive them everywhere and then they're like, oh, can you take me to that place? And you're like, get out of the car, man. We ain't got time for that.

Great relationships, great connections in becoming your greatest version is where the relationship is fully reciprocal. Sometimes it doesn't always have to be 50-50. What's helped me along my journey is to realize, okay, when people can give, they give. When they can't, that's okay too. But see where their intention is, where their heart lies.

For instance, when I was a kid, I'd make a lot of videos for people. And because of that, a lot of people invited me into their homes. They say, Ralph, because your video saved my life, I'm gonna make you a watercress avocado salad. And I'm like, thank you. Because I did for them and they fed me. Well, they fed me so much, I can't even get up now. You fed me too much. Thanks a lot though, all right? It's the law of exchange. Whatever you put out there will come back to you.

And when you're meeting with people and you feel like the relationship is lopsided, then they ain't meant to be in your life because great relationships are always 50-50, 60-40, 70-30, not like 90-10, not like 80-20, not you always giving to people and them not doing anything back, okay? So you gotta learn your value. You gotta learn how to appreciate yourself 100%.

3.	Effort.

Okay, this is, look, some people make a lot of effort and some people just lie on their back and say, oh, I can't be bothered. Hey, that's fine as well. That's fine, because you don't have to always make an effort.

But you see, you would want to make an effort for someone who you feel an effort is worth making for. A lot of people message me and sometimes I message them back. Okay, you might be one of these people. And sometimes I even call people. They're like, oh my gosh, Infinite Waters, you connect with millions of people. I can't believe you're messaging me.

Because I'm just a human being, right? I'm not the Pope. I'm just a human being. So that means I'm not better than you and I'm not below you. We meet each other at eye level. That means I'll talk to anybody. I treat the janitor the same way I treat the CEO. Whoa, we're all equal here, baby. Same effort, right? I'm not going to wear a suit, okay? Just to impress somebody like a corporate person and then take it off when I meet someone else. No, I wear a suit for everybody if I want to, right? Go naked for everybody, if I want to, basically, I treat people the same.

The same effort in becoming your greatest version is when you feel someone is putting in the same energy as you are putting in. A lot of women contact me. A lot of men contact me. My partner isn't pulling their weight. I said, because sometimes people only value your true worth when you pull back, when you disappear, when you leave the scenes, then they know your true worth.

But you've been doing too much for too long. So they take you for granted. You see, I've learned in life, I've got to appreciate everybody. I even appreciate people on Instagram. I see them sharing post after post after post. I'm like, that's a lot of dedication. So if I see that picture, I'm going to like it.

If I see someone's YouTube video, even if they only have like a thousand subscribers and it resonates with me, I'm going to say, hey, that's a great video. Go and check it out. Because I was there. I remember when I only had a thousand subscribers. Now look at us, right? So it's the same effort. Same effort.

A lot of people say, I don't have time. Oh, well, well, I'm busy. I've got to work. I've got to do this. But you've got time to buy those shoes. You've got time to go for the pedicure, the manicure. You've got time when it comes to you. And that's beautiful because self-love is essential. But you see, there is always time. It's only a matter of priorities.

Okay, so same effort is when both people push. They make the effort. Along my early journey, I had to make an effort. A lot of people were making videos. I said, hey, let's collaborate. People like, lots of people check out my videos, right? I said, let's collaborate. We did it. And both of us blew off. Okay, people like Teal Swan, amazing. You've got to realize, you've got to learn how to work with people. Collaborate with people. Put the same effort in. Okay, and that's why things just blossom.

Same effort.

4.   Let people go

You see, to know if someone is meant to be in your life, a lot of us, we surround ourselves with people who we, once again, want to turn around. We want to convince. We want to make them like us when they aren't here to do any of that. So you have to learn how to let people go.

.Okay, and the people who remain are supposed to be in your life. Look at it like this. What is the comfort level when you are with these people? Comfort level is everything.

I've noticed when I'm in the presence of someone else, if I am feeling calm, centered, breathing in that good-ass prana, then that person is meant to be in my life because there is no problem. There is no struggle, there is no stress, and I feel perfectly at peace.

If on the other hand, you're surrounding yourself with someone where you're very nervous, your heart is beating rapidly, and you haven't put down your hand yet, because you're like, oh, what should I do? Then chances are they're not meant to be in your life. You better run. Go that way, not that, that way, go, run.

Can you be yourself around people, or are you always justifying who the hell you are? Right, I accept all people. I've got people with tattoos on the back of their ear. Right, I love all people, right? I've got people who wear clothes back to front. I've got people who walk around naked.

We're still friends, right? You've got to have a sense of humor, okay? If you're someone who likes to relax, and then someone is always serious around you, you want to start question-marking that, right? Say, okay, who is this person around me? I want to just have fun. You see, the people we surround ourselves with, once again, if they're meant to be in your life, they will always take you to the next level. They won't just bring you drama every day.

Ever realize why Infinite Waters, we've never had no drama on this channel, but we're growing every single day, getting thousands of subscribers every single day. Why? What's the secret? Because we're focusing on the higher level, right? Just watch. That's a secret. I don't focus on drama because drama doesn't sell.

Drama is good for nobody. Drama creates negative energy.

Drama, negativity will only delay you. We're about elevation. And the people who are also about elevation, these are the people who are meant to be in my life. I'm not holier than thou. And at the same time, it's not about being positive. And it's not about being negative. It's about being your authentic self. Okay, if you can be your authentic self in the presence of other people and not apologize for it, these are the people who are supposed to be in your life.

Chapter Nineteen

Accept Yourself Before It's Too Late

Do you accept yourself? Are you having a feeling right now that you are finally accepting yourself for the first time in your entire life? So, yeah, I'm often asked, Ralph, how does one know one really loves themselves? Like what are some of the things we all do? How does one know we accept ourselves? You reading this, do you love yourself? Do you accept yourself? It's hard to tell. Let me share with you how I know for certain that I finally accept and love myself.

1.   Enjoy your own company

The first sign you finally accept yourself and love yourself is that you actually enjoy your own company. Now, you can ask my mom. She's like, when Ralph was like a child, he would be happy playing alone. Okay, I actually enjoyed my company back then. And then I lost that, okay? I was like, I need to be around people to be happy. Now, you are accepting yourself and loving yourself if you can entertain yourself. No phone, just you in nature, you in nature surrounded by these beautiful leaves. And for the first time, you actually feel comfortable in your own skin. I actually enjoy my own company.

So many of us, we are trying to run away from ourselves. The human being is on the run from itself. So the moment you actually start to embrace yourself, enjoy your own company, you are finally accepting yourself and loving yourself.

2.   You're celebrating many wins.

Now, you don't have to get the trophy. All you have to do is celebrate each mini victory. You see, all of us on the planet, we all go through so much, so many different things. And what's helped me along my journey is to say, actually, this is a win for me, okay? I've been through, what you could call a tempest, right? I've been through the storm, the thunder... and I'm still here, I'm still able to smile, still able to inspire you and the cat down the road.

If you are able to celebrate your mini wins, be very proud of yourself. And that's a sign you finally accept yourself and love yourself. Because so many times, we're all giving ourselves such a hard time. But if you're not, if you're like clapping for yourself, hey, if you are your biggest fan, you finally accept and love yourself.

3.   You're gentle on yourself

Be gentle, be very gentle when you're stroking the cat down the road. If you are gentle also with yourself, because you know you're doing the best you can, you finally accept and love yourself. Now, there are days when I'm really hard on myself and I know I'm not practicing self-love. I know I'm not practicing self-acceptance.

Then comes the moment I say, actually, Ralph, chill. Ralph, be gentle with yourself. You're doing the best you can with the best you have, okay? Because the moment you turn on yourself, you stop practicing self-love. There's a great African proverb which says: when there is no enemy within, the enemy outside can't hurt you. So if you are gentle with yourself at all times, well done.

4.   Their opinions don't matter.

Society's like, no, not like that. You see, so many of us in this 3D matrix, we fall in the trap of trying to fit into other people's expectations. And that's why so many people have anxiety, depression. You are finally loving yourself. And by loving yourself and accepting yourself, if you're like society, yes, it's like this. I'm gonna do it like that, right?

Many times, self-love comes the moment you forget about what other people have to say about you and just focus on what makes you happy. Okay, every single day, I love to share. Even if I was only talking to the cat down the road, I would still be sharing on infinite waters because I actually love what I'm doing. And that's how I know I'm loving myself and accepting myself.

Don't get me wrong. Don't get it twisted. There was a time when I was afraid to be myself because I was afraid of what other people thought of me. I was afraid that, hey, if I'm talking about different topics, what would they think? What would my mom think? What would you think? And I'm like, ah, who cares? Because once again, the trouble is, you think you've got time. It's now or never. You have to start expressing yourself 100%. And in turn, you will attract the people that will help you go to the next level.

5.   You take your health seriously

Seven-day vegan challenge! Now, shout out to all the people who are really taking their health seriously, who are really eating that plant-based lifestyle day in, day out, going to Whole Foods, going to the local farmer's market, because that's a sign you are actually, finally, for the first time, loving yourself and accepting yourself, okay?

I used to know someone who was like, well, Ralph, we're all gonna die anyway. It doesn't even matter what you eat. I'm like, we are immortal. Don't you know what nerd stands for? Nobody ever really dies. We are energy, and energy can never be destroyed, only transferred. So I'm infinite. Therefore, I need to be consuming the best plant-based foods, okay? So I'm splurging on juices. I'm splurging on beautiful blueberry smoothies, okay?

I'm putting that money up. If you are putting that money up when it comes to your health, your food, your nutrition, you are winning in life. You are accepting yourself. You are loving yourself.

How come on the planet, so many people are quick to buy a $2,000 handbag, but when it comes to food, they're broke? How come people are ready to buy designer clothes, right? Ralph Lauren, this, that. But when it comes to their health, they don't have any money.

So I turned it all around, and I'm like, it's time to start investing in food, okay? Because it will maintain healthy peace of mind for you. Okay, so if you are splurging on pineapples, cold-pressed juice, mango, avocados, rhubarb, you're good okay? Carrot juice, you are loving yourself and accepting yourself.

6.   You have a deeper knowing of who you really are

You see, right now on the planet, there is a tremendous awakening happening. And you know you finally accept yourself and love yourself if you actually know thyself a little bit more than you did last year. Because for me, the true purpose of life is to know thyself.

You see, you've been told and programmed from childhood that, hey, don't worry about it. No, actually do worry about it. What makes me happy? What makes me sad? It's time to know the real me.

If you are in that process of metamorphosis, that change, this massive awakening, you are finally accepting and loving yourself. Because for the first time, you're like, I don't wanna know what's going on out there in the world. You turn off the news and you're like, I'm gonna turn on my mind.

I'll say it again... know thyself. In ancient Egypt, on every temple it said, know thyself. On every temple it said, know thyself. That's what we're here to do.

7.   You're happy with the skin you were born into.

I love this melanin magic, baby. We are all carbon-based beings. If you actually are comfortable with your body, your shape, your size, you're like, hey, I look pretty good. You do look pretty good, okay? I'm feeling comfortable in my own skin. I love the body I'm in.

Ladies, if you love the body you're in, you finally accept and love yourself. Because those people you see on billboards don't even look like that. I helped them Photoshop those images.

Don't worry about it, okay? Be comfortable. If you are so comfortable with the skin you're in, if you're not trying to fit into society's rules and expectations of what the perfect body looks like, you finally accept and love yourself, okay? Because anybody can be a model. You can be your own model and model your own clothes. That's a tip from the cat down the road, by the way.

8.   You are quitting any job that is not a true reflection of who you are.

You are quitting any job, which means just over broke, that is not a true reflection of who you are. You see, most people go to work and they spend all their energy at work only to come home to have no energy for the life they're actually working for.

So I said, okay, if I'm really all about self-love and self-acceptance, for me, it's all about, for the first time, quitting any job. I haven't had a job since 2011, because I'm an entrepreneur, I create jobs.

I'm my own CEO, I'm my own boss. If you have that mindset, you finally love and accept yourself because rich people don't work, they supervise. It's time for you to be on top instead of the bottom. Listen to me, look, I know what it's like. I've worked in so many jobs, but they weren't serving me. And I stayed there to my own detriment.

A lack of self-love made me stay there. Having self-love, right? Having self-love, having self-love made me leave and only start working in an environment that was in my best interest to promote my self-love and self-acceptance. It's time to let go of any job that makes you feel worse about yourself.

It's time to let go of any job that makes you feel worse about yourself. No job should make you complain. It should make you say, gosh, I can't wait to be here. Not, oh, I can't wait to leave. What's the ninth sign? Baby, baby, you finally love and accept yourself.

9. You've got this confidence to actually share the real you with the world.

You see, on social media these days, it's so easy to become somebody you're not. And sometimes we play into the audience. Well, Ralph, this is what they like. But what do you like? Who are you? You can fool the world, but you can't fool yourself. You can fool me, but you can't fool you. And it's all about you.

It's all about how you see yourself and are you keeping it real with yourself. For me, what helped me, what helped me to know, to know I'm finally loving and accepting myself is to actually have the confidence to share the real me with the world. That's why I only do these videos in one take.

I want to see you, I want you to see the raw me, the real me. And that's why I'm connecting with so many amazing, beautiful, deep divers. If you're like, actually, I don't have to start posting these selfies on Instagram, which don't really make me feel happy. I'm going to actually post what I really want. You are actually practicing the art of self-love and self-acceptance. And you should celebrate.

If you are on YouTube and you're talking about topics which may not be popular, it might even make people raise their eyebrows. You are practicing the art of self-love and acceptance because it's all about self-expression. As your self-expression increases, so does your self-love.

10. You wouldn't want to be anybody else.

If that's you, I remember watching something on MTV, right? When I was younger, this guy was so rich, he's like, when I die, I want to come back as me. And I'm like, woo! Right? He was on private jets, living it up.

I'm like, that's a good mentality to have, right? Can you imagine living a life so awesome that when you're out of here, you want to come back as you because your life is the shit? Well, that's how I feel. That's exactly how I feel right now. When I transition, I want to come back as Ralph Smart.

If you have it in you to say, actually, for the first time, I wouldn't want to be anybody else; I don't want to compare myself to other people unless it's for inspiration; I love who I am. I wouldn't want to trade places with anybody. I actually love my life. I'm happy with it, right? That means you finally accept and love yourself. So have a beautiful day.

Chapter Twenty

Stop Chasing Love
And Relationships

Stop chasing love and relationships and instead do this and then they will chase you. They will flock to you. They will be drawn to you. They won't be able to resist you because you're going to be so magnetic. Two words, magnetize yourself.

People often write to me about approaching people. Like, Ralph, I'm not having any luck when I approach women. Ralph, I'm not having any luck when I approach men. What am I doing wrong? It seems like I'm losing an uphill battle because I'm chasing someone around, Ralph. I'm chasing this person around, Ralph. I'm chasing love, Ralph. I'm chasing a relationship, Ralph. And it's just not working. Can you spread any light? Share any light on it?

You see, I've learned one thing about this topic. You don't have to chase someone who is meant to be in your life. Because when you realize whoever is truly meant to be with you, they will be with you. When you are in alignment with yourself, you have to learn how to magnetize yourself.

I don't have to approach women. Why? Because I am a magnet of attraction. We are drawn to people, who are coming from a place of abundance. When I was 19, I was chasing people around. I was chasing love. I was chasing happiness. I was chasing relationships. And guess what? I wasn't manifesting. They weren't coming to me. Until I realized this secret. Ralph, just relax. Ralph, you are chasing someone because you are coming from a place of lack.

Come from a place of abundance. Go within yourself, Ralph. And the moment I started to come from a place of abundance, I had something to offer someone else. I'm not concerned about finding the one. Because I am the one. Oh baby! You find the one you love, doing what you love. When I was 19, in the club all night, okay, with my friends, like always looking for the hottest chick, right? They weren't coming.

Fast forward. I started to focus on what it is I came here to do on the planet. I started to move into my purpose. And guess what? It magically came to me. I didn't have to chase anymore. Bingo! You find the one you love, doing what you love. You don't have to approach anybody. Just make sure you are in alignment with your highest calling. The universe will provide for you everything you need, including the love of your life. The moment I let go, it all came to me.

We all are worthy of love but realize that love is already inside you when you realize that everything you want outside there is already inside you. Your neglect of yourself and wanting to be with someone is why you feel incomplete. You can still be in love even if you're not with someone externally because if you love yourself, if you realize the greatest relationship you can have is with yourself, everything will change.

Magnetize your energy. Magnetize yourself so that people are drawn to you.

I'm married to myself first and foremost before I'm ever going to get married to you, right? And it does wonders, Deep Divers. Stop waiting for love, and instead do this. Stop waiting for a perfect partner, and instead realize this.

They will seek you, every time that you say, I want; you're sending a signal to the universe, that you don't have what you desire, therefore you will always remain in lack. Instead of saying, I want a perfect partner, say, I am married to myself.

Instead of saying, I want love, say, I have love. The universe loves me.

I have health. I'm alive. I can move my arms like this, and this abundance that is born inside of you will make you a magnet of attraction, and people will be drawn to you.

Ultimately do not chase, attract!

Chapter Twenty One

5 Ways To Get Rid Of Anxiety

Are you someone who has panic attacks? Are you having an anxiety attack somewhere right now? Are you looking a bit shaky, baby? Do you suffer from anxiety? And sometimes it feels like the whole world is coming to an end. And people just don't get you. Well, here are five secret ways to make your anxiety history.

Now, I always receive tons of messages every single day about anxiety. Ralph, please share some advice on how to deal with anxiety because I'm having a lot of anxiety right now. Now, this is first-hand experience. I used to suffer from a lot of anxiety attacks and panic attacks. I know what I'm talking about, okay? When someone tells you to snap out of it, that's not helpful. That will only give you more anxiety.

Over time, I've learned that there are certain things you can do every single day that will help your anxiety go away, okay?

1.   Be present

All anxiety emanates from the desire to escape the present moment. All anxiety emanates from the desire, the desire to... Come back here. You're escaping the present moment. Again, that's why you have a lot of anxiety. I had to learn to be present in everything I'm doing. It's called mindfulness. If I'm washing your plates, I'm gonna focus on washing them. I'm not gonna wash your plates, actually. You wash them yourself! But any activity I'm doing, I'm focusing in on it, right? Any activity I'm doing, I'm giving it 100% of my attention. If I'm washing the cat down the road's plate, I'll do the cat down the road's plates, okay? I'm just focusing on doing that.

I'm not thinking of the past or the future. You have anxiety because you are stuck in the past or the future, anticipation, which creates a lot of expectations. The more expectations you have, the more anxiety you have. The less expectations you have, the less anxiety you have. The more you're thinking of the past, the more anxiety you have. The less you think of the past, the less anxiety you have.

It's really simple. So in a very practical way, how to make your anxiety history, seven day vegan challenge, what helped me was to reduce caffeine. I don't drink any caffeine right now, no coffee. I've been to Ethiopia. I love the coffee there though. But I eliminate all caffeine from my diet.

Now I'm drinking a lot of pH 10 water, guava juice, mango juice, papaya juice, grape juice, leafy greens full of magnesium, which is essential for reducing anxiety. So make sure your plate is green. A lot of us, we are looking a bit shaky baby because we have way too much, way too much caffeine in our diet. And combine that with being in a world where we are constantly overstimulated. That's why so many people have anxiety, okay?

So it's all about putting more magnesium through leafy greens on your plate and being present. Develop mindfulness. Pay attention to everything you are doing. Forget about the past, forget about the future. There is only now.

2.   Breathe

To make your anxiety history, what's really helped me along my journey is diaphragmatic breathing. You see a lot of us, we are shallow breathing right from here, right from the top of our chest. We need to be breathing deep from the base of our spines. That's how to reduce anxiety. So every single day I'm doing this. Woo, breathing in that good ass prana baby. I'm breathing in for four, holding for four, releasing for four. Taking these deep inhalations and slow exhalations.

Now if you combine diaphragmatic breathing with intention when you are stressed, you will reduce anxiety. A lot of us, once again, we're not breathing mindfully. It's just an automatic process and that's why you're shallow breathing. You wanna increase the oxygen in your body by having these deep inhalations like this, then holding that breath, and follow with a slow exhalation. Four seconds inhale; four seconds hold; four seconds exhale and let it all out!

When I do this, you'll feel so relaxed, and you won't even know where the anxiety went! Okay? Like where did you go? So start breathing, diaphragmatic breathing with intention when you are stressed, okay?

3.   Total body awareness

Be more relaxed in everything you're doing. The reason why a lot of us aren't relaxed is because we're always in a hurry. Total body awareness has transformed my life. And when it comes to learning how to be relaxed in your body, total body awareness, stop feeling every single emotion right now. Oh, I feel a bit like this. I feel a bit like that. That's great. Get more sensitive.

That will help to make your anxiety history. Like right now, my muscles are very relaxed. My back is straight and I feel good. Reduce the tension in your body to reduce anxiety in your life. Anxiety is not something abstract. Anxiety lives in every single cell of your body. In other words, your anxiety lives in your body. A lot of people, as soon as they wake up, what happens? They check their phone. This gives you anxiety because you're always comparing yourself to other people. This goes in the pocket. And now for the first time, I can relax. I can lose my phone and reconnect with myself.

In other words, have a better connection. A lot of us have anxiety because we are constantly comparing ourselves to other people on social media. It's time to learn how to only compete with yourself. Be in a league of your own and you will reduce your anxiety. In fact, you will make it history.

4.   Have gratitude

Take a moment of silence for gratitude. Are you blowing everything out of proportion? A problem is only a problem because you are putting a magnifying glass on that problem. Now it's huge. It's more than a problem, Ralph. Tell me. It's a matter of life and death. Okay. You see, a lot of us, we have a magnifying glass to each one of our problems.

You see, life isn't perfect. I've got so many dogs running around there, barking every single day when I'm making these videos, but I love dogs. I love the cat down the road. I've got people screaming in the backyard there. I've got airplanes going up there, but it's cool. It's life. I can deal with it. It's not a matter of life and death. I don't expect everything to be perfect.

There are only perfect imperfections, okay? So we have to learn how to stop overthinking, ruminating. Overthinking creates anxiety. And what I love to do is to put everything in perspective, to say, actually, I'm still alive. Touch yourself. That's good. That's good. That's great. And now your anxiety will diminish when you realize, actually, I've got a lot to be thankful for. The moment I started to practice daily gratitude was the moment my anxiety started to fade away.

5.   Focus on meaningful activities everyday

In other words, be excited about the life you're living. I remember, I used to have a lot of anxiety attacks when I used to go to school because I didn't really want to go to school. For some reason, I was like, it's probably all a lie. I'm probably being brainwashed. And I was right. I was having a lot of anxiety attacks on the train, staring at these strange faces. And I just didn't know what to do. I just felt very uncomfortable because the train was so packed.

Ever been on a train and you're staring at a hundred different faces and they all look weird and you're having a lot of anxiety because you just want to get out of the train and more people are coming inside the train and you're like, Ralph, I need to escape right now. Exactly. You're having a lot of anxiety.

So I had to start seeing people on the toilet seat. That's right. I had to start really being excited for what I was doing in life. And every single day right now, the reason why my anxiety has faded away is because I truly love the life I'm living. A lot of us, we get anxiety before work because you don't really want to be there. What you're doing is not really making you happy.

What you're doing is not really making you happy. So deep divers start living instead of existing. Start loving the life you're living instead of hating it. And focus on what matters the most every single day. Spending time with a loved one. Spend time with people who relax your mind, body and soul.

Chapter Twenty Two

Be Brave, Lose The Fear, Go For It

I'm not afraid and this has actually helped me become my greatest version. That's the reason why I'm living my best life. That's the reason why I'm inspiring millions. And this chapter is truly going to help you do the same.

Are you sometimes afraid of going for it? Are you sometimes full of fear? You've got a mind full of fear, deep divers. Are you sometimes wanting to be more brave? We're in a time right now on the planet where you're going to need to be brave. A closed mouth doesn't get fed. We're in a time right now on the planet where you're going to have to become fearless. And we're in a time right now where you're going to have to go for it.

Be brave

Someone said, Ralph, I can't believe you said that. And I'm like, that was nothing! Well, how did I cultivate bravery? First and foremost, just imagine you're 90 years old. You're going to be more proud of the things that you did do than the things you didn't do. That person you want to talk to. That new career change. That country you want to travel to. Go. What are you waiting for? You only live! You've got to have that in your mind. You only live once, even though we are multi-dimensional beings having human experiences.

We are immortal, yes, but it's one life in this body. How are you going to live it? What is your autobiography going to be filled with? Acts of bravery or acts of cowardice? Make sure you have something to look back on. When I look back, even just back to a few years ago, I'm like, wow, I can't believe I did that. And I congratulate myself. I'm proud of myself. I'm doing better than I think.

So when we talk about becoming our greatest version, everything that you truly desire requires bravery. Everything that you truly desire requires some form of bravery. It's not going to be handed to you. Here you go. No, you've got to go out and get it, deep divers. And you're going to be scared and it's okay. Feel the fear and do it anyway. Be brave, lose fear and go for it.

When we talk about being brave, the universe rewards the brave. The universe rewards the brave. Like sometimes we want to do something, but we're afraid. We're timid. We're shy. We're like, okay, let me step back. But the people who do it, we're like, oh my gosh, how come they're receiving all the rewards? In the words of Ralph Smart, the universe reveals his secrets to people who dare to follow their hearts.

How was I brave along my early journey? I was working in a very good job. 300 people applied. I got picked, but I said, you know what? I'm going to follow my true purpose and passion. And that's helping people become their greatest version. And I'm still here. You know why? Because the universe rewards the brave. You got it. And this will help you become your greatest version.

There is no time to play small. There is no time. To hide your dreams under the carpet. The cat down the road is encouraging you to be brave today. Because once again, everything that you desire requires bravery. It's a prerequisite.

When we talk about what's helped me along my journey, become my greatest version. And I'm still becoming that, I had to earn my own self-respect. A lot of people don't respect themselves in the matrix. You know why? Because they're doing what everyone else is doing. They're just trying to fit in. Deep divers, fitting in is so boring. A normal life is boring. What if I told you, I'm custom-made. I came here to stand out. I'm a one of the one. I'm an anomaly. You won't find another me out there or a cat down the road. And that's the reason why I'm winning in life. That's the reason why I'm manifesting. So earn your own self-respect. This is how you actually become brave enough to live the life that you want.

Wake up every single day and say, do I respect myself? We respect ourselves when we're doing something we know is challenging, but we're overcoming it. If we're just playing it safe all the time in the comfort zone, we've got no respect for ourselves. We've got no respect at all. And that's why a lot of people are fed up, miserable. So earn your own self-respect. I want you to do something dangerous today.

Ralph Smart is doing something dangerous every single day. I'm like, wow, that was dangerous. But it was a calculated risk. And that's what's helping me become my greatest version, creating leverage. Deep divers, be brave, lose fear and go for it. The secret recipe to becoming your greatest version.

Lose fear

Look, lose the fear. What if I told you that fear is the greatest energy vampire? Fear, your fear is the greatest energy vampire. Fear is the greatest thief. And you have to stop allowing yourself to be robbed of your joy, happiness, freedom just because you're scared. Everything you want is on the other side of fear. And when we talk of becoming our greatest version, sometimes I'm afraid, deep divers, I'm human.

But I do know that fear isn't real. Fear is not real. It's false evidence appearing real. It tricks you. Your mind lies to you, deep divers. Remind yourself there's something very scary you're going to have to do. Face that fear head on. And you're going to realize that it's false evidence appearing real. You're going to realize that what has kept you hostage is your fear. And what will give you the key to your freedom is not believing in fear. Don't believe in fear. It's not real.

Face everything and rise. Anytime you think of fear, it means face everything and rise. You see deep divers, the truth of the matter is many people are full of fear because they're consuming fear news, fear media, fear from their parents, their friends. And when we talk of becoming your greatest version, ignore everyone. Don't allow their fears to be absorbed by you. Say, you know what? I'm not afraid.

I'm going to start my own business. I'm going to manifest what I want, even though I'm scared. Nevermind, I'm going to do it. And then eventually you're not scared anymore, deep divers. Just like that. It works just like that. Look, be brave.

Lose fear and go for it. Speak your truth, even if your voice shakes. That's what I had to do. I realized that actually our voice is the only part of us that lives outside of us, and it can actually impact everyone around us for the better.

Not only that, by me speaking up for humanity, that's the greatest thing you can do that can help you become your greatest version. Speaking your truth, even if your voice shakes. What does it do? It helps other people speak their truth. Some people say, gosh, Ralph, I listened to that video. I felt so much confidence. I'm ready to speak my truth now. I'm like, that's the point. That's what I'm here to do, deep divers. Let's not get it twisted. And that's going to help you become your greatest version. So be brave, lose fear and go for it.

Go for it

Let's talk about going for it. A lot of... Have you got a procrastinating mind? Are you always leaving it until tomorrow and the day after that and next week? The trouble is you think you have time. That's what Buddha said. And a lot of people think they've got time. You ain't got time. Time is ticking. Tick tock, tick tock, tick tock. Your time is limited. And this moment will never come again. And that's what I tell myself every single day that, hey, I've got to make the most of it right now. And that's why every day counts. Every second counts. And this will help you become your greatest version.

I'm here every single day. I don't take a day off. I don't know what a day off means. But how come I've still got energy? Because I love what I'm doing. And I'm going for it every single day, putting 100% effort in. A lot of people are like, yeah, I'll trust the time. No, no, no, no, deep divers. You don't want to trust the timing. You want to make it happen. Don't wait for it to happen. Make it happen.

Because so many people are waiting. They're becoming skeletons in the waiting room. The cat down the road is concerned about you, deep divers. It's worried about you. You've been waiting for too long. Get up and go, go, go, go for it.

Look, if not now, when? Tell yourself this every single day. If not now, when? When? So what really helped me along my journey was to realize that, hey, I've got to set myself a little challenge. Let me do it. And feel the fear and just go for it. And that's what I did. And I changed my entire life. And you've got to remind yourself every single day. It's okay to have doubts so long as you go for it. Don't have doubts and then do nothing. It's going to be uncomfortable. It's supposed to be uncomfortable.

It was easy, everyone will be doing it. And if you do what 99% of the planet are doing, you will only get what 99% of people are getting. You want to have a 1% mindset. That's what I have. I'm going for it, realizing that actually a lot of people can't do this. So I'm giving myself flowers. Give yourself your own flowers and say, you know what? At least I'm doing something. Do you know how many people just sit on their ass and do nothing and just scroll on their iPhone? A lot of people, but you're doing something. So don't be too hard on yourself. And this is a gateway to becoming your greatest version.

It's time to make it happen. They tried to bury us. They forgot we were seeds who are blossoming and blooming. Don't act small when you came here to shine.

CHAPTER TWENTY TWO

Chapter Twenty Three

How To Accept Yourself 100%

Can you be yourself? 10 signs you're never yourself and don't know it. Do you wake up at four o'clock, trip up before you go to the bathroom, then stare for a really long time in the mirror and then say, who are you?

Now we often get told be yourself and this is so cliche, but you see what's helped me along my journey is to realize that our authenticity is where our real power lies. And I'm not 100% there yet either. Okay, so I'm gonna share with you signs I know when I'm not myself and what's helped me along my journey.

You see, as babies, we were 100% ourselves. We didn't have a filter. When you wanted to cry, you would really cry until you woke your parents up. Ask them about it. When you really wanted to laugh, you would laugh and everybody in the room would start laughing with you and say, oh, how cute. After a few years, things started to change and then we began to move out of our true authenticity.

So in becoming your greatest version, what's helped me is to realize that our authenticity is what will free us, what will strengthen us and what will make us feel really happy. So we can all start laughing like babies again. All right, that would be great. Let's do that.

So what are the 10 signs you're not yourself and don't know it?

1.   Highlights only

You only show people the highlights of your life. That was me along my early journey. I wanted to show the world like how perfect I was. Like I have everything figured out. No, I didn't, no I don't. I'm going through a lot right now, but who wants to say that? Because we all wanna be perfect. Perfect is an illusion.

Okay, sometimes you might post a picture on Instagram and someone might see that and think you've got a perfect life, but you know your life isn't perfect because you still have challenges. And I realize every single day I've got challenges. And when I smile, I'm not smiling because I've had an easy life. I'm smiling because I've had the strength to overcome a difficult one. And it feels fantastic. You see, in diving deep, I talk about all kinds of stuff most people wouldn't even dare to talk about. Indigos, the third eye, past lives. Yeah, and I'm not just showing you highlights.

I'm diving deeper with you. You see, a lot of us, we just show people the cover, the surface, but what about the depth? I'm a Pisces. So that means I know what you're going through. I'm full of compassion. What I have found to be the most helpful to people is to show people that actually it's okay to cough when you make a video. That's fine. Like who said that was a crime? It's okay to go through stuff. You don't have to pretend like your whole life is a hundred percent perfect.

Okay, I talk about every single subject you can imagine. And that's why I connect with so many people because I'm more relatable. People know that my life isn't perfect. They remember me back from 2012 when I was really going through some stuff, baby. And I'm still going through some stuff, but at the same time, I'm always in the process of becoming my greatest version. Therefore, it's moving me in the direction of becoming stronger, in becoming more authentic, in becoming more liberated.

2.   You don't have a problem in the world.

Oh no, you don't. Do you? No problems? You're perfect. I have a lot of problems. Like every day there is a new problem in my life.

But guess what? I've got a solution on standby. You see, a lot of us, we live our lives and we show people only what we feel they want to see. We tell them things like, I'm fine, which only means fearful, insecure, neurotic, and emotional. You've never been fine in your life. Look at you. That's what I had to tell myself.

So now I say I'm evolving. I'm becoming my greatest version. I-N-G, becoming, we're not there yet. What is more important than the destination is the journey getting there. So I'm still working on myself every single day. I'm still evolving and it's amazing because you see what really helps you to grow is to take a look at your problems and ask yourself every single day, is there something I can do that can help me become better than who I was yesterday? Ask the question right now, baby.

3.   You are afraid to show the world your strange eating habits.

Let me share a strange eating habit I have with you. Like I don't eat and drink at the same time. Why? Because it dilutes the hydrochloric acid in your stomach, therefore making digestion a lot harder. That's strange, right? Yeah, it's strange, but I'm telling you because I'm being myself.

You see, I'm a vegan of over 11 years. That's just the label. I eat plant-based foods. A lot of people know that. Why do I keep saying that? Because once again, I am showing you my strange eating habits. Now there are a lot of other people who eat a plant-based diet, but they never talk about it because they don't want people to judge them. They don't wanna be ridiculed. Over 64 billion animals are killed every single year... so I'm proud I'm a vegan, baby.

It feels fantastic. No shame here, baby. I love mangoes, papaya, watercress, dandelion herbs, okay? Now, the more you begin to express and share your food journey with the world, you will start to connect with more of your reflections because it starts with the food. The awakening starts with the food. Do you know how many people have written to me? I get thousands of messages every single day. Oh yeah, Ralph, what? I changed my diet and all of a sudden, I think differently now. Oh, I get it. I told you, that's what happens when you wake up with a bunch of grapes in your mouth.

CHAPTER TWENTY THREE

4.   Every single day, you wear a mask.

Guess what? I wear a mask too. Everybody wears a mask. The only problem though is that you feel you are your mask. You feel you are this person, this label society has given you. In ancient Greece, people would wear a mask in a theater and they would talk through their mask, their persona, which means her through sona, sona, sound. Persona, talking through the mask. But that was the earliest form of acting. That is beautiful because we are all actors.

But what happens when you come home and you don't take off the mask? What happens when the mask now becomes you? What happens when you actually believe you are that role you are playing every single day in society? You can't brush it off when really and truly, that's not who you really are. So what helped me along my journey was to say, okay, it's great to role play, like have an alter ego. That's beautiful. That's another part of who we are, but also realize it's just the role. It's not entirely who we are. And that's what freed me to become my greatest version. So take off the mask, baby. And then, oh my goodness, you see what you look like? I told you.

5.   You are afraid to express yourself in your job.

As a psychologist, I worked in a school. I help people with autism, children with ADHD, and I still do that. People of all races, colors, doesn't matter who you are. If you're an alien, I'll help you, okay?

Look, I was in the staff room one day and we were talking and I'm like, I really wanna talk about the third eye right now, but I wonder what these teachers would think of me. So I didn't, I just said, let me stop, let me stop. I was silent and I was talking about things which I didn't really care about, okay? And ask yourself, am I doing that right now in my job? At lunchtime, you know what it's like, everybody around the table talking about random stuff you're not interested in and you're acting like, yeah, yeah.

No, you aren't resonating with that, admit it. So what freed me along my journey was to say, actually, yeah, let me start sharing a bit more about who I am in my job. But what is my job, Ralph? What is your job? Like, I don't work, I live a lifestyle.

So I said, I'm only gonna surround myself in an environment that complements my energy 100%. So I had to leave that environment to be free, which helped me move more into my true authenticity. Express yourself, baby.

6.   You're never yourself

Because you can't be yourself, express yourself with your friends and family. Are you always in a large crowd and you're the silent one? You're the silent one, aren't you? That was me, I used to be real silent. Everybody would be talking, laughing and I would be like fake laughing and talking too. That wasn't me. I get it, you don't wanna be alone, none of us do. But at the same time, I would rather be alone than with people who don't really know who I am.

That's just me and that's what I learned the hard way. You see, I grew up and I would be around different people, I would be around friends, but they didn't know how weird I was. Like I talk about indigos, the third eye, crystals, all kinds of stuff. And I was thinking these same thoughts when I was like 10 years old, 12 years old, okay? Imagine me saying that to my friends then, okay?

Yeah, you might be going through this right now. You might be in a large crowd, a large group of friends, they're all talking about the game. You're thinking about how I can help the planet, okay? But you're not telling them that, you're just silent. So what freed me was to say, actually, I'm gonna start talking more about what I really am thinking. And once I started to do that, I attracted the cat down the road. I started to connect with more people who are on the same frequency as myself. And it felt fantastic. Your vibe attracts your tribe.

So ask yourself, are you really in the vibe of who you are when you are around people? Or are you just pretending? Like, be honest. Like, I can't fake anymore. Like, it's so hard and annoying. Like, look, this is me, take me or leave me. I'm asking you that, take me or leave me. Think about it.

7.   You would rather other people accept you for who you're not than accept you for who you are.

I'm very different and I accept myself. But there was a time where I didn't wanna accept myself. I just wanted people to accept me. I would do everything. Like, I wanted to be really tidy at work, come in dressed and everything. But then when I would go home, I would just like to wear a bandana, okay? I love Tupac. Look, that's what it's like when a lot of us, we're trying to make our feet fit in the shoe and it's just not happening.

It's really stressful, isn't it? So I made a vow to myself to say, look, no more. I've gotta accept myself 100% because I've gotta live with myself. You see, the reason why a lot of people have a lot of psychosomatic stress is because they're living upstairs.

8.   You're never yourself because you care more about what others think than what you think about yourself.

Don't worry. I used to be exactly the same way. I used to say, look, I only want people to see me in a certain way. Once again, the highlights, not the mid-tones, not the shadows. So why do we wanna control what other people think of us so much? Because we wanna control, period. Control is the greatest illusion. Control comes from the ego, which is the false self. The longest journey you will ever take is from the head to the heart.

So I had to say to myself that, look, the perception I have of myself is greater than the perception other people have of me. And once I realized that secret, I moved more in the direction of my true authentic self. And I'm still working on it every single day because let's face it, a lot of us will become so conditioned.

.Okay, you wanna get the A. You wanna get the top mark. You wanna be perfect. Not perfect, but perfect. Getting influenced by the cat down the road. Okay, look, I'm gonna cough right now. I'm here to show you that it's okay. You see, we are all humans. We are drawn to people who show us the struggle. People know me from back in the day. That's how I connect with so many people because people know that my hair used to be all over the place. I used to just make videos butt naked. Yeah, all of that stuff, right? People know, people know.

9.   You have become disconnected from your true emotions.

What are we talking about when we say emotion? Energy in motion. You can't feel yourself right now. You don't know what you want. That's why so many people can't find their true purpose.

.Don't worry, it happened to me along my journey. I was struggling for a long time, sleepless nights, tossing and turning, and sleepwalking too. I didn't know what I wanted to do with my life because I was disconnected from my true emotions, the energy in motion. As a Pisces, who's really compassionate, as an empath, as a sensitive soul, that is my greatest strength. Why? Because I know exactly what I want.

You see, your emotions are your inner GPS. They tell you what you're going through right now. So imagine turning that off. Now you have become desensitized, disconnected and cold. We have become strangers to each other, many of us on this planet. Some of us don't even know our next door neighbor. Who the hell are you? Nobody knows. Don't worry about it, okay? Get to know your neighbors, but you've got to get to know yourself first. Study everything, but study yourself first. This is what's helped me along my journey.

I realized that I was for a long time in the wilderness, disconnected from feeling because I felt that being vulnerable was a sign of weakness. So I had to dive deep. And I started diving deep and guess what? I inspired so many other people to dive deep because my mentor inspired me to dive deep, okay? And that's the whole secret, people. Get in touch with your emotions. And you can only do that when you are in an environment that allows you to express your emotions.

10.   You think you're a label.

I'm a vegan, who says that? I'm a psychologist, who says that? I'm an indigo, who says that? I'm a doctor, da-da. Yeah, I say it all the time. You see, labels are how we define ourselves. But once again, these are the roles we are playing. You can say I'm a banker. Yeah, you are, but that's not all who you are, okay? You could say I'm a nurse. I'm a physiotherapist. Yes, you are, but that's not all who you are.

So what I've realized, going back to role playing, labels are man-made. We are infinite. So even though I'm a psychologist, I'm a vegan, I'm this, I'm that, I know I am infinite. There are no words that can define me, especially not one word, maybe a billion words, and that still won't even get close. We're infinite, baby. People say I'm black, I'm white.

I'm like, do you even know that race was created by Johann Friedrich Blumenbach. You've got to study, baby. You got to do the research. All this separation to keep you divided, where is it getting you? We are energy underneath everything, and that's what's freed me. That's what's helped me become my greatest version, but more so, that's what's helped me become more authentic. So be yourself, baby. Be yourself.

Chapter Twenty Four

How To Get A Tranquil Mind

So neuroscience and psychology tells us that we have between 50,000 to 70,000 thoughts every single day. The average person, and that's like 35 to 48 thoughts a minute. I can only share with you what's helped me along my journey because I've got a very noisy mind. It chatters a lot. I'm always overthinking a lot of the time, right? I've realized this.

You have to realize that overthinking comes from a desire to control. Are you a control freak? What kind of thoughts do you have? What kind of thoughts go through your mind? You will find that the majority of them are based around control. You want to control how other people see you. You want to control other people. It's a lot of hassle.

You see, our subconscious mind runs over 95% of our lives. That's a lot. So our conscious mind isn't really doing much. So when our mind is very full of a lot of clutter, it is coming from routines that have been etched into our mind over a long period of time. So how did I start to break that routine and hack the subconscious mind? Forget about good thoughts and bad thoughts. That's what's helped me get a tranquil mind. Like I think of the most random stuff sometimes. Someone sitting on the toilet, some spaghetti and the cat down the road. Why? Nobody knows.

Right? I don't label thoughts, like this is a good thought and that's a bad thought. Because the moment you start judging your thoughts is the moment you start creating resistance to certain thoughts. Right? Someone asked, how can I remove negative thoughts from my mind? When you try to push negative thoughts out of your mind, you only create more. It's like a boomerang effect. Get out of my mind. Whoa. They're right back in there because resistance makes them stronger.

You have to start embracing your so-called negative thoughts and see them as disowned aspects of yourself. And that's what's helped me along my journey. I realized this, that we are surrounded by a lot of different frequencies. And every single day I am finding time to do nothing. That's right. Nothing. Right? What do you want to do today? Nothing. That will help get you a tranquil mind.

You see, a lot of us were so bombarded with always wanting to do something. This action, in essence, creates stress in the body. So I'm learning more and more how to not overwhelm myself to get a tranquil mind. By just slowing everything down. OK, I come to a serene setting every single day. Nature. Sometimes I climb a mountain and get stuck up there. Sometimes I go to the beach. Sometimes I'm just not in my room because that's boring most of the time, but I'm just going for a walk. And when you can just consciously feel that chi invade your nostrils. It starts to clear your mind.

Most of us don't have time to do that. Uh oh. If you don't have time to take five minutes every single day just to go for a walk, you're in big trouble. Right? Don't worry about it.

Now, 7 Day Vegan Challenge. What's helped me when it comes to food is to prepare my own food. That helps me get a tranquil mind because at least I know what's going in it. But also when you prepare your own food, like I love making brown rice with tomato sauce with water. Am I making you hungry right now? Good. That's my intention. Right. And the whole process just slows down. Like when you go and eat out, it's fantastic.

It's fantastic, but it speeds everything up because you just get your food, you eat, then you bounce. When you prepare food, you actually start enjoying it. You're like, I'm going to chew this as slowly as possible because it took like two hours to make. And it only takes like two minutes to eat. That's not fair but that's how it goes. So I prepare my own food. And guess what? In nature, you don't have to because mangoes are already prepared for you. Grapes are already prepared for you. Right. I've come to see this.

A lot of people say, how can I block out painful memories? Right. How can I stop thinking about painful memories? And I've got memories which sometimes when I think about them, they sometimes create pain. I don't want to think about these experiences. Getting lost at the airport and things like that. OK. But hard times. Certain times in my life, I wasn't even sure where my life was going. I would wake up every day like this can't be life.

Then the cat down the road would say, yes, it can be life, Ralph. Get out of bed. It was hard. Hard. I realized this, that to get a tranquil mind, embrace your painful memories, too, because they are part of the process of giving you that tranquil mind. When you aren't in resistance to thinking certain thoughts, you realize that you are not your thoughts. They're just clouds that will pass away. They don't define you. They can never define you because you are so much more than that. And that's really given me a tranquil mind.

. Now, I know we are surrounded by tons of people every single day. I'm sharing with a lot of people surrounded by all kinds of energy. And certain times I've realized that instead of me getting pulled into other people's drama and whatnot, I'm going to pull them into my peace vortex. Right. And it helps a lot of us. We are pulled into other people's craziness. Right. The energies around us create disharmony and we've got to take responsibility for that.

Can you speak your mind about what is happening on the planet? For a long time, I couldn't. Until I said, wait a minute. Being free is our birthright. And once I found my voice to express, I could sleep peacefully at night. I could sleep peacefully. I had a tranquil mind because I got everything off my chest. Now, our beliefs, so many of us have. We need to put a massive question mark around them. I believe. Who gave you that belief? You see, a lot of us, we only believe what we think will be socially acceptable.

So every single day, to get a tranquil mind, I am questioning my beliefs because you see beliefs aren't the truth because beliefs can change from one day to the next. A belief is a subjective reality you have created. So I never cling to certain beliefs all the time. I'm always questioning my belief to say, OK, why? When? How? The more questions you ask. The great paradox is that the more you will clear your mind. Right. Can you feel that wind? You can't, but it feels so good.

Now, are you always comparing yourself to other people? You go on social media and you're like, oh, my gosh, their life is so much better than mine. I found that instead of comparing your life to other people, because that will only leave you depressed and miserable, just start collaborating with them.

You see, what we see of people isn't actually the truth of who they are. It's just a tiny glimpse, which they've taken a long time to prepare for before they've taken that photo. Right. Certain times I see people taking photos of themselves and there's like all kinds of crazy stuff going on behind them. But you're just seeing a snap of that moment, thinking it's the entire moment. Right. So you don't have to compare yourself to other people.

You are unique. You are amazing. You are enough.

And work with people. Right. A lot of the times we don't have a tranquil mind because we have a competitive mind state to win instead of to cooperate, realizing we are all one. This is just a game we're playing. Work with each other. Loosen up.

Chapter Twenty Five

How To Let Go Of The Past

How to let go of the past, the secret guide to moving forward. Someone wrote to me saying that they find it hard to let go of not only a negative past, but also a positive one. Sometimes they find it difficult to relive up to what they were before.

How many of us experienced that? Put your hand up. Great question. So let us dive into this, letting go of the past. Goodness gracious, what happened to you? We can't talk about the past without talking about attachment and detachment. Many times if we've had a very negative past, we don't wanna look at it. So we become detached from our past. Or if you had a very positive past in your heyday, right, now you have become attached to who you were.

So let's first start with the so-called negative past. Goodness knows what we've all got in our closet, hey? I always remind myself along my journey that the only time you should look back is to see how far you've come, okay? Many of us, whatever we've gone through, what do we do? We try and run away. We try to avoid the past. That's why it's so difficult to move forward. You start drinking, you start smoking. You're trying to forget what happened. To let go of the past, you have to acknowledge whatever happened.

You have to realize you're not the same person. Look, you don't even have the same consciousness and you're wearing different clothes now. Many times we keep telling ourselves stories about what happened in the past.

The mind we have is the greatest editor ever. So you have to realize that the mind is gonna put all the clips to support your story. So you have to ask yourself, did that really happen to me? Or did I just make that up? How many times have we recalled our story to someone and we've put in a whole load of extra in there? Go on, be honest. We do it all the time because we are secretly editing our life. So we have to realize we have to lose this editor to let go of the past. I've got a story for you.

An old man with his head bowed down, sitting on a bench. A young girl noticed. She said, what's wrong with you, sir? He goes on to say that he's having a hard time coming to terms with his past. He said, once I was a boy. Then I became a teenager. Then I became a man. Then an uncle. After an uncle, I became a father. After a father, now look, I'm a grandfather. Look at me.

Then the girl said, I see you, but I feel you, the eternal part of you, which is your essence, and that never changes. And then they had a good laugh after that.

You see, because we're always changing, I always say embrace change. But before you can embrace it, you've got to prepare yourself for change. You've got to accept change. Change is the only constant in the universe. You were talking about how you had a positive past. Do you know how easy it is to rest on your laurels? It's like that scene from Requiem for a Dream. The woman, she's older now, she's looking back on her past when she was really famous. Goodness, I hope that's not me. But it's terrible.

Okay, now to avoid that situation, you have to see you've got the ability to recreate yourself every single day. That is where we find our true freedom. Stop looking at what you did yesterday. Only use what you did yesterday as a catalyst to propel you to where you are right now. Here's how it works. The past, many of us, we see the past as fear. We see the present as love, and we see the future as doubt. That is how so many of us live.

What about seeing the past as wisdom because you can learn so much from whatever happened to you. Seeing the present as love, because it's a gift, that's what it is. That's why it's called the present. And then seeing the future as possibility. There is no fear. Seeing the future as confidence. Because once you take care of what is happening in the present moment, you've got nothing to worry about.

Many times we get attached to certain labels, expectations we place on ourselves, expectations which are hard to live up to. What happens when you feel you are finished? Every day you are always being updated, renovated, repaired, yeah, a lot going on in there. What helped me personally along my journey was to let go of my past and embrace the now, the eternal now, which is what I call total body awareness.

You see, the past doesn't exist within our minds. It exists in our body. What happens when you're thinking about the past for so long? You're reflecting, it's wonderful, but now analysis is paralysis.

Total body awareness is where you realize all the stress, tension, heartache is all stored in your body. That's why yoga's so powerful, swimming's so powerful, running's so powerful, saying can I get a hug is so powerful. Because you are releasing energy, all of those energetic blocks. That is how to free yourself. Many of us become attached to an image of ourselves in the past.

. So I'll give you an example. I made a video called How to Decalcify Your Pineal Gland. It went viral. Okay, what happens when you've created such a masterpiece? You have to ask yourself, is it a masterpiece, really? For me, it's no different from any other video. Because it's all energy. Just like the old man sitting on the bench, the young girl told him, I see your essence, your energy. So what helped me move forward was to realize you have to have no favorites.

When we talk of these attachments from a positive past, have no favorites in whatever you're creating, how you see yourself, because it's all you. It's all you. Accept everything as the same. That's a secret to really never run out of steam, to keep going. Choo choo.

Many of us, we're so hard on ourselves. Because of this, we get stuck in the past. When you are kind to yourself, you can move forward. How are you talking to yourself every single day? In a nice way? In a horrible way? In a way I don't like you way? The kinder you are to yourself, the easier it is to move forward.

The harder you are on yourself, the easier it is to stay in the same position. So what helped me along my journey was forgiving myself for whatever I've done in my past or whatever other people have done in my past. I'm not gonna forget about it, but I'm gonna release. Because relaxation is what you are. Stress is what you think you should be or what you think should have happened. Accept that it did happen, but move forward now.

Many times I talk of what I call memory assimilation. You see, the past, which is memory and experience, literally shapes who we are. The science of this is that our brain changes based on our experience, neuroplasticity. So we already know the science of it, right? What happens when we are not aware that we're taking other people's memory, their memories, what they're talking about from our environment? Okay, there's a lot going on. We are all energy, and you are absorbing all the frequencies in your proximity.

What does this mean? It means you are a sponge, my friend. We are all sponges. So you have to ask yourself, who is forming my memory? Who is reminding me of who I think I am? And who is helping me let go of who I think I am? For me, it was Krishnamurti. Because every time I read Krishnamurti, I say, I don't know anything. Because enlightenment is knowing how much you don't know.

Let's talk about food. Before 2006, I was on a heavy diet of junk food, eating a lot of meats, a lot of dairy, and I didn't feel so good. But more so, I also realized I was assimilating a lot of memory from the tortured animals. You see, food is information. So when you are eating food from the past, not just one week old, but a couple of months old, something that's been stored in the freezer, you have to realize you are assimilating DNA into your body. The fear that the animals have experienced is transferred into your body. For me, that's the reality I stumbled across.

But once again, I'm not here to tell you what to do. I'm only here to give you a perspective. To realize, you have to ask yourself, are you eating food from the past or are you eating living foods? Fresh fruits, vegetables, pineapples, blueberries, cranberries, strawberries, lots of berries.

Okay? Many of us, we're holding on to the grudge. The grudge is like, we are having a tug of war, not with other people, but with ourselves. For a long time, I thought holding a grudge was a powerful thing to do. I thought holding a grudge was the most powerful thing in the world. Then I realized, wait a minute. Once again, that's what's pulling you down. That's what's weighing you down. And because of this, you ain't going anywhere soon.

Many times, I always remind myself that to recreate yourself, to redesign yourself, you've got to let love guide you and not fear. You see, I could have gone the route of keeping you guys in fear, but I don't do that. Because for me, I'm all about a higher state of living. And that's why once you enter that state, you start taking responsibility for the way you feel, for your internal condition.

.See, many of us, we blame people for our past, which is fine if you want, but also realize one thing. You can keep blaming them, but ask yourself, are you taking responsibility for how you feel right now? Because once again, if you are stuck in the past, the past is right now. The past, present, future, they are all happening simultaneously. Many times, we don't see the bigger picture. The past can become scary because it's all we know.

I used to skate a lot, I still do every single day, actually. If you try a new trick and it doesn't go well, what happens? We say to ourselves, I'm not doing that again. But if you learn from the past, you start rewiring your whole brain. You actually do the thing you are most afraid of. You face your fear. So now, you move past the past to enter a whole new possibility, a whole new way of life.

What's helped me along my journey is really just to see that the people who support you, the people who are always gonna be around because they've seen your essence, those will be the people you have to connect with. Those will be the people that will help you live in the now. And you've also got another group of people, they're gonna remind you of your former self. They're gonna bring up the past. Oh, do you remember when you were 14? Hey, I'm 32 now. I'm 50 now. But they always wanna go back.

So you gotta be very mindful of who you are spending time with. Many times we say, I am a victim of the past. And I always remind people that the story you tell yourself influences how you edit your life because we are all editing our lives. We take and we put in whatever fits our storyline. So many times, if you say I'm a victim of my past, guess what? You're justifying staying in the past. That's your justification.

If you say I'm a survivor of the past, that's a little better, a little better. But once again, you're still caught up in that survival program. That's why you're a survivor. So you're still at war, you're still going up against people. What about if you say I'm a thriver? Okay, now you're entering the realm of abundance, which means you're an alchemist, you're a wizard, you're a sorceress. Okay? Every day is a new beginning, it's a new start.

That means you are forever changing. That means you are now the butterfly because the caterpillar is stuck in the past until its imaginal self starts working and envisioning a better future, a better possibility. But once again, the caterpillar had to prepare for change, accept change, and then embrace change and be open to change. And that's how it changed into the beautiful butterfly. Look behind you right now, there's a butterfly. Realize this every day and we can be whatever we want.

Do you know the amazing time we're living in right now? It's beautiful. So realize the infinite possibilities, use the past for wisdom instead of for justifying how much you've been victimized. And also remind yourself that you've gotta be careful of who you surround yourself with. Are people reminding you of your former self or are people helping you enter into the new?

Chapter Twenty Six

How To Let Go Of What's Weighing Your Heart Down

Do you have something weighing your heart down right now? It's hard for you to get out of bed because your heart feels really heavy, like really heavy. How do you let go of whatever is weighing your heart down? First, before you read any further, let's just breathe in that good-ass prana, baby. That's better. That's what you got to do.

Now, that's the question that came in. Somebody said that every single day, they wake up with a heavy heart. They feel like they can't go on any longer. They can't move forward. Something is eating them up inside. Regrets.

Look, I know what it's like. But as a Pisces, I'm always realizing it's so important to have a light heart. And that's why I swim around like a fish. You've got to be fluid. You don't want to get stuck. And a lot of us who have a heavy heart, we get stuck. We lose our fluidity. So what's helped me along my journey, plain and simple, is to realize this. That whatever is weighing your heart down, it's okay. Just don't stay there. Whatever you're going through, allow yourself to feel it. Just don't stay there.

At the end of the day, you always have to ask yourself, is this helpful for me? Or is it harmful to me? You see, we've all done something in the past which we absolutely regret. If I could turn back the hands of time, you would. But no, you can't. The cat down the road tried to do that. It didn't work. So we've got to deal with what has already happened. It is what it is. And the more you can realize that your peace of mind must be made a top priority, the better you will be.

How I do this every single day is by not overthinking so much. You see, thoughts can't get rid of thoughts. Only silence can. So I've learned that the more present I am, the more I can let go of whatever is weighing my heart down. Many times we think if we think enough about something, it's going to magically disappear. In fact, it only makes it worse. 99 problems already... don't be the 100th one. We do this by letting go of all the thoughts which are holding us back, that are making our heart even heavier than it already is.

You see, it could be a financial situation you're going through, a relationship issue. You said you can't forgive yourself for something you've done in the past. You feel guilty. Right. And I know what that's like. We've all done something that can really eat us up alive. But realize you are work in progress. At the same time, you're also are the masterpiece.

When you can learn that it's OK to not have a clean slate, nobody does on planet Earth. Everybody is wounded, scarred and needs healing. That's what I'm doing. That's why I do what I'm doing, because this is the last hope for humanity to heal those wounds. Realize you want to be proud of yourself, that you actually recognize you've got a heavy heart, because so many times people walk around desensitized, out of touch with their emotions, out of touch with how they really feel. And therefore, their heart grows heavier. Don't be afraid to be sensitive. Sensitivity is your strength in a time like this.

It's your sensitivity that will actually make your heart lighter. Our heart is more powerful than our brain. Five thousand times stronger magnetically than our brain. So if we realize that our heart, we have to take care of it, that is important. And we do this by making our peace of mind a top priority.

Forget about buying a car, buying a house. Ask yourself, how am I doing inside? We're always checking out, waking up, going to work, always going outside of ourselves. What's helped me along my journey to let go of everything weighing my heart down is to learn how to check in, check in with yourself every single day. Say, actually, actually, how am I feeling right now? Get a journal out. Start journaling your emotions and your feelings. I guarantee you your heart will feel a lot lighter.

You see, many times what happens? We don't put our peace of mind first. We don't value it. The greatest form of wealth is your peace of mind, because if you lose that, you lose everything. So always remind yourself to let go of this heavy heart you have. Be kinder to yourself. You're doing the best you can.

I'm very kind to myself all the time because I realize, you see, your heart is your best friend. And if you are mad at yourself, you're trash talking yourself, you now make an enemy in your heart. You become your own worst enemy. And once your heart is your enemy, you're on your own, Jojo. You've got nobody else.

So we have to learn to make our hearts lighter. We have to learn how to make our heart our best friend. We do this by praising ourselves, praising ourselves every single day. Find one thing about yourself you absolutely love every single day and make it known. Because the more you can get your heart on your side, the lighter your heart will become. Be kind to yourself. Be gentle with yourself. You're doing the best you can.

You see, many times what happens? We get stuck because we're ruminating, wishing things never happened in a certain way. But they did. So the best chance you have right now is to let go of everything, everything that's weighing your heart down and to make peace with your past. You have to learn how to make peace with your past. Because if you don't, your past will eat you alive.

How I always make peace with my past is to realize this, the lessons. That's what the past is for. Lessons. Lessons learned. So who cares if this happened to you in the past? It doesn't define you. Never allow your past to dictate your future. And the more you make peace with your past, all those people who did you dirty, they scammed you, they ripped you off. It's happened to me. I'm like, I'm a lot wiser now. And see them as lessons, not defining moments of who you are.

Make it a top priority to start voicing how you feel to other people. Don't drain me. Don't talk my ear off. I'll listen to you though. If you've got a friend, call them right now and tell them what you're going through. The worst thing you can do when your heart feels really heavy is to hold it all to yourself; is to bottle up your emotions; is to suppress your emotions.

Depression is suppression. So what's helped me along my journey? And the reason why I'm so vocal, my throat chakra is open, baby, is because I'm always expressing how I feel. That's why I sleep very well at night. And that's why I'm in equilibrium, mental balance, emotional balance and spiritual balance. So if something is weighing your heart down, talk to a friend. You can phone a friend if you want.

Don't feel you've got to deal with this all alone because you have to be a strong person. In fact, people who are more expressive are actually stronger because you're learning how to let go. To say, actually, I have no shame in saying that I'm going through something emotionally. That's strength. That's vulnerability. And by doing that, your heart feels a lot lighter because now you're sharing the load, meeting up with a good friend and saying, actually, I've got financial issues. Actually, I've got relationship issues. Actually, my life is screwed. I'll listen to you.

When we talk of letting go of everything weighing your heart down, 7-Day Vegan Challenge. Ever been in a state, deep divers, where you're so stressed out, you actually miss meals? You forget to eat. And what's helped me is to always, 7-Day Vegan Challenge, eat regularly, especially when your heart is feeling very heavy, because the more you get into a healthy eating pattern and routine, of eating that beetroot, the spinach. OK, now you start getting back into the flow, the rhythm of your life.

So whenever my heart feels heavy, which is rare these days because I'm always moving in balance, but along my early journey, there were days when I used to wake up with a heavy heart and I wasn't eating. So it made it even worse. Plus, I was dehydrated, which made it even worse. So please stay hydrated. We are over 80% water. If you are hydrated, you're thinking clearly. Your heart will become lighter. When you're feeling thirsty, you are already dehydrated. You've got a heavy heart because not only is your heart feeling very heavy, but also you are neglecting yourself. Preservation, self-preservation, the first law of nature. So you have to practice self-care to let go of everything that's weighing your heart down. And that can be in the forms of foods, right?

Treating yourself to that delicious smoothie. Oh, you're smiling right now. That's cheering you up. All of a sudden, your heart feels lighter because you're taking care of yourself by the foods you are eating. Shout out to everybody who's eating a beautiful plant-based diet, because that's a surefire way to really clear all of those toxins from your bodies, clear all of those toxins from your body. And now you're purifying yourself. You're going on a detox, okay? And that's what will really help you have a lighter heart.

You see, what's helped me along my journey is to never carry past energies into the present. And what I love to do every single day is to find the root of my problem. That's how to let go of everything weighing you down. What is the root of my ailment? What is the root of my confusion? Once again, everybody on the planet is wounded. Everybody needs healing. As a psychologist, as a counselor, as someone who's inspiring millions of people, I see this. That's why I'm making videos every single day, because I know you need healing. I know you are wounded. Why? Because everybody on planet Earth has had some form of trauma. It doesn't mean we're victims.

It just means that we have to find the root cause of our ailment. What is making our heart feel heavy? Many times, grudges make our heart heavy. Many times, we can't forgive somebody. That's what makes our heart heavy. Many times, we can't forgive ourselves. That is what makes our heart heavy. Many times, we are trying to become perfectionists. That is what makes our heart heavy. So you have to find the root to say, actually, why am I waking up with a heavy heart? Not living a life you know you were supposed to be living in the first place. That is what will make your heart heavy. It's time to get back into alignment.

And now, all of a sudden, oh my gosh, my heart is so light, it's going to fly away. It's going to fly away right now, okay? It's all about total body awareness. You see, the root of all our ailments lie in our body. Every single day, I'm breathing in that good-ass prana. So when I'm breathing in that good-ass prana, every single day, I feel healed, okay? Because I'm connecting to the elements.

I'm always in beautiful breathing spaces, no pollution, eco-therapy. And that is what will help you say, actually, the more aware I become, the lighter my heart becomes. The more aware you become, the lighter your heart will become. Self-awareness is the key to having a lighter heart. You see, many times on this planet, especially in this matrix, we're also programmed to just make it. I want more money. I want to become more successful. I want to become more famous. I want more attention.

Screaming for other people's attention will make your heart heavy, because if you don't get it, you feel bad about yourself. Self-love will give you a lighter heart. Start by only trying to win your own approval and getting your own attention. You see, you've been asking for other people's attention for so long, you've forgotten about giving yourself attention and the love you need.

Become your greatest fan and realize that love you're seeking on the outside, you can never get it because it doesn't exist. The love you are searching for so desperately will only be found inside yourself. And the more you form this beautiful relationship with yourself, your heart will become lighter. You have to find the root cause of what is making your heart heavy. And then you have to make peace with that.

You see, in our society, we treat symptoms. If you've got a headache, take some aspirin. Take some paracetamol, right? We're on drugs, man-made drugs, which are the worst. And that's why a lot of people are dying prematurely. And walking around with a heavy heart now. To change that around, instead of just treating symptoms, if you're not feeling well, you take a pill.

Start treating your unresolved issues. And I guarantee you, it always goes back to your relationship with yourself and your authenticity. What is more important than getting attention is authenticity. The reason why I'm making these videos is because it's very authentic. It's a very authentic connection I'm having with myself and with other people. I can do videos for attention, but right now on the planet, it's all about raising the frequency. I'm having fun doing it.

The more you learn to realize that you must place your authenticity above your attention seeking, that will give you a lighter heart. Because you can sleep at night knowing that you stay true to yourself.

Every single day I wake up and I'm like, wow, it feels good right now to wake up with a light heart. My heart is so light, it's lighter than it's ever been, okay? It's lighter than it's ever been. Why? Why does my heart feel so light? Because every single day I wake up knowing I get to do whatever I want. I'm doing what I love. I'm not doing something against my will. I really, really love to do these videos. You don't have to pay me to do it. I'm going to do it regardless.

I'm a Pisces. I'm a natural communicator. This is what I do, right? And the more you can really find peace in the sunrise, as soon as you wake up, do something that sets your soul on fire in a beautiful way. For me, I'm going skating every single day, going into nature every single day. And that's what makes me happy. As soon as I wake up, my heart is lighter.

You see, many of us, we're reaching for our phone. We're going through the newsfeed. Then we're comparing ourselves to other people as soon as we wake up. So, of course, your heart is going to feel very heavy. Comparison is the greatest thief of joy. And we have to really learn to be unique. You see, you have to be different to make a difference. And being different just means you're being weird. And being weird means you're only being yourself.

So learn that if you can find happiness in the sunrise, it's the first thing you do in the day that's going to set the tone for the rest of the day. You see, many times I meet people as soon as they wake up, they compare themselves with other people. They have a very negative attitude towards themselves, right? And that's why you have a heavy heart. Because you can't find peace once again out there. Peace does not exist out there. It can only exist inside of yourself.

That's why every single day you want to be in communion with yourself. Meditation is fantastic for having a lighter heart. Because meditation is when you are in the present moment 100% and in total communion with yourself. Meditation is all about the inner relationship. And the more you practice that, the more your heart will feel lighter. And that's the only way to move forward.

Every single day I'm moving forward because I'm not getting stuck. I don't have time to sit around and say, oh my gosh, look at this video. Look what they said. I'm already on to the next one. Right? Because I live in the present moment. I don't live in yesterday. I don't live for tomorrow. I live for the here and now. You have to learn how to lose your mind and come to your senses.

It's just like the great Yoda said, train your mind to let go of everything you fear to lose. And that really sums it up. You see, many times we're afraid of losing things. Our partner. She's mine, Ralph. He's mine. We don't own anybody. And I've realized this along my journey. Everything we own, our possessions, our car, our house is just on loan. We're just borrowing it. We're going to have to return it. We can't take it with us out of this dimension. So we have to really get into that mindset.

Say, actually, I don't own anything. I don't even own my body. I don't even own the air I breathe because the moment I breathe, I've got to breathe it right back out. OK, so we don't even own the air we breathe. It's an exchange. It's based on the law of exchange, right? Give and take, inhalations and exhalations.

So we have to learn how to train our mind to let go of everything we fear to lose. The good news is that we can't lose our primordial energy, our essence. OK, and that's how to have a very light heart; to realize even if you do lose everything, even if right now you've got financial issues, relationship problems, you don't know what to do with your life. Even if those things are happening, remember you are already a masterpiece in the universe's eyes. You were created magnificently and you can't lose your essence.

You can lose your car. You can lose your house, but you can't lose your internal energy.

It's what I call your inner core. Yes, change. Is the only constant and sometimes things do seem uncertain. The future can look bleak at times, but to let go of everything weighing your heart down is to realize no amount of thinking is going to change the future. You've been caught in a trap of feeling that you can control things that haven't happened yet. You can't. All you can control is your attitude to what is happening.

You can change your response and you can stop reacting to life and you can start responding to life and then you realize life is not something happening to you. It's always responding to you. And then you realize life is nothing more than a mirror of my internal mental and emotional condition. Train your mind to let go of everything you fear to lose. That's how to have a very light heart. Don't get too attached to anything, even your own creation.

When I'm making my videos, I've got so many videos, and I love all of them the same. They're all my babies, right? But I'm not attached to one video. Oh my gosh, you've got millions of views. Who cares? I'm already on to the next one. And that's why through this non-attachment, my heart is very light because once again, I'm just having fun out here.

I'm just having a blast. It's amazing, baby, right? What happens when our heart feels heavy? What happens when we get stuck? We forget to do things that make us smile. We take life way too seriously. And what's helped me along my journey to let go of everything I'm afraid to lose and doing something I used to do before I got so serious, something that used to make me smile. For a long time, I stopped skating because I was like, I have a heavy heart. And whenever we have a heavy heart, we always love to justify our actions.

Then we have a self-fulfilling prophecy. So if you have a heavy heart, you can't do something that makes you smile because now it goes against your belief that you have a heavy heart. So stop justifying your behavior by creating a self-fulfilling prophecy to say, actually, I have a heavy heart, so I can't go and do what I love. I can't go to the gym. I can't go to the beach because if I do, I just might smile, right and I won't have that heavy heart anymore.

Do something every single day that makes you happy. I don't care what it is. It's not about the money. It's about your life fulfillment. Money can't buy that. It can only enhance it. So to let go of everything that's weighing your heart down right now. Learn how to put life in perspective. What you think is the end. Oh my gosh, it's ending Ralph. No, it's only the beginning. In fact, it hasn't even started for you yet. No matter how bad your life seems, always realize there's a brighter tomorrow. But forget about the brighter tomorrow. Realize just by embracing whatever the weather, you surrender to what is. And in surrendering to what is, you find peace. In trying to change what is, you have a heavy heart. So learn how to realize it's all beautiful. The sun, the rain, the snow, the sleep, the thunder. It's all energy.

So learn how to surrender and your heart will become lighter. Stop trying to feel you always, always have to win a battle. You always, always have to be right. No. Allow yourself to release resistance to what is, to how you feel. And then your heart will become lighter.

Your heart should be as light as a feather. And if it is, then you have a lot to smile about.

CHAPTER TWENTY SIX

Chapter Twenty Seven

How To Completely Heal Your Body And Mind

Infinite Waters is not about Ralph Smart. Infinite Waters is a community. And right now, we need to go back to community. We need to start coming together on one accord and coming in unison and vibrating at the same frequency. And this is what's needed. This is the best thing to do when you find yourself in a crazy world.

Because we are all we have. And right now, people are starting to notice that.

We've got to stick together. We've got to band together. We got to do a little samba together, baby. We've got to start raising the frequency together. And of course, we've got to start raising the vibration together, right? The best thing you can do for yourself in a crazy world, in this crazy world, let's take a look at that.

Someone sent me a message. They're like, Ralph, the world has gone so crazy. I'm like, are you kidding me? But what is the best thing we can all do for ourselves? You see, I talk about becoming your greatest version. I talk about living your best life. And right now, a lot of people's dreams have been put on hold. But I'm here to tell you, it doesn't have to be the end of your story. If you are watching this video, please don't allow this chapter one to be your chapter two, three, four, and five. The story is not finished yet. And you can still write yourself in this story as the victor, the hero, the one who triumphs over any adversity. I like that.

People are always like, Ralph, gosh, why aren't you depressed? Why aren't you crying a river? I'm optimistic. Why am I hopeful? Because I know the people I connect with every single day are wonderful beings. And this gives me hope, tremendous hope for humanity.

Now, the best thing you can do for yourself in this crazy world, we all right now have to take a look at our lives. We've got to take a look at our lives, not just what's happening around us, because if we look at what's happening around us, we will only be confused. But if we take a look at what's going on in our own life, we will get the answers we need to solve the problems happening outside of us. This is what we are being called to do.

I'm going to tell you about the 10 Laws of Alchemy because this is the best thing you can do for yourself in this crazy world. It's to become aware of the 10 Laws of Alchemy.

1.   There is no bad weather in nature.

Everything that's happening on the planet right now, the craziness, right? The fear that's being thrown around all over the place. It's okay, because there is no bad weather in nature. Hailstones. It's crazy. No, it's not. It's needed. Snow is crazy. No, it's not. It's needed. 100 degrees temperature. It's so hot. It's crazy, Ralph. No, it's needed. Rain. I don't like the rain, Ralph. It's crazy. No, it's not. It's needed. We need flowers to grow. We need apples, oranges, pears, and peaches. 7-Day Vegan Challenge. We need the rain to fertilize the soil.

So, remind yourself, we have to turn this energy around on the planet. The doom and gloom. Coronavirus. Omicron. Oh, my gosh. New variants. Oh, my gosh. There is no bad weather in nature. So, this is why a crazy world can be a good thing. A crazy world means an opportunity. An opportunity to find out who we really are. An opportunity to come together like we've never come together before. Oh, it's amazing how everything that was happening in the midst of global pandemic is bringing people together.

There is no bad weather in nature. And there are no bad experiences. There are only experiences. We can extract the lesson from what's happening in our lives right now and what's happening in the world right now. And we can use it to work in our favor. We can use this bad weather, times of uncertainty. We can use this to work in our favor because there is no bad weather in nature. So, all of the craziness you see around you, it's the raw material. We can turn the lead into gold. Everything, everything, everything can be used.

Mother Nature is constantly recycling everything. Even waste can be used in Mother Nature to produce flowers. Okay. So, the craziness that we see in the world right now with QR codes and all of this, we can use that to work in our favor. We can find a use for it to say, actually, now I'm going to start to see my true power. I'm going to stand in my power. I'm going to create my own reality. I'm going to say no to fascism. I'm going to say no to 1984.

And I'm going to say yes to myself, right? That's the best thing that you can do for yourself in this crazy world. Check in with yourself, how are you feeling today? Have fun, right?

2.   Namaste

Now, namaste. This is the symbol of someone doing a prayer, right? When you have deep reverence for something, you really communicate with a higher source than yourself, right? People do this all around the world, but you don't have to be religious to do it. You don't even have to be spiritual to do it. You can just be a human being and you're already a spiritual being anyway.

But this practice of just bringing your palms together, closing your eyes is the second law of alchemy. When you close your eyes, you are now able to see clearly. That's the great paradox. You get a better picture when you close your eyes. You get a bigger picture when you close your eyes. A lot of people have their eyes wide open right now, but they're still blind. So how I really love to get clarity about a situation or even myself is to do this. I spend about 30 minutes, actually an hour, just closing my eyes at some point in the day. And it's amazing. When you open your eyes, you're like a new being.

You start raising the frequency. So close your eyes to get clarity on where you need to be with your life, on what you need to do to get there. And you will also invite greater inner peace into your entire life. And this will heal you. Many people are distracted out there on TikTok, Instagram, Facebook, but it's time to look within.

And we can do this by closing our eyes every single day.

Not just when you're going to sleep, but actually setting a conscious intention when you're doing it.

3.   Bring the peace

When there is no peace at the party, you bring the peace. I like that, right? So it's bringing peace to wherever you go. It's learning how to bring peace to the chaos. Right now, all around the world, a lot of people are going through it. Hard times. A lot of people are finding the world very troublesome, chaotic, frustrating.

It's really messing with their minds. We've got to learn how to become this peace we want in the world, because there is no world out there. You see, this whole thing could end today if people realized they are the world. And as we change, we also change everything around us.

4.   Become a transformer.

Transform the energy. Transmute the energy. You see, negative, positive. It's just energy. Negative is also needed. Positive is also needed. If you look at a battery, it's got negative, it's got positive. You need that to create electricity. So you don't throw away the negative. We don't want to do that.

We want to learn how to transform it, to power us up, to take us to where we need to go. So don't throw the baby out with the bath water. Remind yourself we can transform this energy, all of this so-called negative energy around us. We can use this to transform the lead into gold. This is what the alchemist does. So all of the fear that's being thrown around, the doom and gloom, the lockdowns, all of these things happening, even in Australia, Germany, all of these restrictions.

When you can feel all of this sadness in the world, the despair, that's still energy. We have to learn how to transform that energy into an energy that uplifts us. What do I do to do it? Raising the frequency. I can literally make a video about a very depressing subject, but I can turn it into something beautiful. People are like, Ralph, gosh, I even forgot you were talking about something so horrible because your energy is so amazing. I'm an alchemist. I transform the energy.

5.   Spend more time in nature

You've seen me day in, day out in the heart of nature. Breathing in that good-ass prana, baby, in beautiful environments where the feng shui is beautiful.

You see, our environment shapes who we are. We don't actually shape our environment as much as our environment shapes who we are. If you are living in a concrete jungle, come outside, go into nature.

If you are surrounded by clothes on the floor, broken heaters, books everywhere, rearrange your room, get a better feng shui. And this is the best thing you can do for yourself in this crazy world. Surround yourself with beautiful energy in terms of places you visit, people you meet, and the air you breathe. You better be breathing in that good-ass prana, baby.

6.   Do not become like the same energy you are fighting against.

I told you, when you fight something outside of yourself, you become weaker. But when you say, actually, the greatest war is the war within. You see, everything that's happened on the planet has happened for a reason. You've got to find out what that reason is.

I'll give you a reason why. We neglected the inner and we focused on the outer. Many people are at war with themselves. And when you are at war with yourself, it will spill over into a war with other people. And that's exactly what's happened. But if you make peace with yourself and you end the battle within, there can be no war out there. And this is the best thing you can do for yourself in this crazy world. You must remind yourself, you are the world. We are the world.

We are the children. Wasn't that a great song? All of those celebrities singing those songs. And we are the real celebrities, by the way. So you don't have to fight the system. You don't have to fight someone you don't agree with. All you have to do is vibrate higher. And as you vibrate higher, you are now in the love frequency. All you've got to do is just spread love their way.

You see, fear and love are the only two emotions in existence. Where there is love, there cannot be fear. Where there is fear, there cannot be love. So if you choose to embody that love frequency, fear can no longer surround you. How empowering is that?

7.   Smile

Make it authentic. Make it genuine. I'm genuinely smiling at the end of every video I make. Life is beautiful. I chose to smile instead of frown. I chose to smile.

Choose to smile today because when you smile, not only do you benefit yourself, but you also benefit people that see you. They feel good. And this is how to bring harmony into the world. A crazy world, right? Smile more.

.   8.   No longer give it away

You gave it away. Pardon? You gave it away. Huh? You gave away your power, your consent, your freedom. And the best thing you can do is no longer give it away. Don't give it away anymore. Don't give away your future. Don't give away your future to someone else.

.Like when I left the corporate world, the nine to five matrix, I said, okay, I'm no longer going to give away the future of my life to someone else I don't even know. I'm no longer going to live someone else's life. I'm going to live my life. I'm going to do whatever I want every single day, because it's my birthday.

Many people have given over their freedom, given over their consent, given over their power. So we are responsible. And the best thing we can do for ourselves in this world is to no longer give it away. Hold on to your freedom. That's all you've got. That's all you have, right? Hold on to it. Don't give it away. Otherwise you'll have none left.

9.   Love someone

In this crazy world, love someone, love someone, love someone, love a cat down the road, love a dog down the road, and also love a beautiful human being, because love is the only thing, the only force that can save humanity right now.

Many people argue with each other. They argue, they fuss, and they fight, not realizing we are on the same team. United we stand, divided we fall. And this is why right now, more than ever, we need a community, a common unity. We need to.put aside our small, petty differences and move out of the ego. And we need to align with each other in the heart space.

This is the best thing you can do for yourself in this crazy world. Love something, love someone, and stop arguing with people who are on your same team. You see, in the end days, they always talk about how people who should be united are still arguing amongst each other. And this is how the inorganic ones can take over the planet. But the story doesn't end there, because eventually people start to realize we are all we have, and we are all we have. Love someone today.

10.   Take care of your body.

Prevention is better than a cure. 7-Day Vegan Challenge! Eat foods, fresh leafy greens, vegetables that boost your immune system. This is not the time to get sick. You want to make sure you are investing in your health, going to the local farmer's market. And this is the best thing you can do for yourself in this crazy world. Don't allow your health to go by the wayside. Take care of it. Invest in it.

Chapter Twenty Eight

Being Confident

A lot of people write to me and they tell me that, Ralph, I love your confidence, you are so full of confidence. It's like you're afraid of nothing and I want to be like that, Ralph. I really want to find my confidence, my true confidence. Not this fake ass confidence, but true confidence.

I'm about to share with you big secrets about confidence a lot of people aren't going to tell you. Because there is confidence, then there is fake confidence, then there is arrogance... and you have to know the difference. You see, we're often told that being confident means you're the loudest one in the room or you're the loudest one in nature. But really, being confident is all about composure.

How many times deep divers have you been in the presence of someone who is just very loud? And you're like, okay. But then you come to know them and actually they're looking a little bit shaky behind the scenes. They're not actually confident.They're just faking confidence. And that's why you have to be careful that you don't fall into the fake confidence movement. And then there are people who are very arrogant and they're not confident either. They're just arrogant.

Confidence is something totally different. Confidence is not about being the loudest one in the room. It is about being the most composed. Many times we see people and a lot of people say, Ralph, gosh, you're so calm, right? And that's what I equate to confidence. That's what I equate with confidence. Being calm, composed. Roger Federer in his prime playing tennis. So calm, so composed. That's confidence. Usain Bolt running a hundred meters. So calm, so composed. Like it's a walk in the park. That's confidence.

A bird sitting on a branch is not afraid of the branch breaking because her trust is not in the branch. Her trust is in her own wings. That's confidence. The cat down the road falling from a nine foot story building, landing on his ass. That's confidence because the cat has nine lives. It ain't worried.

We sometimes think being confident is about your materialistic things, your material possessions, your car, your house. While they can add to your confidence, they can't truly make you confident. The reason why is because confidence, true confidence comes from within.

When you actually break down the word confidence, confident, confident, right? Its etymology goes back to the Latin confidere, which means to trust. So in essence, if you really want to learn the first steps to be confident, like Ralph's smart in the heart of nature, breathing in that good ass prana, you have to trust yourself because that's what confidence actually means. It means trusting yourself 100%.

Now we can pretend we trust ourselves, but you see, there's a difference between really trusting yourself and actually faking it. So we have to embark on this journey, to trust ourselves. How are we going to do this? So we have to prepare. We have to be ready. We have to train. Look, if you are a pro athlete and you have a football match, Ronaldo is confident because he is training every single day, even when he's not playing football. So to be confident, you must train. You must go into the gym of confidence because confidence is a muscle. You've got to train it.

Ralph smart is confident. I trust myself because I'm training every single day. I'm in the heart of nature, inspiring millions of people. I'm consistent. If I was saying, you know what? I'm never going to make videos again. Once a year when I make a video, I'm going to be looking a little bit shaky. But because I'm doing it every single day, I'm confident in what I'm doing. So confidence is linked to your ability to trust yourself, to be consistent, to really be enamored with what you're doing every single day. So you're not worried. So you don't have a mind full of doubts.

You see, when we talk of confidence, a lot of people think they can be confident without action. No, nothing could be further from the truth. If you want to be as confident as Ralph smart and the cat down the road, you're going to have to act. You're going to have to act until you make so many mistakes. You figure out the ways how to not do something. That's the beauty of making mistakes. They actually make you more confident. The more mistakes you make, the more failures you have, the more confident you become.

Because every failure, every mistake is showing you a way of how not to do something. Therefore, that leads you to the correct way of doing something. If you want to be confident, don't be afraid of your mistakes because they are stepping stones that will help you become your greatest version. If at first you don't succeed, try again.

Just say it. We are attracted to people who just say it. They're straightforward. They don't sugarcoat it. They speak their heart and mind. Even if their voice shakes, they are confident. You know why? Because they just say it. If you want to be confident, you have to just say it. Ralph smart just says it. I don't beat around the bush. I just say it. I say what I mean and I mean what I say.

This is how to cultivate confidence. It is about being truthful to yourself, being authentic, and not being afraid of the truth that you stand on. There are so many people out there who are shy, who hide their truth, who hide behind closed doors, and they have a low self-esteem, a low confidence level because they're afraid to speak their truth. If you really want to cultivate confidence, it's going to be scary. You're going to feel very uncomfortable, but that's good because growth happens in discomfort.

Growth happens and confidence is formed in discomfort. Leaving your comfort zone, speaking your truth, just say it. Ladies, fellas, if you feel a certain way about someone, just say it. If you feel a certain way about your job, express yourself. If someone has treated you poorly, let them know. This is how you build confidence.

Just do it. Don't think too much. Just do it. If you want to start that business, just do it. If you want to start a YouTube channel, just do it. You want to become a scientist? Just do it. You want to become a rocket scientist? Just do it. You want to become a doctor? Just do it. You want to help people around the world set up a non-profit charity? Just do it. And you will get confident because the more you do it, the more your confidence grows. Let me tell you this about confidence.

What actually helped me to become really confident was realizing how will I be remembered? We remember people who stand out. And this is how to be confident. Stand out. And standing out only means you are honoring your uniqueness. Nobody is you and that is your power. Once you place value on your uniqueness, you will become confident. So, I embraced my uniqueness.

I don't want to be anyone else. I became my own Picasso. And that's what you have to do to become confident. Become a unique Picasso. And I guarantee you, you will become confident. So, we've got to remind ourselves, confidence is not about being like someone else. Confidence is about honoring who you are.

Remind yourself, confidence comes from getting in shape, having a better diet, eating to live, looking your best. Why do people feel confident when they dress nice? People say, Ralph, you're dressing so smart. I'm like, wait a second. This is nothing new. We've been dressing like this for like 10 years because that's my last name. Smart. Ralph Smart. But it helps you become confident when you're feeling good about the way you look. The way you dress, the food you're eating.

Once you feel good, it helps, because once again, confidence is a feeling. It's an internal feeling cultivated from within. It's got nothing to do with outside. It's got everything to do with the feelings you're generating. The feelings you're generating about yourself. Confidence.

If you really want to become confident, you must accept yourself. You must, under all circumstances, accept yourself for who you are. Love yourself for who you are and respect yourself for who you are and realize it's okay to be the work in progress and the masterpiece at the same time.

Many times we think that confident people have it all figured out. No. Even me, I'm confident, but sometimes I'm still like, okay, which way am I going? Cat down the road, help me. But I know that I'm moving in the right direction because my heart is in the right place. I know that along the way, I'm going to figure it out, right? So being confident is not about having it all figured out. It's about realizing one step at a time. It's okay to be the work in progress and the masterpiece at the same time.

Now, talking about confidence, it's about composure. Like I said, you've got to be calm, composed and realize everything is under control. We link confidence to a demeanor, a calm demeanor, someone who has it all under control. And you can only have things under control once you know what you're doing, once you're practicing daily, day in, day out on your craft and talents and your skills, because you have to master the arts, master the crafts to become confident in what you do.

If someone has been doing something their whole life, of course, they're going to be confident about what they're doing. If someone is just starting out, they're going to be looking a little bit shaky. So confidence is a timeline. The longer you do something that you love with passion and heart, the more confident that you become.

.The famous Bruce Lee said, someone asked him, are you good at martial arts, Bruce? Bruce Lee said, if I tell you that I'm good, you will say I'm boasting. If I tell you I am no good, then you know I'm lying.

Are you good at inspiring millions of people? If I tell you that I'm good, then you will say I'm boasting. If I tell you that I'm no good, then you know I'm lying. Humble confidence is a term that I coined, and it relates to realizing confidence comes from a reserved demeanor, a calm demeanor.

A lot of very confident people are very unassuming because they are so full of talent and creativity and all of these things, but you would never know. They're not the loudest ones. Once again in the room, they have a certain humility, and that's what I have.

A lot of people say, Ralph, you have a certain humility because I'm in circles and I don't even tell them what I do. I just keep it moving, right? Because it's not really important. I know what I do, and when you can learn to adopt humble confidence, you will become an ambassador of true confidence. You will develop this true confidence.

So how do we generate this true confidence? It starts with facing your fears. What if I told you your greatest fear is a lie? You know why? Because fear stands for false evidence appearing real. You've got a choice to focus on the false evidence appearing real or face everything and rise. The moment you start to face everything and rise and realize that actually, there's actually nothing to be afraid of. Fear is your worst enemy, and once you can face fear and overcome it, you start becoming confident.

Okay, so it's linked to that. I want to remind you, confidence doesn't come overnight. You can read as many books as you want. It's a process, and you must remind yourself if you really want to become confident, don't be too hard on yourself to be confident in 24 hours. Realize confidence comes from within, and it's developed when you've been doing something for a long time, and you trust yourself when you do it.

Chapter Twenty Nine

Stop Being Nice, How To Gain Respect

I would rather hear a bitter truth than a sweet lie. What would you take, a bitter truth or a sweet lie? I would rather you tell me a bitter truth than a sweet lie because I'm tired of people smiling at me when they're lying to me through their teeth. It happens on the news.

Stop being nice. I see it time after time how so many people feel they have to be nice to everyone they meet. But in that process, they deny the world of who they really are. They suppress their feelings. They go home knowing that they weren't being authentic. I don't care about being nice. My only concern is about being authentic.

Someone contacted me. They're like, Ralph, I love your videos, but sometimes you scare me when you talk about everything that's happening in the world. I tell them, I didn't create this. I'm just here to give you a message. I'm not here to put a smile on your face because life is rough. The world is a horrible place at times. It's also a beautiful place. But I'm not here to tell you what you want to hear. I'm here to tell you what you need to hear. Right now, there's a great awakening happening. And it's only happening because people are coming out, speaking their heart and mind.

Enough of sugarcoating it. Enough of filtering. Enough of pretending. Right now, we all owe it to ourselves to be real and authentic. Are you ready to do that, and stop being nice? Because I guarantee you, you will gain more respect.

The amount of people who tell me, Ralph, you know what, your videos have changed my life because you just tell it like it is. You don't give us that fluffy stuff. You're just straight to the point, real organic. And that's why I resonate with your messages, Ralph. You see, if I had focused all of my energy on just pleasing everyone, the truth would not come out.

My culinary teacher told me back in high school, Ralph, the word nice means stupid. Pardon? Yes, the word nice means stupid in old English. You don't want to be nice, Ralph. Ever since, I've been terrified of being nice. I remind myself that I didn't come here to be nice. You didn't come here to be nice. You came here to be authentic. And authenticity includes positive, but also negative. And we owe it to ourselves to show the world who we really are.

It suddenly dawned on me that the reason why a lot of people have such a hard time being themselves is because they don't want to offend people. Not me. I don't care how you feel. But I love you anyway. I'm not concerned with how you feel, because I do not control how you feel. Stop being nice.

You see, I've got my Soul Tribe, family, and they tell me the truth. They tell me like, Ralph, your lips were crusty today. Oh my gosh, really? Yeah, you should have put some lip balm on your lips. Oh my gosh. Thank you. You hurt me, but you told me the truth. I would rather a bitter truth than a sweet lie. Because sometimes we meet people who tell us lies just to please us. They tell us what we want to hear, but it's not the truth. And we need people who can tell us the truth according to them.

Every single day, we want to remind ourselves we have to allow our light to shine. And it can only shine when we choose to be unapologetically, notoriously ourselves. I don't care how you feel about what I'm telling you, about the global pandemic, about leaving your comfort zone and coming outside to do a little Samba baby, to live your best life, to stop making excuses for why you can't live your dream life. I'm going to be hard on you, because that's what I'm supposed to do.

I'm not supposed to tell you what you want to hear, because I remind myself of all the people who helped me grow, who helped me grow, growing up, they told me the blunt truth. And that's what actually served as a catalyst for me to become my greatest version. The bitter truth, not the sweet lie, because sometimes when people are nice to you, they're actually hiding the truth. They're actually keeping you in an arrested state of development. But when people are real to you, when people tell you the truth, they can actually help you evolve.

Now, stop being nice. Here's how to gain respect. Instead of being nice, be truthful in anything you do, with anyone you are with, be truthful. Say, actually, I'm not going to tell you what you want to hear. I'm going to tell you the truth. We're living in a world where the truth has been hidden. And we have to actually say, wait a minute, I'm only interested in the truth. I don't care about nice. Like, if you are dating someone or in a relationship with someone, you want the truth. You were snoring last night. Not that, oh, you were singing beautiful lullabies. That's a lie. No, you were snoring. You were farting. Oh, my gosh.

The truth will help you change. Lies will keep you in the same position. 7 Day Vegan Challenge. I remember watching documentaries about what was really going on with farms, animal farming. The horrid truth about what happens in these cages, what happens to these chicks. They just go through the grinder one by one, get sliced up. I'm like, oh, my gosh. But that truth said, you know what? I want to go plant-based. I want to start helping my friends. I want to wake up every single day with a whole bunch of grapes in my mouth. You see, sometimes when we are faced with a truth, we can now get a new perspective. When we are just shown things that make us feel comfortable all the time, we never level up.

Stop being nice. Here's how to gain respect. Be fearless.

You see, sometimes I'm like, gosh, should I really say this? Should I really express how I really feel? I don't want to offend people. I'm a Pisces. I like to please people. But I realize that we've got to impress ourselves. We've got to please ourselves. We didn't come here to kiss ass. Ain't nobody got time for that. Not even the cat down the road. I'm not here to be a circus entertainer and make you smile and make you clap. I'm here to show you the truth according to me. I don't care about how you feel about it, because I can't control that. I'm here to stay true to me. So we have to be fearless. This is how to stop being nice and how to gain respect. Be fearless.

You see, I've got people who contact me, deep divers, and they're like, Ralph, your videos woke me up to the truth. It was a rude awakening, but it acted as the catalyst for me to change my life for the better. You made me see myself, Ralph. You made me see things I weren't doing that now I am doing. You gave me the biggest wake up call ever, and I'm so thankful. It was hard. It was painful. But thank you for not being nice to me, Ralph. I needed that kick up the backside.

You see, I would rather someone disagree with me if that's how they really feel, than go along with me if that's not how they feel. I don't want a yes man, a yes woman. I don't want someone just to nod their head. I want someone to have their own unique way of seeing the world. To stop being nice, to gain respect, you must learn how to stand for something. I've been telling you, being free is our birthright. I've been telling you, let love guide you, not fear. I've been telling you to wake up from the matrix and reclaim your power. I've been telling you, they are turning the world into a 1984 Orwellian state, and it's time to take back your power. Oh, you're scaring me, Ralph. I don't care. I'm not here to sing kumbaya to you every single day. You're living in a world of polarity.

To stop being nice, to gain respect, to make people respect you, you must learn how to stand for something. If you don't stand for something, you will fall for everything. You must have a backbone. You must have a value system. You must have a value system. You must not externalize your power. You must internalize your power and say, hey, I'm going to be me. Take it or leave it. This is how you love yourself. This is how you accept yourself.

Come from a unique perspective and keep the same energy and stand in your truth. Own your truth. Stop being ashamed of your truth. Stop hiding the truth of who you really are. Let the whole world see it. Let the whole world see it. And when you stop being nice and focus more on authenticity, you will gain more respect. People don't have to like you to respect you.

People say, Gosh, she's so confident. Gosh, he's so confident. I wish I could say that, but I'm afraid because I'm just being nice. You see, nice keeps you scared and in fear and afraid. Being authentic makes you free.

What is more important than being nice is being real and staying true to yourself. You aren't here to please people. You cannot please everyone because not everyone loves mangoes. I know it's a strange thought, right? I love mangoes! But I am not here to get on your good side. I am here to express my unique, authentic truth. When you make that your aim every single day, you will gain more respect and you will influence more people than you can imagine. Stand in your truth. Stand alone. Because now you will inspire other people to stand in their truth and they will stand with you.

Chapter Thirty

Why People Try To Bring You Down

There are only three things guaranteed in life: the cat down the road going missing, Ralph smart not having breakfast, and people trying to bring you down. Key word, trying, because they're not going to succeed.

You can't bring down the sun. Not going to happen. But they try. Yes, they try, don't they? We all know someone who tries to make our life hard, difficult. And if that's happening to you, I want to remind you, it's okay. In fact, it's needed. Don't be alarmed. Don't stress about it. Don't worry about it. I want to remind you, just remember, many people are drawn to light. They are drawn to success. They are drawn to people who are doing things.

People don't care about people who aren't doing anything. So if you have someone trying to bring you down, it means they're already beneath you. But it means they also secretly admire you. Because you are awesome. Yes, you are.

Now, nobody can bring me down without my permission. Always remember that. Nobody can bring you down without your permission. Now, someone asked me, Ralph, why are people trying to bring me down? And what can I do about it? And the other day, I was literally making a video. And someone I know I haven't seen for a long time, they're like, Ralph, thank you so much for encouraging me to start my YouTube journey. But someone left a comment on my video and it really upset me. Really upset me. They started to laugh at the way I was talking because I stammer sometimes. And I told them, don't worry about it. This is normal. In fact, it's going to keep happening.

They're like, oh no. I said, don't worry about it. Don't worry. Because when people are trying to bring you down, it's only going to make you stronger. And they're like, really? I said, yeah, don't worry about it. I've been making videos for like a little while now. People have tried to bring me down. Then they realize you can't bring down the sun.

Except at sunset, Ralph. But you still can't bring down the sun!

Take that reassurance I'm sending you. Stop allowing people who do so little for you to take such a large space in your mind rent-free. Why are you allowing people to steal your inner peace, your happiness? We know that life is filled with different characters, different kinds of people. Some people love us. Some people support us. And some people are envious of us, jealous of us. They try and bring us down.

And I want to remind you, when you are faced with someone who's trying to bring you down, don't think that it's a bad thing. In fact, it's a great thing. Why? Because this person is showing you something. They're showing you who you don't want to be. Thank them. They're showing you who you don't want to be. You don't want to be the kind of person who's trying to bring people down. I don't have time for that. Ain't nobody got time for that. Why? Because I'm too busy lifting people up, raising the frequency.

That's my only focus. And many people who are faced with people at work, at home, when you're out and about, who are trying to bring you down, remind yourself that it is because you are holding up a mirror to them. And this mirror could be of your success, your happiness, your relationship, something they don't have. And this is the reason why people try and bring you down, because in their mind, they don't have what you have. So they need to bring you down to their level.

But you've got to be like that bird up there. Hey, it's flying so hard and so high. I can't bring it down. You've got to fly high in life, becoming your greatest version, living your best life. Keep flying higher. Be out of their reach, out of their grasp. Don't pay them attention. Don't focus on them because whatever you focus on grows. Focus on the people who love you, the day ones who've been there for you. Focus on where you're going.

But let's be honest, we're human. Sometimes we're going to be affected by what people think of us, what they say to us. It's going to bring us down. Why do people try and bring you down? You have to understand this first before you can know what to do about it. The reason why is because many people are hurting inside. When they see you, they see a missed opportunity. They see what their life could have become, and you are going places. You're doing something with your life. And for a lot of people who don't support that, it's hard for them to take. It's a hard pill to swallow.

When you've changed your whole life around, you both grew up together, but now you're on a better path, manifesting, looking fantastic. If they see you, they are seeing a missed opportunity. And this is why people try and bring you down to their level, because misery loves company. What you've got to do about it is realize that not everyone had a hug today. Hurt people hurt people. And you are dealing with many people who are hurt, who wake up in a bad mood because they chose to be in one. They don't see that there's enough to go around.

. You see why people try and bring you down? It's because they believe in a limiting belief system which goes like this. There is not enough to go around. Nothing could be further from the truth. Because abundance is everywhere and everyone can live their best life. That's why when I see people, I've mentored students, manifesting, inspiring millions of people as well. I'm excited. I'm happy. Because it doesn't take away from me.

I know they can never be me. No, they can't be infinite waters. I'm comfortable in my own skin. That's why I've never made a video trying to bring anyone down. People have tried to bring me down. Key word, tried. They didn't succeed. Because you can't bring down the sun. What's the easiest way to get on, deep divers? What's the easiest way to get on? It is to hold the tail of a big fish and ride the wave. And that's what a lot of people do. They say, hey, the only way I can make it in life is to try and bring someone down who's going places. Maybe I can get in the spotlight that way.

But if you are sure of yourself, you don't bring anyone down. When you are a success, you don't bring people down because you're too busy going to the next level. Anyone who's trying to bring you down is already beneath you. You scared them. Yeah, they're afraid of your greatness. Why? Because they can see what you're becoming.

When I was first even making videos, sharing, making films, sharing with the world, I had many people trying to bring me down because they knew, hey, if that guy continues, one day he's going to be a superstar. That's what happened. And it always happens at the beginning of your journey.

When you are on the road to doing big things, people are going to try and bring you down because they're afraid of your greatness. They can see what you are going to become if you have enough time. They want to throw you off course, off track. They want to distract you from where you need to go. It's all a trap. You've got to be smart and realize nobody can try and bring you down without your permission, attention and focus and consent. Realize this as well.

We are dealing with people in life. We think it's personal. If someone is trying to bring us down, we think it's about us. But it's got nothing to do with us. It's got everything to do with what they want to do. And you don't control that. So you aren't responsible for that. You're not responsible for that. And it's not your issue if someone is trying to bring you down. That's their issue. Let them deal with it. Don't deal with it as well. You didn't wake up trying to bring someone down. They did. Let them deal with it. Don't pay them no mind, no attention. They don't deserve it.

Focus on the people who do deserve it. Because you will see that there are people who are supporting you who deserve your attention. Not those who are trying to bring you down. Remind yourself. It's a sign. Why are people trying to bring you down? It's a sign that you're going to the next level. Soon they'll be asking, are you hiring? Can I work for you? Happened to me along my journey. There was someone who was trying to bring me down. Some years passed. They were like, Ralph, I love your videos. Are you hiring? I want to work for you. I'm a changed man. I said, ain't nobody got time for that. No. You had your chance. You blew it.

Why do people try and bring you down? What can you do about it as well? Realize this. It comes with the territory. When you are going places, when you are changing your life for the better, every new level you have new adversaries, new people trying to bring you down. But that's okay. Welcome it. Because you need these people. Why? Because this is part of the training to show how strong you are. Many people bring us down in life because their own life is a mess. The only thing they can do with their time is take a look at your life because it's not a mess. It's everything they wish their life was, but it's not.

They wish they were you. They wish they had your life. They had your smile. They had your relationship. They had your swag. They had your... They don't have it. All they can do is say, hey, come down to my level. Ain't nobody got time for that. Learn from the birds in the sky. Fly high. And remind yourself. It's okay. And it's not going to change.

You will always have people who support you and you will always have people who see you as a missed opportunity. Because when they look at you, they see a missed opportunity. They see what their life could have been, should have been, but wasn't. It's a compliment. But focus on the people who are lifting you up, who are telling you how to eat to live. 7-Day Vegan Challenge. Who are making you feel like the sunlight.

Chapter Thirty One

Alkaline Drinks To Flush Out Toxins And Mucus

I still haven't had breakfast yet, but I'm cool because I've been playing this fun drinking game all day. What you've got to do is take a shot of water, that's right, every two hours so you can stay healthy, hydrated, and glowing. Are you ready? Let's take the shot right now. That's good.

It's the seven-day vegan challenge, it's that time of the week where we talk about everything: food, health, because health is wealth, and nutrition. I'm going to talk about seven alkaline drinks that will flush mucus and clear toxins out of your body. Forget about eating to live, it's time to start drinking to live. Seven alkaline drinks that's helped me to flush mucus and toxins out of my body, really cleanse the blood, let's go.

First and foremost, let me give a huge shout out to Dr Sebi, my food mentor, who really helped me learn about the importance of eating to live.

Now, what color is your pee? If it's bright yellow, uh-oh, your urine should be crystal clear. It should be so clear the cat down the road can see through it. Okay, that shows you've got a very good pH level. Zero on the pH scale is highly acidic, seven is our body, 14 is highly alkaline. We need to be drinking more alkaline drinks to really stay at a good pH level internally, and this promotes good wellness and health inside of our body.

1.	Water

So the first alkaline drink that will flush mucus and clear toxins out of your body is water.

Got water? Yes, Ralph, so do I. Wait a minute, so do seven billion people on this planet. Over 70% of it in our bodies, that's pretty cool. But not all water is good water. Some water, you've got to be like, ain't nobody got time for that. Tap water, ain't nobody got time for that. Full of fluoride, ain't nobody got time for that. So what water do I drink? That's alkaline, fresh mountain spring water, a high pH. This keeps the body stay alkaline, it helps to flush out mucus from the body, it cleanses the blood, it's got all the vitamins and minerals you need. Now, I'm drinking about one gallon of water every single day.

That's also what Dr Sebi recommended to me. And ever since, I feel healthier, clear skin, more confidence, more energy. Now, the reason why mountain spring water is so powerful is because boiling water, hot boiling water, the temperature is 212 degrees Fahrenheit, 100 degrees Celsius. Spring water is coming out of the ground at 200 degrees Fahrenheit, 200 degrees Fahrenheit. So it's purified, it's clean, it's healthy. And this is why it's so good for us.

Also, I'm drinking water pH 9 and pH 10. You see, the problem with tap water is that it's highly acidic, mainly because of the water passing through the pipes, picking up bacteria along the way. And it gets to your glass and you're like, oh, what is this? Just throw it away because it's no good. So fresh mountain spring water is a good way to go. And alkaline water pH 9 and 10 is fantastic. Okay.

2.	Kale and watercress smoothie or juice

What's the second alkaline drink that will flush mucus and clear toxins from your body? Kale and watercress. My two favorite words right now. Okay. A kale and watercress green juice smoothie. Okay. Kale packed full of vitamin K, vitamin C, vitamin A. Watercress packed full of magnesium. Good for your central nervous system. Okay.

But not only that, they help to get rid of mucus out of the body. They are blood cleansers. Now, Dr Sebi often would tell me, Ralph, the biggest cause of disease, dis-ease in the body is mucus. The more deep divers you can start eating and drinking foods that can help you clear the mucus out of your body, the more you will heal yourself. And kale and watercress are powerful together. Like they've got to be together. Okay. And all of a sudden, you're alkaline. You feel well. Put some lemon juice inside there and some lime inside there as well.

Okay. But they're acid, Ralph. No. Lemons and limes actually have a large acid high in vitamin C too. Once they come into contact with the body, they actually become alkaline. Also you can put lemons in water. And that's also a fantastic choice.

.   3.   Green tea

Green tea is packed full of all the vitamins and minerals you need. But also it's alkaline. So once again, if you are eating a heavy acid diet, you need some green tea right now. Packed full of antioxidants. Okay. Green tea is 99.5% water. So you are definitely going to be hydrated. It's detox time. It's detox time anytime you have a green tea. Okay. It's super powerful.

So if you are somebody who has a lot of inflammation, green tea is anti-inflammatory, anti-virus, anti-fungal. It's got everything you need to be in optimum health. And it smells fantastic.

4.   Ginger.

Got ginger? Yes. I used to take ginger beer, Ralph. So did I all the time. But ginger, root ginger is so powerful. The benefits of ginger is that ginger has vitamin C. It's got all the antioxidants you need. It's also anti-cancer.

Did you know that you can use ginger as a natural aspirin? Because it thins the blood. It's anti-inflammatory. Once again, it helps you to remove that mucus. Do you sometimes do that when you've got a cough or a cold? When you take some ginger and it' like, it just came out of me, Ralph. Exactly. It gets rid of all of that junk, all of that mucus inside of your chest. And now you're good to go. It's also a blood cleanser, okay? So ginger tea is fantastic.

5.   Burdock root.

Burdock tea is fantastic, okay? Burdock is packed full of antioxidants. One of Dr Sebi's favorites too. Packed full of all the vitamins and minerals you need, but it's a blood cleanser. It helps to remove toxins out of the blood. It helps to remove toxins out of the blood, okay? It helps to remove mucus out of the blood. Anti-viral, anti-fungal, anti-inflammatory.

.   Start drinking burdock tea and tell me how you feel afterwards. I feel so alive, Ralph. I feel so good to be alive, Ralph. It feels so good to be alive, Ralph. And it's alkaline, okay?

6. Beets.

Got beets? I'm not Dr Dre, but I've still got beets, baby. Beetroot juice, okay? Packed full of vitamin C, vitamin A, packed full of antioxidants, okay? Beetroot juice is so good, the cat down the road drinks it all the time, okay? It will help to cleanse your blood. It's so red, Ralph.

Exactly. That means it's good for your blood, okay? It will help to get rid of all of that mucus, okay? And it's not that expensive. For what it can do for you, full of anthocyanins, which actually help to prevent cancer, it's a good go-to. So it's alkaline as well. It's a great choice of drink instead of soda.

7. Coconut water.

Got coconut water? I do now, Ralph. So do I, okay? Coconut water. I thought that's acid, Ralph. No, it's not. Once it comes into contact with a body, once again, because of the allergic acid, it turns alkaline.

Coconut water is healthy, packed full of potassium, packed full of magnesium, okay? Potassium actually helps to lower your blood pressure. Magnesium is good for your nerves. But also, coconut water is packed full of lauric acid. Lauric acid actually helps to boost your immune system. Once again, fighting off dis-ease. It's a blood cleanser, helps to get rid of mucus. And once again, it's alkaline.

So there you have it, seven alkaline drinks to flush out mucus and toxins. After I drink some kale, I'm just like, peace. Because it's just so full of goodness.

Chapter Thirty Two

Alkaline Foods To Flush Out Toxins And Mucus

People always ask, Ralph, when are you ever going to have breakfast? Never. Simple answer.

Today is the day when we're going to talk about food, glorious food. Are you eating right now? Are you eating to live? Do you eat and say, woo, I feel so good? Or do you eat and feel like, oh my gosh, I need to go to the toilet right now? Here are seven alkaline foods that flush toxins and mucus from your body.

This is the seven-day vegan challenge. It's time to eat to live. A lot of people say, Ralph, please share with us your secrets. What do you eat every single day? Well, I'm about to share with you seven alkaline foods that have completely changed my entire life for the better.

Health is wealth. Now, many years ago, I came across Dr Sebi, who really mentored me, really helped me learn even more about food. I've been a vegan for over 14 years. I've been eating the plant-based diet. A lot of people say, Ralph, gosh, you look 15. Well, thank you, thank you, thank you, thank you.

You're far too kind, deep divers. Now, something that Dr Sebi told me was that disease, dis-ease, starts in the small intestine. There is only one cause, Ralph, of disease, dis-ease, and that is mucus. You see, if you get rid of the mucus, you get rid of the disease.

You see, if you have a lot of phlegm all up in your nose, we call that sinusitis. If you have a lot of mucus in the lungs, we call that bronchitis. If you have a lot of mucus in your joints, we call that arthritis. Yes, mucus.

Mucus is responsible for disease, dis-ease. Now, there are foods that you can take that will flush the mucus out of your body so you can be well again, so you can kiss the cat down the road.

Let me just say this first and foremost. Our body, we've got to keep it alkaline, at a pH of 7.3. Now, pH stands for the potential of hydrogen.

Zero, highly acidic, processed crap, processed hot dogs, right? Then you have 14, which is very alkaline. But deep divers, you also have PRAL, and that stands for potential renal acid load. So that's the actual pH level inside of the food.

So plus 18 would be like cottage cheese and minus 14 would be like spinach. Okay, we got that. Great. Now, let's look deeper into the seven alkaline foods that will flush toxins and mucus from your body.

1.   Oregano

That's right. Cultivated in the Mediterranean. Now, I love the herb oregano. I love the smell of oregano. Doesn't it smell so good? Deep divers, yes. Well, it's also good for you. It is a blood cleanser. It removes toxins from your blood. It has one of the highest antioxidant ratings in any food. Let's clap for oregano. Not only that, it has 42 times more antioxidants than apples.

It is a superfood, but it is great for removing all of that mucus from your body so you can be well again. You see, we need to be eating more alkaline foods because our body is slightly more alkaline. Okay, so oregano, highly alkaline, very good for you. Doctor's recommendation.

2.   Parsley

Now, parsley is a work of art. Once again, a fantastic herb full of iron, potassium, copper. The British Journal of Nutrition has shown in studies that parsley actually prevents free radicals. So parsley is anti-cancer. It is full of antioxidants. It also has the triple A, antibacterial, antiviral, anti-inflammatory. So it removes all of that mucus from your body. Highly alkaline as well.

.   3.   Limes

That's right. I love limes. Do you like lemons as well? Well, limes are even better. Now, I love lime tea. Limes are packed full of vitamin C. They are also packed full of antioxidants. They also help cleanse the blood from all the toxins that build up there. So if you want to get rid of mucus, take some limes.

.But I thought limes were acidic, Ralph. No, no. When they come into contact with the body, they actually become alkaline because of the potassium, phosphorus, manganese, zinc, copper. Yes, limes are alkaline once they are in the body. You need them in your life.

4.   Burdock roots

.

That's right. Now, Dr Sebi always used to tell me about burdock root, that it is fantastic. It's very, very alkaline. Okay. It is a diuretic. It also has a lot of minerals and vitamins you need. It removes the toxins from the blood, antioxidants, antibacterial, antifungal, anti-inflammatory.

Burdock root, you can take it in a tea. That's what I do. Fantastic. Once again, the herbs are for the healing of the nation. Grab yourself some burdock root, but more so it is highly alkaline. We have to keep our body alkaline to be in optimum health.

5.   Watercress

One of my favorites, right? Now, watercress is so alkaline, it's unbelievable. Okay. Watercress.

Did you know that watercress is the most nutrient-dense vegetable on planet earth. One of the most nutrient-dense vegetables on the planet. Did you know that it has more iron than spinach, more calcium than milk, more vitamin C than oranges? Why isn't anybody talking about watercress? Well, I am.

.

It is highly alkaline. It's a blood cleanser. It will remove toxins from your blood. And it is low calories. It is fantastic. Get yourself some watercress.

6.   Peaches

Life is like peaches and cream. Ok, we don't need cream right now.

We only need the peaches because they are packed full of vitamin C. Also potassium, which regulates the fluid levels in our body. Peaches, which are high in antioxidants, removes toxins from the blood, and it is a diuretic also. So peaches will help you remove all of that mucus from your body.

7.   Soursop

Okay. Guanabana, also another name for it. Packed full of vitamin C. Soursop is so nutritious. It's unbelievable. It removes toxins from the blood. Once again, that is key to really removing mucus out of the body. It's high in antioxidants, high in potassium, magnesium, manganese. Soursop is a miracle food. And if you want to keep your body alkaline, soursop is alkaline.

So there you have it, those are the seven alkaline foods that will remove toxins and mucus from your body.

Don't forget, PH 10 water is fantastic for keeping your body alkaline.

If you're not eating right, you're not thinking right. If you're thinking right, chances are you're eating right and stuffing a whole bunch of grapes in your mouth.

Chapter Thirty Three

10 Secrets Marijuana Smokers Won't Tell You

Ten secrets marijuana smokers won't tell you. But why, Ralph? I have no idea. They're too busy getting high.

Now, I don't smoke marijuana. But I did growing up. I tried it. And recently, I tried two weed cookies. Yeah, I didn't even know they were weed cookies. I'll talk about that later. Kind of funny what happened next. Dun, dun, dun.

So, I'm going to share with you, with my psychology background as a psychologist, but also as an infinite being, some beautiful things about marijuana, but also some things that might get you to look at marijuana in a totally different way.

So, let's take a look at the secrets marijuana smokers won't tell you.

1.   It's a cultivated plant

They won't tell you that, do you know, cannabis, the cannabis plant, is over 6,000 years old. It's been cultivated. Okay, it's one of the oldest crops cultivated by human beings. Now, that is fascinating to think that we've been growing it for 6,000 years. That's a long time.

So, people have been using it for a long time. In fact, over 5,000 years ago, you had the emperor Shen Nung, the emperor of China. He wrote in a book on marijuana about the benefits it had, the medicinal qualities of the plant, how it was used to cure PMS, menstrual cramps in women, also diarrhea, constipation, nausea, a whole list of benefits.

We can talk about ancient Egypt or Kemet, the Ebers papyrus, one of the greatest documents documenting all the herbs, how they can be used to help us become our greatest version. Yeah, that talked about marijuana too. So, even the ancient Egyptians were getting, like, super high. That's probably how they built the pyramids.

Now, it's been around for a long time. But, you see, marijuana is still illegal in many countries around the world.

And it was actually in 1937 that in the US, they had prohibition. But before then, before 1937 in the US, people were using marijuana as a pain reliever for medicinal purposes. Okay? So, marijuana has been used for thousands of years in the Indus Valley, Tibet, Brazil, Peru, I could go on and on and on, all over Africa.

People have used this powerful plant to heal themselves. And now, all of a sudden, it's illegal. I'm sorry. We're sorry about that. It's just illegal. We'll come to why it may be illegal later. In some countries, it is legal. For instance, Uruguay and a few other countries. But most of the world, yes, it is still a Schedule 1 drug. You'll get arrested for it.

Now, thank goodness in California, though, you can actually use it for medical reasons.

2.   They won't tell you about getting high.

Now, this is where my weed cookie experience comes in. You see, I was in Venice with a friend and someone gave her weed cookies and then I took them and I just forgot they were weed cookies. So, I ate both of them, just thinking they were cookies. Yeah, I know. I was hungry. I had the munchies and then I was in Whole Foods and then it kicked in.

I was like, what the hell is happening to me? Because I'd never, ever taken weed cookies. And I was like, in Whole Foods like, where the hell am I? I was asking people for directions. I was feeling really thirsty. Anybody who's taken weed cookies knows what I'm talking about. And then I was like, trying to drive home. I couldn't drive home and then I had to pull over.

I went to the hospital, got a big bill. It was a crazy night but then I woke up and then I said, can I get a hello there? I'm infinite, baby. But, marijuana smokers, there is a key ingredient in marijuana called THC. Okay, this is what gives people the high. Now, I got very high and I started to experience and see the world in a different way. Like, it was almost as if reality was dissolving and a lot of people who smoke marijuana, I know people who smoke marijuana like I eat strawberries. Like, big time. It gives you that natural high.

But you see, a lot of marijuana smokers I know, sometimes we're in a circle in Venice Beach, they will tell you that they don't just use marijuana, the THC element in it to get high, they use it to connect with their higher selves. Okay, so the THC is known for giving people that high, but also, it is a wonder ingredient for helping people even with cancer and all kinds of other ailments. We'll come to that later.

3.   Nobody has ever overdosed off marijuana.

Now, my weed cookie experience, I thought I was overdosing. I thought, somebody help me. Then I realized, no, that's the moment I was supposed to just chill out, Ralph. Do you know ancient shamans in Peru have been using marijuana for thousands of years to, once again, connect with their higher selves, but also, it takes them into different dimensions, other realities, and no one's ever overdosed.

Okay, in ancient Egypt, they also had the lotus flower. In the murky waters, the lotus grew, which also may be one of the reasons why they were so advanced. But, we often think that people are going to overdose big time on marijuana, but nobody has ever died from taking marijuana.

But if I say, tobacco, marijuana, which one do you think is more dangerous? Think about it. Uh-oh, you see, and a lot of people, millions of people, have died from tobacco. So, we are programmed to think that marijuana is very dangerous, but in actuality, nobody has ever, nobody, absolutely nobody, not even the cat down the road who gets high all the time, has ever died from marijuana.

Isn't that something? Okay, and do you know the American Medical Association was actually against prohibition in 1937? Because they actually saw this as a wonder drug, a wonder herb.

4.   Marijuana is a natural pain reliever, analgesic.

Okay? A natural algesic. And that means that it can be used to treat pain. Are you going through something right now that's very painful? Yeah, marijuana can be used to treat it. But also, people who have a lot of chronic pain, okay, use marijuana.

In California, scientists have even seen how it has relieved a lot of people with chronic pain. So, for a long time, marijuana was used instead of aspirin as a natural pain reliever. Okay, and people have died of aspirin related diseases, but nobody has ever died of marijuana. So, it's great for pain relief.

5.   Cancer.

Let's talk about cancer. Do you know in 1924, Dr Otto Warburg said he had the cure for cancer and he did, because he talked about how cancer was created from a lack of oxygen in the cells. Okay, the journal, the British Journal of Cancer found that marijuana actually slowed down tumor growth. It inhibited tumor growth.

So, therefore, marijuana is fantastic for cancer prevention. Right, lots of people are treating themselves through naturopathic medicine with cannabis and it's helping them heal from cancer. Isn't that something?

6.   It's safer than alcohol.

How drunk did you get last night? Look, they know that once again, nobody dies from marijuana. Now, let me give you the psychology of counseling people who take marijuana. There are some side effects, and there are some people who say they have paranoia.

Let's dive into it. Reduce dopamine levels, that's why some people say, you're a pothead, you're lazy, okay? But, the benefits definitely outweigh the negatives and I definitely feel each case is different. Maybe you can enlighten me on that. Because, once again, I don't smoke marijuana. I need you guys who are always smoking wherever you're smoking. I won't show your location out.

But, once again, some people do experience paranoia, forgetfulness, but the paradox is that marijuana has been found by scientists in California to actually treat Alzheimer's. But, marijuana is safer than alcohol. In 2012, 3.3 million people died of alcohol-related diseases. Okay? So, it's safe, but there are side effects. Safe side effects. That works.

7.   Hemp, the hemp plant, can be used for practically anything.

Do you know it was like the first kind of paper? The textiles industry? Hemp seeds. Seven-day vegan challenge, packed full of protein, a complete source of protein.
But, hemp is responsible for over 25,000 products out there. Anything you can think of, hemp made it. From building materials, yeah, it goes on and on and on and on. So, hemp is part of the cannabis family, and hemp is amazing. Okay? Like, amazing.

8.   It helps people with seizures.

Okay? Now, it is an anti-spasmodic herb. Right? It produces anti-spasmodic qualities. That's why people who have a lot of seizures, they take marijuana. It's a muscle relaxant. So, they're a lot calmer, and it actually helps them. Okay?

9.   A natural alternative to ritalin

I used to work with people with ADHD, ADD, and do you know what? They were given, we would administer to them, Ritalin. Okay? And, I could talk about Ritalin, and what it actually does, the side effects, which aren't too good at all, but you see, cannabis is actually a natural alternative to Ritalin, and it can actually be used to treat people with ADHD, ADD, and I just feel these are all labels anyway, but, it can be used as an alternative to Ritalin.

10.   They just feel amazing a lot of them when they smoke it.

They feel like their ego is dissolving. Now, in our society, we have created so many rigid laws based around separation. And, a lot of cannabis users won't tell you when they smoke it, when they use it as a, when they ingest it, any way they consume it, okay, it's almost as if their ego dissolves.

Now, my short experience on those two weed cookies, I was like, who the hell am I? Sometimes, you can probably see these memes of people who smoke a lot of marijuana, they just want to hug people, right, and that's probably why it's illegal, because it's so beneficial.

Now, as I see it, you've gotta do your own research, like, my weed cookie experience wasn't the best. So, I would never say, okay, just go and smoke marijuana, go and take a lot of weed cookies.

You've gotta know why you're doing it. And, for some people, it's gonna help. But, for me, I get on a natural high every single day.

At the same time, I definitely realize how beneficial cannabis is, the hemp plant, marijuana, because it's been used for thousands of years, and the science is there that it cures so many ailments. We can even talk about multiple sclerosis, okay, we can talk about glycoma, once again, the intraocular pressure, it reduces it. You want me to break down the science?

So, why might it be illegal? You see, the pharmaceutical industry is a big business, and can you imagine if everyone started hugging each other? And, if it was made legal, a lot of people might start seeing reality in a whole different way. Okay, so, you've always gotta do your own research and ask yourself, should I be taking this? Will it help me become my greatest version?

I say that God's pharmacy, the universe's pharmacy, whatever you wanna call it, the force's pharmacy, is in nature, but also in your body. A bonus one for you.

Do you know that our body produces natural cannabinoids? Once again, that ingredient found in marijuana, but also, it has its own endocannabinoid system. Isn't that fantastic? So, it's almost as if we have our own pharmacy in our body. That is incredible. So, once again, our body mimics nature.

Anything, any herb out there, our body can practically produce. It's all in us. So, what I always love to say is that through meditation, I'm getting on that natural high and it feels fantastic.

Chapter Thirty Four

How To Stop Feeding Your Fears

How to stop feeding the fears. Please stop feeding the fears. Every day I get a whole load of questions about fears, literally thousands from all around the world.

So I'm going to share with you some tips which have helped me along my journey in becoming my greatest version. To stop feeding the fears, can you imagine if you were driving around town and instead of seeing 40 or 50, no, you see this massive sign which says, please stop feeding the fears. Thank you.

Wouldn't the world be a much better place? Of course it would. Now, a couple of years ago, when I was faced with a great challenge, a skate trick, which was really fearful, I would play the soundtrack for the film Requiem for a Dream. You know the one.

It almost feels as if the world is coming to an end and it's a matter of life or death. And whenever I used to play that music, I would get so pumped up, I would get so charged that I would just do the trick because for me, it was all or nothing. I was going to die. I didn't care. I didn't care what was going to happen. Facing your greatest fear will be your greatest liberation.

What is fear? Fear is a self-created feeling. Based on the pseudo-realization, you don't have the capacity to overcome a perceived experience. In other words, fear is false evidence appearing real.

Now, here is where it gets really tricky. Your subconscious mind can't distinguish between what is real and what is not. So this imaginary thought you have in your mind of me stealing all of your vegan cookies, don't worry, I won't touch them, is now a reality within your body, which is the subconscious mind. You're feeling nervous. You're like, Ralph, please don't take my vegan cookies. I won't, don't worry. I will actually. I'm going to eat all of them.

The first tip is to air out your dirty laundry. A lot of us, we only show the world what we think the world wants to see. Many of us don't post a selfie when we're taking a dump on the toilet, do we? Right? That would be socially unacceptable. It would be a tragedy to say the least, right? But you want to post a selfie when you've got your makeup on, when you're smiling.

Hey, that's me. I would admit, I'm going to admit it right now. But I've realized that to stop feeding what you are most afraid of, you have to throw yourself, that's right, into, wait for it, the lion's den. Don't get eaten. So imagine you are a gladiator right now, okay? And you've got the crowd, everyone's screaming for you to, they hope you don't get eaten by a lion. And those lions which are coming towards you, which are your fears, are you going to run away from the lions or are you going to stand and face them?

Well, guess what? You don't have a choice. I'm sorry. Those lions in actuality are your unresolved issues. So once you address your unresolved issues, you stop feeding the fears.

I wrote down in my diary today, fear only exists when you believe in it. Let me say that again. Fear Only exists, capital O, when you believe in it, when you give it power, when you externalize your own power.

So when you face those lions, you now realize the secret that you are the lion. That's why you've heard of many stories, gladiators, sometimes the lions wouldn't do anything to them because the gladiators earn the lions respect. They were one of them. They were one of them. So that's a wonderful thing.

Now, when we talk of fear, so many of us, we are overthinking. The secret to stop overthinking is to let go of who you think you are. But what happens, wait for it, when you are wearing this facade, this mask, you've been wearing the mask for so long that now you don't even know who the hell you are. And guess what?

Neither do I. Don't worry about it. We're going to get a detective. We're going to find out who the hell you are. Okay?

When you realize assumptions make bad conclusions, you stop feeding the fears. Because once again, fear is memory. It is a belief system, a perception, which we confuse with the absolute truth of what is taking place. So when you assume, for instance, that flying is a dangerous experience, that a spider is dangerous.

Look, I used to be afraid of bees or wasps, both of them actually. And then recently, what happened? I released that fear. How did I do that? I said, look, if you're going to sting me, at least do it here. Do it on my hand. Okay? I surrendered. I stopped assuming that this was a negative experience.

To stop feeding our fears, we must let go of what we think is good and what we think is bad. And realize that our attitude shapes our experience. So our attitude shapes and governs what we are afraid of.

I love coming out into nature, breathing in that beautiful prana. So just surrounding myself in a very earthy natural environment has helped me to stop feeding the fears. But what happens when you are around certain friends or family who trigger certain fears you have? Happened to me along my journey. I said, I want to start talking about becoming your greatest version. People said, oh, what's that? Now they know what it's about. Oh yeah, because we are going worldwide, baby.

But there were people who encouraged me. They believed in me. So guess what? I stopped feeding the fears. Once you connect with those who remind you who you are, you stop feeding the fears. You see, many of us, we focus on problems. Oh, the world is coming to an end.

Look here. Look here, son. Look here, daughter. I don't fear. Why? Because fear creates more fear. I focus on solutions. I show you the problems, but I will always give you a solution out of your untidy room. The Hoover's downstairs, guys. Clean it up.

Many of us love drama. We love gossip. We love fear, scary movies. Not realizing this is affecting our subconscious mind and trickling into every aspect of our lives. I love meditating. Meditation is the subtle art of allowing thoughts to come through you without judgment. And that has helped me to stop feeding the fears.

Look, it's so quiet here. Silence. That is what meditation is. It is when you absorb yourself into the present moment 100%. Many of us, we feed our fears because we're thinking about the future, which I'm sorry, guys, doesn't exist, or the past. Now, I look back only to see how far I've come. That's the only time to look back. Right? But you see a lot of us who, those of us who feed our fears, we hold the past against ourselves. We say I was a very bad person.

Right? I don't deserve it. I am not worthy.

One of the most common fears we all have is the fear of not being good enough, which goes back to fear being memory, fear being a belief system. Show me the evidence for that claim. I'm your lawyer now. No, I'm a lawyer against you. Okay, listen, write down and say, show me the evidence. Grab a piece of paper, whatever you are afraid of, say to yourself, show me the evidence.

Many of us can't release fear because we are justifying our fears. We give ourselves the excuse for holding onto our fears. No excuses.

In a very simple way, the moment you become vulnerable and show the world who you really are, but you must show that to yourself first, you stop feeding the fears. You are not in this world to live up to other people's expectations of you. You are in this world to be who you are authentically. And trust me, once you do it, you get so much confidence that fear now becomes your support. Because when you are afraid, it means you are getting ready for the big jump.

When you are afraid, what does it mean? It means you are going to the next level. So the gladiator, which is you, which is I, who walks, the gladiator who walks closer towards the lions, when you walk in the direction of your fears, now your fears become smaller.

One more thing, fear exists within the body. The body is the subconscious mind. So to stop feeding the fears, start breathing deep from the base of your spine. Breathe in for four, hold for four, release for four. Okay. And see if that works. Also realize that when you are afraid in your mind, you are afraid in your body.

The great psychologist Fritz Perls is with a client. He asks her, are you anxious, madam? And she says, no, I'm fine. He laughs. He says, it doesn't look like it. You look very anxious to me. Because he observed that there was an incoherency between her words and actions. So to stop feeding your fears, become more coherent between your words and actions.

Develop a very powerful, high power pose, right? Once you develop a high power pose, you now reduce the cortisol levels, which is that stress hormone linked to fear. And then my friends, you stop feeding the fears. Most of us are afraid of making mistakes. Most of us are afraid of not being perfect. Many of us, we feed our fears because we are in the pursuit of excellence. Not realizing we are already a perfect masterpiece.

Be who you are. Accept yourself a hundred percent. Love yourself a hundred percent. Let love guide you, not fear.

Chapter Thirty Five

How To Stop Living In The Past

Do you wake up always ruminating, overthinking about your past? Is your past holding you back? Well, you've come to the right place because this chapter is all about how to stop living in the past and move your ass forward. Because we have to move forward.

Are you always living in your past? Do you wake up blaming yourself for how badly you screwed up in the past? For how you didn't get it right? The job that you never took. The relationship that you were unavailable for. The missed opportunities. The friendships that you let go. Are you mad at yourself? Trash talking yourself? Blaming yourself?

I'm gonna give you the secrets to how I stopped living in the past and how I was able to move forward with the help of the cat down the road.

Oh, I'm moving forward and life is a lot better because you see the past can be your liberation or it can be your prison. And after this chapter, it will no longer be your prison.

Look, there's a saying and I love it: "Yesterday is history. Tomorrow is a mystery. Today is a gift and that's why it's called the present."

Yes, indeed. Today is a gift and that's why it's called the present.

But let's face it, we're all human. And sometimes the past can beat us up, get the better of us. And we're stuck there.

Like, is anyone there? No, no one is there because you're in the past right now. And you're thinking about how badly you screwed up, how you messed up, the missed opportunities, how you failed miserably and you can't forgive yourself. So how on earth are you going to become your greatest version and move forward? Well, you're going to do that with the help of Ralph Smart.

Because you see, I used to also get caught up in my past and just overthink and daydream of like how scenarios could have worked out differently. Then it suddenly dawned on me, I can't turn back the hands of time. And that's a good thing because you see, a lot of the times we don't even realize everything that we have been through has made us who we are today.

Let's just say, if you could change your past, something else could have happened to you that may not have led you to where you are right now. You see everything happened for a reason. This is what helped me along my journey. I had to realize that there's no mistakes, accidents or coincidences in this universe. Everything is happening for a reason. Everything is happening in divine order.

Now I know some people are like, Ralph, how come some people had such a terrible past? Surely that wasn't meant to happen. Well, some people have had a gruesome past. What's helped me along my journey is to be a realist. And a realist is one who realizes that there's no need to cry over spilt milk. Accept what is, that's my mantra. And it has helped me to stop living in the past and move forward.

Accept what is, not how you would want it to be, not how you would change things. No, accept what is. It didn't happen to you, it happened for you. And this is how to stop living in the past and move forward. We have to learn how to forgive ourselves. Please, forgive yourself today.

I forgive myself every single day, because I'm like, okay, whatever happened to me in the past or whatever I did, it was only because of my level of awareness. Now I know better, I'm a whole new person, right? A whole new being. Do you know what's really helped me to stop living in the past and move forward? Don't look back, Ralph, you're not going that way.

I realized this, that truth be told, it's okay to live in the past for like a split second and then move forward. Don't hold your past against yourself. Make your past a friend, a healer, a teacher. And this is how you can actually stop living in the past and move forward. I have this exercise, which I call, make peace with your long lost friend, which is your past. And once you reconcile with your past and make peace with your past, it will help you to move forward.

Do you know why a lot of people can't move from their past or move forward in life and let go? Because they haven't made peace with the past. I want you to imagine the past is a long lost friend that screwed you over. Now you can continue to hold a grudge or you can say, hey, let's squash the beef because the cat down the road said so.

.Let's all get along. And I don't have to forget, but I can forgive and I can move forward and free myself from all of that heavy energy. So once you see the past as a long lost friend that screwed you over and say, you know what? I'm going to let it go and I'm going to move forward. I'm no longer going to allow an experience that happened in the past to control what is happening right now. I'm no longer going to allow an experience that happened years ago to rob my peace of mind in the present moment.

You know why? Because my peace of mind is the highest form of wealth. And sometimes we don't even realize if we are always caught up in the past, it robs us of the joy of being in the moment. We've got to remind ourselves, yesterday is history. Tomorrow is a mystery. Today is a gift. And that's why it's called the present. You can only unwrap the present if you've let go of the past.

You want to say to yourself and affirm to the universe, I am no longer going to allow the past to rob me of this gift, the present. I like that. Are you always caught up in the past? Are you blaming yourself for what happened? For what shoulda, coulda, woulda, but never happened? Well, here's how you move forward.

First and foremost, stop blaming yourself. You see, when we blame ourselves, we do nothing except make it worse. Instead of blaming yourself, ask the universe for guidance to see what you could have done differently and then make it right moving forward. Okay? This is how you let go of the past. Stop living in the past and move forward. Take accountability if you messed up and say, you know what? How I can heal from my past is by making it right, right now.

Moving forward, I know better. I'm going to do better, but I'm no longer going to hold the past against myself. I'm going to free myself from that. And I'm going to realize it's a different me. It's a new me. I've got more wisdom. I'm not going to do that again. No mistakes in life, only lessons. Right?

I say this. The past is your greatest teacher. Learn from it. But don't be held captive by it. Okay? Realize that the past is not a waste. Even if it didn't serve you, it's not a waste.

If you can learn from it, only look back at the past to learn from it. If you've had a bitter past, treacherous past, arduous, exhausting past that's caused you a lot of stress and you've lost all your hair and you want to throw a temper tantrum right now, learn from it. Don't hold it against yourself and remind yourself to move forward.

You have to realize that each and every one of us has a past. Okay? If you're a human being, you have a past. Eight billion stories. Okay? Sometimes I'm just watching documentaries of people's lives and I'm like, wow, they've had a crazy ass past. And even myself, I'm like, gosh, Ralph, you've had a really eventful life and I'm still alive. I'm still alive, I'm still living.

But so much has happened to me so fast, right? And I can only imagine what your life's like. And each and every one of us is going through it.

.What really helped me though was to realize it's okay to be the work in progress and the masterpiece at the same time. I'm not focusing on who I was yesterday. I'm focusing on who I am today. I'm not focusing, on the broken version of myself in the past. I'm focusing on how strong I am right now and focusing on becoming my greatest version. What doesn't kill you will only make you stronger.

And so far you have survived 100% of your worst experiences. Take that into consideration that as bad as your so-called past was, it didn't take you out. You're still here to tell the tale. And that means you have another opportunity to move forward. Some people get lost. Sometimes alcohol takes them into a low frequency and vibration. Sometimes their life spirals out of control. And then they're thinking about that time and it's causing them a lot of pain, a lot of suffering.

Sometimes you've had a family dispute. Sometimes you've had a divorce. Ladies, fellas, I don't know if you've had a divorce. The cat down the road said you did. But what happens when we think of the past. We start reliving these same emotions. And this is the trap of being stuck in the past. Not what happened, but the emotions that we are reliving that are not serving us. So listen, to move forward, remind yourself that you want to stop reliving these emotions that aren't serving you. And how do you do this?

By breathing in that good-ass prana. Inhaling all of that good-ass shit and exhaling all the bullshit. Breathing in that good-ass prana. Meditation, being in the here and now. Losing your mind and coming to your senses. What keeps us in the past is a wandering mind. What keeps us in the present is losing our mind and coming to our senses.

This also stops us living in the past and helps us to move forward. Look, make your past a friend, not an enemy. How do people make their past enemies every single day? They hate their past. The past is going to hate you too. It's going to make it very hard for you to be in the present moment. So you've got to say, okay, my past wasn't great and that's okay. It's okay if my past wasn't what I wanted it to be, but that's not going to get in the way of what I'm going to make my present reality. I'm a co-creator. I can make it right again. And you have to affirm that to the universe.

. I can make it right again. Say it with me. I can make it right again. A little louder. I can make it right again.!

Some people have been abused. Some people have been abandoned. And what we've got to do is to really be here for ourselves. When people weren't there for us in our past, we must not neglect ourselves. Realize you're not alone.

Talk to people, heal yourself, take time out. And this is how you can actually move forward. Sometimes you've got to slow down so you can move forward and realize that everyone falls, not everyone rises. And what's really helped me along my journey is to not focus on the fall, but to focus on the comeback. To say actually, no matter what my past did to me, it's not going to dictate who I become right now.

With me as a case study. Like I remember just working a regular job thinking, gosh, this is crazy. I'm never ever going to be able to manifest my dreams. I remember people looking down on me. There was a job I had when I was like 16, just like collecting rubbish, right? In a retail store. And I remember going past a woman who said, oh, here comes the rubbish man.

I felt bad. I'm like, oh my gosh, she's abusing me right now. And I remember saying that this is going to be my motivation to create a better future for myself. Now, fast forward to today, two words: Infinite Waters

My YouTube channel is inspiring millions of people. By book, Feel Alive is a number one bestselling book. I got the YouTube Gold Award. I'm helping millions. The same woman is like, Ralph, gosh, I can't believe it. Can we hang out? I'm like, no.

I realized that actually, I'm not bitter about that experience because it actually helped me get to where I am today. You see, I don't know a strong person with an easy past. Let me repeat that. If your past has been bad or hard, use it as fuel to power you up to go to wherever you want to go to. Remind yourself, get your wings back. Start flying because you came here to fly. You came here to shine. Don't allow what happened to you back then to stop what you can become today. So make peace with that past.

Use it as motivation to get to where you want to go to and realize what doesn't kill you will only make you stronger. Don't allow yourself to be held captive by your past. Instead, give yourself the key and the permission to move forward in the present.

Chapter Thirty Six

How To Stop People, Situations Destroying Your Peace Of Mind

It was all good just a week ago. It was all good like just two days ago. It was all good just like a second ago. Now look.

Do you have someone who is very negative in your life right now? Are you dealing with a negative situation right now which feels like you're never ever gonna get out of? And was it all good just a week ago? Was it all good just two days ago? Was it all good just a few seconds ago? But now things have taken a turn for the worse and you're like, Ralph, will I ever get through this? In this chapter we're going to talk about how to stop situations and people from destroying your peace of mind.

Let me share with you what's helped me along my journey. I know what it's like when you're well dressed, everything is going so well and then someone gets on your nerves. A negative person comes into your life. They're testing you right now and you're looking a bit shaky baby. I know what it's like when everything was all good but all of a sudden a situation came up and now you want to pull out your hair. Now you don't know if you're going to come out alive because this situation is so irritating.

It's draining your energy right now. Well over the years, I've learned how to stop situations and people from destroying your peace of mind. It all starts with this. You have to realize that you are bigger than any situation. You are also bigger than any person trying to hold you back and trying to pull you down.

You see what happens when we are thinking, overthinking, ruminating about a situation that is negative, a person that is holding us back, a negative person, a person who we are losing sleep over. We spend all of our time focusing on this one person. We spend all of our time focusing on this situation and a lot of the time it's all about how this person is destroying my peace of mind.

This situation is destroying my peace of mind. So therefore it actually becomes a self-fulfilling prophecy. I've realized that over the years, you can learn how to change your focus.

Whenever I'm going through a trying situation, whenever I'm dealing with someone who is trying to pull me down, I stop focusing on that person because the moment you focus on that person, you breathe life into them. The moment you focus and you keep focusing on that negative situation, you breathe life into it. It does not mean you have to ignore that person or ignore that situation.

It just means you now have to start focusing on something a little bit more uplifting because that will, in the end, create your amazing new reality. I've seen over the years that I am bigger than whatever is happening to me and life is never something happening to you. Life is always something responding to you. It's responding to the thoughts you have. It's responding to the words you use. It's responding to your own energy.

So every single day to stop people and situations from destroying my peace of mind, I stop externalizing my power. I take back all of the power and say, actually, I am responsible for how I respond. I'm not responsible for what has just happened because many times we aren't. It doesn't mean that we have to see ourselves as victims though. It's just that we are responsible for how we deal with the situation. We are responsible for how we deal with a person.

So if you can start to really tap into your true power to say, actually, I am bigger than this, I'm not going to let this stop me, I've got way too much more living to do and so does the cat down the road.

Your peace of mind is the highest form of wealth. So that means I'm investing in my peace of mind every single day. How do I do this? I come out into nature. I practice daily ecotherapy. I meditate. I listen to 432 hertz music to get my brain-wave frequencies in the alpha state. So I'm going to be more calm throughout the day. So when a situation seems unbearable, it's going to be a walk in the park.

When I'm around a negative person, I'm an alchemist. They are no longer negative to me because I'm not focusing. I'm taking all of my power back and I'm focusing on people who I actually like, who actually helped me along my journey and I help them.

. Ask yourself every single day, do I want to feel like this? Do I want to feel like a victim every single day? Like, do I really want to feel like that? Or do I want to feel like a hero of my own story? You've got two choices. You can be a victim. You can be like that person who everyone is picking on. Situations are picking on you. People are picking on you and you're totally helpless.

Or you can become the hero of your story. You can triumph out of any situation that is seeming unbearable right now. And that's what's helped me along my journey. I've chosen to be the hero of my own story. We have to move out of this victim mindset. I know what it's like.

Many times life's going great and then all of a sudden it takes a turn for the worst. Sometimes in the forms of undesirable people or situations. But if you can realize you are never a victim, you are co-creator of your reality and the best is yet to come.

I've learned over time to be an alchemist which is the art of making the best out of the worst and never allowing situations or people to govern your internal condition. We have to take responsibility over how we respond to things and we have to take responsibility for our emotions and how we feel.

Don't treat people as bad as they are. Treat them as good as you are. And that's how to stop people and situations from destroying your peace of mind. Every single day I say actually I'm going to keep my composure. I'm going to remain authentic and I'm also going to rise out of this situation or this circumstance which is not serving me. But what happens? A lot of us, we lose our cool. All of a sudden we get into react mode. I just want to scream right now. I just want to throw a chair around. Be careful of the cat down the road. I told you that.

All of a sudden we're just into reacting. We just want to scream and that's good up until a certain point where now it actually becomes detrimental to our own mental health. So instead of reacting, I've learned how to respond. How you respond to a situation literally has the power to change the situation itself.

A lot of the time people say Ralph, should I just be silent? Maybe that's the best thing to do because if I'm silent then they'll go away. No. Many times you actually do have to speak your truth even if your voice shakes. You've got to learn how to speak your truth even if your voice shakes. You've got to learn how to get it off your chest. I'm never concerned about what other people think of me. If I'm dealing with an undesirable person or a testing, trying, challenging situation, I'm going to express how I'm feeling.

The more you can really express yourself, the more you can speak up, even if you are dealing with a person that is destroying your peace of mind, tell them how you feel and then move on. Don't just bottle up all your emotions. Stop suppressing your emotions because depression is suppression. It's time to get it off your chest and that's how to stop people and situations destroying your peace of mind.

7-Day Vegan Challenge! Every single day I'm eating a plant-based diet to become mentally strong. How do I do this? By daily fasting, intermittent fasting, but also check this out, I don't eat dairy, I don't eat meat. That in itself is a fast. That's discipline. I've learned over the years to let go of foods which weren't serving me.

That means I can also let go of people no longer serving me and situations no longer serving me. So to really stop situations and people destroying your peace of mind, learn how to practice food discipline. Even if you really want those greasy fries and that processed meat, say actually I'm going to sacrifice that for more health within my body.

And instead you can eat a beautiful pineapple, papaya, whatever it is. But by you learning how to let go of certain foods that aren't serving you, you can also learn how to let go of certain people who aren't serving you, as well as situations.

Vibrate higher. You see the only way negative energy can affect you is if you are vibrating at the same frequency. We have to learn how to rise higher. People sometimes write to me saying something like, yeah I was arguing with this person for four hours Ralph and they're a terrible person. I'm like wait, wait, wait a minute. It takes two to tango. You also had a part to play and that's how to stop situations and people from destroying your peace of mind. Realize you also have a part to play.

You aren't a victim and if you can learn how to vibrate higher, rise higher, those so-called negative people or situations will no longer affect you because you are at a different frequency and vibration. What happens when someone's mean to you? Are you always really mean to them back, very reactionary and in your reptilian brain? I've learned that actually, you must stop copying other people who are mean to you. Stop mimicking them. Stop imitating them because it's a temptation there I know.

. Just like when a situation is really crappy, we become like really crappy but we have to learn how to become an alchemist. If someone is negative towards us, we've still got to smile at them. A lot of people say Ralph, how come you're always smiling? I say because it's good for my health right? So stop imitating people who are negative towards you or situations that are negative towards you.

Learn how to keep your own authenticity. Smile even when you're in a storm and that's how to stop people and situations from destroying your peace of mind. And realizing once again we are never victims. We are never ever victims of circumstance. We have to see what this is bringing out of us.

If you put a glass of water on the table, you bang it down, water is going to shoot up. Meaning that if someone gets on your nerves, they are only bringing out of you what was already there. So we have to start working on what they are bringing out of us. All the unresolved issues that they are highlighting within us, we have to start working on them.

I remember back in the day when I would have really hard situations to deal with and people to deal with. It would make me feel a certain way. Sometimes irritated, annoyed. Then I'm like actually this is a good thing because I've got to work on my emotions, on the way I feel. I've got to find more inner peace right? So that's how to stop people and situations from destroying your inner peace. From destroying your peace of mind.

Start working on what they are bringing out of you. Choose to respond instead of react. How I respond is just by breathing in that good ass prana baby. In a very calm way. Choose to not let it destroy your happiness. And every single day I'm making sure I'm taking care of myself mentally, emotionally and physically. And that means happiness has to be at the forefront.

So you have to say, is this really worth it? Is it really worth me losing sleep over this? Okay? Never allow someone to have that much power over you because whoever angers you controls you. It's time to stop externalizing your power.

Realize you will overcome any situation and any person that is destroying your peace of mind.

Chapter Thirty Seven

How To Stop Procrastinating

It's now or never. That's how I live my life. Like it's now or never. Are you always waiting for life to happen? Are you always procrastinating? I'll do it. No, you won't.

Someone asked me, they're like, Ralph, how can I stop procrastinating? Why do I always leave it until the last minute then end up regretting it? Ralph, I always see you sharing, doing a little Samba baby. Like you just do it, Ralph. Help me.

Don't think about what could go wrong. Just do it. I've learned the art and the formula, the blueprint for never procrastinating ever again. I just do it. I just do it. I don't care how freezing the swimming pool is. I'm just going to jump inside.

That's my mentality. That's my motto. Just do it.

You only live once. Like I told you before, why so serious? It's just a ride. So, it's now or never. Are you waiting for life to happen for you? Are you waiting for everything to be perfect? Keep waiting, keep waiting... I'll see you in the waiting room later on though. I'm going to live my life right now, right?

A lot of people are stuck in a prison, which we call a comfort zone. Growth can only happen in discomfort.

Do you know that I've made some of my best videos when it is pissing it down, hailstones, or when it's like a hundred degrees temperature, or when the wind is swaying all over the place, leaves are blowing all over the place. Yeah. Some of my best content has happened outside with me battling the elements of nature. It's so exhilarating, so exciting. And the best comes out of me.

In a comfort zone, you get stuck. And so many people live their lives in a bubble. It's safe. And that's the reason why you can never level up. When we talk about actually making stuff happen for yourself, you're going to have to go out there into the wilderness. Hyenas, cats down the road, bears. I'm scared, Ralph. Good. Feel the fear and do it anyway. Just do it.

So I said, you only have one life to live. Yes, we are infinite. We are immortal. But in this incarnation, in this body, it's only one life to live. You might come back in the next life as the cat down the road. So you better appreciate who you are right now. Okay? Look, carpe diem. It means seize the day. And that's what we have to do every single day to stop procrastinating. You see, Buddha said, the trouble is you think you have time.

Ever met someone who's always telling you their plans like, yeah, next year I'm going to do this. What? There's only right now. What are you talking about? There's only this moment. And therefore you have to maximize the moment. You have to realize that this moment will never, ever, ever come again. So you better maximize the moment and realize it's called the present because it's a gift.

Back in the day, I had a dream to inspire millions of people, to help people become their greatest versions and live their best life. And I'm like, okay, I don't want to think about this any longer. I've got to get out there. So I actually started to buy a camera and then a tripod, set it up. And then I said, peace. I stepped into radical action. As time went on, I realized that this is the way. This is the way deep divers. You have to just do it.

Don't think too much about it. Don't be concerned if it works out or not. Learn the lessons in the process and say, actually, this is all an adventure. What have I got to lose? Nothing. What have I got to gain? Everything. It's now or never.

Do you want to start that business? Do you want to talk to that guy, ladies? That woman, fellas? Do you want to travel the world? What is it you want to do right now? It's now or never. Are you waking up every single day with that in your mind? Because whatever you focus on grows. There are so many people who don't realize their words and their actions aren't matching. They say one thing, but then they do another. And this leads to procrastination. You've got to be strict on yourself to say, look, my words and actions have to be married to each other.

Give your words and actions a hug today. Look, life is a journey between B and D. B stands for birth and D stands for death. Oh no, Ralph. Don't worry because in the middle of that deep divers, you have C, which stands for choice. You see, life is all about the choices that you make. And therefore you can choose the life you want by making a better choice. You don't have to settle for that life that you hate. You can change it. That's what I did.

I'm living my best life looking only 19. Sometimes they're like, gosh, Ralph, you look so young. What's your secret? And I say, well, you know, a little Samba baby and raising the frequency.

It's now or never. There are so many people who sit on the sidelines of their own life. They observe, they spectate. No, this is your life. This is your game. You should be involved in it. Get your ass off the sidelines. Say it with me. I'm getting my ass off the sidelines. That's good. Get out of the waiting room. You've got to live life like you're on the run.

You've got to live life like there's fire up your backside. You've got to live life like you've only got 24 hours left to live. What are you going to do? If you only had 24 hours to live, you're going to do everything that you want to do. Well, that's what you've got to be doing right now. If not now, when? Just a question. If not now, when? Next week, Ralph. Next week doesn't even exist.

What are you talking about? If not now, when? So I actually bought a watch, and it says, now. That's the watch you want to buy to stop procrastinating. Buy a watch and write now. That's all you need. That's the only time you need.

Now, do it right now. Just do it. A lot of people always start catastrophizing and this stops them from actually acting. They think about the worst possible scenarios. Instead of what could go right, they think about what could go wrong and that prevents them from actually going out there and crushing it. So I always say, hey, it's going to work out for me.

Even if it doesn't work out for me, it's going to work out for me, period. I'm always thinking about the best scenario because this allows me to move with positive energy. A lot of people are procrastinating because they wake up with a doom and gloom mindset. It's not going to work out. And your wish is my command, it's not going to work out. Are you giving yourself excuses right now to stay in that arrested state of development?

I meet so many people who have a whole load of excuses. They've got a whole load of excuses of why they can't do it, of why they can't be there. It's too hard. I'm unlucky, Ralph. They're better than me. I'm not enough. Do you want to keep trash talking yourself or do you want to say, actually, I'm going to find one reason why I can do it? What is my reason I can inspire millions of people?

Let's keep it real. Who can do this better than me? Raising the frequency. Exactly. I was born to do this. And therefore, the seas will part ways. Look, stop waiting for life to happen and start making it happen. I had to learn the art of stepping into radical action. I don't talk a lot. Like when I'm making videos, I do. But after that, I'm quiet because a wise man once said nothing and got to work.

But I see so many people talking, tricking themselves on the gram on TikTok. Yeah, I made it. What have you made? You haven't even made your bed. And this is the reason why you're waiting for life to happen because you wake up with entitlement. You think you've made it. You're tricking yourself. You've given yourself trappings of wealth and delusion of grandeur. Get off your high horse and get to work. I'm so happy I didn't grow up with Instagram or TikTok because I actually had to do work. Like these days, a lot of people post like a 30 second video and think that's work.

Oh my gosh. You better get to work. I wanna see you're tired. I wanna see the blood, sweat and tears because you're gonna live to see another day. This is how to stop procrastinating. It's now or never. How to stop waiting for life to happen and how to make it happen for yourself. We sometimes get caught up in comparing our lives to other people's lives. Comparison is the greatest thief of joy. I know I'm in a league of my own and this allows me to do what I'm doing right now. I focus on myself.

I don't focus on comparing myself to other people I've never even met. Ain't nobody got time for that. So focus on yourself today and focus on being better than who you were yesterday. A lot of people start procrastinating and waiting for life to happen because they're waiting for a perfect moment. Ah, isn't that beautiful? Kumbaya, no, doesn't exist. Life is beautiful and ugly at the same time but it's all about how you choose to respond.

How you respond to a situation literally has the power to change the entire situation itself. Just imagine how far you would be in two weeks if you started what you wanted to do today. Well, you can be that far in two weeks if you start right now. You've got to remind yourself, life moves real fast. Life is like that. It's like a blink of an eye. That's how fast life moves. So don't think you've got all the time in the world. The game is going to change. The universe is going to send obstacles your way, trials and tribulations. When you've got the energy right now, you better do it.

When I said, hey, I want to write a book, I wrote a number one best-selling book, Feel Alive. I didn't say, hey, let me wait for 10 years. Ain't nobody got time for that. I've got to do it right now. Now. Now. You want to start eating better, 7 Day Vegan Challenge? Take the first step right now. It's not about how fast you go. All you've got to do is take that first step and just go. Start with a green juice, then a pineapple, then a whole bunch of grapes in your mouth.

Do you want to be a skeleton in the waiting room, growing cobwebs over your face? Or do you want to go out there and say, hey, I'm going to be brave because the universe reveals its secrets to people who dare to follow their hearts. It may not work out, but at least I've done something. And I'm going to be more proud of the things I did than the things I didn't do. You've got to remind yourself, the more you do, the more you create, the more you learn, the more you grow.

The more you fail, the more you grow. The more you make mistakes, the more you realize and find out other ways of how not to do something, you become incredibly smart. You just stop procrastinating right now. Take a look at your environment right now. Are you distracting yourself? Eliminate distractions, things which aren't helping you grow. I'm not a distraction, deep divers. You know why? Because I make you do a little samba, baby. I bring you joy and smiles and I help you level up. But there are distractions in your life that aren't taking you anywhere. And you've got to get serious with yourself and have fun at the same time and say, oh, I don't want to be distracted from what I'm here to do. I want to be inspired with what I'm here to do.

Every single day, remind yourself, like I said, this moment will never come again. This moment will never come again. Sometimes you might miss the boat. If you keep staring at it, you better jump inside. You better just do it. Hit that like button right now, deep divers, if you support The Real. Just do it.

Stop waiting for life to happen. Start making it happen. Feel the fear and do it anyway. Get out of the waiting room. If not now, when? This moment will never come again.

Chapter Thirty Eight

How To Stop Taking Things So Personally And Caring What People Think

Look, are you someone that takes everything so personally? Is that you? Be honest. The cat down the road is like, just be honest. Are you someone also who cares what people think to the extent of your own happiness and inner peace? It's really bothering you right now. That's a problem. Well, that problem is about to be solved because we're gonna talk about how to stop taking things so personally and caring what people think.

First and foremost, if you are doing something big, you're gonna have a lot of people who have a whole lot to say about you. That's a good thing. You know why? Because people only talk about what's worth talking about.

Now, if someone says something to you and you feel a certain way, remind yourself, it's not all about you. It is not all about you. And you gotta get off your high horse and realize that actually, it might just be about what they're going through. So I had to learn this along my early journey. When I first started making videos, people would say stuff. And now I'm immune to it. You know why? Because I realized it's got nothing to do with me. Ain't got nothing to do with me. It's got everything to do with you.

So if you are someone who is taking everything so personally and caring what people think, remind yourself it's not about you, it's about them. And oftentimes people project onto you their fears, their dislikes, their likes, whatever it is, they project. You have to learn that there's something called ascribing intent. And people who ascribe intent care what people think. They take everything so personally. And you have to learn how to not ascribe intent.

What am I talking about? So let me give you an example. You're talking to someone and they don't text you back. Now you're taking this personally and you're like, oh my gosh, maybe they don't like me. Maybe I'm a bad person. Maybe I'm not desirable enough. You don't feel loved right now. You're looking a little bit shaky, baby.

But what if I told you that they're in an important meeting and they can't actually text you back? What if I told you they lost their phone? What if I told you that they're driving on the freeway, on the motorway and you don't want them to text you while they're driving, do you? No, of course not. You don't want an accident. Don't be silly.

So when you learn the art of not ascribing intent, you realize not everything is about you. Okay? Not everything that someone does is in response to you.

So oftentimes it's about what they're dealing with, what they're going through. And if you are someone who's always caring so much about what people think, remind yourself that it's none of your business. Whatever someone has to say about you has got nothing to do with you. It's their opinion. It's how they see you, not how you see yourself.

So you have to learn that the perception that you have of yourself is greater than the perception other people have of you.

To stop taking things so personally and caring what people think, you have to realize the perception that you have of yourself, the inner mirror, is greater than the perception other people have of you. You have to live with you and therefore focus on yourself. Focus on yourself. And this is how to stop taking things so personally and caring what people think. I'm not paying attention to anything that's not helping me evolve.

Sometimes people wanna bring me gossip. I'm like, why are you bringing me this? Because I told you, if it's not helping me evolve, it's a distraction. Take it away, you keep it.

Why do we take everything so personal in the first place? Many times it's because we feel we're being attacked. Many times it's because we're insecure about certain things. Look, a glass of water on a table, if you bang the table, water is gonna shoot out of the glass. In other words, if they triggered you, that's because you still have lessons to learn. Remind yourself that their opinions of you won't break you. You know why? Because they didn't make you.

You have to remind yourself, in life, we take things so personally. You know why? Because we're focusing on the small things. You've got to focus on the bigger picture to stop caring what people think. That's what I did.

When I first started YouTube, I would start my intros like peace. And someone said, Ralph, I don't like your intro. And I took that personally. I thought maybe there's something wrong with the intro. And I was caring so much about what this person thought. But I was wise enough, because the cat down the road gave me some advice. And the cat down the road said, Ralph, why are you taking things so personally from people that you don't even know personally? What? Say it again, cat down the road. Why are you taking things so personally from people you don't even know? Like who are these people? So I had to realize that.

And then sometimes you actually do know these people and it's personal and you take these things personally. Then you have to remind yourself whose life is it? Whose life am I living? You didn't come here to live someone else's life. You came here to live your life. Everyone is gonna have an opinion about your life, but it's your life. And that's why you have to live it and let go of society's expectations. This is how to stop taking things so personally.

So many people, when they get told something or when someone does something to them, they take it personally, they feel a certain way. Never give other people the power over your internal condition. Never give people the power over your inner feelings and emotions. Why are you doing this deep divers? To stop taking things personally. I don't care what anyone thinks of me. Not even the cat down the road. You know why? Because I am in control of my inner emotions and feelings.

I'm not gonna allow someone on the outside to control how I'm feeling on the inside. Because you have to master your emotions. Otherwise they will master you. You have to remind yourself it's all on you right now. We take things personally. You know why? Because we're always focusing on what's going on out there, distracting ourselves. We should be paying attention to cultivating more self-love. Because once you cultivate more self-love, you won't take things so personally.

People are like, oh, I don't like what you're wearing. I love what I'm wearing. You know why? Because I love myself. People say, oh, people might tell you, oh my gosh, I don't like who you're dating. I don't like who you're married to. But wait a second, I know them more than you. Stop being nosy. I'm happy with my choice. This is how you stop taking things so personally. Why is everyone telling me how to live my life? I just want to live my life. Therefore you have to know thyself because if you don't know who you are, you're going to be very fragile.

Someone's going to come along and tell you what to do and how to live. And you're going to take things personally when they tell you things. And now you're going to care about everything they have to say. In ancient Egypt on every temple it said, know thyself. Because once you know who you are, you will come to know the secrets of the universe. And the secret is: all is mental. One of the seven hermetic principles, all is mind. And the more you focus on yourself and love yourself, other people's opinions drown out. And you stop taking things so personally.

I remind myself when I used to take everything so personally, it was because I didn't find myself. I hadn't found myself yet. I was still searching. I was still like a little lamb lost in the woods thinking other people had the answers. Now I have the answers. You ain't got the answers. I've got the answers. Look, you know what the answers are? That I had to own who I am. This is how to stop taking everything so personally. You have to stand up for yourself. You have to speak your truth. Even if your voice shakes, you have to believe in yourself. You have to know thyself. You have to be confident. You have to be emotionally strong. You have to be emotionally resilient. This is how to stop taking things so personally and caring what people think. You must practice emotional resilience.

Well, how do we do that, Ralph? So look, when people tell you things that you may not like to hear, remind yourself that it's okay. Let anyone say whatever they want. Because it's got nothing to do with me. Remind yourself there are no statues of critics. This is how to stop caring what other people think. I don't have time to put down people. You know why? Because I'm too busy lifting people up.

I don't have time to critique what someone else is doing. You know why? Because I'm too busy creating. Have you noticed that deep divers, people who are really doing big things, creating, they don't have time to critique people, nitpick.

They don't have time. You know why? Because they're manifesting. You know why? Because they're becoming their greatest version. You know why? Because they're going to the next level, raising the frequency. If you are someone who's taking things so personally, you must have a whole lot of time on your hands. Focus on where you need to be.

Focus on where you need to go. Focus on becoming your greatest version because any moment you spend thinking about what is not serving you, you are missing an opportunity for an experience that can inspire you. Every moment you care about what someone else thinks, you're missing the moment of thinking about someone who is really rooting for you. Like, why do we as human beings spend so much time on people not serving us? Caring about what they think. Spend time focusing on people that love you.

I learned this and it changed my entire life. I've got millions of people who support me. Well, truth be told, I only need to support myself and believe in myself because those people may change. And it happens because how people treat you has got everything to do with how they feel about themselves and this ties into not taking things so personally.

Let me explain. So if someone tells you they love you, you're amazing, that's great. You're not taking that personally. But we focus when someone says, hey, I don't like you. We're like, why? So a lot of people have this need to be loved by everyone. Well, not everyone loves mangoes and that's okay. Once again, it's got nothing to do with you. So as I was saying, deep divers, how someone treats you has got everything to do with how they feel today.

I've had people who've said, Ralph, I don't like you. Next day, Ralph, I love you. Got nothing to do with me. I'm not focusing on your flaky behavior. I'm not focusing on your changing mind. You know why? Because I love me, I accept me. Ain't nobody got time for that. This is how to stop taking things personally and caring what people think. How people treat you is about how they are feeling right now.

If they woke up on the right side of bed, they're going to treat you fantastic. If they haven't slept, really grumpy, I feel sorry for you. And you're going to take it personally thinking it's got everything to do with you. No, it's got everything to do with them because they woke up on the wrong side of bed. So you've got to learn this valuable lesson. How people treat us is not about us. It's about what they're going through, what they're experiencing. And this is how to stop taking things so personally and caring what people think.

You must remind yourself, deep divers, if you are someone who cares so much about what people think of you, you can never truly be free. And therefore, to stop taking things personally or caring what people think, prioritize your freedom .because being free happens the moment you stop caring about what people think. Being free happens the moment you stop taking things so personally and realize that, hey, you can't please everyone. And you don't have to focus on people who may feel a certain way about you.

.Keep it moving and become your greatest version. So, my friend, remind yourself, if you are taking things so personally, caring what people think, listen, stop allowing people to live rent-free in your mind. Stop allowing people who do nothing for you to live rent-free in your mind.

It's on you now because once you stop giving them that limelight, you stop taking it so personally and you stop caring about what people think and you focus on your dreams, visions, and goals.

Sometimes you gotta say, okay, I was terrific. Sometimes you have to give people the benefit of the doubt. You know why? Because sometimes people just didn't know that. Sometimes there's miscommunication and sometimes it happens. And therefore, it wasn't personal. They didn't mean to offend you, but somewhere it got lost in translation. You misinterpreted it. There was a misinterpretation of what they did and now you took it personally. They just meant to give you some love. Now you thought they were dissing you.

You have to have a sense of humor. This is how to stop taking things so personally. I've been making videos for a little while. People have said amazing things to me, weird things to me, crazy things to me. It's all okay because I know who I am and this is how to stop taking things so personally and caring what people think. You've got to know who you are

Chapter Thirty Nine

How To Stop Resistance To Move Forward: 10 Breakthrough Solutions

Are you in resistance to something right now and it's driving you crazy? Let me share with you what's helped me along my journey.

I used to work 12-hour days. Yes, can you imagine? I used to wake up, it was dark. And then when I left for work, it was dark. I had no life. It was terrible. Don't work 12-hour days. And nowadays, I just chill in nature and stuff and wake up with a bunch of grapes in my mouth. I'm a fan of Bruce Lee and he had the one-inch punch. What I learned from Bruce Lee was that he gave his one-inch punch to someone and then they went flying. Like, where the hell did you go? Even the cat down the road was surprised.

Now, what's the secret of that when it comes to resistance? You see, what I found myself doing for a long time was using a lot of force, working 12-hour days and getting very little back in return. A lot of force, little power. Bruce Lee's one-inch punch, little force, lots of power. And then I realized that sometimes you just have to relax and everything will take care of itself.

So I'm into, I love sports. I love watching athletes that drive the determination, the motivation, the perseverance. More so the passion. Okay, I train athletes. As a psychologist, I talk about the subconscious mind, how to go to the next level. The greatest athletes in the world have the perfect cadence. What am I talking about? Cadence is the perfect rhythm. If you watch someone running a race, or maybe it's you or me. Like when I skate, if my facial expressions are a certain way, it means I'm not gonna land the trick. When I relax and find the perfect rhythm, the perfect cadence, I usually land it. Most of the time.

Okay, so I'm gonna talk about the 10 breakthrough solutions that I use every single day that have helped me along my journey. And you've heard me say resistance makes you stronger. Okay, that is true. And when I talk of resistance, sometimes your immune system, you need resistance when it comes to certain diseases out there. That's beautiful. But that's not what I'm talking about. This resistance, I'm talking about how it affects our lives in so many ways, and it doesn't help us to become our greatest version. So the 10 breakthrough solutions, let's start with the first one.

1.   Stop editing your life

This is what's really helped me along my journey. When I first started making YouTube videos, nobody was making it, like in terms of what I was talking about. So I was like, oh, that's pretty strange, but that put a lot of pressure on me because I'm like, I'm a pioneer of this stuff. So I would try to edit videos as much as I could, like cut here. Oh, I messed up a word, cut there. It was a nightmare. And it would take a long time just to edit one video, sometimes five hours. And I would miss the beautiful sunshine coming to yours, going to the beach. Yeah, it just wasn't fun.

So fast forward a few years where I am right now, I don't edit videos. And people always ask Ralph, gosh, why not? Because I say, I don't need to. I would rather show people my mistakes to show people it's okay to make mistakes. Oh, man. Do you think I really care about messing up a word? There are far more serious things I've got to worry about. Actually, I don't worry that much, but I do sometimes.

Okay. Like when I stopped editing everything, abundance came. As soon as I stopped editing videos, everything took off, but more so in my life.

Now I want you to ask yourself, are you editing your life out to the extreme? It's okay to edit. Like I'm a cinematographer, okay? You need to edit sometimes to create a more cinematic effect. But are you editing every single aspect of your life? Like are you Photoshopping your face and feathering your face? I used to do a lot of that, but then I realized it's okay from time to time.

But how we edit our lives is that sometimes we only want to show people what we think they want to see, okay? Because a lot of the time, people are so preoccupied with their own stuff. Ain't nobody got time for that. They are not thinking of you. They are thinking like, oh my gosh, I've got to pay the rent, right? Goodness gracious. But you're so selfish. You're so self-centered, okay? You feel that the whole world revolves around you.

That was me along my early journey. And I said, it's really, really, it's just not that serious at all, okay? So that's the first breakthrough of how to let go and move forward, how to release resistance, okay? Stop editing your life. Live an unedited, organic lifestyle. That's what's helped me along my journey. It might help you, it may not. Depends who you are.

2.   Release controlling

I'm into control. Are you? I used to be into control in a big way. Now I'm releasing. The universe is like, Ralph, you don't control anything. You really think you're in control? Okay, I'm going to show you. I'm not in control anymore. Okay, I was in control like a few seconds ago.

I realized I'm not in control of anything. Externally to me, I can't control if you're going to watch my video or not. I don't even care, okay? I'm not in control of what you're wearing right now. I don't control that. We often think we're in control. Sometimes we think we can manipulate certain situations. A lot of the time it happens in relationships. It happens in our interactions. We try to convince people, win them over. I don't really care about even who connects on this channel because I know that the right people will.

That's all that matters. And when I started to let go of control, like I can't control how other people perceive me, I realized a secret. The only thing that matters is how I perceive myself. That's the only thing that matters. Like get a mirror. If you think you are so amazing, I can't control that, baby. I can't control what you do. I don't want to control what you do. And therefore I release resistance, okay?

Resistance is like this. You're trying to control the situation. When you release it, just relax, okay? If you notice what your body is doing in resistance, a lot of the times we're very tense. You see, resistance doesn't just happen in our minds. It happens in our whole body, okay? A lot of the times I tell people, when I'm in resistance, I see my muscles tightening up because I want to control a situation. When I say I, it doesn't even matter, my whole body just relaxes, okay?

3.   Eat what works for you

Now, seven day vegan challenge, okay? How I release resistance is by realizing that just because it tastes great, no, it doesn't taste great, actually, does it? Right, you're like, what is that? Well, Ralph, you said it's good for you.

Do your own research. Hey, I don't like watermelons, but I like papaya and I love mangoes. Now, watermelons are very, very good for you, but I've just never been attracted to watermelons in that kind of way. Like, I love the smell of watermelon, don't get me wrong, but I'm not really like, oh, I've got to eat a watermelon today, okay? So I don't eat watermelons, and that's fine.

Like a lot of us, we're putting things in our mouth that shouldn't be there. A lot of us, we're eating foods, we're in resistance to it, but we say, well, it's healthy, that's fine. But once again, it's not just about what you're consuming, it's about how you feel when you are consuming what you are eating. So what do I do instead? I just buy loads of strawberries, okay? But hey, go with what works for you.

4.   Resistance makes stronger

When we talk of resistance, a lot of us don't realize how much resistance governs our life, okay? There are so many ways we are in resistance, we don't even know. I'll give you an example.

Along my early journey, I wanted it real, real, real bad. I wanted to make it. I was tired of living the routine life. I said, enough is enough, I don't want to do this anymore. I want to be like those people, okay? Who appear to be more successful. I wanted it. What do you want, Ralph? I don't know, I just want it. I want the good. Certain people with lots of money in their bank account may be very depressed and miserable. And certain people have both, right? That's probably the ideal life.

Like I have both, internal happiness, high bank balance, internal bank balance and outer bank balance.

Look, it starts like that. You have to start embodying the frequency you desire to attract into your life. Now, I know we're trying to package ourselves for people. I was along my early journey. I said, okay, I've gotta make a video which is like under three minutes. Why? Because, well, I want people to watch the video. Resistance makes stronger.

Nowadays, once again, I don't need people to watch these videos because once again, I've connected with so many people and so many people know about Infinite Waters, millions of people, that we're good. Every day is abundant, baby. But when I was first starting, there was a lot of resistance because I was trying to package something. I wasn't being who I was 100%.

So what happened? I was trying to make people laugh. See, I just did that. Just fun, you gotta be yourself, baby, right? I was trying to make people laugh. I was trying to do the cartwheels and stuff because I was trying to make it. See, when you have nothing, you're trying to do everything. When you feel you have everything, you don't have to do anything.

5.   Don't cater to the crowd.

You aren't a gladiator in an arena, okay? You've gotta start catering to yourself. A lot of people say, respect me, put some respect on my name… Look, you've gotta respect yourself, baby. People say, they don't treat me right. They don't respect me. Nothing is ever as personal as you think. You've gotta start respecting yourself. You've gotta start cultivating the love within.

Now, a lot of the times, along my earlier journey, I used to try and convince people, like even say, okay, this is how the universe works and this is the right God, and da-da-da. What are we talking about? Like, you're going back and forth. We're arguing right now.

6.   We don't need to argue about it.

That's a great way to release resistance, okay? Resistance is created because we are trying to convince people because we're not secure about what we believe in, what we know about. Once you're secure and once you know what you know about, you don't have to argue with people, okay? We can, we can agree to disagree, baby.

We don't even have to do that. Like, you go your way, I go mine and we'll just have a beautiful day, okay? So you don't have to argue. That releases resistance, okay?

7. Move out of your comfort zone

Now, how I release resistance is always reminding myself that you got to move out of your comfort zone. You see, a lot of us, we have a, we've got a massive block and we're in heaps of resistance to going to new places. I was for a long time.

You know, I thought along my journey that I was in the best place ever, that there was no other place that would make me more happy than where I am right now.I just thought it was the bomb, right? It was so amazing until I got on a plane, right? I've traveled to over 30 different countries, okay? I've been to nearly every continent on the planet. I've been to a lot of places. And I realized that by being open to new experiences, the resistance subsides, okay?

A lot of us create a lot of resistance because we are closed off to new experiences. Therefore, we stunt our own growth. So what helped me along my journey was just to say, hey, hop on a plane and don't look back. Now, it happens like this. A lot of the times we go through life and we are really afraid, okay, to show the world who we really are. Why? We suppress a lot of emotions, okay? We try to put on this very hard shell like, oh, I'm Mr. Strong, I'm Mrs. Strong. We try so hard and we create so much resistance.

8. Stop suppressing emotions to release resistance

So what helped me along my journey was to really become more vulnerable. See, that's the paradox of releasing resistance. Like, the more vulnerable you are, the more you release resistance because you aren't suppressing emotions, okay? You're actually opening up yourself. You're actually becoming more transparent, more honest. And I found that when I started to share with the world, I was releasing resistance. I talked about my panic attacks. Okay, I'm not afraid of talking about that, but it feels so amazing inside.

9.   Stop forcing relationships

Now, we can talk about relationships for a second. Uh-oh, does the shoe fit? Have you ever tried to get someone to fall in love with you and it's just not happening? It's what I call the Cinderella effect, baby. The shoe doesn't fit, but you're trying to force it. Once again, lots of force. It's just not happening, is it? Little force, it's happening.

A lot of the time, I've seen along my journey, we want the people who aren't meant for us. Why does that happen? Why do we want the people who aren't meant for us? Sometimes a lot of women want guys who aren't even interested in them. Sometimes guys want the same.

You've got to know your true worth of realizing you don't have to do anything to attract the right people. I don't, right? Every single day I get approached, I get stopped because the right people will find you, okay? So, hey, don't worry about trying to get your foot inside. It should always be a perfect fit. That's how to release resistance, how to let go and move on, okay?

10.   Focus on the now

Building on the previous point about relationships, a lot of people say it shouldn't have happened. I could have done this. I would have changed that whole situation. If only I had, wait a minute. You want to release resistance. What's helped me along my journey is to say, forget the shoulda, coulda. It doesn't matter, okay? The only thing that matters is what is happening right now, this beautiful, magical moment, okay? And that's what releases resistance. Stop trying to control the past through our thoughts, we're overthinking.

We create a lot of resistance, what I call energetic blocks. That's why a lot of people, they're eating great, but once again, they're not in optimal health because they've still got past unresolved issues. I am as free, as light as a bird because this is what I deal with as a psychologist, as a counselor, as an infinite being. I'm always looking for the hacks, the solutions. So I always realize that if I'm holding onto the past, I'm in resistance. If I can let go of the past and say, okay, the past is the past, today's a new day. I say: it feels so good to be alive. Can I get a hello there? And I automatically release resistance. You can do it.

Chapter Forty

Why I Stopped Watching Porn

Confession time, I'm spilling the beans. 13 years old, raging full of hormones. It's new, it's exciting. Tapes and magazines are being passed around and one of them just happens to land in my hands. And at this age, I'm so impressionable. I am mesmerized by all of these exotic women, fantasies in my mind. And what happened is that I was seeing women in a different way.

I thought they were like this in real life. Oh, how I was wrong. And what happened is that after a few years, I just stopped totally, but I learned so much. And the biggest reason why I stopped is that in a lot of pornography, we are not seeing the bigger picture.

First of all, to each his own. If you love pornography, wonderful, I'm happy for you. I'm just sharing my own journey. So we have male domination where it's always about putting women under subjugation. Also, you have a whole genre of the dominatrix where you have female domination. So there's always a power control going on. And whenever I used to watch porn, I would always feel like this was not being done in a loving way.

When I was in my teens, about 15, I got introduced to my mentor, Omran Mikhail Ivanov, a Bulgarian master teacher. And he had a book called Love and Sexuality. And this is one of the biggest reasons I stopped at the age of 15, because he spoke of women in the most amazing way. You have to read some of his books, mind blowing. But when I was just watching porn at 13, I thought, okay, women are supposed to be treated this way.

It couldn't have been further from the truth. We had jokes in our school, like beating the meat, choking the chicken. The three S's, spit, swallow, suck. But you see, a lot of us, we won't admit that we have ever done something like this, but it goes on.

As a psychologist, I speak to people every day with porn addiction. Even women who are in the industry. And what do they tell me? They tell me that it's not real. It is fantasy. Because that's why you have a lot of women always looking at the camera. Are they really enjoying it? Or are they paid actors? But when you are 13, you don't know the whole history of many of these women, some of them may have parental abandonment issues.

You don't see that many times, they have to have so many takes, cut, cut, cut. But you're just seeing the beautiful lighting, the makeup, the nails, or the guy with the big penis. There are false expectations for men, false expectations for women.

A lot of women feel that if they don't look like a porn star, they're never gonna be good enough for their boyfriend. A lot of guys want their girlfriend to perform like a porn star. That's every guy's fantasy. Not every guy's, but when you're 13, that's how you're thinking because you are under mind control. What's even worse is that many of these porn stars are under mind control. And yes, some do it out of choice, but a lot of people do it because they wanna make money. They wanna make a name for themselves. They wanna be famous. It's not really coming from a heart space.

More so, you have to ask yourself, are you seeing these people in their authentic state? Because what I discovered is that true love is about intimacy and you don't see that in pornos. It's just penetration, but intimacy is about foreplay. It's a dance and that's why Tantra is about the union. When you are watching a porno, it's just to get off. Oh, I got mine, yay, you got yours. There is no sharing. There is no trust. There is no compassion. So I am so happy that I made that choice at 15 years old.

Many times we are not seeing how it's impacting our health. Mantak Chia, a fantastic sexologist. Every time you are releasing your DNA, you are losing a part of who you are. But if you are doing it with someone you love, you are giving it to them. That's how children are born. But when you are just throwing DNA samples left, right, and center, we don't even know what we're doing.

I had to step into higher consciousness and realize what if that person you are masturbating to was your sister, someone else's sister, a close family friend, a relative. Would you still be doing it? But because there is no connection, you see, now you can do it. Many times it's become a bit of a circus show and it starts off soft. You start really soft with soft core porn. Then you go to bondage, rape, incest, all kinds of crazy stuff. Anal, it goes so far that you've got to be careful.

So if you are someone who is just watching porn, remind yourself, are you loving yourself 100%? Because at 13, when I was watching porn, I never loved myself. More so at that age, I was single as well. That's why when someone catches you, you close your door. And if they do catch you, you feel so embarrassed. You say, no, I wasn't watching it.

When you love to do something, you are proud of doing it. You're like, yeah, I was watching it and what? That's what you should be doing. If you love porn, love it 100%. But don't just do it when you're ashamed of what you're doing, because deep down in your heart, you know it's wrong.

More so, we have to start seeing that many times the whole porn world is a business built on supply and demand. Therefore, they are giving you a product and that product is not organic. Ask yourself, do these people really want to do that? Would they do it for free? Some of them would, but many of them wouldn't.

So in just taking responsibility, it has changed my life in the most phenomenal way. Because many times porn will impact your relationship. You can't communicate with women. You don't even know how to interact with a real woman. When I was 16, I got involved with my first serious relationship. And that's when porn had to stop. That was a long time ago. And I felt such a deep union. That's what Tantra is all about.

But if you are just watching porn, you don't even want to get into a relationship or you're in a relationship, but now your energy is being dissipated. You're sleeping with your wife or your girlfriend or your boyfriend because women do watch porn. Yes, they do. Trust me. Now you're sleeping with them, but your mind is somewhere else.

Yes, I say it is wonderful to explore sexual energy. Feel the energy going through you and how it opens you up. It can release stress. It can even help depression, believe it or not. But a lot of the times it creates addiction, you see? And it starts off small, it grows larger. It starts off soft, now it grows harder. It changes the very essence of who you are.

So in becoming your greatest version, you have to ask yourself, do I want to do something which is not going to serve me in the long run? Because whatever we do now echoes on into eternity. And more so, whatever we see with our eyes goes directly into our subconscious mind. There you have it. We're here in nature. We're taking a very lighthearted approach. Do what you love. More so, love yourself 100% because the birds certainly do. Can you hear them singing?

Chapter Forty One

7 Signs Your Manifestation Is Near

Have you been wishing on a star to follow where you are? Have you been wishing on a dream to follow what it means? Have you heard that song, by the way? It's an amazing song. Listen to it. But we no longer have to wish on a star because we're about to manifest.

We're about to manifest. Your manifestation is so near. I can see it, Ralph. I told you! Seven signs your manifestation is near.

Have you been waiting to manifest for the longest? Well, it's near. And I'm going to share with you how you know a powerful manifestation is near and coming your way. Let me share with you what's helped me along my journey. Recognize the seven signs that a powerful manifestation is near. That a powerful manifestation is about to enter my life.

I started from the bottom. Now I'm here in nature, living a life of infinite abundance. And this is only possible because I was aware of the seven signs a manifestation was near.

1.   If you don't give up, the miracle happens

That's how to recognize a powerful manifestation is near. You see, just when you want to give up, that's when the amazing manifestation comes into your life. It's just like when you're looking at your phone, oh my gosh, yeah, an amazing person just goes by and you will never ever get to talk to them ever again. It sucks, right? So don't look at your phone, keep your head up, and don't give up now. And if you aren't giving up, that's a sign your manifestation is near.

Do you know how many timesI wanted to give up, even on YouTube? I'm like, this is too hard. But a small voice was like, Ralph, hold on. And it started to talk to me like, Ralph, you love this. And I'm like, yeah, I do love this. And I kept going. And that's why I'm reaping the benefits. So if you aren't giving up, if you are realizing the day you plant the seed is not the same day you eat the fruit, that's how to tell a manifestation is near. I see so many people starting something and then stopping something.

But if it's in your heart to do something, for instance, to inspire other people or be a hairdresser, be a scientist, why give up on your dreams just because it's hard? You see, Deep Divers, I knew my manifestation was near because I didn't give up. And when it was really hard, because it's going to get hard. Oh, it's going to get really hard. I asked for help. Ask and it is given. So if you feel like giving up or you're holding on, well done, a manifestation is near. To speed up the process, start asking for what you need. Because those that ask will receive. And those that don't will just be left wondering.

It's better to ask than to assume.And if you keep asking and you don't give up, a manifestation is near.

2.   You aren't just thinking about it. You are actually thinking really hard about it.

You have a clear vision. You have a crystal clear vision of what it is you want in life, of what it is you want to do with your life. Because a lot of us think... but some of us really think about what it is we are here to do on the planet. And if you have a clear vision, I always say, live with purpose.

Live with a vision. I had a vision many, many years ago that I wanted to inspire millions of people. You see, you have been told that desire is bad, right? But even the desire to have no desire is still a desire. So a little exercise, okay, to really speed up that manifestation and a sign a manifestation is near, is to really start having desires. Say, actually, I envision a life like this. And a great exercise for this is something called scripting, okay? Scripting, I want you to start writing. Get a journal. Borrow one from the cat down the road, okay? And start writing how you want your life to go.

The vision you have in your mind of how you want your life to go, okay? Like, my life was pretty bad. At first, I was like a victim. I was like, going to fall on my ass a hundred million times. And then I actually started changing the script and saying, actually, Ralph, in this story, you wake up every single day with a whole bunch of grapes in your mouth. Ralph, you can spend time on the beach every single day and have a beautiful family with love, health, happiness. Keep writing.

And then it actually manifested, right? So you know a manifestation is near if you are starting to change your story. There is no change in your life without a change in your storyline, okay? And that means you've got to have a clear vision, start writing down what you want to see in your life, okay? Because that's actually a form of alchemy. The alchemist would turn lead to gold and that's what a lot of MCs do. They write something down on a piece of paper and then they get a gold plaque. Or they go platinum. That's alchemy.

So start getting a pencil, use the lead to turn it into gold, okay?

3.   You are getting off your ass.

If you are getting off your ass, congratulations because that's the only way to speed up the manifestation process. You see, I see a lot of people telling me what they're gonna do. I always say, don't tell me your plans, show me your results. Everybody can talk a good talk. I'm gonna do this, I'm gonna do that and you haven't done shit. So get off your ass, get off the sidelines and start being involved in life. Start being involved in your true calling. Start investing in yourself and that's a sign your manifestation is near.

If you have the courage to start following your dreams today, you're gonna make mistakes. So what? We all do. I always make mistakes but I learn from them. So if you are getting off your ass, not being distracted, you're like, Ralph, what? If it's not helping me evolve, it's a distraction. If you are doing that, a manifestation is near. So near, be ready.

4.   As above, so below

You see, the law of attraction, which is actually the law of correspondence, one of the seven hermetic principles going back to ancient Egypt or Kemet, states that as above so below, as within so without. You see, we never attract what we want, we always attract what we are. I see a lot of people praying, Ralph, please, I'm not God. Actually, I am.

Never mind. I see a lot of people praying to the cat down the road because the cat down the road is God, right? And they're like, cat down the road, please give me more money. Please let me find the love of my life. Please let me find a better job than this crappy one I'm at right now watching paint dry.

You know, a manifestation is near. If you are no longer praying for it, you are working for it. If you are no longer wishing for it, I wish I had this, I wish I had that. No, you are doing what it takes to be worthy of it. You see, you always see me creating, even on the weekends. I don't take a day off. Why? Because I love this. Why? Because I know I was ordained by the universe to do this. And that's a sign a manifestation is near. Whenever you do it, not just talk about it, not just pray for it, but actually do it, whenever you actually step into radical action, you get the job done.

If you're doing that, congratulations. A manifestation is near. It's actually behind you. Look around. Oh my gosh. Yeah, it's there, right?

5.   You are going the extra mile.

If you are going the extra mile today, deep divers, congratulations. If you are doing what most people are afraid to do, congratulations. Why? Because a manifestation is near. Nobody said it would be easy. But deep divers, you're already in pain. You're already hurt. You're already tired. You might as well get a reward from it.

It's the determination. If you've got it, congratulations. Your manifestation is near. Anytime you can go the extra mile. You can sacrifice, right? Anytime you can go the extra mile, you can sacrifice a weekend, a nice sunny day. Do you know how many times when it was like 100 degrees, so beautiful and everyone's at the beach and I'm like, oh, I've got to start creating. And that was back in the day. But guess what? Now I can actually enjoy time at the beach because I took care of that. Now I can live in this beautiful moment.

Sometimes you've got to do the work. You've got to be in the trenches. You've got to put your boots on because it's time to work. There's a time for work and there's a time for play. If you are keeping your head down, staying focused, keep the focus, deep divers. My eyes are on you right now. A manifestation is near. Okay. So just remind yourself, if you are going the extra mile, if you are doing what most people aren't doing, a manifestation is near.

You see, a lot of people say, a lot of people tell me, Ralph, I want to start a YouTube channel. A month later, Ralph, I want to start a YouTube channel because actually starting a YouTube channel takes effort, deep divers. You've got to buy a camera. You've got to edit. You've got to upload. And it's not just about talking.

It's about being about it. So if you are being about it, if you are going the extra mile, if you are sweating, congratulations, your manifestation is near.

6.   You are learning like your life depended on it.

Law of attraction, manifest, manifest, manifest. You are learning what you need to know like your life depended on it. Let me repeat that one more time, deep divers. You are learning what you need to know to level up like your life depended on it.

You see, we've been programmed in this matrix. The thing is that actually, back at school, we would take exams and we would think they were really serious. No. What's serious is your life purpose.

That's the real exam. And if you are learning what you need to pass that test, a manifestation is near. If you are into content creation, if you are learning about different cameras, if you are learning about sound engineering, congratulations, a manifestation is near.

If you are a makeup artist, you're learning about the business of the makeup industry, a manifestation is near. If you are a scientist and you are constantly reading journals, learning, expanding your mind, a manifestation is near. If you are somebody who is just a truth seeker, a manifestation is near because once again, knowledge is power. No, no, no. Wisdom is power. Because wisdom is knowledge applied.

So if you are reading more, learning, having a mentor, learning from other people's mistakes, like the best way, I used to work in a library, read autobiographies. They will make you feel so good about yourself when you hear about everyone's fuck ups. Whoops. Did I just swear I don't care. It's a beautiful day. Loosen up. Right? So that's how you know a manifestation is near. If you are learning and expanding your mind daily.

7.   You're taking care of your inner world

Seven day vegan challenge! Shout out to everybody who's eating to live. If you are taking care of the inner world, a manifestation is near. And that's through what you are eating. If you are eating to live, if you are having self care and you're not working yourself to death. You're actually going on a holiday, recharging.

You see, I knew a manifestation was near because where is my workspace? This is not a job. What I'm doing is not a job. I don't have a job. I've got a lifestyle. I just make videos and go to the beach and stuff, and then sip mango juice full of vitamin A. So my skin keeps glowing and glowing.

Okay. That's how to tell a manifestation is near. You can't control what is happening out there, but you can definitely control what you put in your mouth. You can definitely control if you are breathing in that good ass prana or not deep divers. You see, once you take care of the inside, the inner world, the outer world will take care of itself and you will start to manifest anything you desire.

You there, who says, I want this and I want that. No, don't want! Realize you can have it when you work for it. You can have it when you realize you already have it.

Chapter Forty Two

____

8 Life-Changing Affirmations For Success, Wealth And Happiness

That one friend who's always saying their affirmations and you get tired of hearing them. You're like, please be quiet. And then the moment you realize, wait a minute, wait a minute, those affirmations are actually working out for them. And you're like, hey, what did you say again?

Do you say affirmations? Do you believe in saying affirmations? I do. Because I've seen them actually work out for me.

Every single day I'm saying affirmations and that's why I'm living my best life. I'm about to share with you eight life-changing affirmations for success, wealth and happiness. Look, the cat down the road is already saying it's affirmations.

Your words have power. Every single day I'm speaking what I want into existence. The universe works in my favor.

Let me share with you what's helped me along my journey. The affirmations I say every single day that have helped me to live my best life. Now why are affirmations so powerful? What is an affirmation? An affirmation is a statement you say to the universe, you proclaim to the universe. And if you keep repeating these affirmations, they will manifest. Affirmation emanates from the Latin affirmare, which means affirmation. To make steady or to strengthen.

So any time you say an affirmation, you are strengthening your intention. Your words have power. If you say something enough, it will manifest. Now let's take a look at these affirmations.

1.	I am responsible for the energy I am bringing into this space. And I will leave it better than I found it, than I met it.

That's what I say every single day. And it has helped me to attract more success, more happiness, more joy. And more wealth and more love. I am responsible for the energy I bring into this space. When I'm making videos, I'm taking responsibility for the energy I share with you. No fear, it's only pure love vibrations. I'm only here to uplift you. I'm only here to help you grow. I'm only here to help you become your greatest version.

I could pull you down. I could say really nasty things about you. But that wouldn't be friendly, would it? And it wouldn't help me either. When you take responsibility for your energy, you will change your life. Because we are energy.

So every single day, I affirm to the universe: I am responsible for the energy I bring into this space.

If you see someone, send them some good energy. Even if you don't know them, say hi, how's your day going? Right now, you are actually spreading good vibrations everywhere. And they will return to you. I am are the two most powerful words in the universe. Because whatever you put after that, you will become. I am!

In ancient times, in the mystery schools, in Egypt. Sages would ask the divine creator, what is your name? And the divine creator would say, I am that I am. I am is such a powerful phrase. But it's what you put after that, that matters. So when you say I am responsible for the energy I bring into this space. Now it's all on you. Because for the first time, you are realizing that you can affect everything around you. And also within you.

2.	I am ready to not be reactive, but instead be proactive.

Are you somebody who's always reacting to people and situations that don't serve you? They're getting on my nerves, Ralph. When you can realize it's not about being reactive, it's about being proactive.

If there is a negative person in your life, who is not serving you, instead of reacting. Learn how to be proactive to say actually, I'm not going to allow this person to control the way I feel. I'm not going to allow this person to steal my happiness. That's proactive, right? That's when you are being proactive. Reaction and being reactive is saying, oh, they did this to me. They did that to me. I'm going to do this to them. So every single day, I say this: I am ready to not be reactive, but instead be proactive. And that has helped me attract success, wealth, and happiness.

3.   I am ready to invest in the tools that I need that can help me become greater.

I got a YouTube Gold Award. But I wouldn't have got a YouTube Gold Award if I didn't invest in my dream. We have to realize we need tools to help us become our greatest version. We need to invest in tools, the equipment that we need.

I had to invest in a camera. I had to invest in a microphone. I had to invest in a laptop, a PC. All of that costs money, but in return, I received even more abundance. Are you ready to put that money up for your dream? Are you ready to invest in your passion? If you are, then say this. I am ready to invest in the tools I need that can help me become greater. And that will help you in turn attract more success, wealth, and happiness.

4.   I am ready to no longer be controlled by other people's opinions.

I say this as soon as I wake up. I see too many people caring so much about what other people think of them. Stop allowing people who do so little for you take up space in your mind. When I say this affirmation to the universe, I am ready to no longer be controlled by other people's opinions, I start to ask myself, Ralph, whose opinions actually matter? Whose life is this? Then I realized, only my opinion matters.

How you see yourself is more important than how other people see you. Your opinions of me, didn't make me. Therefore, they won't break me. Your opinion of me does not cut me a check. Right? So say the affirmation and I guarantee you, you will become happier, wealthier, and more successful. You have to stop caring about what other people think of you. They aren't you. They're not living your life.

Only be concerned with what you think about yourself. And yes, we can listen to what other people think of us. Sometimes, they can help us. But we have to remind ourselves, it's all about how we see ourselves. Stop waiting for other people to validate your existence. For goodness sakes, deep divers, realize your value is internal.

5.	I am ready to improve my health.

I went from rags to riches. No, I was born rich. Because I woke up with a whole bunch of grapes in my mouth. 7 Day Vegan Challenge. Shout out to everybody who is actually on the road to eating to live. On the road to improving their health. I say this every single day, I am ready to improve my health. I am ready to go to the next level of health. Mentally, physically, and emotionally. And spiritually, of course.

You see, a lot of us, we don't pay attention to our health until it's too late. Then we're like, oh Ralph, pass me the grapes. Pass me the kale. Full of antioxidants. No, prevention is better than cure. So I proclaim to the universe, that universe, hey, I am ready to take my health more seriously. I am ready to become healthier. I'm ready to eat better foods with more nutrients and live enzymes. And I guarantee you, once you start to change your diet, when you are eating healthier foods, You will attract more wealth, because health is wealth.

6.	I am ready universe, to let go. And trust you.

Trust the process. It's not here yet. And now you're looking a little bit shaky baby. You see, I've learned how to become patient. How to be patient. To realize that you don't get it when you want it.

You get it, when you are ready for it. You get it, when you are worthy of it. A baby is in the womb for nine months. You can't rush the process. A cake has to be baked at a certain temperature. For a certain amount of time. If you do it any sooner, it's not going to be good. Say: I'm ready, deep divers, to let go and trust the universe. I know that there are forces, benevolent forces, working in my favor. Every single day.

Every single day the universe is helping me. Because I'm letting go. I'm surrendering. I'm saying, actually, the universe's plan for me is better than my own. I'm trusting the process. Even if you're not there yet, it doesn't mean that you never will be. So don't be so impatient. That's what I remind myself every single day. I'm like, Ralph, be patient. Good things are heading your way. Then I just get a bunch of grapes.

So I am ready to let go and trust the universe. I am ready to let go and trust the process. Life is a process. What is more important than the destination... is the process. It's the traveling. It's not about getting there. It's about how you feel when you are traveling there.

7.   I am ready to venture into new frontiers of learning.

I'm ready to expand my mind. I'm ready to read a book I've never ever read before. I'm ready to go to the next level of learning. You see, I've graduated already. But nature was like, Ralph, you don't know anything. So I'm like, okay, nature, teach me. Because enlightenment is knowing how much you don't know.

I don't know anything. That's why I'm wise. Like Confucius said, the great philosopher. True wisdom is to know the full extent of one's own ignorance. So when you can say, actually, my cup is empty, my mind is empty. Now you can learn more. If you think you know it all, you stagnate. You stop learning. I'm an eternal student, deep divers.

I'm learning every single day. I've read over a thousand books on psychology. And I'm still reading more. Why? Because I have a hunger to learn. Like Warren Buffet said, the more you learn, the more you earn. So when you can say these affirmations, I'm ready to venture into a whole new frontier of learning and higher wisdom and knowledge. You will attract more wealth, more success, and more happiness. If you don't know, deep divers, now you know. Now you know!

8.   I am the work-in-progress universe and the masterpiece at the same time.

I say this every single day: I am the work-in-progress and the masterpiece at the same time. I ain't no saint. I'm a wizard. I'm also human. I'm work-in-progress. I'm also a masterpiece. So when you can realize that it's okay to be human and brilliant at the same time. It's okay to be flawed and flawless at the same time. It's okay to be perfectly imperfect.

You see, a lot of us, we are so hard on ourselves in this matrix. It's never ever good enough. You didn't get the great grades you wanted in college, right? So now you're still stressing over it. You don't have the job you want. You're not where you want to be at in life. You think you're falling behind and everyone is moving so far ahead of you.

I've learned how to forgive myself. I've learned how to love myself. I've learned how to realize that actually, Ralph, you're doing better than you think. Be gentle with yourself. You're doing the best you can. Learn how to forgive yourself. When you say this, I am ready to be the work-in-progress and the masterpiece at the same time. You will attract wealth.

More wealth because you are already rich. More happiness and more success because you are saying that actually, I'm going to work harder on myself than on my business. Working on myself every single day. It doesn't stop because I have a lot of things to work on. So do you. So does the cat down the road. That's how you become your greatest version. That's how you are becoming, ING, your greatest version.

It never ever ends and that will help you live your best life. When you can take an honest look at yourself and say, actually, I need to work on this about myself. Sometimes I react to people. I need to be proactive. Now, you are in the process of becoming your greatest version and you will attract everything you need.

Which is your favorite affirmation?

Chapter Forty Three

12 Secrets To Attract Anything With Your Mind

So I've actually done it. I wake up every single day seeing what I once thought about now right before me. And it feels amazing. Just a small seed, one small thought, I'm living the dream, but it hasn't always been easy. And I'm gonna share with you what I learned along my journey.

1. You have to know your design.

I see time and time again, many people say, I want this, I want that. But were you designed for that? Peacocks wanting to be gorillas and gorillas wanting to be peacocks. It's not gonna happen. So for so long, I was like, I want this, I want that. No, I can't have it because I wasn't designed to have it.

It's not about attracting anything with your mind. It is about attracting your greatest potential. And that is what people who have attracted with their mind realize. They know their needs. You have to know your needs. What did I come here to do? What was I designed to do on this planet? And I found it because one day I just realized I was talking to a friend for five hours and I still had energy. I love talking. I love being in nature. I love waking up every single day knowing I can do whatever I want. Go to the beach, go hiking. But I honor my design. And that's why I have attracted anything with my mind because I am attracting what I know I already have. It's not about saying I want, it's about visualizing yourself already having it.

2. Words are everything.

In a lot of ancient texts, they talk about how in the beginning was the word. Word is bond. Whatever you say, you become. What is the most powerful statement? I was, I am, or I will be. Which one? Think about it. I used to think it was "I will be." Then I used to actually think, wait a minute, I was so great once.

No, "I am" is the most powerful statement because I am pulls you back into the present moment. It allows you to attract. If you say I am good enough, you start behaving like you are. If you say I was good enough once, you now start to doubt yourself. If you say I will be good enough in five years, what are you doing right now but distracting yourself from your highest potential. So I always am very mindful with the words I use.

I say I am amazing. I am all of these uplifting words and as I use them right here in the now I start creating my reality and attracting my highest potential.

3. Seven day vegan challenge.

There was a time when I used to reach into my pockets and there was nothing in there but pieces of paper. So I learned a secret. You can actually eat like a billionaire. And it's really simple because just think if you are a billionaire, what do billionaires eat? Maybe some beautiful organic tomatoes. Well, I've got news for you. They aren't that expensive. You can go to the farmer's market, get the most delicious tomatoes in the world, get the most delicious mangoes in the world, get the most delicious guavas in the world. You can eat like the richest man alive, like the richest woman alive. And then you start to realize, oh, I get it now.

Health is wealth. Haven't you Googled the price of a heart attack? I used to work in a hospital. It's expensive. A lot of people when it comes to splurging on healthy organic food, that's the time so conveniently they don't have money. Oh, it's too expensive. Wait until you see these medical bills. So I started to attract anything with my mind by not being so stingy when it came to eating amazing plant-based foods. I invested in my health.

I don't care if it's $100, I'm gonna buy it. Why? Because health is wealth. By me eating that hemp, I am gonna attract abundance because I'm gonna feel so recharged, so energized, and so revitalized. Health is wealth. It starts with the diet. We attract what we eat. Junk in, junk out. Wellness in, wellness out. A different mindset.

4.   Have allowing thoughts

That's the fourth secret I learned along my journey. You see, so much is floating in our minds. A lot of us, we have goals, we have dreams, we have aspirations, and then we see that we haven't even tidied up our room.

I said do away with goals for me. It was more about creating a theme. When I first started to share with the world, I said, I wanna, woo, breathe in that good-ass prana every single day. Come into nature, do whatever I want. That was the theme. My goal wasn't to inspire millions of people.

No, it was only to have fun doing what I was doing, and that's still happening. A different mindset happens when you realize the secret to becoming your greatest version is when you have thoughts which are allowing. When you have thoughts which are allowing, you allow greatness to take shape. If you have thoughts which prevent you from becoming your greatest version, it's gonna be hard. You see, so many of us, we have thoughts, we have thoughts which go against us. We have thoughts which go against us. We've got distractions. Some people were just walking along there, but my thoughts, which are allowing, are like, we've got a video to do, we've got the birds out, and it's a beautiful day. You can't stop the rain. And you can't stop the sunshine. It's a mindset.

Change your thoughts and you change your world. We've heard this time and time again, how do we do it? I started to realize this. It's a choice. This thought says, I can do it. And this one says, I can't do it. Most people say, I can't do it. And they wonder why they can't do it. Some people haven't done it yet, but they say, I can do it. Thoughts create reality, a subjective reality. They influence us in ways unimaginable. So it starts with a different mindset. To have a different mindset, you have to start thinking differently.

If you are thinking like how everybody else is thinking, you will only go as far as them. You don't wanna be lost in the crowd. It's no fun. And that was me along my early journey. Just thinking what everyone else was thinking, my life wasn't going anywhere. Then I realized it was because I was not able to think outside of that limited mindset.

To become more expansive in the way you think, you have to begin to allow more expansive thoughts, which means you have to begin to change your focus, your attention, but more so what you are tuning into. I started to read more, I got a mentor, researched around what it was I wanted to do. I studied the lives of highly successful people.

Then I realized what made them attract that amazing life for themselves was their mindset. They thought differently. Everybody around them told them they couldn't do it. And that's why they did. They had perseverance, determination, consistency, but more so passion, because passion is the catalyst which helps us manifest our true desires. And look at it like this, that thoughts can take you to places you have never gone before, but thoughts aren't enough. I realized, which I'll come to later, you need action, radical action.

5.   Priming.

Priming is how to attract anything with your mind. It is how to attract your highest potential. What is priming? Priming, for example, I'll give you an example of priming. Think of a green crayon right now, got it? Great. Think of a green flower. Great. Now think of a fruit. You've thought of a fruit. Great, what is it? Avocado, fantastic. How did I know it? Because our mind, our subconscious mind puts things in categories, sometimes according to colors, shapes, sizes, right? It links things together. So think of the yellow sun, think of a fruit, you probably say banana.

But subconscious associations. So how to use priming in a very practical way, how I started to do it was, I remember a long time ago, walking into a bookshop and it was before I had written my books, I was starting out. I said, give me the best pen you have. They gave me a Parker pen, okay? All of a sudden, I had even more passion to start writing because I was priming my subconscious through this pen that I have the best pen in the world, which will mean I will write the best book in the world.

Turquoise, this is priming. Turquoise is a symbol of royalty, prosperity, good fortune. So every day, every single day, when I look in the mirror, I see this turquoise, it reminds me that I can do anything and I can attract anything. Subconsciously, because certain times you just walk past the mirror and trip up on all of those clothes you need to wash, right? But subconsciously, it goes into the subconscious.

Our subconscious mind works through imagery and that is how to prime your brain. For example, certain people, they've got pictures of their children on their fridge, that primes their subconscious mind to give them a hug every day, okay?

6.　　　　Radical action.

You're reading a lot and that is fantastic. But action is the next step. To achieve your goals, dreams, aspirations, you've got to start moving your butt. Most of us don't want to step into radical action. We only want to talk about it. Don't talk about it, be about it.

I don't really talk about what I'm gonna do, I just show you the results. I never wanted to be that person who was just talking about, oh, I'm gonna do this, I'm gonna, just do it. And it's a lot harder just to do it because now you've got to go into the trenches. You've got to start being creative. You've got to put down the books and start testing yourself on what you've learned.

Radical action is everything in terms of attracting with your mind because thoughts can only take you so far. Certain people, they've never even read books on the law of attraction, yet they have attracted everything they need. In essence, they have attracted their highest potential.

7.　　　　Attract anything mentally.

I've spoken about the seven hermetic principles, which are mentalism, everything is mental. Correspondence, how you are feeling inside is what you will attract outside.

Polarity, in this universe you have hot and cold, yin and yang, masculine and feminine. Gender, in everything you see there is masculine and feminine. Rhythm, everything has a rhythm to it in this universe. Vibration, everything is vibrating. Everything is moving. Quantum physics. Cause and effect, what we do now echoes on into eternity.

It goes back to Egypt. Tehutti wrote down those seven hermetic principles. Certain people now refer to them as the Qabbali. Sacred wisdom that will help you attract with your mind. Because if you don't understand and overstand how the seven hermetic principles work, you will never attract your highest potential. Because we think if I think about something, I will get it. No, there is a rhythm to when you will get it.

There is a vibration to when you will get it. And you have to ask yourself, have you put in to get back? Have you planted the seeds to now enjoy the fruits of your labor? We never attract what we want. We always attract what we are. And that's what's helped me along my journey. See, most people who talk about attracting only talk about one principle of the seven hermetic principles. Law of correspondence. Just think about it. No, you forgot about polarity, rhythm, vibration. That's why you can't attract anything.

You can only attract your highest potential. And it frees you because you stop competing with other people and then you realize I am in a league of my own. And that's really how to attract anything with your mind.

8.   Simplicity is everything.

So many times in life, we complicate things. We make things harder than they have to be. And I learned this because there was a time when along my early journey, I was a bit of perfectionist. I was a bit of a perfectionist. Perfectionism will make you doubt yourself, make you not trust yourself. Give it your best, that's all you can do.

But don't hate yourself for it. So I started to realize that simplicity creates effi-ciency. Efficiency creates productivity. Productivity creates creativity and creativity creates connectivity. So because I started to simplify everything, a practical way to do this is focus on one thing at a time. A lot of us have a lot of priorities. We don't have a priority in our life. We don't really know what we want because we don't know our design. You've got to know your design, focus on that one priority and you will manifest it.

9.   Have concentrated focus.

Concentrated focus is everything. You have to know what you are distracted by. I know sometimes I hear a song and I'm like, I'm distracted. I'm not going to do what I set out to do today because I'm just listening to a lot of low vibrational music and it's cool. Sometimes you just let yourself go, but don't make it a repetitive day-to-day thing you do. You've got to know what distracts you.

Concentrated focus is where you focus on what makes your heart smile. Most people don't attract what they want because they're not doing what they love. They know they're not honoring their design because they go to work, they work in places which don't bring them anything. In fact, they work in places which rob their energy, their precious life force. What helped me get it back? I said, I have to come to nature. I have to start rewriting my story.

I have to start changing what I think reality is. I began to mold my reality by concentrated focus. I'm just going to do this today. One thing, don't overwhelm yourself. That's why most people are slipping and sliding and they're not even ice skating, but it looks like it. Whoa! Keep it simple. Focus on one thing every single day and you will see how it grows. That's what's helped me along my journey. Wake up in abundance. I'm living the dream right now.

10.   Create as much as you consume.

As soon as you wake up, ask yourself, am I just going on the computer or am I just watching the television? You're consuming so much, but what are you creating? Are you working on your business, on your vision, on your dream, on your goal, on your aspiration? Or are you just eating popcorn, watching TV?

It's about the law of exchange. You create as much as you consume. That's the perfect equilibrium. That's what's helped me along my journey. I love watching other people's videos. I love supporting people. At the same time, I'm in that process of creation because I know if you don't bear fruit, you will wither away. You have to find a creative space. That's how to create as much as you consume. Find the right environment. That's what's helped me along my journey.

I create in nature. I create in feng shui environments where the energy just flows around very freely.

11.   Ignore people who don't believe in your dreams.

It doesn't mean you have to run away from them, but just don't take everything they say to heart. Realize many people project their own version of reality onto you. They say you can't do it because they didn't do it. They missed out.

Don't make them make you miss out. They had their time. It's too bad. And along my journey, I was around a lot of people who were saying, it won't work out. Just go and do this, get a regular job. And I did, but then I realized I wasn't going anywhere because I was listening too much to people who weren't on the same frequency as me.

I started to look at their diet and realize, okay, they don't even care about animals the way I do. So why am I taking advice from them? When you start ignoring people and start listening to yourself, you're well on your way to attracting anything mentally.

12.   Be around the right energy

This is where being in a loving relationship is so fantastic. But a loving relationship, not someone who drains your energy, but someone who's there to support you in helping you become your greatest version.

A friend who's not there to distract you, oh, let's go to the club, get you drunk and now you're all over the floor. Get up, right? But a friend who actually gives you information to help you go to the next level. A parent who doesn't discourage you, but encourages you to go to the next level.

It's a choice who we surround ourselves with. Are you listening to someone who's just talking, but they're not giving you anything, telling you how to improve your life? I listened to mentors. I had a mentor and his book was so long, but I knew after reading it, he helped me. The great Omran, okay? He helped me. So my mother helped me, right? She was a mentor. The birds were a mentor.

And then I found that I was a mentor to myself by living in my higher nature. And then once you surround yourself with the right energy, friends that encourage you, friends that don't judge you for being you, you get more confidence to actually be yourself, to move into what we call self-actualization.

And then you will see, you will naturally attract everything you need. When you have a loving partner that encourages you, that supports you, you go even further than you could ever imagine. When you get a friend who doesn't want to hold you back or wants to propel you forward, you go further than you could ever imagine.

Chapter Forty Four

How To Manifest Breakthroughs And Make Good Things Come

If you are reading this chapter, remind yourself to rest your mind. It is all manifesting. Rest it. Rest your mind. It is all manifesting. And I promise you, you don't have to worry. No, you don't. Because every little thing is going to be alright.

Breakthroughs come like crazy for me. And I want to share with you what's helped me along my journey to manifest and attract breakthroughs and make something good come your way each and every day for eternity.

Now, a lot of people come up to me. They're like, Ralph, thank you so much for your videos. Your videos have changed my entire life. It's that time for summer madness again. And I'm like, thank you so much. And they're like, how, Ralph? How are you able to be so consistent? How are you able to attract these breakthroughs? And why does it seem great things are always coming into your life and not mine? Well, I told them, you have to realize life is not something happening to you. It is responding to you, to your words, thoughts, and actions.

You know, sometimes it's hard for me. My life isn't perfect. This is not the breakfast club, the Brady Bunch. Real shit happens in my life. Ups and downs, trials and tribulations. Sometimes I want to pull out my hair. And I know sometimes you want to pull out your hair. Don't do that because it's so beautiful. Keep it in the bun though. Listen, let me tell you this. I'm an alchemist. What is an alchemist? Who is an alchemist? Because this is the secret to attracting breakthroughs every single day, even when things aren't going your way. The secret of alchemy is making the best out of the worst and never allowing external events to govern your internal condition.

I'm an alchemist. Regardless of the craziness, the chaos that's happening out there in this crazy, mad world. I realize I can choose how I want to feel. I can choose to do a little Samba, baby. I can choose to say peace, love, and ice cream. And that's what I'm doing. I'm not a victim of circumstance. I'm a co-creator of my own circumstances. And I didn't come all of this way just to stop. I came all of this way to keep on going. Breakthroughs will come like crazy.

This is what's helped me along my journey to manifest breakthroughs and attract something wonderful into my life every single day. A lot of people talk a lot. I want to do this. I want to do that. And you still haven't done shit. Because talk is cheap.

So I realized along my early journey to stop talking about what I'm gonna do and just do it. Don't tell me your plans. Show me the results. Every single day I'm stepping into radical action. I'm putting my money where my mouth is. I'm making sure that I'm in the act of doing something. Don't talk about it. Be about it. 10,000 hours. Are you putting in the work to live your best life today? I am. That's why I'm still here after all these years, looking 18.

How I made something great come my way every single day is by realizing that good and bad things are happening to me every single day. But what makes them good and bad? Good or bad is my attitude towards the experiences. What makes an experience good or bad is your perception of it. You see, even in a bad experience, if you can extract the lesson, it is no longer bad. It is your greatest teacher in disguise.

So when you're in a storm, dance, do a little samba, baby, and say, I'm going to make the best out of it. When things aren't going your way, say, hey, it's part of being human. There's an Egyptian proverb which goes like this. A beautiful thing is never perfect. I'm telling you this, because in 2006, I had a breakdown and I realized that, gosh, this is terrible. But you see, my breakdown was actually the catalyst for my breakthrough.

Sometimes you need to be at your lowest to rise to your highest. Sometimes a fall is what you need. A fall on your ass, that's what you need. Just to show the universe you can get back up.

You see, what's helped me along my journey, to attract breakthroughs and make something great come my way every single day is to realize this: Thank you. Those two words, thank you, are probably the greatest words you can speak every single day. Because gratitude shifts you into a higher frequency and vibration. You see, this is the secret to breakthroughs. Life is an emotional mirror. The whole world is an echo. And if you wake up saying, I hate life, nothing is going my way. The universe says, my dear, my dear, your wish is my command. It grants you everything you are saying.

So when you wake up and say, thank you, universe, the universe says, my dear, your wish is my command. It sends you more things to be grateful for in your life. That's how it works. Word is bond. Life is not something happening to you, it's happening for you.

You see, I'm not special. I just realize every single day, the only thing in my way is me and my limiting beliefs. Once I move out of my way, the breakthroughs can manifest. What is holding you back today is your bullshit story of why you can't do it. Tear it up. Ain't nobody got time for that. No, cancel the pity party. I'm not coming. I'm so sorry. You see, I've realized this. I embrace adversity. I embrace things not going my way. And I've learned to still say thank you. Because this is the lecture of life. And this is how you attract the breakthrough.

Every single day, see yourself there. Where do you want to be? A lot of people don't know where they want to be because they don't know themselves. So first and foremost, you have to know what you want in life. If you don't know what you want, someone else will choose a shitty life for you. If you're not living your life, someone else will live it for you. So you have to know what you want and be in your purpose and then see yourself there.

That life you want, that wonderful experience you want, you've got to see yourself there. And then you've got to act like it's already here. Feel yourself already there. And then you have to let go of your old self. That's the secret. You've got to let go of your old self. Shed that old skin and get some new skin.

In the words of Ralph Smart, feel alive. You have no obligation to your former self. That person you used to be, let it go. Let that old you go and embrace the new you where anything is possible. This is how to attract breakthroughs into your life. I have the imagining exercise and it goes like this.

Imagine you living your perfect life. What would it look like? How would you feel? Well, visualize that every single day because when you visualize, you materialize. Imagine you living your dream life. You have wonderful health, a beautiful relationship, and a wonderful family. You love what you're doing every single day in your work and profession. And keep visualizing that because whatever you focus on grows and you turn into whatever you're tuning into. This is how to attract breakthroughs. Let me explain.

In our body, we have DNA. We also have blood chemistry. And when you wake up in a bad mood, full of frustration, frustration and rage, no gratitude, bad body language, it changes your blood chemistry in a negative way. And that's why you can't manifest the breakthrough. However, if you wake up in euphoria, joy, even if it's not going your way, but you say, I'm going to choose to feel good because the emotion is the energy in motion.

All of a sudden, you will attract a breakthrough because it's changing your blood chemistry, DNA repair. And when you start feeling good, you start attracting better into your life. When you start feeling good about yourself, loving yourself, accepting yourself, you start attracting better into your life, including breakthroughs.

You see, a lot of people are settling, they're settling for a shitty, shitty, mediocre life. You have to stop settling for mediocrity. And you have to start taking the leap of faith to infinity and beyond. That's where you've got to go. And you have to say, today I am losing fear. Fear is the greatest energy vampire. Let it go and embrace this new you. And then start feeling worthy that you can live this life. Feel worthy that you can live the life you've always dreamed of. This is how to make breakthroughs come like crazy. This is how to make something good come your way. Feel worthy of it.

You see, universal law states, we never attract what we want. We always attract what we are a vibrational match to. So, this is the reason why you have to start embodying the feelings and the emotions of the life that you want. This is how to bring it closer to you in this present reality.

It's happening for me every single day. It's working out for me every single day. I can't lose, deep divers, because I'm not playing their game. I created my own. And in my game, there are no losers. Even if I fail, it's not a loss, if I can learn something from it. Switch off your phone, and you can hear more.

In the words of Ralph Smart, switch off your phone, and you will hear more. Take a break from your phone, and really connect within. And listen to that voice inside of you, because it's always guiding you to the right place. And then learn how to trust the timing of your life. There are seasons and cycles for a reason. This is how the breakthroughs start coming.

This is how to make something great come your way every single day. And I want to remind you of this, deep divers, 7-Day Vegan Challenge. When you take care of yourself, this temple, I wake up every single day with a whole bunch of grapes in my mouth. When you realize every 35 days, your body makes new cells from the foods you are eating, you are literally what you eat, everything changes. So this is how to attract breakthroughs. Stop eating from the dollar menu, and start realizing you are royalty, a king, a queen. And when you start putting life into you, you will get life out of you. I like that.

Remind yourself, in our darkest moments, we become illuminated. If you are going through a hard time right now, I'm here to remind you, don't give up. You didn't come here to go out like that. Your story is not finished, and it's okay to be the work in progress and the masterpiece at the same time.

Just remind yourself, the moment you want to give up is the moment the breakthrough is about to happen. If you can hold on that little bit more, the gates are going to be wide open for you. Happened to me along my journey. I was ready to quit. I was ready to quit, throw in the towel. Cat down the road said, don't do it Ralph, because so many things are going to manifest for you.

So many beautiful things are on the horizon, like peace, love, and ice cream. I want to remind you, the breakthroughs come when you work on yourself. When you heal these unresolved issues.

Take a look at the man in the mirror. Take a look at the woman in the mirror. You should be working on yourself harder than you work on your business. And if you have people around you right now who aren't doing anything for you, let them go. If you're not helping me evolve, you're a distraction. Everything is energy, and energy is contagious.

Make sure you have the right people around you, the right environment, and make sure you believe in yourself to feel worthy that you can live the fabulous life.

Your breakthrough is coming. Your breakthrough is coming. Your breakthrough is already here. Feel what it would feel like. Embody what it will feel like to be there already.

Chapter Forty Five

The 'Thank You' Secret

I get a lot of people writing into me saying, how do you attract anything? And I'm going to tell you, it is through the thank you secret. It is that simple.

I meet a lot of people who are very grateful every single day. And their gratitude mirrors other areas of their life. Their lives are more fruitful, more abundant. And I also meet people who are very ungrateful and that also mirrors certain areas of their life. They're not really manifesting, not a lot is going on. I'm always seeing this subtle correlation between one's level of gratitude and what one is attracting into their lives.

Every single day, I am waking up in infinite abundance and it's only going to grow more. So I started to realize with a thank you secret, if you practice saying thank you every single day, what happens? First of all, those words are higher frequency words. Thank you makes you... Thank you for what? Okay, now you have to appreciate what you have.

A lot of people say I want, I want. When you say I want, you are sending a signal to the universe that you don't have what you want. Therefore, you will always be in lack. Saying thank you, which is part of the thank you secret to attract anything, what happens? You now appreciate all the blessings that you do have. I'm thankful right now. Then I say, wait a minute, I've got this beautiful turquoise on. I actually woke up today. Did you say thank you today that you're even alive? Okay, you're still sleeping.

Are you alive? Get up. Okay. If we look at this, the thank you secret teaches us that people who feel more appreciated always do better. When you tell someone thanks, you pay them a compliment. They do so much better. We need that support. Have you ever been around someone who's just like, thank you so much, you're just so amazing. And all of a sudden you're like turning into Superman or Superwoman. Out of nowhere. Nobody saw it coming. But that's what happens when you have the right support behind you. So I started to realize with the thank you secret, I uplift people, I inspire people. And therefore people feel better about themselves.

So that means they also respond to you in a better way when you start showing them gratitude. And this now makes your connection even stronger, better, and deeper. People always do better when they feel loved and appreciated. The thank you secret taught me that just those few words can do so much. It's got a powerful, long-lasting impact. On whoever you say it to, even yourself. Thank you so much for these beautiful strawberries. A long-lasting impact.

Most people don't have time to say thank you. And if that's you, what's your life like? Take a look at it and you will also see that there is a pattern between your level of gratitude and what you are attracting into your life. Just a small thank you to someone, showing them that they are somebody. They will never forget that. That might stay with them until they're 80 years old. They'll be like, I remember you. You said thank you. We never forget people who touch our hearts. We never forget people who touch our hearts.

Now, the reason why a lot of people can't say thank you is because when you say thank you, the ego has to dissolve. Many of us, we are still in our egos. So if you were to say thank you to someone, it's like you have to now lay down your guard. You have to surrender. In essence, you have to be in the heart space. We never forget people who say thank you.

Just like you never forget a kind gesture, 7-Day Vegan Challenge, you never forget someone who buys you all of those blueberries and you're like, how could I ever repay you? And they're like, don't worry about it. And you're like, you're my blueberry friend right now. Let me just, let me just give you my car. Just take my car, go for a spin. You see what you just attracted? Just because you bought that person blueberries.

Now, being thankful has to come from a very genuine place. And when it does, it can be one of the most powerful acts in the world to help you attract your deepest desires. The thank you secret taught me that it gives you a good heart. It gives you a good heart because once again, it keeps the heart light. Our heart is very heavy when we are in the ego, when we don't want to uplift anybody. We don't want to admit that someone has helped us along our journey. We want to take all the credit for it.

I'm so thankful to my mentor, to my mom, to the cat down the road, to certain friends, but more so to you, beautiful deep divers. And that's what keeps me in the heart space. You've got to be careful of moving to the ego because that's when you begin to move away from the thank you secret. It keeps you humble.

I've met people, I know a lot of superstars. You are a superstar, right? And a lot of them are like, Ralph, I watch your videos. And I'm like, wow, I just found out Prince used to watch my videos. So I'm like, oh my gosh, he's a legend. When people are grateful, it keeps you humble. When you are grateful, it keeps you humble. When someone says thanks to you, what comes to your mind? You're like, thanks as well. Okay.

So just by saying thank you, we can break down the boundaries and the borders we have created. There is a lot of separation on the planet. Separation comes from the ego. The ego creates separation. Through the thank you secret, we now start realizing we are all connected. Borders begin to break down and now we can really attract the truth. That we are all connected. What happens when you realize this? I've seen along my journey that when I focus on gratitude, on things I'm grateful for, on people I'm grateful for, I now end up attracting more of those things and people to be grateful for.

It's like a weird kind of cycle. I'm so thankful for my hand and then all of a sudden I get a whole load of strawberries in it. Thanks. That's how it happens. I say whatever you focus on grows. I'm so thankful that every single day, I never have to work a day in my life again. I'm set for life. Why do I say that so boldly? Because I've already seen it. I'm already doing it. I'm already living it. And that's why I keep attracting more of this beautiful abundance.

But it's not just about me. It can happen for you too. If you take the time out to say thank you. Right now, there's probably someone you haven't said thank you to. Say thank you to them right now. And then see what happens in your life. Many times, what happens? People open up to us when we say thank you. We make people vulnerable. You don't have to people please. But if saying thank you is coming from a genuine place, people will open up to you a lot more.

In a deeper way, people close up when you point the finger at them. When you judge them. When you don't show them appreciation. People open up when you show them appreciation. Just look at the comments. Right? Look at the comments of most of my videos. You're only going to see a lot of positive comments. Because this is the beautiful space we create on Infinite Waters.

I realized just by saying thank you, I started to attract more authentic people into my life. People who I could count on. I could trust. We could become vulnerable to each other. It goes a long way. It brings you closer to someone. That's a thank you secret. A lot of people are like, Ralph, I want to attract my dream partner. Learn to say thank you a lot more.

Happened to me along my journey. Saying thank you brings you closer to people. When you have no appreciation in your life, your life will begin to fall apart. Did you say thank you today? It costs nothing to say thank you. But the returns are so great. It's free to say. But the returns are so great. This investment doesn't cost anything. But the returns are so bountiful. So abundant. So, that's how to attract anything with the thank you secret. Don't underestimate the power of gratitude.

Chapter Forty Six

How To Manifest 33 Magic

The reason why the number 33 was so powerful in ancient mystery schools was because it's in correspondence to the 33 vertebrae spinal column. Right. So it's transformation, elevation.

How to manifest three, three magic. Well, let me just talk about sound syncing. Ever been thinking about something and then you turn on the radio and then a singer says the exact word you're thinking about. Oh, my gosh. Really creepy. Right.

I say that synchronicity is where your dominant thoughts align with your life and become your dominant experiences. That's why sometimes you're thinking about a fruit and then someone walks in the room with a T-shirt saying banana. Wait a minute. I was just thinking about bananas. That's what happens. Right. Sometimes you meet a random person. But guess what? You find out they're not random. They're actually an old family member.

Three, three magic is all about realizing that word is bond. Right. Many years ago, I went by the name of Kemet Prince One. Now, if you're a deep diver, you should know that. If you're not, don't worry about it. Right. And that was powerful because once you connect back to the ancient mystery schools of Egypt, it's powerful energy. But at the same time, I was keeping myself in a box because I was just at the one one stage. Right.

The 11th stage, which is the first gateway, then the two, two, then the three, three leading on to infinity. So it was great. It made me feel empowered to know all of these ancient secrets. But at the same time, the magic wasn't happening like it should. So I said, OK, walking down the ocean, I said, whoa, the ocean is super powerful. Infinite waters. As soon as I connected with that force, the force of infinite waters... game over. I manifested the three three. I manifested the three three magic, which is all about transformation.

No borders, no boundaries. That's why I connect with millions of people every single day, because once again, it's all about the names you use and the energy you embody. You see, once you change one area of your life, all other areas change. Right. There was a time where I used to feel really sorry for myself. Right. I used to be all tucked in bed. Didn't want to go out. Didn't want to see you. Definitely not you. But then one day. The sun shone on my face and I got inspired. And I said, it's time to go out. It's time to realize there's more to life. And as I changed my perspective, as I changed my inner experience, feeling better about myself. All other areas of my life became aligned to that.

You see, that's why I always talk about the inner experience as a psychologist, I'm giving consultations daily. I'm talking with people all around the world that you've got to take care of your emotional bank balance. Three three magic is about realizing how you feel. We never attract what we want. We always attract what we are. So it doesn't mean that if you think negative thoughts, negative things are going to happen to you. No, you've got to become an alchemist, a wizard.

Where if you're stuck in an avalanche, you use your wand to get the hell out of there. Three three magic is really about a higher level of who you are. Now, many times I talk about becoming your greatest version and people say, Ralph, wait a minute. We already are perfect. And I say, actually, you're right. We don't have to become anything. We already are amazing. We already are enough at the same time. Gosh, I love saying that at the same time.

That should be a meme at the same time. Windows has new versions every year. Every couple of months, they've got a new version out. Goodness gracious. Because you need to update yourself. You need to upgrade yourself. Let me upgrade you. Three three magic right now. This being the year of unity on the planet is where you're going to see a lot of content creators come out of the woodworks.

Right. That's what I'm seeing right now is the March 3rd Pisces. Pisces know what I'm talking about. Right. There's going to be a hell of a lot of content creation that's going to help humanity rise even higher to their limitless nature. Right. What else? We're also going to see that. Races are going to break down. The concept of race is going to break down even more in this year. And nationality as people begin to see the truth even more manifesting three three magic, which is what I call alignment magic.

You see many artists, a lot of people get stuck. Once again, wiping the trophy is biggest trap ever. My mentor said, look, don't rest on your laurels to manifest three three magic. You've got to realize once again, every day's a new year. Look right now, as I write this, it's New Year, you're probably just rolling out of bed. Probably drunk so much last night. Ate so much. You can't move. You see, that's how many of us live.

Look, I've got viral videos. I've got over 42 million views. Right. Over nearly half a million subscribers. But at the same time, it doesn't matter. It doesn't matter at all. Because once again, every day we're creating the magic is everyday magic. I'm not saying, gosh, yeah, look at everything I've done. That's how you get stuck. That's how you get trapped, because once again, you're resting on your laurels to manifest three three magic. You have to see that every day is a new start, no matter what's happened to you.

You can be anything once you start deleting the programs you have in your mind. Once you start realizing, hey, just as long as you are in alignment, you will be taken care of. All I have to do is just share. Right. I'm set. And that's all you have to do, too.

If you're a dancer, just dance. Don't worry about it. If you're an artist, just draw, paint and you will be taken care of. That's how three three magic works. You've got to be in alignment. The right people will find you when you are in the right place. And that's what I've seen along my journey. I know exactly who I'm connecting with. Right. Because once again, you know what time it is or what time it isn't. Right.

How the world is shifting to such a powerful place right now as we speak. But let me just tell people who are doubting themselves right now for the new year, because sometimes when you don't realize every day is a new year, you go with the program and you might feel inadequate. You might feel useless that your life isn't going according to plan.

Don't worry about it because I was just like you. There were days where I thought, goodness gracious, life won't get any better. What happened? I took a small step. I did a little bit every single day and I believed that things would get better. I know they did. They got tremendous.

Only through connecting with people who reminded me who I was. Your vibe attracts your tribe. You see, I'm not here just to make videos for everyone to say, oh, my gosh. No. I've already gone past that stage. Right.

I went past that stage long, long, long, long, long, long, long, long, long, long, long, long, long, long, long time ago. I'm here right now as a wizard to, once again, trigger. And be the catalyst for my former selves out there. Right. Because everybody you see is you in a different space and time. So once again, if you've got a crazy idea, share it, because it will probably change your life. That's what we call three, three magic. It's not about just doing what people want to hear. You've got to do it for yourself.

If people don't like it too bad, go and eat some grapes. And just realize that, hey, you're good enough. Your message is good enough. I was skating yesterday and someone said they wanted to get into content creation. And I said, look, your presence alone is enough. Let me repeat that. Your presence alone is enough. That is ultimately three, three magic. So go out there, share, have fun, dance around, and have fun with the cat down the road.

Chapter Forty Seven
____

How To Manifest Magic Money

Stay close to anything that makes you glad you're alive. Now, a lot of us, we open up our wallets and we see a piece of paper and no, a lot of the times it doesn't make us feel alive, right? It just makes us feel like, okay, I have some kind of power right now.

We have this idea, many of us, a belief system that money is negative, that rich people are evil and poor people are humble. So what I had to do along my early journey was reprogram my subconscious mind, because guess what? I've met a lot of very nice rich people and some pretty awful poor people. And guess what? I've met a lot of very unkind rich people and some super kind poor people.

Getting rich has nothing to do with money. It has everything to do with self-worth.

1.   Sell stuff you don't need

The first secret is what I call look around. Uh-oh, what are we looking for? An airplane? No, not that exciting. Go into your room, take a look around at what you have, right? Move the dirty underwear out of the way first, right? What are those? You're going to have a lot of those kinds of moments.

Don't worry about it. You're going to find something of value, right? You're going to find something of value that you can offer to your fellow human being. And once again, now you enter the law of exchange.

You see, a lot of us don't realize we collect so much junk and it's time to sell it. That's what I did recently, right? I had all of these camera lenses I wasn't using and they were really expensive and they were just lying there for years. And I said, light bulb moment, it's time to get rid of them, right? So once again, when we talk of magic money, I'm talking about manifesting money out of thin air, just like the fiat currency it actually is.

So look around at what's in your room. You got a lot of clothes there, I know, and you don't wear them. Now you can give it to a thrift shop, which is wonderful, or you can sell it on eBay or wherever you want to sell it, right? I always have this little joke.

A lot of us don't like money, right? And the people that attract the most money, love money, or are very neutral, the artists. But the people that absolutely hate money, their pockets are empty, right? Their pockets are empty. These are the kinds of people who say, money is terrible. And at the bottom of their page, please donate, right? That used to be me, not anymore. Now, I don't ask you for anything, don't worry about it. Okay, right? So sell stuff you don't need.

Just like George Carlin said, a lot of us, we've got a lot of stuff. And you will be surprised once you start selling things you don't use, right? Now you start generating magic money.

2.   Find something money can't buy

The second secret of manifesting magic money is what I talk of as, you have to find something money can't buy. For me, it's skating, it's surfing, it's sharing with the world, connecting with millions of people every single day. Money can't buy that, right? So once again, I've manifested magic money, which is energy, right? You are the money. There's a reason why they call money currency.

Look at it like this. A lot of us, we sell ourselves very short. Now, I used to work 12 hours a day, and I was getting paid peanuts. Now, I only have to work one hour a day, or even less, and I get paid more in one hour than I used to get paid in the whole 12 hours, right? How did I do that? Because I realized a very simple secret. Because money holds no intrinsic value, what they're paying you for is your labor. Your labor.

What does that mean? It means, for instance, if you say, I'm only worth $30 an hour, really? Really? Well, that's all you're going to get. If you say, wait a minute, I have a lot of talent, I know my worth, you can put the price up, right? When you realize you have something money can't buy, you start attracting, manifesting magic money.

3.	Purpose

Now, purpose is the third secret. I say, the moment I began to follow my true life purpose, I became rich. Thank you very much, right? I'm not talking about just financially, because I get tons of questions. How can I create more financial wealth? And I always say, that's not your problem.

You've got to take care of yourself mentally, emotionally, and physically, right? So, once you move in the direction of your true life purpose, you start manifesting magic money. A lot of us, look, we're on these social media sites, just wasting time. Oh, what's that over there? What's that? I don't know, but I've just spent the last four hours doing this, and well, what the hell am I doing? Terrible.

That was me, right? Sometimes it still is. Don't worry about it, right? But time is money for a reason. Because in that time, you're just browsing other people's lives and photos. And it's really cool sometimes, but what are you doing to move into your true life purpose, more so, become your greatest version?

4.	Money is linked to our self-worth, our health and our emotions.

If someone wants to put five million dollars into your bank account right now, well, you're going to say, thank you very much, right? If they were to take all the money out of your bank account, you're going to feel not so good.

So, once again, the external money governs our internal emotions. So, how do we override that? You've got to start becoming healthy without no money, without letting money, the numbers, the numbers give you self-worth, right? I meet people every single day who know their self-worth and I call them walking billionaires, right? Yeah, they're walking billionaires. No, they're not. No, they're not. They're priceless.

5.   Mastery

The fifth secret is what I call mastering your craft, right? That's what helped me along my journey. I've been doing this for a very, very long time. A lot of people say, gosh, that guy's still doing it. Absolutely, right? Because as a psychologist, I love helping people become their greatest version.

Why? Because I'm helping myself in the process. Now, when we talk of your craft, ask yourself, how much are you willing to invest in your craft today? When I first started making videos, right after I quit my job, I said, okay, I'm going to invest in a very expensive camera. And it was a sacrifice I had to make. I thought I was really crazy. But guess what? Years down the line, it's paid for itself. Because when you realize the importance of investing in your craft, you know the secret of all the greatest billionaires.

The money you earn goes back into what you're doing, right? A lot of the times when I get money, it just goes back into it, right? And then you manifest even more. But I don't worship money, right? I don't say, oh my gosh, it's money. I don't care, right? But it's the principle of self-worth to realize you came here to live in supreme abundance, right? Once you start investing in your craft, buy a new microphone, buy those new trainers, those shoes that will help you walk to different places.

Does that make sense? Of course it does, right? Buy that new software program, right? Go on that trip, which is going to give you a new lease of life in a nutshell.

6.   Sharing

When you can share everything you have, you start manifesting magic money. Now, just like you, I was guessing, is that really a secret of how people do it? Okay, I've got a story for you. Years ago, I'm a cinematographer and I'm also a graphic designer.

So I've been working in After Effects for years, right? But when I was first starting, there was a guy on the internet who was giving all his tutorials and project files away for free. Now, taking into consideration, each project file is probably about $100 each. And he had over a hundred of them for free, right? And because he would give his project files away for free, he would create such a wonderful relationship with his clients that people would just give him money, right? Because he had given away so much for free, right? He had given away so much for free.

So the more you share, the more abundant you actually become. A lot of people are hiding away their secrets and that won't help you out.

7.   Health is wealth, right

I didn't call it that, but that's just obvious, right? And when you realize the kinds of foods you eat are so important, you begin to realize a tiny secret. What is that? That it's not about the money. It is not about the money. Sometimes you see these billionaires, right? Same shirt, same t-shirt, same shoes, just like they haven't got any money.

Because once again, after you start manifesting money, you realize it's just a piece of paper. Once again, going back to the second secret, you've got to find something money can't buy. For me, it was falling in love with you guys, right? Being in a loving relationship. I put these over money, right? Because once again, they helped me raise my energetic bank balance, which helps me externally manifest my bank balance, right?

8.   Studying is everything.

I always say study, study, study, study. Oh yes, you gotta study. Because when I realized that just this information, everyday diving and diving and diving, it's helped me to create multiple streams of income, but also passive income. I give consultations every single day, but I could happily live off my videos alone. I could happily live off the books I make.

I could happily live by realizing I don't have to hunt for money. No, the money comes to me through wisdom. Give me wisdom over money. Why? Because with wisdom, I can always get the money, but not the other way around, right? So once again, I could go on and on about different secrets.

9.   Another bonus secret: money is linked into your mood, right?

Your psychological mood. When you are feeling very, when you have a lot of, when you have a lot of self-hatred, it's very hard to manifest magic money out of thin air. When you're just having fun, I always say the people that have the most fun attract the most magic money.

It's what I call effortless creation. So once again, realize the attitude you have towards money is the same attitude money has towards you. And that the more you study specifically in the area of your craft, that will help you as well.

For me, it's psychology, relationships, being a vegan. I promote that message, but more so I concentrate my focus. When you do one thing well for years, consistently with a heart connection to who you are connecting with, you cannot help but manifest magic money out of thin air.

Chapter Forty Eight

____

How To Manifest Money

Money, what comes into your mind when I say money? Maybe it's greed, maybe it's fear, power, freedom. When I think of money, I think of a tool, a means and not an end. And that's what's helped me along my journey. I see money as a collective belief system.

Money is currency, currency is energy, therefore we are the currency we are working for. We are the original money, we are the value. The intrinsic value within yourself is the true money.

How you feel emotionally, mentally, physically, this affects how you manifest money. I see money as a piece of paper and I treat it that way. I pass it around, I ride on it and I use it to wipe my butt because what's empowered me along my journey is to use money, not to become used by money.

To see that money does not have power. Money is neutral. We give money power and it's liberating because a lot of us worship money. And now I just see money as a slave to me. So I use it that way. I don't look up to money, I look down on money.

Here are seven principles which have helped me manifest money along my journey.

1.	Have fun

Being detached from the pursuit of money I have seen along my journey, I just manifest more of it. Because a lot of us, we are placing so much emphasis on getting it and that creates worry, concern, anxiety. So we end up losing energy. But this laissez-faire approach I'm taking these days is beautiful because I see that the moment you stop caring too much about money, then you step into the realm of abundance.

And that's what I say along my journey. I am money, don't worry about it. Do what you love, follow your passion and it will appear.

2.   Know what you want

Because a lot of us, when we have a concentrated focus on whatever we desire, it manifests. If you are unsure of what you want, what's gonna happen? It happened to me along my journey.

My head was all over the place and because of that, you dissipate your energy into different areas instead of it being concentrated into one place. And that's why I love doing one thing and doing it well, more so investing all my energy into that one thing. Invest in what brings you the most happiness and you will receive that same energy back.

What I love to do is see the storyline with money. For instance, someone wants a Ferrari. Okay, do you want a Ferrari? Yes, I want a Ferrari, but you don't.

You see, the universe doesn't respond to what we want. It responds to how we feel. So the person that really wants that massive supercar, that Ferrari, they are doing everything in their willpower to attract it. And they are having that synchronicity because synchronicity is where your dominant thoughts within your life, they become your dominant experiences. And what I've seen along my journey, you just have to know what you want, as simple as that. Know your needs.

3.   Attitude

Number three is all about the attitude we have. Some people, and that was me along my early journey, I used to say money is evil, money is negative. But no, ideally we have to see that money is a medium of exchange.

It's an illusion we've created. Once I changed my attitude to see that money is my servant, it now works for me because I am happy for people with money and I see that I came here to live in pure abundance. It's all a mindset.

How we see money is how money sees us. It's all about moving out of the poverty mindset, making sure we have everything we desire, everything we feel we are worthy of.

4.   Honoring your worthiness.

How many of us have passed someone in the streets and we've just said, wow, wow, wow. They're so beautiful. They're so handsome. They inspire me deeply because within them, you see something precious. You see something that money can't buy. When I'm skating, I am learning a new trick.

No amount of money can give me that. It takes hard work to reach that level of mastery and it's beautiful. But once you see that you are priceless, then you can manifest any dream you desire because you see it's all coming from you.

You are the source. You are what you are seeking. So a lot of people who know their true worth, these are the wealthy people because there is no price tag on them. You can't bargain with them. Can't give them that small change. No, they are priceless. And because of that, we place ourselves in environments which compliment our own energy.

5.   Gratitude consciousness.

I found it along my journey. That's why I love the love I receive from people. And I love giving it back because everything I am doing with my life is about helping people become the greatest version of themselves. In the process, I'm learning too because I don't have all the answers.

But when I'm connecting with my divine reflections, they are triggering and helping me remember who I am. So once we can appreciate and focus on what we have already instead of just complaining, a lot of people say, I want, I want, I want. But we have to see ourselves already there.

When you say to the universe, I want a bigger house. I want a million dollars. You are sending a signal that you do not have what you desire. Therefore, you will always remain in lack. When I land a skating trick, it feels like I am a billionaire. In fact, I am priceless because can a billionaire do that? Can a billionaire do what you are doing? That creative gift you have inside yourself, whether it's singing, whether it's drawing, money can't buy that.

So you have to be thankful for the gift and then you see it multiply.

6.   Letting go of limiting belief systems.

I've come to see that it's all BS: belief systems. And when we talk of manifesting money, which goes back to talents, the gift we have, it's all about passion. But more so to get that passion, we have to stop doubting ourselves. We have to see that it's all a test to see if we are who we really say we are.

Because what I always do along my journey is say that anything is possible. The only limitations I have are the ones I create for myself. Therefore, nobody is doing anything to me. I use words that empower me to say that I am worthy to live in abundance. That's my daily mantra. Thank you. I use thoughts which empower me. And right now I am letting go of thoughts and stepping into the knowing because thinking is an interference with our natural flow. And then I use actions. Words, thoughts, and actions.

Multiple streams of income. A lot of us are focusing and placing all our eggs in one basket. That's what I was doing. I was working in a school and I loved it. Helping people, helping the school children. It was fantastic. But at the same time, I knew the universe had a greater vision for me and a plan. And that I could do multiple things to generate multiple streams of income. And that's what I'm doing right now. I'm counseling people. I make videos, Google AdSense.

I'm a cinematographer. I rent out camera equipment. But more so, I have knowledge of self. Your true wealth is your wisdom. You can have a big house, a big car, but that's nothing if you don't really know who you are. Give me the wisdom any day because with the wisdom, I can get the money. With the money, I can't get the wisdom. So there it is.

CHAPTER FORTY EIGHT

7.   Radical action

One thing about the law of attraction is that it doesn't happen by thinking. It happens by moving because the body is the subconscious mind. I was sitting in the psychology lecture room and heard about Fritz Perls who said "lose your mind and come to your senses."

It didn't mean anything to me at the time. Now I understand it. I overstand it. I understand it. Because when you start stepping into the flow, start moving your body, get up early. Start exercising. Start eating beautiful plant-based foods, drinking fresh mountain water that will give you the energy to get whatever you desire. And realize even when you have what you want or what you've always dreamed of, there is always more because the universe is always about expansion.

However, once you say, I have it all and I am open to whatever the universe brings me, then you start to fly. And that goes back to that detachment. Let the money work for you. Don't be a slave to money. Let money be your slave because we came here to be free and being free is our birthright.

So I talked about being playful to attract money, abundance, wealth. So what I do along my journey is the abundance dance because you have to have fun. So have fun. I love to see my emotions, which is the energy in motion, as my bank account. So when I am feeling sad, I have no credit. When I am feeling happy, I have a high energy level. I am living in abundance because everything is connected and it works like that in the universe.

A great way to live that's helped me along my journey in terms of money is to always realize that you become super powerful when you are okay with being alone. Can you handle freedom? That is the question. You see, a lot of us, we say, I don't wanna work in a nine to five job. I want to be free. But then we are faced with an existential vacuum, what Kierkegaard talked of. Now we don't know what to do. That's what it was like for me when I stopped working in 2011 and started my own business. But now I embrace it. I love this alone time to create.

And that is the only way to manifest abundance, to form this intimate relationship with yourself, to see that what you have to offer the world is unique. Therefore, you have to place value on what you have to offer the world. The secret I've learned in manifesting and living in abundance is that whenever you create something which is of value, not only to yourself, but of service to humanity, then you will always live in abundance.

Some videos I made two years ago, people can find it in the archive and it's still valuable because there is life-changing information there. So we have to see that right now, there are two ways to live. Some people say, okay, I wanna sell my soul to become rich. But in the process, you destroy your soul.

So if you can make money helping people, putting value into their lives, it's a win-win because you manifest abundance, you also help other people manifest abundance. We have to see that, like Tyrese said, those that can see the invisible can do the impossible.

Dream big because dreaming big and dreaming small take the same amount of energy. My mom always used to tell me that if you keep watching the TV, the television, it tells lies to your vision, hey, that's their money they're earning. So what are you doing? And I have discovered the secret along my journey that you just have to create, create, and create.

That is how to manifest abundance. Be a producer instead of just a consumer. You're listening to your favorite musician, but what message are they putting in the lyrics to help you become the greatest version of yourself? Because otherwise, you are just supporting someone who is not even giving you anything back in return.

That's why I can listen to Bob Marley and all of these other great singers because they give me so much. But we have to see that once we start disconnecting from anything no longer serving us, whether emotionally, mentally, physically, then we start to live in abundance because it's all about seeing that this is all a game. This is all a massive game. And the only way to rise above it is to one, get angry at the game, two, play the game, or three, become a creator of your own game. And that is how to manifest your own unique reality.

For me, what I came to see is that don't limit yourself. See that it's all yours. Is it spiritual to be rich? That's what I asked myself along my journey. And the answer I've come up with is yes. Spirit emanating from the Latin spiritus, meaning to breathe. So I see that we are all spiritual beings having a human experience. So when we talk of manifesting abundance and money, I see that each one of us is a note in this universal orchestra.

I am a C, you may be a D or maybe an F sharp, but we all have a core frequency we are resonating with. And because of that, everything in our life is aligning to that core frequency. You see, the big point people forget about the law of attraction is that it is based on our core frequency. So that's why we have to see that certain people attract certain things because it's in alignment to their core frequency. I love free line skating, you may not. So you're not gonna attract that into your reality.

Many people ask, how come all the powerful people, all of those villains in those films, had all of the biggest mansions and lived the most lavish lifestyles possible. While all of the good people with the good hearts, they were living in poverty. We have to be careful about words. And that's why I don't get confused with words. I don't get stuck on words like I'm spiritual. Because for me, the universe doesn't care if you're spiritual, you are a source energy.

So the universe does not have favorites. Once you know how to hack the reality matrix code, that's what I'm seeing along my journey, you can live in abundance because the universe doesn't care if you want all the money in the world because money is just an illusion. You are the money. But a lot of us in the spiritual paradigm, in the religious paradigm, we are told that desire is a negative thing. We are told that wanting something is negative. Therefore, we fail to see that once you have a desire, you are now all about expansion.

Growing up and along my early journey, I used to see that desire, it had a negative connotation with it. Wanting something was bad. Just be grateful for what you have. Now I see the secret, that desire serves as the catalyst for your own expansion. And the universe is all about desire. That's how it was created in the first place.

A big bang. It's not just about being humble. It's about stepping into your true authenticity and asking ourselves, how are we spending our time every single day working on ourselves? Because once we love ourselves 100%, we start manifesting abundance because we don't wait for the world to love us. Yes, money is not perfect. And that's why I don't worship money. Because money is just an idea created by a group of individuals.

So we have to see that we can create a new form of money, a new medium of exchange. This could be where we trade our talents, bartering. But to do that, we also have to have the financial resources to bring that into existence. So it's all an attitude. And we have to see right now, we are living in a new earth internally. But if we wanna see that in our physical reality, for it to make a huge impact in society, then we have to step into radical action.

The same thugs and gangsters who are creating wars around the world, they are doing this and they are able to do this because they are stepping into radical action. So we have to see and ask ourselves what motivates them. And that is why I love working for elevation. It's an elevation for the human nation. Do you get my drift? We are the only species that has to pay to live, but we are supposed to be the most intelligent?

Once again, this is all a perspective. This is what's helped me along my journey. For you, it may be different, but we have to start putting ourselves out there. If you have a gift, look at YouTube, make a video, share it with the world, who knows where it will take you? Because other people, when you can start connecting with other people, they will help manifest your dream and your vision. Connect with those who remind you of who you are. And we are here in nature, using that money to wipe our butt.

Chapter Forty Nine

How To Successfully Manifest Your Dreams And Goals

What my mentor told me, he said, Ralph, once you make it, you must help other people get there. So that's what I'm here to do. Everyone has a dream. Everyone has a goal that they want to fulfill, that they want to achieve. And this chapter is going to help you out. You see, truth be told, you're going to have to be in the 1% to manifest your goals and dreams. Because you see, 99% of this planet, they settle.

They settle for mediocrity. They settle for a shabby ass nine to five that's not serving them. And if you truly want to manifest your specific goal or dream or vision, start thinking like the 1%. We've got a whole lot to talk about.

I've done it. People say, gosh, Ralph, I've seen you from back in the day and you're still going strong. Yes, I am. And I'm never going to stop because I found the blueprint to manifest a specific goal, dream or vision. I can't stop. I won't stop.

Where you are right now, you've got to be brutally honest with yourself. Are you achieving the goal or goals that you set out to achieve, or have you thrown that in the rubbish dump? Well, in this chapter we're going to pull that out of the rubbish dump and we're going to start successfully manifesting a specific goal or dream that you have.

A lot of people have big dreams, but then they get crushed, they get buried. And I'm someone who realizes that there's a formula. And if you follow this formula that I'm about to share with you, you too will successfully manifest a specific goal or dream that you have right now. So let me share with you what's helped me along my journey.

First and foremost, we've got to remind ourselves when we talk about successfully manifesting goals, a goal, a vision, a dream. A lot of people. They have a whole long list. And I always tell them. Start with one goal, start with one dream first. Don't overdo it. Don't go crazy. Like my one goal was just to help someone. That was it. That was it. I just wanted to add value to someone else's life.

So, that was a humble goal, but it served me to be where I am right now. You see, a lot of people have these grandiose goals and dreams like I'm going to save the whole world and free everyone. And that's fantastic. But give yourself a break. It's going to be hard for you to do that immediately. So I always say start small. Everything you do, start small and be consistent. The reason why I'm still here, is because I set one priority. And this is how to manifest a specific goal or dream that you have.

Don't have priorities. Have one priority. One priority every single day. Say this is what I'm going to lock in on. This is what I'm going to focus on. And you have to know what that goal is. That is key. You have to know what the goal is. You have to know what the dream is. You have to know what the vision is. If you don't, how on earth are you going to manifest it? You have to be specific. You have to have a fine tooth comb just to go over everything.

Remind yourself, don't overwhelm yourself. Start small. And it doesn't matter how slow you go, just as long as you go. The truth is, you can have as many goals as you want. Have as many dreams as you want. But the reality is a lot different. Because when you get into this world, people don't care about your dreams or goals. Well, maybe your mum or dad do. But a lot of the world, they've got problems of their own.

They have problems of their own. So you have to realize that first and foremost, be mindful of who you share your dreams and goals with. Because there are dream killers out there. There are people that you tell your goals to, your dreams to. And they put a whole load of negative energy over it. They're like, oh, that's not going to work out. No. It's going to be terrible for you. It's going to be bad for you. And now you feel discouraged. You're like, OK, I'm just going to stay in bed.

This is how to successfully manifest a specific dream or goal. Ignore everyone, including the cat down the road and listen to yourself. Listen to your intuition. What is it that you want? What is it that you came here to do? Don't allow anyone to get in the way of that. And you're going to have to be about action. You're going to have to say, you know what? Right now, I have to go out there. I know what I want right now. I'm going to have to go out there. I'm going to have to fall flat on my face and eat the dirt every single day.

That's what I did. I would wake up and make a video and realize, OK. This camera is not working. Fantastic. And it was hard to take in the early days of me just sharing with the world. There were so many problems occurring, but I didn't stop. I realized that I had to complete this mission. I had to fulfill this goal. I had to fulfill the goal. And this is how you start successfully manifesting a goal, a dream, a vision, whatever it is. You don't give up when things aren't working. In fact, you use that as motivation to carry you through.

If you think it's all going to be easy. You're in the wrong profession. Because when you're in the profession of successfully manifesting, successfully manifesting a goal or vision, expect things to go wrong. But it's your attitude that essentially determines the outcome. Have a PMA, a positive mental attitude. Every single day is when we talk of goals.

When we talk about successfully manifesting any goal or vision or dream that you have. Yes. Start with the number one goal first. Before you move on to the number two, before you even write down number two, make sure you're just on number one. Once again, one goal, one dream. Don't say, hey, I want to start this seven figure business.

Hey, I want to travel the whole world. Hey, I want to meet the woman of my dreams, the man of my dreams and a cat down the road. No, that's too much, too much. And this is why a lot of people throw all of their goals and dreams in the trash can because they overdid it. Start with one, one at a time, one at a time. And remind yourself once you've done that, once you have one goal, one dream.

Look at this. The word smart, right? I love this, here is an acronym, a powerful one, I love it. Smart: Be specific about what you want. Make sure it's measurable.

Make sure it's achievable. Make sure it's realistic. OK, and then make sure it's timely. So that's smart. And what's your last name, Ralph?

Right. So it's: Specific. Measurable. Achievable. Realistic. Timely.

OK, my goal every single day is to breathe in that good ass prana, baby. And also to raise the frequency and also to raise the vibration and also take that, take that, take that good ass energy I'm sending off the page. That's just one goal.

So when we talk about manifesting a specific goal or dream that you have, realize that. Your focus is everything. Whatever you focus on grows. And let me give you an example of what I did. Every single day I would wake up and just focus on abundance. Just focus on living the life that I'm proud of, that I love, that I chose. The more I would focus on this, I would start acting like it's already here. I would start seeing myself already there. I would start placing myself on the throne. And now we're here.

When it comes to manifesting a dream, turning that into a reality, when it comes to achieving a goal. Remind yourself you have to be your biggest fan. You have to be your cheerleader. You have to be your greatest friend because people aren't going to believe in you if you don't believe in yourself. If you don't support yourself. People can't help you if you can't even help yourself. Put yourself in position.

Know what it is that you have to do to get what it is that you want. I said, OK, I want to inspire millions of people. First of all, I need to buy a camera. I could use a potato, but that probably won't work out right. I need these tools and I'm going to buy these tools and I'm going to learn how they work. And I'm going to master it. And that's what I did with Infinite Waters. And that's the reason why I got a YouTube Gold Award. I had a goal to write a book, Feel Alive by Ralph Smart on Amazon.

Number one bestselling book. And how I achieved this goal was to learn from other authors. Like, OK, how do they write a book? What's the process? What's the structure needed? I was studying under authors. Mentors. And then I said, OK, I've got it. So I didn't say I can do it all by myself. I said, I'm going to ask for help when it comes to manifesting a specific goal or dream. Don't think that you can do everything by yourself. You're going to need help. You're going to need people who have already been there, done that, got the T-shirt like Ralph Smart. Do you know there are so many people out there who think they know it all?

I'm praying for you. I really am, because I don't know it all. I'm still learning. And that's the reason why I'm leveling up. There are people who could ask for help. They don't want to ask for help. But the people I see who are manifesting their goals and dreams are asking for help. They're studying under a mentor, a teacher. They're saying, actually, teach me, fill my cup. When it comes to successfully manifesting a specific goal, dream, vision that you have, you must take a risk.

You must realize that nothing good comes when you're in a comfort zone. All you will receive is everything you've always known. It's when you get out there, when you're uncomfortable, when you place yourself in the lion's den and eventually become a lion, start roaring and say, oh, my gosh, I've been battered and bruised and down and out. But I've learned something in this process. This is how you specifically manifest the goal, a vision, a dream. You must embrace failure. It's inevitable. You must embrace the hard times. It's inevitable.

You must embrace when things go terrible and they will. And you're going to want to give up and you're going to have to realize that's part of the process because the universe wants to see how bad you want it. You're going to have to realize as well that when it comes to manifesting a specific goal, when it comes to manifesting a specific vision, dream, realize every single day.

Once again, be specific, make sure it's achievable, make sure it's timely, make sure it's measurable, make sure it's realistic. Some people have unrealistic goals. They want to be the best violinist in the world. They've never ever played the violin. It's not going to work. Right. You have to honor your talents and invest in your talents and stop wishful thinking. I love this. Your future is created by what you do today. Right. Your future is created by what you do today. I love that. And this is so true that your future is created by what you're doing today.

Every single day when it comes to dreams, when it comes to manifesting a goal, you must plant the seed today that your future self will thank you for. You must plant the seed today that your future self can eat from. What you do today, it is what you do today. That matters because your future is created by what you do today. And therefore, when it comes to goals. Start now. Realize that it must be now. You must start now. Don't say, hey, I'm going to just party on the weekends. I'll start on Monday. It's too late.

Monday is already here. Tuesday is already here. Wednesday is already here. Thursday is already here. Friday is already here. Oh, my gosh. Then it's the weekend again. You have to make sure that you're once again in the 1% club. That means working on yourself, working on your visions, your dreams on the weekend. When everyone else is partying, you're locking in, focusing on what it is you want to manifest and getting out there because you're going to need time. And you're going to have to be patient because your dreams won't fall into your lap. No.

They will come to you when you have done the work. Your goals won't be achieved overnight. They will come to you when you have done the work and it's work. People say, well, it shouldn't be hard work. No. But it's still work. Even if it's smart work, it's still work. And it's hard work. And it's also smart work that you need. It's a combination of both people who are manifesting like myself and who are achieving goals and big dreams. We're putting in the time we're putting in the hours. We realize it's a marathon. We realize that actually there's no such thing as overnight success.

Rome wasn't built in a day. It's going to take a lot of time. When we talk about goals and how to successfully manifest a dream or a goal, remind yourself, deep divers, that timing is everything. Timing is everything. Trust the timing of your life. Now, that doesn't mean that you're passive and you just let things just flow by. No, it means that you are in the right place at the right time. That's what I was when I started to share in my back garden. I was in the right place at the right time because timing is everything. Timing is everything. And this is how to successfully manifest a specific goal, dream or vision.

Timing is everything. Make sure you realize this. Don't say, hey, I'll leave it until next week. You've missed the time. The time is now. It's now to do it, to become your greatest version and manifest the dream, the goal, the vision. I love this. If the plan doesn't work, change the plan, not the goal. That's fantastic. Sometimes people throw away their dreams and their goals. You know why? Because the plan isn't working.

It's not the goal that's wrong or the dream that's wrong. It's the plan that's wrong. And that has to be ripped up. And now you have to create a new one. Deep divers, if the plan doesn't work, change the plan, not the goal. It's now time for you to get smarter. Raise the frequency and find another plan. And this is how you can successfully manifest a specific dream or goal. Always remind yourself, you can change the plan. And I love this as well. A little progress each day adds up to big results. This is huge.

You know, once again, a lot of people overwhelm themselves. They're trying to do everything all at once, trying to fulfill all of these dreams, trying to achieve all of these goals. No. One goal. One dream. A little progress. Every single day will add up.

A little progress each day adds up to the big results, deep divers. And remind yourself that when it comes to successfully manifesting a specific dream or goal, realize why you're here, who you are, and why this is important to you. Once again, recognize who you are, why you're here, and why this is important to you.

Why this is important to you. Because you see, a lot of people don't manifest their goals or their dreams because they haven't actually answered that. They don't know why they're here, what they're here to do, or why it's important to them. Why is it important to Ralph Smart to inspire millions of people? Because I realize that that's the greatest gift you can give someone. Helping them along this life journey. Helping them along the way. Being a part of their life in a positive way. I'm like, yes, that's what's important to me. And this is how I started to successfully manifest this dream, this goal.

Chapter Fifty
____

How To Move Out Of A Scarcity Mind

So let's talk about the abundance secret. Let's talk about how to move out of scarcity mindset into a wealth and abundance mindset.

Do you wake up with a scarcity mindset? Well, after this chapter, that's going to be no more. Because we're in a world right now where a lot of people are realizing what's getting in the way of them attracting abundance into their life in all areas is a scarcity mindset. And a lot of people don't even know they have it. So we're going to talk about how to move out of that scarcity mind, the scarcity mind, and move into an abundant mind.

We came here to live in abundance. Wearing my turquoise piece. Sitting on my throne in the gold room. I came here to live in abundance. And I own it, it's my birthright.

But so many people have been programmed in this matrix to fail. They've been programmed in this matrix to always live in a state of lack. They've been programmed in this matrix to think that abundance is bad. Nothing could be further from the truth. And we're going to talk about the abundance secret and how to move out of a scarcity mind into a wealth and abundance mind.

The gold room, first and foremost, the gold room is not the most expensive room I've been in. Do you know what the most expensive place I've been in is? Mother

Nature. I've got over 5,000 videos in the heart of nature that you have not seen. I'm in nature every single day. You should be saying, oh my gosh, I can't believe you're in the heart of nature, Ralph. With your rich self. Yeah, because Gaia is rich.

There are so many people out there who have programs, beliefs, and ideas that abundance is bad. Abundance is evil. And this is the reason why they keep abundance away from themselves. They wake up wondering why their life is not changing. Why they're not living in abundance. And it's got everything to do with your attitude towards abundance.

I've heard people say, Ralph, people who live in abundance are evil. People who live in abundance, who take care of themselves, who like to be in nice places and eat nice food and chill with a cat down the road. These are bad people, Ralph. You should be poor. Because, blessed are the poor, Ralph. I'm like, who taught you that?

First and foremost, this is the reason why abundance is staying well away from you. You see, the abundance secret is to realize abundance is the natural state. I said, the abundance secret is to realize that abundance is the natural state on this planet. When you take a look around at nature, it is full of abundance. But someone has programmed you to believe that abundance is bad.

No, it is your birthright. Along my early journey, I also had a program that money was evil, that abundance was bad. That those people living their best lives on beaches, palm trees, sipping a mango juice, yeah, they're terrible people. And the really good people are the people who have nothing. I was programmed. Then I came across the abundance secret. And everything changed. And I started to wake up, all magical and fly, to raise the frequency.

I realized that abundance is our birthright. When you remind yourself, it's all yours anyway. You are supposed to be living in abundance. You know why? Because you are a god and you are a goddess. You are a king and a queen. You're supposed to be sitting on the throne. You're supposed to be living in a palace. You're supposed to be waking up every single day with a whole bunch of grapes in your mouth. Why do some people say abundance is bad? Because that was the greatest trick the inorganic ones played on you.

They told you that scarcity is a good thing. When you don't have anything, that's fantastic. No, you are supposed to realize that we don't own anything anyway. We are not the ones who own anything. We are only here for a brief moment in time in this life journey. And therefore, we are supposed to have the most fulfilling life experience. It's not about being infatuated with materialism and hope.

No, it's about realizing you are the wealth. You are the abundance. And you came here to have the resources to live a wonderful life. That means you've got to eat good. That means you got to feel good internally. That means you've got to feel rich. What does rich even mean? Realizing I create happiness. And this is the abundance secret. It's about the moment you realize abundance has nothing to do with money alone. It's got everything to do with how you see yourself.

You've got to realize abundance doesn't have something just to do with a Ferrari car or a Malibu mansion. No, abundance is your own self-worth. It's how you treat people. It's how you see yourself. It's all of these things. It's the energy that you have. Sometimes you meet someone and they have a poor spirit. We say, oh, that's a poor spirit. Why do we say that? Because they have nothing to offer. Abundance is when your spirit is rich. This is the abundance secret.

How to move out of a scarcity mind into a wealth and abundance mind. I found a pot of gold. Not out there, but inside here. Find the inner treasures that lie buried deep within you. And you will live in abundance forever. I said, find the hidden treasures that lie buried deep within you. And you will live in abundance forever.

So this man right here is on a yacht. If you're in a scarcity mind, you say, oh my gosh, look at him. He's evil because he's enjoying his life. I hate rich people. I hate people who have managed to get out of the matrix and hack the whole system and actually enjoy life. That's a scarcity mind. But if you say, wait a second. That's what we're all supposed to be doing. We're supposed to be having the most fruitful, soul-nourishing experiences. We're supposed to be realizing that we came here to live it up.

We came here to live it up. Anyone that tells you otherwise is lying to you. Anyone that tells you you came here to be poor is an enemy. You came here to have everything you need and more. The abundance secret is about realizing every single day you can have that. It's also about realizing money is energy. And that's what I realized along my journey. Wow, boy, did that change my whole life. When I realized that I don't worship money. Money is just a piece of paper. It's fiat currency backed by nothing. So I'm not going to worship money, but I do know that money is energy. That's why it's called currency.

The attitude that you have towards money is the same attitude it has towards you. You got some people who say I hate money. I hate abundance and they're always broke. You've got some people who say I'm open to receiving the energy. Because they realize money is energy. That's why it's called currency. So this is the abundance secret that's going to help you become your greatest version. That's going to move you out of the scarcity mind into an abundance mind.

Remind yourself. Don't think that because you have nothing, it makes you more righteous. Don't think that because you have no money, you're a saint. No, sometimes a lack of money is the root of all suffering. Do you know how many families have been broken up because of money? A lack of it? Do you know how many fathers and mothers never provided for their children because of a lack of funds? But do you know how many people who have helped their family out with the abundance secret? Oh, now you're listening.

Let me keep going, right? The abundance secret, move out of the scarcity mind into wealth and abundance mind. Once again, we've got to remind ourselves. When I talk about the abundance secret, I'm not just talking about money. I'm talking about feeling rich in all areas of your life, realizing I create happiness. And this is the greatest abundance secret. This is what has freed me.

I'm extremely happy because I know my worth and I'm living in abundance every single day. Okay, so we have to remind ourselves there are programs not serving us that keep us away from our true abundance. And once we delete them, we now move into our true abundance.

We now move into our true abundance, right? Once again, don't worship money. You know why? Because it's just a piece of paper. You are greater than money. And that's the reason why a lot of people who are manifesting abundance, they realize that it's just a piece of paper. The real wealth is me, you, raising the frequency.

Realize you can be on that yacht. You can have the most soul-expanding, mind-altering life trips. You can sail around the world. Because abundance is your birthright. Don't feel bad about living in abundance. Be glad that you woke up to the reality that this is how we should be living. A lot of people with abundance actually help more people than those that don't have anything. I'm one of them.

I'm making videos every single day in the heart of nature in the gold room, inspiring millions because I'm abundant. I can give. When I was poor, I couldn't give anyone anything. Isn't that something? Let's talk about it. The abundance secret, how to move out of scarcity mindset into wealth and abundance mindset. This waterfall here is the personification of abundance. It's a metaphor for abundance. Abundance flows. And this is what mother nature is showing you.

Abundance flows everywhere you look on this planet. Look at how that water is just gushing down the waterfall. It's amazing. That's what abundance is like. When you tap into the abundance secret, abundance flows. Scarcity stagnates. People who have a scarcity mind, they start stagnating. People who have an abundant mind, they start flowing. Oh yeah, they start flowing deep divers.

Health is wealth. Eat to live. Eat to live. Every 35 days, your body makes new cells from the foods you are eating. Realize you are literally what you eat. And I realize this, that part of the abundance secret was realizing abundance is also health. It's linked to health.

I've been making videos day in, day out in great health and that's abundance. Health is wealth. If I was eating junk food every single day, I would not be able to share with you deep divers and that wouldn't be good, right? So the abundance secret is realizing that health is wealth. And as you begin to eat to live, you also begin to manifest financial freedom, wealth, prosperity, riches, and abundance in all areas of your life.

Chapter Fifty One

How To Attract A Water Relationship

How to stop attracting a Coca-Cola relationship. A lot of people message me every single day. I get over a thousand questions, and about 50% of those questions are about relationships. And many ask, how can they stop attracting the wrong mate? So I'm gonna share with you what's helped me along my journey to move into water relationships.

So there is the Coca-Cola relationship, which is the toxic relationship, the karmic relationship, and there is the water relationship, which is about soulmates and twin flames. Now, along my early journey, all I was attracting was Coca-Cola relationships. And these are the 10 secrets to stop attracting a Coca-Cola relationship.

1.   We don't meet people by accident.

It's either a lesson or a blessing. So if you are in a relationship right now, ask yourself this, is this relationship a lesson or a blessing? If it's not a blessing, then it's a Coca-Cola relationship that you are attracting. So I realized that I was ending up in relationships where I was learning so much about myself. And that's why I was attracting this relationship in my life at this specific time, because I had lessons to learn.

Ever been around somebody who's in a relationship and they keep complaining about that person? And you're like, why the hell are you with them? And they're like, I don't know. Because they have lessons to learn. So once you learn the lesson solution, now you begin to move into the water relationship.

2.   You've got to stop blaming people.

Like whoever you are with right now, stop blaming that person. Or maybe you're single. Okay, stop blaming yourself. Stop blaming that person, because now you actually reclaim your power, thus pushing you further into a water relationship.

We stay in Coca-Cola relationships and toxic relationships when it's always tit for tat. You're always blaming each other. In essence, you are as bad as each other. That's why you both need each other.

Okay, so I realized this along my journey. And I was like, okay, I get it. The moment I stopped blaming that person for where I found myself, then I just realized I had the power and I was choosing to be in this relationship.

Someone asked, how do I know I'm dating a psychopath? That's a great question. But I always say, once again, you've got to stop blaming that person you are in a relationship with. You have chosen to be there. You said, okay, sometimes he gets angry. Once again, you are choosing to enter that contract because that's what a relationship is.

You don't have to be there. But if you are there, there are lessons to be learned.

3.   Intuition.

Ever walk into a room and get a sense that you shouldn't be in there because it's on fire? Ah, run outside right now. We meet people. They always say the first meeting sets off a lasting impression.

And I meet certain people and instantly I get a vibe about this person. Now, let's just say you want to cultivate greater intuition. You are going to keep meeting people who don't have your best interests at heart because you weren't intuitive enough. In essence, you are in the relationship for the wrong reasons. I was in so many relationships for the wrong reason.

Sometimes, I get it, we are in relationships because it's convenient. What I call relationships of convenience. Sometimes, you can't afford the rent so you've got to stay with someone. Sometimes, they look so good that you just want to wake up to their face but they don't make you feel good. Once again, you've chosen looks over feels. Okay, it's all about the feeling first and then the looks second.

So for me, it was about intuition to say, okay, is this a heart-based relationship? Do I feel it in my heart or do I feel it in my wallet? Do I feel it in my mind, my ego? You see, the Coca-Cola relationship is ego-based because what happens when we are in our ego? We defend, we attack. Defense and attack. We justify.

We prove. So to stop attracting a Coca-Cola relationship, ask yourself, is that all I'm worth? Do I have to always prove myself to this person? Don't they trust me? You're better than that and that's when you start to move in the direction of a water relationship. Now, intuition is everything. The more intuitive you get, you will ask yourself, okay, yeah, I get this vibe about this person. Is there any hope of evolution together? Yeah, there is. Great, then walk off into the sunset. Wonderful.

4.   Know what you want

The fourth secret that helped me to stop attracting a Coca-Cola relationship and start moving towards a water relationship? Is knowing what you want. Most people don't know what they want so they settle. They end up with the wrong person, which in essence is actually helping them learn more about themselves. And that's what happened to me along my journey. I didn't really know what I wanted.

I didn't really know what I wanted because I didn't even know who I was. I meet people every single day who say, I don't wanna be single, Ralph. So they end up with a person they're always complaining about. I say it's better to be single than keep tearing my ear off like with your complaining, right? Don't do that. So what helped me along my journey was to say, I've got to know what I want. But before I can know what I want, I've got to know myself.

So to stop attracting a Coca-Cola relationship, come into nature, baby. Start meditating more to say, okay, what is it I actually want from a relationship? What are my core needs? And is this other person providing me with core needs? More so, am I providing myself with my core needs? Because the greatest relationship you can have begins with yourself.

5.   Honor your needs.

Seven day vegan challenge. I realized that when I used to eat a lot of meat, I was going out with all meat eaters, which was fine at the time. And then when I was transitioning to become a vegan, moving towards a plant-based diet, my relationship was going through a rocky stage because I was trying to influence the other person to get them to eat like me and it wasn't happening.

And I get so many people messaging me saying they're doing the seven day vegan challenge and their partner is still on another diet and it's really difficult sometimes. Of course it's gonna be. So when I was actually dating a vegan for the first time, I noticed a total difference. And it was only because I started to honor my needs. You see, if you don't honor your needs, chances are you're gonna end up in a Coca-Cola relationship based on the diet. For instance, if you are eating a plant-based diet and they're still eating bacon, it's gonna be hard. Because once again, the water relationship is about resonance, especially when it comes to eating.

So if you've got a bowl of kale, I've got a bowl of kale. If you are eating cranberries, I've got a load of cranberries in my hand right now offering them to you. Take them, take them, eat them, eat them.

6.   Expression.

Many people in toxic relationships, in karmic relationships, in Coca-Cola relationships have very little expression. Meaning they don't really express themselves fully to that person they're with. They're hiding. They have a lot of secrets. And that was me along my early journey. When I started to move into the water relationship, it was only because I was learning how to express myself even more. Expression is all about authenticity.

Authenticity is where you move out of the ego. Because the ego, once again, it's all about defending itself wearing a mask. So to stop attracting a Coca-Cola relationship, learn to express yourself more. And if that person doesn't accept you for who you are, bounce.

7.   Evolution.

Now, what helped me along my journey was this. To ask yourself, how much can I evolve with this person? Many people, they lie to themselves every single day in a relationship. I did when I was in a relationship and it wasn't going anywhere. And I'm like, this is cool.

No, it's not. I had to get real. And the cat down the road was like, Ralph, get real. This relationship isn't doing anything for you. And the longer you hold onto a toxic Coca-Cola relationship, the more you miss the opportunity to be in a relationship that helps you become your greatest version.

So evolution is everything. Like the person you are with, or if you're single, the person who you wanna be with, ask yourself, how are we gonna look like in like 10 years? Can I see myself with this person? Are they a good father or a good mother? That's what you gotta be thinking of for the water relationship. The Coca-Cola relationship is like, oh my gosh, they've got a great body. That's short term, baby. That's why a lot of people are screwed over because they went for the bait.

Relationships are a lot deeper than that. You gotta start thinking of the spiritual connection both of you have, more so the heart connection.

8.   Be more transparent.

Transparency is like where you're gonna be like a crystal clear glass of water. And I'm gonna be able to see right through you. So can you see through this person you are with? Or is it looking really murky right now? Along my early journey, I didn't know the person who I was with, right? And it didn't feel good. It felt very uncomfortable. And I didn't know I had a choice to be with someone where I could get more transparency with.

But it was because I didn't really know who I was. I wasn't transparent with myself. So what helped me to stop attracting a Coca-Cola relationship was to become the energy I wanted to attract within that person. And it happened. And then I started to see... my reflection.

If you aren't transparent within yourself, you are gonna see a distorted image of yourself in another person. If you can see yourself clearly, your values, what you represent, when you see someone, you will instantly recognize your reflection.

9.   Honesty.

Now, honesty is difficult because let's face it, none of us are saints. All of us, including me, have got a dirty little secret we're not exposing. That's fine.

Even the cat down the road has a dirty secret. When I talk of honesty, it's not about being a saint. It's just about being honest with yourself to say, okay, is this all I'm worth? Most times in relationships, we're not honest with ourselves, let alone the other person.

If you're not honest with yourself and your feelings, saying, okay, am I happy here? That's all you gotta say. Am I happy here? Four words. Am I happy here? If the answer's no, what are you doing there? Because you see, you begin to move into the water relationship when the answer's hell yes. Like, it's gotta be a hell yeah. Not a, I don't know. You're looking a bit shaky, baby.

Okay, that's how I knew I was in a Coca-Cola relationship because I wasn't even sure of what I felt. Water relationship is where you absolutely know you feel fantastic. They bring out the best in you and you bring out the best in them.

10.   Appreciation.

What helped me along my journey was to realize this. I was with a person who wasn't really appreciating me 100%.

They weren't really supporting me on my mission here on planet Earth, okay? And to stop attracting that kind of relationship, you only wanna be around a person who is gonna be your personal cheerleader. And guess what? You are gonna be their personal cheerleader. You're gonna be happy for their success and upset at their sadness. And those are the people who you should hold dear to your heart because those are the people who only ever cared about you.

I mean, everybody else didn't care. So that is the secret. The water relationship is surrounding yourself with someone who really appreciates you, who doesn't really wanna change you or wants to grow with you. And then both of you say, feel so good to be alive!

Chapter Fifty Two

How To Attract Someone You Want

How can I get someone to like me? How can I get them to be into me the same way I am into them? Has that ever happened to you? Sometimes you just really love someone and you're like, I want them to be attracted to me the same way I am attracted to them. And then you've got like 5,000 other people who are really interested in you. But you're like, I'm not having it.

I realized this, that you've got to be willing to give to someone the same love you so desperately crave from them. Wanting is coming from a place of lack. They won't love you. You've got to start embodying that love within yourself. You've got to start embodying that love within yourself.

I realized along my early journey, the long way, the hard way, that the greatest relationship exists within yourself. You can beg people to love you. Please love me. Please love me. But the greatest love comes from within. And that's really how to start manifesting the love you want.

You see, once you love yourself, everybody's going to love you, including the cat down the road. I talk of the water relationship and I talk of the Coca-Cola relationship. The water relationship is when you say, okay, what can I give to that person to help them evolve and become their greatest version? The Coca-Cola relationship is where you're like, how can I take from this person? Right? Big difference.

And a lot of people on the planet are in the Coca-Cola relationship. That's why they are not manifesting the love they want. So ask yourself, how can I give to someone? And then, my oh my, you're going to start manifesting the love you want. I've learned this, that not everybody that's passing through your life is going to stay. Not everyone you meet that you are so desperately in love with is truly meant for you. Sometimes you go shoe shopping and you enter the store and you're like, okay, I just need one fit.

My foot is not going to fit all sizes. And then you find the perfect fit and then you're like this. Yippee! Okay, that's the same thing as love. It's all about resonance, which means returning to sound. It's when someone is singing the same song as you. You've got to keep your ears open, baby.

Okay, are they singing the same song as me? Oh, they are. It's a perfect fit. You see, some people are passing through and they are just passing through. You've got to let them, let them go, right? Don't force, don't try and hold them back. Come back here. No, no, no, no, no, no. Let them go. We don't need them. Let them go. Let them go. Let them go. But some will stay. One person will stay. Don't force. Allow the flow. And that's what's helped me along my journey. I never beg someone to stay in my life.

Oh, love me. No, no, no, no, no. I realize I am love and I realize you've got to allow the flow. Whoever stays, let them stay. Whoever goes, let them go. Whoever wants to say, I'm not sure. Well, let them say, I'm not kind of sure right now. But you don't have to force anything, especially when it comes to love. Allow the flow. Give people that freedom. I've learned this, that you've got to stop playing games.

Now, a lot of people in the Coca-Cola relationship are always playing games because games come from the ego. This mask so many of us wear. The ego is cloudy. We can't see through it. The water relationship is about transparency. Now you can actually see through someone. And for the first time, you actually stop playing games, like games, like, oh, I text them. So I'm going to wait for them to text me. Do you ever say that? Like you're waiting, like who texts first and stuff? Like that's all the ego. And I learned that along my journey.

Look, if you want to text someone, text someone. If you want to call someone, call someone. You want to meet someone eye to eye, do it. You want to go skinny dipping with that person, do it. And please take the cat down the road with you.

So I've learned that you've got to stop playing games and start to bear your soul to that person. Allow yourself to be vulnerable with that person so they can actually see you. Your entirety, the pleroma, an ancient Greek word, which means a divinity, a totality of divine powers. And that can only happen once you stop playing games. Just bear your soul, baby.

7 Day Vegan Challenge. Shout out to everybody on Snapchat who is sharing beautiful food, making me really hungry. I've learned that if you really want to manifest the love you so desperately crave, start taking your health seriously. Start eating your fruits and your veg, the dates, the apricots, the watercress, the cacao, arugula. Get your body right by eating right. Because if you aren't eating right, chances are you aren't thinking right.

Quote me on that. I've learned this, you've got to go to the gym, get your body in shape so you feel better about you. Once you feel better about you, you will start to attract other people who feel better about you. I've seen it along my journey. And food is like such an easy way to get a confidence boost. Like once I'm drinking vanilla almond milk, I feel so confident, I feel so attractive.

And I feel like I can fly in the sky, right? And that's how to manifest the love you want. By getting confident, by knowing that you are taking care of your body, mind and soul by putting the most delicious plant-based foods in your mouth. Ask yourself this, would I date myself? Am I sexy? Okay, and if the answer is no, we've got a whole lot of work to do because you should find yourself so gorgeous.

That's how you should see yourself. Always see yourself as attractive. And that also comes from authenticity. Nothing is sexier than authenticity. So start eating that spirulina, baby. I've learned this, don't lead people on. If you really want to manifest the love you want, don't lead people on. Ladies, you know what I'm talking of. Fellas, you know what I'm talking of. If you don't want to be with someone, just say, hey, you're totally not my type. Sorry about that. It's nothing personal. But you see, a lot of us, we get caught in love triangles because we start leading people on. We're like, I like you. I love you.

No, you don't. You're just afraid of saying, actually, can you please leave me alone? Because I just want to like do this. Breathing in that good-ass piranha, baby. So I've learned that you've got to be very straightforward with people. Don't worry if you might sound like an asshole. Look, be yourself. And the right person will find you. You don't have to change for people. Just be yourself, your true, authentic, beautiful way.

And the right person will come into your life and give you a really, really, really big hug. Okay, and the cat down the road is going to join in, by the way, right? Don't lead people on. Now, what's helped me along my journey is, I never make finding a partner my primary focus.

Because I realized so long as I am in my purpose, it will come. Many, many years ago when I was making a video in nature, afterwards, I got a message from someone and then we started to go out because they had seen me in my purpose, right? That's the secret of how to manifest the love you want.

Be in alignment with the truth of who you are. Then people are going to be like, oh my gosh, they're taking my breath away right now. But sometimes the more you search for love, the more elusive love becomes. Because love finds you when you find love within yourself first. Can I get a hello there? And that comes from being in your purpose. What's helped me along my journey is this, that you've really got to know what you are looking for in people? See the best in people. That's how to start manifesting the love you want.

So many times we just focus on their flaws, their imperfections. Nobody is perfect. Deal with it. I realized that, hey, I'm not looking for a perfect partner because I'm not perfect. I realized that everyone's pretty screwed up on the planet. I can deal with that. I'm looking for authenticity. So start to know how to see. And then see beyond the body. Can you imagine if we only saw souls and we didn't see bodies?

Start to look beyond the body. That's how to manifest the love you want. See beyond the body. Nice backside, beautiful. Nice shoulders, ladies, beautiful. Fellas, your muscles are so big. Great. But what else? You see, once again, the water relationship is where you allow yourself to be seen in your totality. Therefore, allow yourself to be seen. Okay? And you can only do that when you say, I've got a beautiful body. I love my body. That's great. I accept who I am. But I'm also more than a body.

I've got a message to share with the world. I'm talented. I can play the piano. I can draw. I love science. I love ballet. I'm not just this physical body. Allow that other person to recognize, baby, that you're not just the backside. That's how to manifest the love you want.

Because ladies, you write to me all the time saying, Ralph, why does he only want me for my body? Well, you are so much more than your body. Give him something else to meditate on. I've learned this, that love is not about possession. And so many of us, we enter relationships trying to control someone else, trying to make them ours, just like a piece of property. You manifest the love you want when you stop trying to possess someone, control them, when you let go.

Say, hey, fly away. And if they come back to you, then they're yours. But if they don't, then they were never yours to begin with. So loosen up, baby, right? Being so clingy all the time sometimes creates a lot of resistance. It goes back into the I want program. Realize you are love. Love is everywhere. It permeates everything in existence. Start respecting people. You see, what do people want in relationships? Respect. It's so simple.

Men want respect. Women want respect. To manifest the love you want, start respecting yourself. Start recognizing yourself. Start appreciating yourself. Respect, appreciation, love only comes from inside. Respect, appreciation, and love, they only come from within.

So people always say, Ralph, why isn't it happening right now? And I've realized you've got to be patient. You see, just like in nature, there are cycles, seasons, and it's the same thing with love. Yes, just because it is not happening now, it doesn't mean it will never happen. You've got to be patient. And in that time you are patient. Well, what am I going to do, Ralph? Work on yourself, work on yourself, work on yourself.

It's what I call training day. That's what I was doing, okay? I was like a teenager saying, I want to manifest love into my life. This beautiful princess. It wasn't happening. Then I realized there is a perfect time for the perfect reunion. Slow motion on this side. It may not be now. It may not be in five minutes. It may not be next month or next year. Could be in three years. But it's going to come. Hold your horses, right? Be patient. And that's how to manifest the love you want. What's helped me along my journey is to appreciate the contrast you see in other people. You see, and it goes back to letting go off.

You've got to let go of perfection. Nobody is perfect. Realize that even if you do find someone, they're probably going to fart in bed. Don't worry about it. They're probably going to pick their nose, okay? And they're also going to have really weird habits. Deal with it. But through it all, you will live to see another day with them. And both of you will dance off into the sunset. How amazing is that? And then both of you just trip up, okay? Saying a fairy tale.

Saint Rapunzel. Look, I started to realize this, that what it boils down to is this. So many times we have to realize your vibe attracts your tribe. So what I love to do to manifest the love you want, start analyzing your own vibe. What kind of vibes are you sending out? Okay, because that is the same kind of vibes you are also going to attract into your life. Positivity.

Positivity is contagious. When you see someone who is highly positive, highly positive, we are captivated by them. Because we're like, okay, if they're so positive, it means we're going to have a great time. We're actually going to go somewhere really hot and tropical and go skinny dipping somewhere, okay? That's great. But what is more important than being positive? I'm asking you right now. Being authentic.

Okay, to manifest the love you want, make authenticity a priority. And realize this, that look, it's nothing personal. If someone isn't loving you the same way you love them, it means they aren't meant to be in your life.

Because someone who is truly vibrating on the same frequency as you, what we call sympathetic vibration, when you are vibrating towards each other, you ain't gotta chase a whole lot. Both of you have to start recognizing each other's greatness. You see, to manifest the love you want, ask yourself, am I paying people compliments? Am I uplifting them or am I just putting them down? Many times also in a relationship, we ain't finished yet.

People are afraid to love because they have been hurt in former relationships. I was for a long time. I was scared to love again, right? I had been hurt, okay? Don't let that stop you. Start to see new relationships with new eyes and new lenses. And start to realize this, that don't be afraid to love.

Because it's only when you love a hundred percent that you know, this is the one, this is my forever someone. Because you've put in a hundred percent effort. When you do things half-heartedly, then you're only going to get half back.

It's mirrors here, reflections, right? So I started to realize you've got to love with all your heart. And even if someone abuses your heart, at least you know, okay, well, it doesn't matter. Because they weren't worthy enough in the first place to really appreciate it. But someone will, I guarantee you, someone will love all you have to offer.

Right now, there's probably someone about you, right? Start to appreciate the people you have who love you in your life. That's how to manifest the love you want. And start to realize love permeates everything in existence. And it starts when you start cultivating the love within yourself.

Chapter Fifty Three

The 7 Hermetic Principles

This chapter is about the power of your mind. How to attract with your mind. What's helped me along my journey is to see that, if you can change your thoughts, you can change the world.

There are seven hermetic principles which I live by. Hermetic principles, okay, what are we talking about? Let's take a trip in a time machine and go back in time. In ancient times, in ancient Egypt or Kemet, you had the god Tehuti, the god of writing, really the patron of scribes, the master architect; his companion was Ma'at.

And when the Greeks were in Egypt, they identified a lot of the qualities Tehuti had with their own god Hermes because he also was a divine messenger and writer. So, the wisdom from Greece and the wisdom from Egypt, you had Hermes Trismegistus. The Greeks called Tehuti Thoth and one of Tehuti's titles was Three Times Great.

So, that translated to Trismegistus, Hermes Three Times Great. So, fast forward to 1908, you have a book called The Kabbalion, which talks about hermetic philosophy, the seven principles that govern the universe. Now, these principles are powerful. They have changed my life and they have made me see the world in a different way. The Kabbalion was written by the three initiates. Here are the seven hermetic principles.

1.   The principle of mentalism

The ancients believed that everything is mental and once we can see how powerful this is, we can even use it in our own life to see that it is one mind. We are all in. It is a reminder that everything is connected. It is a reminder that it's all BS: belief systems. Once we can see the significance of the mind, we realize that this is the catalyst which governs every single action. It always starts in the unseen realms before it appears in the seen realms.

2.   The principle of correspondence.

One of Tahuti's sayings was, so above as below. The macrocosm, the microcosm. As within, so without. This means that everything taking place within our minds is a reflection of what we will experience in our physical reality.

Therefore, we have to become aware that how we feel inside governs the experiences we attract on the outside. Once we can see that there is no separation between the inner world and the outer world, the correspondence, then we can understand this.

3.   The Kabbalion is the principle of vibration.

Once we can see that nothing is static, everything is moving, everything is oscillating, everything is frequency; I always say it's never what you say, it's the energy behind that matters. That is why we have to become mindful of how we talk to people because it's not the words, it is the energy behind the words. If you're a singer, you know that drinking water can help get your voice in divine alignment.

We have to see that the vibration can also change through our lifestyle. It is the energy flowing because the emotion is the energy in motion. So, once we see that we are living in a universe filled of frequencies, it becomes clearer.

Nikola Tesla said, if you want to understand the universe, think of frequency, sound, vibration.

4.   The principle of polarity

This is that everything is dual. There are poles within everything, that everything has its opposites. Hot, cold, high, low, light, darkness, good and evil. However, once we delve deeper into it, we begin to see that good and evil are two sides of the same coin and this is what the ancient alchemists and hermetic masters knew. They talked of mental transmutation, turning evil into good.

The ancient hermetic masters saw good and evil as poles of the same thing. So, they used mental alchemy to transform and transmute evil into good and we do this all the time. Once we have a negative emotion, by becoming more conscious of it, we can have more harmony within our bodies. That, in essence, is alchemy.

I look at it as, when we talk of polarity, I don't say opposites, I say complementary. So, hot and cold are complementary. Light and darkness are complementary. In essence, they are one in the same.

5.   The principle of rhythm

There are cycles in the universe. There are seasons. We even have our own bio-rhythm.

You might wake up at six in the morning, it may be five, but it is something which is intrinsic to you because you are unique. The principle of rhythm is that everything is in movement and I always say there is no time, there is only movement. So, once we see that the whole of the universe is a dance of energy, we begin to free ourselves.

We don't have to take ourselves so seriously, but rhythm is all about getting into divine alignment and we do this by yoga, by any exercise that resonates with you to move more into our bodies, getting into rhythm because our bodies are miniature universes. We have a whole planet inside of us and it is fascinating. Even once we start changing the kind of foods we are eating, all of this helps us to get back into divine alignment, to find more harmony and rhythm.

I call it the grand orchestra and the breath is the conductor of this beautiful song. So, once we begin breathing deep from the base of our spines, we develop a greater rhythm, moving us more in tune with the true universal frequency of planet earth.

6.   The principle of cause and effect.

You reap what you sow. The seeds that you plant right now, they will harvest.

But ask yourself, are you planting seeds of positivity or seeds of negativity? The principle of cause and effect states that every cause has an effect and every effect has a cause. There are no accidents or coincidences in the universe. I call it divine mathematics.

Even from the time we are born, there is a divine agreement that we make even before we get to this planet. The law of cause and effect is that every action has a reaction and every reaction is caused by an action. When we talk of karma, I love this definition of karma. Absolute actions of absolute results. Absolutely. To see that whatever we think, whatever we do, creates that ripple effect. And that butterfly effect which is created will come right back to us. Almost like a boomerang.

Cause and effect, we can talk of karma. We can talk of reincarnation. A lot of people ask me, what is reincarnation? Do you believe in it? For me, I say that what you do now echoes on into eternity. Therefore, as we are energy, whatever we go through now will remain with us. That is why there is no escape. You can't run away from the matrix because where you left off is where you have to pick up from. Whatever we do now stays with us.

Therefore, we always have the opportunity to become the greatest versions of ourselves. Sometimes, you see someone playing the piano at the age of 8 and you say wow. How come they can play this to such a high level? Because they are coming in with information. Cause and effect. Cause and effect for me is about becoming aware of radical action. And when we talk of manifesting your desires, your goals, your dreams and aspirations, thinking is not enough. We have to realize that it takes action. We have to see that our beliefs shape our thoughts. And our thoughts govern our actions. So, whatever we do has a consequence.

7.   The principle of gender.

This is that the masculine energy exists within you. Also, the feminine energy exists within you. We exist within each other. It doesn't matter if you are male or female. It is a reminder that it even goes beyond human beings. We see this all throughout nature.

That the masculine and the feminine exist within everything. So, it is a great way to see the world. That gender is an illusion. Because beyond your gender, you are energy. Gender is a separation. However, it is also essential to experience the contrast which is needed for our expansion.

So, right now, on the planet, we are living in a time where people are questioning, people are manifesting. Here are some practical ways to use the 7 Hermetic principles in your life. This is what's helped me along my journey. First of all, we have to remember that focus is essential. Because whatever you focus on grows. I see the mind as a magnet. Thoughts are magnets. They draw in what we are putting out.

I also see the mind as a filter. As a sensor ship. So, therefore, once we begin to free our mind, we release the sensor ship. So, we become infinite. The mind is a powerful tool. However, we have to start living more from our heart space.

Once we can see that, focus is the catalyst for manifesting your desire. Concentrated focus. Ask yourself, are you focusing on what you want or are you focusing on what you fear? Because whatever you tune into, you become. You turn into whatever you are tuned into. And that is why it is so powerful once you enter the realm of imagination, which is image in action. Once you see that, you don't have to watch the television.

You can if you want. But ask the greater question. How is this serving me? The television tells lies to your vision. Once we start telling our own vision, we move into the principle of mentalism. That is why the artist is so powerful right now on the planet. Because the artist lives in the realm of infinite creation where there are no boundaries. There is only pure expression. There is man-made law. And this law is written down. But it is fictional because it is forever changing.

They can rewrite the law. However, universal law does not change. It is versatile though. But if you place your hand on a cooker, ouch! It is going to hurt. Because it is a universal principle. And I found it to be so powerful just to see how much power we have. You are powerful beyond measure. But you can only realize this once you start loving yourself 100%. Because once you can accept yourself 100%, then you start to manifest your true desires.

Otherwise, you don't know what you really want. So we spend our time in jobs which don't serve us, in relationships which don't serve us. Once you start listening more to your heart space, you move in the direction of your true calling, of your true passion. The mind is the software. The body is the computer.

To start rewriting the program, we have to start changing the words we use. Because words are the commands that govern every single action in our life. I am no good. I am good enough. I can't. I can. We have to start using words that give us a new lease of life. We have to see that words are spells. Therefore, we have to become the magicians of our own story.

To start attracting with your mind, we also have to take responsibility that we are creating with our mind. We have to see that nobody is doing anything to us. We have supreme power. Once we acknowledge this, then we can begin to fly. We can heal ourselves. We came here to play because once we can see that the limitations we place on ourselves are based on our tradition, how we were raised.

More so, how we see ourselves. The only way to change the perception of yourself is to let go of who you think you are. People ask me all the time, where do you come from? And I say, I am a planetarian. In fact, I am nature's indefinable. You can't label me, so don't even try. We have to see that to attract the mind, we have to start connecting with those who remind us who we are. Kindred spirits, because that is the true fusion. It is powerful. We don't all have to be similar, but we can find a great beauty in the contrast of our talents.

I want another job. I want more money. I want to find my dream partner. The moment you say I want, you are sending out a signal to the universe that you don't have what you desire. Therefore, you will always remain in lack. We have to start using the power of visualization. To see ourselves already there.

Start loving yourself if you are single and you want to be with someone. That is the secret. Start becoming what you are dreaming of. See yourself already there. That is the power of the mind because the biggest secret of the seven hermetic principles is that the first three principles govern the last four.

So, the principle of mentalism, correspondence, and vibration. They govern the principles of polarity, rhythm, cause and effect, and gender. Once we can see this, we become more conscious that what we think affects how we feel and this affects what we manifest.

Everything is connected. Once we can see that from the sound frequencies we are listening to, ask yourself, how is this promoting wellness within my body? Because this will govern what you can manifest. Even from how you talk to yourself to the music you listen to.

Are you living in a busy city or can you go to nature and hear yourself? That's why I love being here in California because by the ocean it is so peaceful just to see the waves roll in and out. You feel alive and more so you see the secret that you deserve abundance. We have to start changing our mental state.

It all starts there because the moment we begin to doubt ourselves is the moment we begin to lose out on manifesting our deepest desires. Once we can let go of this fear, which is one of the biggest programs, it's intrinsic to one extent, fight or flight. But after that, ask yourself, how is this serving me? You can live the life you want, you just have to know what you want and see yourself already having it.

That's what I do along my journey. I visualize myself already there. Before I came to California, I had dreams of coming to Venice. I saw myself there and guess what? I'm here. The biggest revelation along my journey was to see that we don't attract what we want, we attract what we are. Once you change your vibrational frequency, everything aligns to that same frequency.

Therefore, the universe cannot help but mirror back what frequency you are emitting. So, we have to see that if we are miserable, that is what we attract. Once we start to become elevated in our spirit, it happened to me along my journey, everything aligns to that same frequency that you embody. The magic is within you and once you see it, everything becomes magical. So, there you have it.

Realize that your mind has supreme power over your actions and realize that your actions are needed. Your radical action is needed to manifest the world you desire to live in. You live in the world you are thinking of. Be aware, be present and be happy.

Chapter Fifty Four

9 Passive Income Ideas - How I Make $28k Per Week

Your soul knows when it's time for a new beginning. It just knows. Go forward and welcome it today and remind yourself the world is your oyster. You can do anything, be anything. It's all yours, but you have to see yourself there. Are you ready? I'm ready.

Now, I want to talk to you today about passive income, nine passive income ideas. We've got a whole lot to talk about. I am truly rich, realizing I create happiness. Realizing I can start raising the frequency. I can start raising the vibration. So let's talk about how you can generate thousands per week. The cat down the road is doing that.

Now, rich people don't work. They supervise. I had to learn that. And they supervise their passive income. You see, to become truly wealthy, to become truly wealthy, you have to learn about passive income. And I've been learning this for over a decade. Ralph, passive income is the secret. And a lot of people don't know this. You see, we want to generate money in our sleep. That's what I do. I wake up. Oh my gosh, I didn't even do anything, but it still came in.

So, first and foremost, your inner peace is the highest form of wealth. Now, let me talk to you about the nine passive income ideas that are about to change your life, how you can generate thousands per week.

1.   Publish a book

The reason why publishing a book is one of the best ways to generate passive income is because a book has many forms. You can have an e-book, a paperback, or a hardback. You can have an audio book, right? Feel Alive by Ralph Smart has sold hundreds of thousands of copies worldwide.

And when I actually wrote this book, it wasn't to make money. It was to help people. So if you can learn to say, actually, I have a gift, I have a talent, I have knowledge, write a book. All of those posts on Instagram, you could have written a book by now. Okay? So we must never underestimate the power of writing, okay?

The Bible has sold nearly 4 billion copies worldwide. J.K. Rowling's Harry Potter series has sold 450 million copies, right? One of the highest selling books, a great book, The Alchemist by Paolo Coelho, sold 65 million copies worldwide.

So we often forget that when you publish a book, people can read it at any time. There are billions of people on the planet waiting to read your book full of knowledge that can help them become their greatest version. So start publishing a book today, okay?

2.   Start a YouTube channel.

Start a YouTube channel. Now the gift of YouTube is that you can monetize your content and you can produce as much content as you want, okay? I remember 2017, I made a video on the third eye and it went viral. 4 million views and I'm like, whoa.

And I realized that once again, I just wanted to share a message and I did, but YouTube pays its creators and there are tremendous avenues. On YouTube, you can have a membership there. You can also introduce people to who you are and they can support you.

So a lot of people have great ideas, but they forget about YouTube. They forget about saying, actually, let me start a YouTube channel because people can go back in the archive, they can watch a video that you made two years ago and that video can still generate revenue for you.

So on YouTube, it takes time. There is no such thing as overnight success. I've been doing this day in, day out, day in, day out, okay? And I love what I'm doing. But if you keep doing it consistently, you will start to reap the rewards and benefits.

And YouTube is a great passive income revenue stream because once it's out there, now it's up to the algorithm. It can flow this way, that way, and people can see it for as long as that video is up, which can be forever, okay?

3.   Online course membership.

Online course membership. And this is huge. You already know deep divers, I have the membership on YouTube right here. I used to have a membership.

I used to have a membership section on my website. But then I'm like, wait a minute, a lot of people are coming to watch my videos from YouTube. So have a membership. And before you can have a membership, you better be really good at what you do. You have to have credibility, credentials. And the people that do are making thousands, tens of thousands every single week. Because people see the value in what they do. Once you have an online course, once again, just like the book, you have scalability. You can have as many people in that online course as you want.

Also, when you have a membership, people can feel part of a community. So that is a great passive income revenue stream. Only fans. Did someone say only fans now? Sometimes, ladies, fellas, ladies, I don't know. Only fans. I say, hey, if that is your hustle, do it. I'm not going to judge you. I actually met a woman who was doing only fans and she was making some serious money. And she's like, people want to see me. I'm like, that's good. You value who you are. Go for it.

So an online course. Monetize your expertise. OK, and membership, put value on what you do. And all the people who are making tens of thousands every single week are doing that. In some shape, form or way.

4.   Clothing store.

Clothing store. Kanye West. Yeezy. People often think that money can be found in the music industry. No, the true money is in the fashion industry. OK, I saw a Versace T-shirt for like five thousand dollars once.

I'm like, what people are buying that apparently. But clothing, a clothing store is fantastic because this is a passive income stream. You don't have to do anything once the print is there. It is full automation. They can send it to where you want it to go. They can ship it out for you. And once again, scalability. So that's huge. As you know, I have an Infinite Waters clothing store. Good ass Prada shirts. And there's a story behind that.

I was almost involved in a lawsuit suing someone because of this woman who started designing good ass Prada T-shirts. And I'm like, oh, I want one. She actually came to me. She's like, Ralph, I want to design T-shirts for you. And I said, go ahead. Then I realized, wait a minute. You're not giving me anything.

Right. So I had to say, oh, thank you, because you've made me see an opportunity. And sometimes it takes other people to see it before we can see it. And then I said, hey, I need to trademark that and I need you to stop doing that. And she's like, OK, Ralph, I'm going to stop doing that. I'm going to stop using your name to make money.

So I got together with some designers and I started to design. I started to design good ass Prada shirts, different T-shirt designs, hoodies, women's dresses, caps, mobile phone cases. And it's on Spreadshirt. Also, Teespring is everywhere. So that's huge. That's a huge passive income revenue stream. OK, so look into that. Look into your own fashion brand. Forget Fashion Nova.

Have your own name on it. Your own logo. Your own logo on it. Your own design. Wear your own clothes.

5.   One to one consultations.

When you have a client base, who value what you do, you could do one to one consultations. I do one-on- one counseling. And it's huge. But once again, for you to be able to do that, you must be an expert in your field. You must be someone who is highly sought after.

You must know what you're talking about as a psychologist, as a criminologist, as a counselor, as an influencer, as someone who's been doing this over a decade. I have tremendous experience in all areas. So this is what I'm doing. So when you become a master of what you do, now you can start coaching people. There are coaches who charge ten thousand dollars just for a session. It's out there. It's out there. So become aware. That is a great passive income revenue stream. One to one consultations.

6.   Public speaking engagements.

Now, I did a public speaking engagement in Orange County. And. Oh, thanks. Right. Because they saw my value. And they gave me thousands just to talk, for 45 minutes. It wasn't even an hour. But they valued what I was doing for the planet.

They said, here you go, Ralph. And there are some people who charge one hundred thousand dollars just for a public speaking event. OK, so. Before that can happen, before you can get that kind of passive income, because the reason why it's passive income is because even after the public speaking engagement is done, you can still get paid off the royalties. You can still generate wealth. It can go to a DVD. You can download it. You can go to Blu-ray. You can go to an audio CD. So you can do many things after the public speaking engagement.

And this is why it's a great passive income revenue stream. You can make an agreement to say, actually, every time you play that video, I want a percentage. You remember Friends, right? That song. The musician said every time that song is played on Friends at the beginning. They want to check. Passive income, right? Bright idea.

7.   Sell your music, art, photos, NFTs, food and drink supplements

Now, non fungible token, NFTs, Beeple sold an NFT, digital art, 69 million dollars. And people are doing it today, making thousands a week off of NFTs. It is happening. Music. iTunes, Spotify. People are making a lot. There's something called producer royalty checks. And if you are a producer, OK, I'm a producer.

You can make thousands a week because you can make one beat. And you can sell it on BeatStars. And you can have 50 people buying your your song, you can sell that song for 50 dollars with the stems, the WAV file and the MP3 file. Some people even sell a hundred dollars. Right. So just giving you some gain.

As a producer, you can start monetizing your beats. Oh, you can sell your artwork. Don't sell your soul, though. Slow motion this time. And also you can get your own food and drink supplement. That can really help people now for me.

I have the audio CD of Feel Alive, which is selling like hot, hot cake, hot, hot, hot cake every single day. And. The possibility is endless. So just remind yourself, be knowledgeable about NFTs, be knowledgeable about cryptocurrency, invest in crypto if you need to learn about that market, because that's huge. Huge.

8.   Selling ads on your website, selling ads on your website.

Now, someone actually came to me. They gave me this idea. They're like, Ralph, you have this website, www.ralphsmart.com, but there are no ads on your website. So. I have the WordPress ads. But that's not enough because I realized I was missing out on an opportunity. So this company contacted me, they contacted me and they're like, Ralph, we want to put ads on your website. So I started to realize, oh, that's another way to generate passive income.

Depending on how popular your website is, you can generate thousands per week. And this is passive income because you can go to sleep and wake up with a check. And we ain't even had breakfast yet, OK? Take a look at that and your website and the opportunities that it presents you every time to say, actually, I can incorporate ads, sponsorships, all of that stuff.

9.   Rent a room

Buy a house, rent a house, renting something that you own. That's huge. Now, I'm a cinematographer. And for instance, I have the Canon. C500 Mark two. I actually at one point had a Sony Venice camera. Which I was using. But I sold it. But I rented it.

If you have equipment like cameras, lenses, you can if you're not using it, you can rent it out. There are some lenses which cost five thousand dollars, ten thousand dollars, twenty thousand dollars. Right. You get into the airy lenses. Very expensive.

Now, when you buy these things, you can rent it out to someone, other filmmakers for a thousand dollars a day. Two thousand dollars a day. If you have an expensive camera, you can rent that out. Right. So renting something that you own. Of value, that's a great passive income idea for you today, because if you have something of extreme wealth that you're not using. Why not rent it out? And when you wake up, you've got the check.

I want to remind you, it's all about diversifying your portfolio. Remind yourself you came here to live in abundance. Don't sell yourself short. Oh, I like that. I like that. I love you. The world is your oyster.

Chapter Fifty Five

How To Think And Grow Rich

There was a time when I'd make a lot of my videos in front of a beautiful maple tree that would often make cameos in so many of my videos. This maple tree was so beautiful, and red, with such pretty leaves. And anytime I'd look at it, I would think, that's what wealth is. You see, that's what being free is, true expression.

And a lot of people are feeling a certain way right now all around the world.

Someone wrote to me, they're like, Ralph, I lost my job. There's no future for me and I don't know what to do. How on earth am I gonna make money? How am I gonna survive, provide, provide for my children? It's over Ralph.

I wanna remind you, two books to check out. The first one, Napoleon Hill, Think Rich, Grow Rich. And Feel Alive by Ralph Smart. I had to plug myself, deep divers. It's all a mindset, change your mind and you change your world.

The reason why I'm thinking rich and growing rich every single day is because I learned how to change my entire mind. And everything you do in this life is based on your choices. And your choices are based on your beliefs.

And what you believe is based on what you have been programming yourself to believe about this matrix. What if I told you there is more than enough to go around for everybody? What if I told you, you can manifest any life you want?

I wanna remind you deep divers, a little exercise, okay? A little exercise. Now, I want you to visualize what your best life looks like.

Then I want you to visualize what becoming your greatest version looks like. Okay, let me do it. To me, it's waking up every single day with a whole bunch of grapes in my mouth. It's being wealthy and happy and in love. And I've attracted that life deep divers. So you can continue to sing, I'm locked up, they won't let me out. No, they won't let me out. Living in lockdown. Yeah, talk to me.

Ralph, I lost my job. Really? No money to show, what else? And I've got nowhere to go. I'm in lockdown. No, you wanna stop saying that. You wanna stop saying that. It's time to be free. It's time to think rich and grow rich.

I'm in my favorite place. That is nature. And every time I'm in nature, it reminds me to think rich and grow rich. It reminds me I can manifest the life I truly want and nothing can stop me but myself. If you are someone who is feeling hopeless right now on the planet, peace, I'm sending you that. Infinite waters, diving deep once again.

We are out here in the heart of nature, baby. If you feel hopeless because you're stuck indoors, maybe you've lost your job, maybe you are unemployed and you're like, Ralph, how on earth am I gonna grow rich in these desperate times of economic collapse? Hold on right there, deep divers. I'm proof it is possible.

Let me tell you this. Ever been around someone who's always telling you what they're gonna do? I'm gonna do this, I'm gonna do that. Don't tell me your plans. No, please don't do that. Show me your results. And this is the mantra I carry with me every single day. Every single day, don't tell me your plans, show me your results. It's always the people who tell me what they're gonna do who never do shit. Jeez, it's time to stop talking so much and it's time to get down to business.

Imagine your best life. What does it look like? What does your best life look like? For a lot of us, if we're honest with ourselves, it's about wealth, happiness, being with that beautiful person you can walk down the beach with every single day. It's about being happy, it's about having fun. And I've attracted that lifestyle. And how I've done it is to learn how to think rich and grow rich. Every single day, remind yourself, we all have got the same amount of time, 24 hours, but it's what you do with your time that matters.

Are you always just scrolling down the newsfeed on social media? When instead, you could be writing a book. Time management, that's how to think rich, grow rich. Our thoughts, are things, they help us create our reality. And when we realize this, we realize that a thought can uplift us or it can destroy us. The reason why I'm wealthy every single day is because I'm mindful of the thoughts I'm thinking.

I only think about what I wanna draw nearer to me. I only speak about what I wanna draw nearer to me. I speak what I want into existence. Then I put my money where my mouth is. I start stepping into radical action. I have a clear vision of what it is I want. You see, a long time ago, I said, I wanna help people. I didn't say I wanna be rich. I just said, I wanna help people. Money is the by-product of me doing what I love. But I'm not just focusing on money. I wanna be rich, Ralph. I'm already wealthy because wealth is a mindset.

Wealth is when you realize I create happiness. Oh baby, and that's what I do. Wealth is love. Wealth is when you have something money can't buy. COVID-19 has ruined a lot of people's plans. A lot of people blame COVID-19 for not manifesting. You know, Ralph, I lost my job. Ralph, I've got no money because of COVID-19. These are excuses. These are excuses to keep yourself in an arrested state of development.

Let me tell you this. Nothing is in my way of manifesting, not COVID-19. Because do you know what COVID-19 actually stands for? Check this out, Certificate of Vaccination ID. That's one definition. The other definition of COVID-19 is creating our vision in-depth. Let me repeat that, creating our vision in-depth. So always remind yourself, that's what COVID means.

Creating our vision in depth. And that's what I'm doing. Pay attention to what's going on in your life, not what's going on out there. Make your life more interesting every single day. This is how to think rich, grow rich. Learn that you have been given a talent, a gift. Talent emanates from the Latin talentum, which means a sum of money. In other words, our talents should bring us everything we desire. The question is, are we using them? If you don't use it, you lose it.

So remind yourself, you have been given a gift and you have to learn how to share your gift with the world. I don't focus on making money. I focus on serving other people. Instead of thinking about how you can make $1 million, think about how you can serve 1 million people. And that's how to think rich and grow rich.

Now, there is a meme floating around of Mark Zuckerberg and Bill Gates, okay? And it says $150 billion in this picture, not a Gucci belt in sight. Oh my gosh. So wealthy people don't flex on the gram all day. They wear simple clothes, no designer clothes, no Gucci, no Fendi, no Versace. No, it's simple clothes. I had to learn that. And I realized that true wealth is not about bragging about how many cars you have on social media, how big your mansion is. It's about, once again, providing a service, being a service provider for humanity and providing value to millions of people's lives.

Therefore, the universe is taking care of me. To think rich, grow rich, realize the power of your thoughts to create your reality, your words, and your actions. Never feel like a victim. Life is not something happening to you, it's responding to you. We are co-creators. COVID actually stands for co-creator of visions in depth. Let me tell you this, we are co-creators.

We have producers in society and we also have consumers. Now check this out, deep divers. How much time do you spend on your phone? The reason why a lot of people are not thinking and growing rich is because they waste time, hours every single day on their phone when in that same time, they could have done something more productive.

To think rich, grow rich, remind yourself that you wanna learn how to be a producer. Okay, what do producers do? They create, producers always create. And this is how to think rich, grow rich. Learn how to be a creator every single day. Most people watch the TV, the television which tells lies to their vision. Now it's cool to consume, but if that's the only thing you're doing, you're missing out on the opportunity to be a creator.

You become wealthy by learning how to be a creator, not just a consumer. So I have this saying, always create twice as much as you consume. Listen, if you want to think rich and grow rich, learn how to listen. That's why I'm in this position. Okay, so there is an extremely wealthy man with a cat down the road, that is me. Two people come and meet me. One tells me everything. They're like, Ralph, you know what? I'm starting a business. Ralph, you know what? I'm doing this, I'm doing that. Check out my website. Okay, cool, cool, cool.

The second person just listens. They're like, Ralph, tell me how you managed to get over a quarter of a billion views on YouTube, how you got a YouTube gold award. And then I tell them. And that second person is thinking rich and growing rich because the first person didn't learn anything. When you open your mouth and speak, you are only repeating what you know. But if you close your mouth and listen, you will learn something new.

There's a reason why you've got two ears, one, two, and one mouth. You should listen twice as much as you talk. A wise man once said nothing. Oh, I like that. A wise man once said nothing.

Now, when we talk of thinking rich and growing rich, every single day, learn how to do what the rest of the population are not doing. If you wanna be in the 1% club of wealth, you're gonna have to be willing to do what the 99% of people aren't willing to do. What is that? Many people are not willing to embrace their authentic uniqueness. And that's what I've done. There is nobody like Ralph Smart in the universe. I own who I am. I love who I am, who I am becoming. I'm happy in my own skin. I love myself. I'm different. I'm unique. Because of that, I've actually got the golden ticket in my hand.

The golden ticket is the winning ticket of life. And that's how to think rich, grow rich. To say, actually, nobody can do what I'm doing. Nobody is me, and that is my power. To think rich, grow rich. If you're doing what 99% of the population is doing, you're only gonna end up with the same results.

If you're just working a job every single day and complaining about it, job means just overbroke. So you're only gonna get what other people have got. And if you always do what you've always done, you'll only get what you always got.

So what you have to do is learn how to be original, learn how to be unique, but also learn how to bring something different to the table. The people who are rewarded with the most wealth in the universe are people who are one in a billion. You have to learn how to become one in a billion.

You have to learn how to offer people something that can help them in their life. If you don't learn how to do that, then they will always come back to you. When we talk of thinking rich and growing rich, learn that the only one in your way is you. Nobody's out to get you. Nobody wants to see you lose. We have to learn how to root for ourselves.

Every day when you wake up, ask yourself, am I truly living my best life? If not, don't settle for anything less. Be happy with what you do instead of complaining about it. A lot of people say, Ralph, I hate my job. I hate my boss. I'm in lockdown with everything happening. Instead of complaining, get your ass up and do something about it. And realize that you don't have to focus on money. You don't have to focus on becoming rich.

All you have to do is focus on loving what you're doing, trusting the process, innovating, reading a book. Instead of Facebook, why not put your face in a book? Instead of spending all of that time on Facebook, put your face in a book so you can learn the skills you need to level up, to change your life, to attract the wealth you know you are worthy of.

The greatest investment you can make, I learned this along my early journey, is in yourself. Your mind is the greatest piece of real estate you will ever own. I repeat, your mind is the greatest piece of real estate you will ever own. Make sure you are investing in your mind by increasing the knowledge you have, by being willing to learn from people who are already there.

Ask and it will be given to you. Ask and it will be given to you. If you really wanna think rich and grow rich, read people's autobiographies. They already made a ton of mistakes you can learn from. And that's how you level up. Also, if you wanna upgrade your life, live the better life, you're gonna have to upgrade your friends. Really? Yes, you're gonna have to upgrade your environment.

You're gonna have to upgrade your mindset. And this is how to think rich, grow rich. Every single day, remind yourself, the level of wealth you attract is linked to your level of giving. Think, that's the great paradox. The more I gave away, just like videos every single day, the more I was able to start living the life I truly want. So learn how to give freely because it's called the law of exchange. You scratch my back, I'll get the cat down the road to scratch yours.

So you can never become wealthy without giving anything. You're gonna have to learn how to give. You're gonna have to learn how to provide value. You're gonna have to learn to stop being distracted by these celebrities who aren't doing anything for you. Learn how to stop being distracted by this matrix, which isn't doing anything for you. And you're gonna have to learn how to focus on your vision every single day. There are no shortcuts, no overnight success. If you want it, you gotta work for it.

Stop wishing for it, start doing the work for it. It's time that you shine because

I believe in you. I wanna tell you this. If you really wanna think rich and grow rich, 7 Day Vegan Challenge, it starts with your plate. I repeat, it starts with your plate. Health is wealth, you've heard that expression, right? So when I was eating junk food, I was broke, spiritually, emotionally, and physically. I said, hey, I gotta start eating to live. Pass me that acai bowl.

I went to Brazil. If you haven't tried them, try acerola cherries, delicious, full of antioxidants, vitamins C, everything you need. I ate that and became Superman.

Woo, I'm flying right now, I'm wealthy because the food you eat is the fuel you need to take you to where you need to go. So, donate off the dollar menu. To think rich, grow rich, say, actually, my health has gotta be the greatest investment because health is wealth. To think rich, grow rich, realize stress makes you poor. You're always stressing, always in a low frequency. That makes you poor. So, start taking a trip into nature. Now you feel rich.

Because being wealthy hasn't got anything to do with money, even though money is energy, it's called currency for a reason, but it's got everything to do with your peace of mind. Your peace of mind is the highest form of wealth. So, invest in your peace of mind, have a loving relationship. Spend time doing more of what makes you happy.

This is how to think rich, grow rich. I don't want any trouble. Listen, every day, make sure you want more for yourself. You owe it to yourself to live your best life every single day by saying, actually, I can be like this beautiful maple tree behind me, full of exuberance, grace, beauty, magnificence. But the life I want is the life I have to work for. Because there is no free lunch pass in the universe. There is no overnight success. You have to be in your purpose. You have to be patient because great things take time.

It is all a mindset. You change your mind and you change your world. It all starts with you. You can be as wealthy as you want. You can attract everything you want. But remind yourself, we never attract what we want.

We always attract what we are. If you wanna be wealthy today, if you wanna attract everything you know you came here to attract, you're gonna have to learn how to embody that energy, put out better energy, and it will come back to you.

Chapter Fifty Six

How I Quit My Job And Replaced The 9-5 Wage Salary For Freedom

Another beautiful day. Another day in the office. Like, nature is literally my office. It's the best workspace ever.

Now, the world we live in is full of people who don't love what they are doing every single day. It's got to be at least 80% of people who are just doing something for a paycheck. If you ask them, what do you really want to do every single day? They'll be like, I want to go to the Caribbean. I want to play the piano more. I want to take the cat down the road for a walk.

I want to spend more time with my family. But you see, most people, like all of us, myself included, once upon a time, I was caught up in what we call the wage slavery system. Working every single day somewhere which I didn't want to be at. But I'm like, hey, I've got to eat. And then I said, wait a minute, there has to be another way out of this. There has to be another way. And I found the way. And I'm about to share it with you.

Someone sent me a message. They're like, Ralph, your videos are so inspiring. I just got promoted, but I'm still trying to escape this wage slavery system. I want to start my own business. I want to do big things, Ralph. Most people die at 18 and don't get buried until 75. Most people settle for a mediocre life. Most people have a job, "just over broke," and they're living from paycheck to paycheck. Most people are caught up in the rat race.

I'm not a rat. Most people are caught up in the conveyor belt lifestyle. Going around and around, but not really going anywhere. Most people have traded their happiness for a paycheck. Their time for a paycheck. Their energy for a paycheck. I wrote down many years ago, don't go to a job and use all your energy and put all your time there only to come home to have no energy or time for the life you're working for.

But I know what it's like. I was there in the wage slavery system working 12 hours a day and I was thinking, how can I get out of this? Bingo. Right now, we need a plan, Ralph. We need a POA, which is a plan of action. We need a clear vision because if you don't live your life someone else will live it for you. I wasn't living my life. I was merely existing. Someone else was living my life for me. And this is where a lot of people find themselves doing something which they complain about. And you might say, Ralph, you know what? I'm not even in the wage slavery system, but you're still hustling on OnlyFans. That may not be what you want to do.

I'm doing what I love to do and that's the goal. So to escape the wage slavery system, we've all got to remind ourselves every single day we need a clear vision. We need to be doing things that are true and authentic to who we really are. I don't work for money. I work for a cause. Money is just a byproduct.

Most people at a job they don't want, at a job they don't like, they're working just for the money. And this is why they're miserable. But when you learn to work for a cause, to be of service to someone, everything changes. But you've got to start somewhere. I had to start somewhere. I had to leave it all behind and take the leap of faith to say, okay, let me try this out. Let me start making videos. Let me start writing. I wrote a book. Who's going to read it? I had to believe the cat down the road would.

So this is why a lot of people cannot escape the slavery wage system. Because they know they've got to start from scratch. And you do have to start from scratch. But in the end, it will be worth it.

Producers, consumers, let's talk about it. Most people in the wage slavery system are consumers. They only consume Netflix and chill. That's cool. But you see, to escape the wage slavery system, you're going to have to learn how to be a producer. Every single day, ask yourself this question, what am I producing? What am I producing? Because the more you produce, the more that will return to you.

It's called the law of exchange. You can't receive this marvellous life if you're not putting anything out there. I did a four-hour live stream, and we ain't even had breakfast yet! But I love to give. I love to share. And guess what? People invite me into their homes all around the world. They're like, Ralph, come into my house. There's an African proverb which says, when you take care of the village, the village will take care of you.

So to escape the wage slavery system, every single day, have a clear vision of where you are heading to. Have a clear vision of where you want to be. Of where you want to be.

Look, I see a lot of people doing something, but it's only short term. Let me explain. You're doing this because of the bag in the end, some money in the end. But you don't want to be there next year. Then why are you there right now? You see, if you can't see yourself doing that in the next 10 years, stop doing it. Because whatever you are doing, you are building up momentum.

So I had to see, oh my gosh, I get it. I can see myself doing this in the next 50 years. I will be doing this in the next 100 years. Because I'm doing what is nourishing my soul. This is also a part of therapy. Everything we do should be healing us mentally, emotionally, spiritually, physically. It should be helping us evolve into the magnificent being we truly are.

We don't want to be somewhere complaining. Because now we've wasted a moment to count our blessings. To escape the wage slavery system, you're going to have to put in those 10,000 hours. There is no free lunch in the universe. Sometimes you walk around, you see the postman, the postwoman, people working. They don't want to be doing that, some of them. Some of them don't want to be doing that. But they've got to eat.

So if you want to escape the wage slavery system, you're going to have to learn how to be a super creator. You're going to have to learn every single day that if you do what the 99% are doing, you're only going to get what they get. You're going to have to learn how to think like the 1%. So produce twice as much as you consume.

If you read a book, write a book. If you watch a video, make a video. If you read an article, write an article. If you read an article, write an article, right? Now this producer mindset will help you escape the wage slavery system. Most people want instant gratification. Life is a marathon. You're going to fall on your ass. It's not going to work out. And you have to be able to pick yourself back up.

Put your head up, stick your chest out, and move forward. There are going to be days of drought, no harvest. Days where you're going to be alone. Most people don't want to be alone so they follow the crowd. The crowd is the matrix. This is why a lot of people are stuck in the wage slavery system. You've got to think outside of the box to realize there is no box. And I can do whatever I want. I can manifest the life I want.

But I can't do this if I'm looking at what everyone else is doing. I created Infinite Waters because as I was in the forest meditating, I said, okay, I'm going to be so unique. I'm going to be me. And that's what happened. Magic happens when you let go of society's expectations. They told you it's not going to work. They told you it's impossible.

Don't listen to them. Find out yourself. Take that leap of faith. And if you have that vision, even if you don't know how it's going to work out, follow your intuition. That first voice, that internal voice is your greatest guide, your inner GPS taking you to where you need to be.

Now, you see, to escape the wage slavery system, you might say, hey, Ralph, I've got this get rich quick scheme. I'm going to hustle. But if you're not happy doing that, you're still wasting time and you're still trapped in it.

A lot of people are pretending they've made it. Celebrating on the ground like, yeah, I made it. What did you make? What have you manifested? What have you done? So you don't want to trick yourself and fool yourself into thinking you have arrived somewhere when you ain't even done the work. You ain't even done the work. You've got to get your hands dirty. You've got to be in the trenches. You've got to sometimes work those late nights to work on your vision, to get this thing off the ground. Can you do that? It's not all peaches and cream. Some days you're going to be thinking, gosh, can I continue? It's harder right now. And it's not going to get easier. You just get stronger.

There was a time when I was like, hey, I might as well go back into the matrix. But then my voice, my inner voice told me, Ralph, the universe reveals its secrets to those who dare to follow their hearts. The rest is history. If you want to escape the wage slavery system, expand your mind, read new books, get new information, change your daily routine. There is no change in your life without a change in routine. A lot of people are caught up in the same routine every single day, expecting different results. That's the definition of insanity.

Become your own brand. What is my brand? Breathing in that good ass prana, baby. My brand is life. And when you create your own brand, when you become your own brand, you escape the wage slavery system. A lot of people might buy Gucci, Louis Vuitton. But have you ever thought of becoming your own designer? You might listen to Joe Rogan. Have you ever thought of making your own podcasts and being a producer? This is how you escape the wage slavery system.

Every single day is not about working hard. It's about working smart. It's about turning work into a lifestyle. I don't have a job. What I'm doing is a way of life. This is part of who I am.

I'm just being myself and manifesting tremendously. If you want to escape the wage slavery system, stop listening to friends and family telling you it's not going to work out. Go and work in the bank. Go and work here. Go and work there. No, do what you want. At the same time, you must know it's not going to be easy. If it was easy, everybody would do it. If it was easy, everybody would have it.

The truth of the matter is you're in the squid games. Only 1% is going to make it out. And the 1% are the people who trust themselves, who have this big vision, who play at the big level, who take these calculated risks, who wake up every single day and say, hey, I've got to do something.

If I don't do something, if I don't live this life, someone else is going to live it for me. 7-Day Vegan Challenge. Make sure you wake up every… and do what I do. What do I do? I wake up every single day with a whole bunch of grapes in my mouth.

That's how to escape the wage slavery system. If you are eating junk, the whole world is going to bring you down. If you're eating to live, you're going to want to feel better about yourself and everything you do is so connected. If you've just had a beautiful guava, mangoes, grapes, now you're feeling like royalty. And when you feel like royalty, you want those royalty checks. That's right.

Feel Alive by Ralph Smart on Amazon is selling every single day. I'm getting a royalty check every single month because I planted something long ago that is now growing to tremendous heights. You've got to do something right now. You've got to plant the seed today that your future self can eat from.

I know we're in the midst of a global pandemic. If you want to escape the wage slavery system, start thinking about how you can utilize this online space, cryptocurrency, whatever it is, but learn that there's always a plan B. Learn that right now you have to focus your energy on utilizing this talent you have and then sharing it with the world.

Don't work for money. Work for a great cause. Money becomes a byproduct. Don't stay somewhere where you complain constantly. Stay in a place which helps you evolve mentally, emotionally, spiritually. That's how to escape the wage slavery system.

Chapter Fifty Seven

Stop Chasing Money
& Financial Freedom

You can win just by being yourself. I'm proof of that. Financial freedom is here. Wealth is here. Prosperity is here. Health is here. And the cat down the road is over there.

Now, are you someone who's chasing money? Are you someone who's chasing financial freedom? Well, I've got news for you. Stop chasing money and financial freedom and instead do this. It will come to you.

I'm about to share with you the secrets of how I manifested so much abundance. I wake up every single day with a whole bunch of grapes in my mouth. I'm living my dreams out every single day.

I wake up blessed. I don't have to worry when it comes to finances. Why? Because it just comes and comes and comes and comes. Now, let me share with you what's helped me along my journey.

To manifest financial freedom... I stopped chasing money. I stopped chasing financial freedom. Then it came. How did it come? Because I started to realize that money is energy. Okay, money is energy. That's why they call it currency. Once you realize this, you start to realize how money works.

You see, a lot of people, especially in the spiritual community, sometimes feel that money is bad. Money is evil. No, that's poverty. We came here to live in abundance. Abundance is a state of mind. So is poverty. And when I started to attract heaps of abundance, money, financial freedom, it came because I changed my attitude towards money. I changed my attitude towards money. I said, I'm neutral.

To me, money is not good. Money is not bad. Money is just a tool that will give me more of what I already have. It's just a tool. And a lot of people, as soon as they wake up, their mind is just on money. Their mind is just on, hey, I need to make money. And this is how money stays away from you. Why? Because the more you focus on just trying to make money, the more you will distract yourself. Let me explain.

You see, I don't wake up saying, oh, how can I make more money? I wake up saying, oh, how can I inspire more people? Hmm. Oh, baby. Instead of waking up thinking about how you can make more money, wake up thinking about how you can serve more people.

Go on your YouTube, go on your Instagram, okay? Go on your social media. And I want you to look at what you're posting. Are you just posting selfies? Is it just all about you? Or are you helping me out? You see, that's how I attracted financial freedom, because I'm a service provider to millions of people. Therefore, money now becomes a byproduct. Are you understanding these words you are reading?

You see, I started to realize one thing. Money is a byproduct of me living this lifestyle day in, day out. I love what I'm doing, deep divers. I'm in the best shape of my life. I'm having the most fun ever.

Why? Because every single day, I get to do what I love. A lot of people, they wake up, they go to a job which is just over broke, and they're chasing a check, working for money. Deep divers, I don't work for money. The money works for me. Let me repeat that. I do not work for money. The money works for me. Stop chasing money and financial freedom, and instead do this. It will come to you.

It will come to you while you're just doing a little samba, baby. Act as if it's already here. Let me repeat that. Act as if it's already here. I don't think you read that enough. Act as if it's already here, deep divers. That's how I started to attract financial freedom. I told you, rich means realizing I create happiness. Abundance is a state of mind. I had to change the way I was thinking. Therefore, great things started to come my way.

Think rich, grow rich. The famous works of Napoleon Hill. You have to think rich to grow rich. You have to speak rich to grow rich. Start changing how you are speaking to yourself. Start changing how you are speaking about your dreams. Some people wake up saying, this will never happen for me. Some people wake up saying, I'm the chosen one.

I literally was saying I'm inspiring millions of people before I was actually inspiring millions of people. Because I know that word is bond. Words are spells. Therefore, you can speak what you want into existence. You can start attracting money and financial freedom to you when you begin to speak it into existence. I am always wealthy. I always attract prosperity to me, love and wonderful connections.

I started to act as if it's already here. I started to embody the energy of wealth, of abundance. Let me tell you this deep divers, it's no good fooling yourself. Once you act as if it's already here, you've got to back it up. You can't just say, hey, law of attraction, it's already here. All I've got to do is close my eyes, visualize and then the life I want is here.

No, it doesn't work like that deep divers. You have to now back it up, which comes about through stepping into radical action to say, actually, okay, I've been talking about it. I've been acting as if it's already here. Now I've got to back it up through actions.

You see, there is no overnight success. Life is a marathon. You have to put in the work, put in those 10,000 hours. You have to wake up with a mission statement every single day. What is my mission statement? Every day I seek to empower other people and help them live their best lives. That's my mission statement. What's yours? I'm waiting. Stop chasing money and financial freedom and instead do this. It will come to you and there it is.

Scripting. Okay. Scripting every single day as an author who has a bestselling book on Amazon. I'm always writing and I'm also scripting. What is scripting? I'm writing out what I want to experience in my reality. Some people have vision boards. I have a whole diary of how I want my life to go. I already wrote this into existence. I didn't only speak it into existence. I wrote it into existence. I said, okay, chapter one, Ralph Smart wakes up with a whole bunch of grapes in his mouth. Ralph Smart is in nature. Ralph Smart meets a wonderful soul. Ralph Smart inspires millions of people.

And when I'm writing this, it's amazing how my entire life aligned with what I was writing about. So start scripting your life out. Start realizing there is power in the pen. There is more power in the pen than in the sword.

Work your ass off. Let me repeat that. Work your ass off. I don't think you heard me. Oh, you did. Okay. Work your ass off because I don't know a wealthy person who just acquired wealth without doing any work. Now, yes, I know there are trust fund babies, but the majority of wealthy people, people who are people who have attracted financial freedom, they work their ass off. Okay. They're putting in hours. They're putting in time. They are waking up early, at four o'clock. They're taking time every single day to invest in their dream, to invest in their vision. I'm doing that deep divers.

I'm increasing my knowledge. I mean, I'm increasing my knowledge every single day, reading books that can help me go to the next level. Okay. Getting the information I need to go to the next level. I'm putting in the work, making videos in 4k resolution. I'm doing the work.

That's why I've attracted so much financial freedom. So remind yourself, there is no shortcut. A lot of people want to get famous and then get wealthy. There is no shortcut deep divers. You're going to have to do the work. And it's not going to be all fun and games.

Sometimes you're going to have to learn how to be alone, how to focus on your dreams. Like when I was writing a book, I had to focus. I had to turn off social media. I had to turn it off. Right. No more posting on the gram to say, actually, I've got to focus on this book right now.

That's how I manifested financial freedom. I want to remind you of this. Time management, the two most important words to manifest financial freedom, time management, how are you using your time? What's the first thing you do as soon as you wake up? A lot of people, they distract themselves and that's why you will never be financially free. So that was me along my early journey.

I would just wake up, distract myself, go on the gram, go on Twitter, go on even YouTube. Then I said, wait a minute, I've got to start creating. As soon as I wake up, I've got to start exercising. As soon as I wake up, I've got to start meditating. As soon as I wake up, and what happened? I started to become financially free because I was free in my mind.

Financial freedom begins with freedom in your mind. I don't think you heard me. I said, financial freedom begins with freedom in your mind. There is no greater wealth than your peace of mind.

Stop chasing money and financial freedom and instead do this deep divers, it will come to you. Always remind yourself how you use your time is everything. As soon as you wake up, if you just want to flex on the gram, then you're fooling yourself. You might fool other people, but you can never fool yourself.

Look, in that same time of you just trying to show off on Instagram, you could have written the first page of your upcoming bestseller. You could have actually produced a YouTube video. You could have done something productive. That's how I manifested financial freedom. I have no business trying to show you my Rolls Royce on Instagram. It doesn't do anything for me. I could do that, but I don't have to.

Seven-day vegan challenge. Shout out to everybody who has been changing their diet, eating plant-based foods, getting their fruits, their vegetables in. You see, I realized deep divers, the better I ate, the more I attracted to me. I started to attract more when I started to change what I was eating. When I ate junk, I only attracted junk. When I ate a delicious apricot, mango, some figs, and an acai bowl full of vitamin C, I felt good about myself, and this in turn allowed me to manifest more financial freedom.

The food you are eating is the fuel that will take you to where you need to go. Make sure you are refueling with the best fuel. Junk in, junk out. Goodness in, goodness out, deep divers.

Realize we all have emotional currency. This is our actual true bank account. Let me explain. When you are in a low vibration, your emotional currency, which is energy, is going down. When you are in a high vibration emotionally, when you are embodying peace, love, tranquility, serenity, your emotional currency increases, your emotional energy increases, and therefore, you will start to attract money, wealth, health, and financial freedom. It happened to me. That's why every single day I just say this: feels so good to be alive, baby!

Okay, financial finances going up, emotional bank balance going up. I'm feeling good about me. I've counseled so many people who have a lot of money in their bank account, but they don't feel good within themselves, so they're not winning in life. I'm feeling good within myself every single day, and I'm also financially free. So, I want to remind you to start taking responsibility for how you feel. Start protecting your energy. Start cultivating wonderful feelings within you every single day. Start feeling good about you. Start loving yourself.

For goodness sakes, and all of a sudden, okay, there financial freedom comes along with self-love, with self-acceptance. When you aren't distracted, when you aren't comparing yourself to other people, when you are focused on where you need to go to, deep divers, stop chasing money and financial freedom, and instead do this. It will come to you, and it's coming, and it's coming.

Provide value to those around you. I repeat, provide value to those around you. Enter the law of exchange. You see, there's an African proverb which says, when you take care of the village, the village will take care of you.

Yeah, I take care of the village, and therefore, the village takes care of me. When you impact people's lives in a positive way, when you give to people, just like how the sun gives to us every single day, somewhere around the world, the sun is shining on someone's face. They're just chilling like, oh, this feels so good. Thank you, sun. The sun is the giver of life. Therefore, it's always abundant.

To manifest financial freedom, you have to learn how to become like the sun, the giver of life. Every single day, I'm giving you amazing content, life-changing content, videos that will change your entire life. And therefore, by giving freely, the universe takes care of me.

The community takes care of me. The village takes care of me. That's why I don't have to chase money or financial freedom because it's already here, just by me giving of myself to the community every single day.

Learn how to give every single day. Wake up saying, what am I giving to the world? What am I sharing with the world? That's how you enter the law of exchange. And the more you enter the law of exchange, you will begin to manifest financial freedom. I want to remind you of this, to manifest financial freedom, learn how to be patient. Great things take time. Rome wasn't built in a day.

You may not have it now, but if you keep working on your dreams, if you keep loving what you do, it will come. I told you, I don't work deep divers. I haven't worked in the matrix since 2011. I don't have a job deep divers. I have a lifestyle I love. This is a lifestyle. I'm having fun deep divers. I'm like, oh my gosh, I've got the golden ticket, baby. That's right.

The golden ticket to financial freedom every single day lies in my hand. Why? Because I love what I do. I'm not complaining. I'm just grateful. I'm just saying thank you universe for another day of abundance. Feels so good to be alive, baby!

This can happen for you too deep divers, but you've got to start getting grateful. You've got to start saying, actually, I'm thankful for my life. I'm going to start using my talents and talent emanates from the Latin talentum, which means a sum of money. Your talent should always bring you financial freedom. The question is, are you using them? I'm using mine. You better start using yours.

Learn how to create without expectation. I meet some people who are like, Ralph, I really want to start making YouTube videos so I can become very wealthy like you and just travel all around the world and sip a delicious mango juice on the beach.

I'm like, cool. Okay, cool. Okay, cool. That's great. But I just looked at your first video and already you're telling people that they have to pay X amount to sign up to your course. You have given me no value whatsoever. That's why you will always be struggling. So learn how to create without expectation.

I did over a thousand videos without promoting anything just to help people. And that's why they've put me on the throne. That's why the universe is always providing financial freedom for me because I'm giving from a pure place without an ulterior motive. So learn how to create without expectation, learn how to create without expectation. You might have to create so much before someone says, thank you. That's okay. Know why you are doing it.

That's how I'm manifesting money. Lots of it. That's how I'm manifesting financial freedom. Remind yourself, never place all your eggs in one basket. Learn how to have multiple streams of income. Okay. That's how to manifest financial freedom. Get good at what you do. Be one of a kind. Start smiling more. That's how to manifest financial freedom. Start being real. That's how to manifest financial freedom. And then start saying, feel so good to be alive, baby. Can I get a hello? That's how to manifest financial freedom.

I was wearing suits, nice jackets before I was manifesting. Then I started to manifest because how we dress can impact what we start to attract into our lives. Dress the part before you get the part. May you manifest what you have been patiently waiting on. You've got to act as if it's already here. You've got to feel like it's already here and then you've got to back it up. You've got to start doing the work.

No more wishful thinking. Don't wish for it, work for it. Work your ass off and then it comes baby.

Chapter Fifty Eight

10 Reasons You Should Never Open Your Third Eye

Now, my third eye opened a long time ago. When we talk of the third eye, what are we talking about? We're talking about what the ancient people would call a gateway into higher intuition, wisdom, and knowledge, what the ancient Hindus referred to as the Ajna Chakra. People now realize we're talking about the pineal gland.

This is not some imaginary concept; the third eye actually governs our circadian rhythm, our melatonin and serotonin levels. So the pineal gland, the ancients would refer to as the seed of the soul. I've made videos on how to open your third eye.

To do that, change your diet, seven-day vegan challenge, stuff a whole load of watercress in your mouth. Different things like that. But is opening the third eye for everyone? Well, I'm gonna give you 10 reasons you should never open your third eye.

1.   If you love and don't wanna give up this current reality, opening your third eye is totally not for you.

If you don't think a normal life is boring, don't do it. Don't do it at all because opening your third eye shows you different levels, different dimensions and new realities. Happened to me along my journey. I didn't say, what are those? I said, where am I?

A lot of people who open their third eyes, what happens? Reality gets turned upside down. They have clairsentience, clear feeling, clairaudience, clear hearing. It's almost as if they've got new superpowers, baby. Now, it's fascinating because what scientists are saying is that don't even see 1% of all there is out there. We see less than 1% of the electromagnetic spectrum. Less than 1% also of the acoustic spectrum. So we're not seeing anything and we're not hearing anything either.

If you are happy with that, if you wanna stay like that, don't bother opening your third eye. But if you wanna tap into the 99% of what you're not hearing and what you're not seeing, then you really do wanna open your third eye.

2.	If you don't wanna give up this nine to five grind every single day and you feel it's the only way because you gotta survive, don't bother opening your third eye.

What happened to me along my journey? I went to university at 17 years old, graduated, became a psychologist. Not only that, I became a criminologist. Not only that, I got a job working in a school with people with ADHD, autism, bipolar disorder, and I did that for many years. It was fantastic. At the same time, I realized I didn't wanna be stuck in a nine to five, but I thought that was the only way for me.

And if you don't wanna give up a grind that you feel you have to do, if you feel it's a duty, oh, I gotta go to work, then you don't wanna open your third eye because the moment I started to dive deeper, my third eye opened, I realized how many other possibilities were out there. This life could be anything I wanted.

I realized the possibilities were endless. Now it's great to have a nine to five but your third eye will show you there is more to life than just a nine to five. You can actually create any lifestyle you want.

3.	If you don't wanna give up processed junk food, sausages, bacon

By the way, the World Health Organization has come out saying, yes, these meats and junk foods do cause cancer. But wait a minute, we already knew that years ago. Nevermind, don't worry about it. But if you don't want to give them up, then don't open your third eye. If you don't wanna give up processed junk food, don't open your third eye.

Let me repeat that. If you don't wanna give up processed junk food, don't open your third eye because, seven day vegan challenge, over half a million subscribers moving so fast, every single day we're getting over, I think it's nearly 150,000 views every single day on this channel. A lot of vegans on this channel, a lot of plant-based eaters and we're proud to be plant-based eaters. Do you know what they write and tell me? The moment they changed their diet, their third eye started to open. The moment they started to embrace a more plant-based diet, their third eye opened.

Because you see, when you open your third eye, you start to see the interconnectedness between everything. You start to see that animals are precious, just like the cat down the road.

Yeah, it's real precious. And your dog of course is precious. So therefore a sheep is also precious and definitely a pig. But you start to realize that I have to eat better. Why? Because there is more choice out there for me. Your third eye will make you take responsibility for your life.

Now as a psychologist, if you don't like the term third eye, that's cool. We can go with the psychologist Maslow who talked of transcenders. People in our society who had transcended the normal way of living. We'll come to that later. So when we come to realize when your third eye is opened, all you wanna eat is healthy stuff. That's all you want on your plate.

4.   If you feel animals were solely created for your consumption, you should never open your third eye.

If you don't wanna give that up, if you don't wanna give it up, don't bother. Because when you open your third eye, once again, you realize a life is a life... is a life. So don't bother to open your third eye, which is the seed of the soul, intuition, higher wisdom and clairvoyance.

The life of a living, breathing animal is no different from the life of a living, breathing human being. Therefore you have the wisdom, more so the intellect to realize all life is sacred.

5.	If you don't wanna give up everything you read, everything you see on the TV, you're there scratching your nuts, eating popcorn, don't bother opening your third eye.

That was me along my early journey. I'm no saint. I was there scratching my nuts, eating popcorn, watching Sunset Beach. It was terrible. Actually, it was actually quite fun, but I was asleep.

But if you are addicted to that lifestyle and don't wanna give it up, you should never even go on that journey to open your third eye. Because once you open your third eye, it's gonna lift you out of that chair. And it's gonna make you think.

It's gonna make you question what you're watching in a more analytical way. It's gonna make you read between the lines to realize this is nothing more than what the Hindus called Maya, illusion. What's helped me along my journey is to realize that the third eye can never be fully opened. It's a whole process going up the four levels of consciousness. You start to realize that the media, the goddess Medea, whose main trait was to be very cunning, deceptive, that's what a lot of the media does. Not all the media, but as your third eye is opening, you have more discernment, which is the ability to judge well what you are taking into your body, not only through eating, but also through what you're watching on TV, realizing, yeah, it's just a film, but a film also has subliminal messages in it. You see, films weren't just created for entertainment. They were created for indoctrination.

And when your third eye is opening, you feel bliss, you feel euphoria, but more so you start smiling every single day because you can see it from a mile away. You don't believe everything you read and you don't, you definitely don't believe everything you see.

6.	Never, ever, ever open your third eye is if you definitely don't want to give up doing everything your masters tell you to do.

Don't bother. A lot of us, we are governed by oligarchy, the authoritarian rule. We have masters, not realizing when you open your third eye, you start to realize, wait a minute, we are all masters.

Every single human being you see is a master, is a giant, or sometimes a sleeping giant. They don't even know their true power. But as your third eye is opening, you start to realize how much power a human being really does have. But if you aren't ready to have that kind of power, don't bother opening your third eye.

7.   TNever open your third eye if you feel like you know everything.

I've been there. We all pretty much feel we know everything and we don't wanna give that up. When your third eye is opening, it makes you realize you're just stepping, touching the surface of what we call enlightenment. What is enlightenment? Enlightenment is knowing how much you don't know.

That's why a lot of people who open their third eye, some people do it through dance, music, DMT. By the way, the pineal gland naturally produces DMT. We'll come to that later. Marijuana. But you can even do it just by, woo, breathing in that good-ass prana, baby. Getting high naturally.

But you begin to get more clarity to realize, wait a minute, we don't even know what planet Earth is. We don't even know what we are. You begin to realize since birth, you've been told what to think, what to believe, and who to trust. Therefore, how many thoughts are actually your own? How many? Look, you start to realize, I know nothing.

A wise man once said nothing. And I'm not wise, because I'm still talking a lot, right? But then again, like Confucius said, that true wisdom is knowing the full extent of one's own ignorance. When you think you know everything, what happens? As a psychologist, I always say it shuts down more learning. Because then you say, okay, I've arrived, then you stagnate.

The smartest people in the world are always hungry for new information. And that's what happens when your third eye is opening.

8.   Never, ever open your third eye if you like being separate from your fellow human being.

Like, what's up? What's up? Like, your neighbors are there and you're here and you don't even say hi. Hi, hi, hi, how you doing? No, no, no, you don't even look at each other. We've become strangers on planet Earth due to the ego, which is the illusory self.

Therefore, a lot of us believe in the mirage of separation. We believe that I and them are very different. As your third eye is opening, which really can be done through meditation, transcendental meditation, what happens? Oh my God. It's almost as if you have a psychedelic experience with someone else when you connect with them. Because there is no I and there is no I. There is no you. There is only the experience happening.

Therefore, one must come to realize that as your third eye is opening, you realize that separation is the biggest illusion on the planet. Do you know how many wars are caused because of separation? People have low self-esteem because they say, oh, my skin color is different. When you're opening your third eye, you start laughing and stuff because you realize what NASA's not even telling you.

Do you know how many other life forms exist in our universe you know nothing about? But don't worry about that. Because when your third eye is opening, you start to catch glimpses of it, what I call the glitch in the matrix. But hey, if you don't want to give up that feeling of separation, forget about it.

9.   Never open your third eye if you don't want to give up trusting your doctor.

If you feel your doctors are going to save you from overeating a lot of junk food and they are the only cure and remedy for you, then don't open your third eye. Because opening your third eye is a trip, boy, or girl, or woman, or man, or cat down the road. You start to realize that actually, like the great Jewel Pookrum said, physicians heal themselves.

What are we talking about? You have to become your own doctor first. Yes, it's great to have other doctors who can help you heal holistically, allopathically, and naturopathically, but ultimately it's you, you've got to know thyself, what it says on the Temple of Delphi, Temple of Apollo. You've got to realize that you can heal yourself by learning your thought process.

Yes, it's great to have support because we aren't here to do everything by ourselves. I've got people who help me heal, but I'm not going to place all my hands like that. Help me, doctor. I'm not going to throw all my eggs in one basket. I'm not going to place all my trust in someone I've never even met before. They don't know your ailment, but you do. That's why you've got to study medicine. You've got to become your own doctor first.

See, when you're opening your third eye, you start to realize that actually, like the great Dr. Bruce Lipton talks of epigenetics, our perception is controlling our DNA. Like the great psychiatrist, Mr. Deutsch said, the brain changes itself, through something called neuroplasticity. New experiences give us a new brain. And when you're opening your third eye, you realize that this body is pretty much incredible, amazing, outstanding, awesome, because it can heal itself when placed in the right environment with the right mindset.

But you don't want to do that, so stay with that doctor. Or you do, and then realize you are the doctor and we are helping each other heal.

10.   If you don't want to give up your nationalistic mindset.

If you love thinking, my country is better than your country. Now, a long, long, long, long, long time ago, I was also brainwashed with that mindset. I've traveled to nearly every single continent on the planet. Many, many, many, many countries, including Brazil and everywhere. Just say Brazil, that's everywhere. Lots of places, all of Europe. So many countries in Africa, North, South America, everywhere.

I travel every single year to so many different places. I'm always on the go, always on the move. So I begin to realize that there's a huge problem with the way we think as human beings. As a psychologist, I know that we love territory. That is why we fall for the trap of being nationalistic. Let's just say I say my country is better than your country.

What happens? That means I've got to fight to protect mine, and you've got to fight to protect yours, which means it ultimately leads to a war. But if I say, actually, I don't have a country, I am a planetary citizen, shout out to the planetary citizens out there. Hmm, I don't want a British passport, an American passport, a German passport, a Japanese passport, an Ethiopian passport.

I want a world passport, a planetary passport. How about that? When you're opening your third eye, these thoughts come into your mind that I get it. I don't see any borders. Do you? But that's a trap you fall into. When you're opening your third eye, you realize, like Da Vinci said, everything is connected and you learn to realize everything connects to everything else.

So it's a beautiful, beautiful time to be living in right now if your third eye is opening and you're getting a more expanded way of thinking, feeling, but more, so being.

Chapter Fifty Nine

10 Signs You're Highly Awake

Someone asked me if I could talk about my awakening experience and some of the signs that I noticed during that period. Right now, we are in a monumental time of change on the planet. And a lot of people are experiencing a paradigm shift. And they don't even know it.

I've been talking about this for a long time. But you see, what happened to me, took me to the next level. But when it was happening, I didn't know what the hell was going on. What's happening to you?

Let's take a look at the signs you're highly awake, but don't even know it.

1.   You walk into a room and then leave three seconds afterwards

Huh? Why? Why do you keep doing that? You have increased awareness levels. What I call the super awareness right now. And you don't even know it. You just get a vibe about certain things, people and places. Yes. You go into the room and then you leave. And your friends are like, what are you doing? And you're like, I just don't want to stay here anymore. Huh? And then you leave it at that.

You see, we are in the age of Aquarius. The information age where people are experiencing paradigm shifts like never before. Due to the level of information now, you are having increased levels of clairvoyance, which is the ability to see well. Clairaudience is the ability to hear more clearly. Clairsentience is the ability to feel things more deeply. You aren't just seeing things. You are feeling the energy behind the things you are seeing. And you don't even know it.

That's why a lot of the things you feel you can't explain. You're even like, I don't know why, butl just feel it, baby. It's just like that. That's the first sign.

A lot of people, their third eye is opening. The ancient Hindus talk of the Maya. How a lot of reality we observe is actually an illusion. A lot of the reality we observe is actually an illusion. So the truth is subjective. The truth, your reality, becomes reality. A lot of people are starting to see that. Based on the increased awareness levels. We create our reality based on our thoughts. Change your thoughts and you change your world.

2.   Right now, you have more questions than answers.

The cat down the road is saying, look at you go. Like, what happened to you? You're like questioning everything. Like someone says something, and then you have like a thousand questions. No, two thousand. You might read something. You might watch something. And you have more questions than answers afterwards. That's a sign of your awakening.

I realized I am very ignorant. Because enlightenment is knowing how much you don't know. And true wisdom is knowing the extent of one's own ignorance. A wise man once said that. We have terms like ignorance is bliss. Don't worry about it. Ignorance is bliss. You see. in many ancient civilizations and cultures, ignorance was not bliss. Ignorance carried a heavy price. In ancient Kemet or Egypt. They had the mystery schools. Where they realized this entire universe was built upon sacred geometry. There were no accidents or coincidences.

Everything in this universe is built on a mathematical design with such intricacy. It would blow your mind away. And that's why you're probably questioning stuff. Don't worry about it. You have a lot of discernment. For some strange reason. Like somebody might tell you something. Like oh the moon up there is just so and so. It's just like this. It's just like that. And you are not really gravitating towards a certain answer for something. You have more questions.

Like what really is the moon? What is this planet we call planet earth? How many other more planets are out there? How well do I know myself? How well do I know the cat down the road? How well do I know you? More questions than answers. You don't even know why that's happening right now. You are awakening to your highest potential.

3.   You have a better food choice than ever.

And you don't even know that. You haven't even realized. Check in your basket. All of a sudden you've not only got strawberries. We actually put the bananas with the strawberries. You put blueberries inside. You got the kale. You have a better food selection choice than ever. Right?

Even your friends are like, what happened to you? And you're like, I have no idea. I'm just taking all of these fruits and mixing up all of these colors into this beautiful smoothie right now. And just like going around my daily business like I don't know what's happening, baby. No, you are going through an epic awakening.

You see, food is information. Food carries information. And that is why the more organic you eat, you are now activating more neurogenesis, which is the activation of brain cells. Foods with live enzymes like the great Dr. Sebi spoke of. We are electrical beings. Therefore, we need electrical food.

Now, seven day vegan challenge. A lot of people are awakening as soon as they start eating a more plant based diet. A lot of people say, gosh, my third eye is opening. That's right, because food is information.

Downloads like you might just be drinking a hemp smoothie. One of the greatest sources of protein, or spirulina. And all of a sudden you start saying stuff and everybody around you is like, what the hell are you talking about? And they're like, I've never heard that before. That's the spirulina doing that.

4.   Numbers you are seeing.

Eleven eleven two two two three three three. Oh, yeah, baby. You're like, whatever. You keep seeing it now.

It's getting to the point where you're seeing it at least like every single day, at least like one kind of eleven eleven or two two two or three three three or three three three. Right. And eleven eleven. We talk of the numbers. You see, numbers are signals. Nature symbols.

Numbers are how nature expresses itself. Music is the universal language. But music is built on numbers. Numbers are realities. So if I say eleven eleven, that's the gates. That's why a lot of people, if you see eleven eleven, you are now seeing the glitch in the matrix. We'll come to that later. But more so, you are entering a portal of higher awareness and consciousness. A lot of indigos, a lot of crystals.

These are just labels. We are even beyond that. The numbers are showing you that this universe is built on mathematical design. Almost like a simulation holographic universe. People tell me they keep seeing three three three, which is based on transformation. Two two two.

You're building. Okay. What are the chances of you seeing eleven eleven? Not once, but like a thousand times. Not once, but one thousand one hundred and eleven times. What's the chances of that? No accidents. That's a sign you're awakening. You don't even know it. You are beginning to realize that life isn't random. Life is highly intelligent.

Do you think we are the only intelligent beings? Do you think we are intelligent? Do you think we invented that word? No. Nature has been more intelligent before us. You think nature waited for us to invent maths?

5.   Synchronicity

Synchronicity is everywhere. Sometimes you're just thinking of a guitar and then someone plays it behind you. Who the hell was that? Sometimes you're thinking of something and then someone just says it. Sometimes you just are awaiting something and then it magically appears. That's synchronicity.

Where your dominant thoughts align with your life. They align with every single experience. Your thoughts now become your experiences. Many people are shocked when they have synchronistic experiences. But that's a great sign you're awakening. Because the universe is showing you that what you think matters. What you think you are creating. You are a co-creator through the thoughts you are thinking.

So I always think that I want to become my greatest version. I don't want to, I'm doing it. And that's what happens. I said a long time ago I want to help inspire a lot of people. We got over 74 million people diving deep. Getting the message. Growing at a phenomenal rate. Synchronicity. I said I want to meet loads of vegans. They arrived at my house, baby. Right outside as well. Synchronicity.

6.   You realize that positive people also have negative thoughts.

But they don't allow those negative thoughts to control their entire life. You are now becoming an alchemist. You don't even realize it. Like someone shouts at you. And you're like whatever. Going to the beach right now. Going to drink a nice coconut juice. Coconut water. Papaya juice baby. Right, you are becoming a master alchemist. Where even if you've had a really crappy day, you come home and you start dancing. And everybody's like what happened to you? You start smiling for no reason. Yeah.

Wait a minute, I just got a car ticket. Yeah. Okay, you're starting to realize how you can actually create whatever experience you want. By changing your attitude towards it. You're also realizing that nobody is perfect. There are no positive people I always say. There are no negative people. We go through things. And it's not about being positive. And it's not about being negative. It's about being authentic. And that's a sign you are highly awake and don't even know it.

Like someone might say you're a really negative person. But you're just being you. Someone might say you're really positive Ralph. You're always happy. I'm just being myself to be honest.

8. You are drawn to nature spaces.

Eco therapy. You love to breathe in that good ass prana baby. Okay. The concrete jungle just doesn't appeal to you like it used to. And that's what happened to me along my journey. I was just ending up in random parks and beaches. And I'm like what am I doing here? Okay. That's a sign I was awakening and I didn't even know it. Okay. You end up on someone's beach. Wait a minute. Can people own beaches? Have we gotten that crazy on this planet where people own beaches? Okay.

You are drawn to nature spaces. Whether it's mountains. You are drawn to what I call healthy breathing spaces. Getting the right chi. Okay. And yes, people are like what happened to you? Because you're just not in the office anymore.

8. You have changed your career, your job.

Wait a minute. You don't even have a job right now. Don't worry about it. You've changed it. Whatever you are doing, you've changed it. Okay. Why have you changed it? Because you have new information that yes, we are immortal. But in this present setting and environment, you only live once. So that means I'm only going to live a lifestyle, which is your job. That serves me. That helps me become my greatest version.

I talk about the best eight hours you have every single day. The nine to five, the daylight hours where you have the most energy. You are highly awake and don't know it because you say in those eight hours, I just want to party. I just want to dance, baby. I just want to do whatever I want to do. That's a sign you're awake.

I realize that. I said over a decade ago, I never want to work in a man-made job ever again. I'm going to create my own job, my own lifestyle. I'm going to live it, breathe it, and create abundance. And that's what I'm doing right now. It's a mindset. You've got to visualize to materialize, baby. Visualize to materialize. Visualize to materialize. Say it three times. Three is a lucky magic number. Okay, so you've changed careers all of a sudden.

And people, even your parents are saying, huh? Why did you do that for? Even your partner. You went to go and work in a local farm somewhere. Look, at the same time, you also realize that you're learning to play the game. It's not saying that, okay, these people are bad. These people are good. No, you're learning the matrix we live in and how it operates. But more so, you are placing your happiness at the forefront. And that's why life feels so fantastic.

9. You don't have time for drama anymore like you used to.

You don't have time to distract yourself like you used to. You have this urge to help people. What I call a willingness to help people. And that's a sign you're awakening and don't even know it. Happened to me along my journey.

There was a time where I was just so self-absorbed. Then I realized that I just want to share with people what I know. And that's why things are growing so fast right now. That's a sign you're highly awake and don't even know it. You've got a lot of people right now on Instagram. They're sharing great pictures, inspiring people.

It's not about just saying, oh, look at me, look at me, look how great I look. That's amazing. But you see right now, being the age of Aquarius, people are even taking a backseat. Now the message is even more important than the person. People are now realizing that their message is so important. It's not just about them. It's about the collective.

That's why people all of a sudden... they're making documentaries, making films, using art to inspire.

10. You realize that you don't have to impress anybody.

Okay, you realize this. What are you doing? What are you doing? What are you doing? What are you doing? You don't even know it. Okay, you just have that kind of vibe about you right now. And people are like, what happened to you? You're starting to realize that you didn't come here to please people. You came here to be real. And that's why a lot of the time you might, your parents might want something for you or your partner.

How old are the people that dive deep? We've got people from like three years old. No, babies actually. Yeah, babies to like 80 plus. So pretty much everybody. They're realizing that they don't have to impress people like they used to. The only concern, the only concern is to be as authentic as possible. Okay, that's a sign you're highly awake and don't even know it. If you don't feel the need always just to impress people.

Like I don't make videos to impress people. Because I already made so many videos like we got over 1000 and something videos on this channel. After a while, the novelty wears off. Trust me. I do it because it's just fun. Right? It's just fun. But also I'm learning along my journey and it's helping heaps of people. But that's why it feels so great doing it.

Chapter Sixty

How To Lucid Dream

What is a lucid dream? This is any dream where you are actually aware that you are having a dream. You're in the dream world like, I'm actually dreaming right now. And I'm aware of it. I am aware of it. You can control your dreams. You can be anything in the dream. You can go anywhere in the dream. You can even see Ralph Smart in the dream and the cat down the road. There are infinite possibilities.

Lucid dreaming has helped me become my greatest version because it's allowed me to see the infinite possibilities that lie in existence. So you've probably seen Inception, the great film. In one part of the film, they're dreaming, lucid dreaming. And they're like, oh, you come here to sleep. And the other person's like, no, I come here to wake up. And that's how lucid dreaming feels like when you keep doing it.

You actually become so alive and you have this limitless potential, which when you wake up now becomes a reality. Your dreams are real. Okay, now, before we actually get into it, we have to share some very important information. It starts like this. To begin to lucid dream, you have to be in alignment with your true circadian rhythm. To begin to lucid dream, you have to be in alignment with your true circadian rhythm, meaning you need to have a proper sleep schedule.

I know it's hard. I know it's super hard, right? What time did you go to bed? Okay, this is key because our brain produces melatonin. Melatonin governs your sleep and wake cycles. In fact, melatonin is the secret to lucid dreaming. Goes into the pineal gland. Right? Melatonin, the magic of everything.

So I started to realize I have to be more in tune with my true bio rhythm. To even contemplate lucid dreaming, you need to be in a smooth, regular sleep and wake cycle. And once you get into the groove, you're on the first step towards having a successful lucid dream. Once you've done that, I've got a lot of viral videos which are 432 hertz frequency, which is the universal frequency, super powerful DNA repair brainwave states.

You've got gamma, beta, alpha, theta, delta. Harvard studies show that you will have more lucid dreams in the theta brainwave state. So I put out music, binaural beats, theta, waves. And if you play that before you go to bed, you will have more of a chance to have a lucid dream. So look for theta music and play it before you go to bed. That will increase your chance of having a successful lucid dream.

Now, the next step, we're gonna look at the seven day vegan challenge. Tryptophan, that powerful amino acid. Tryptophan is the secret to having more lucid dreams. If you are eating a lot of tryptophan, you're gonna have more lucid dreams. Now, I've been a vegan for over 13 years and I'm eating a lot of tryptophan, which is in cacao. Cacao has tons of tryptophan. And that's why I'm lucid dreaming pretty much every other day, right? So tryptophan produces more serotonin in the body. Serotonin produces more melatonin and melatonin will give you more lucid dreams. It's that simple.

What other plant-based foods have tryptophan? Flax seeds, spirulina, spinach, chia seeds, okay? And check this out. If you really wanna eat melatonin, a great plant-based source are almonds. Almonds are a great plant-based source for melatonin and you will be lucid dreaming. You are what you eat. Now, we're getting there.

Dream journaling. Before you even start to really learn how to lucid dream, what I want you to do is buy a dream journal, say Ralph Smart sent you, and start writing what you see in dreams. You see, the problem is most of us can't even remember our dreams. What did you dream of last night? I have no idea. Don't worry about it.

So what helped me along my journey to really master lucid dreaming was to actually learn how to write down my dreams. And that is an art in itself.

Like dream recall, writing down your dreams. What do you see? What do you hear? Where are you going right now? What are those? Nobody knows, right? So write down everything about your dream.

If we look at the next step, we're talking about MILD, which is mnemonic-induced lucid dream. Now this is a powerful way to lucid dream, right? It consists of four stages. You're like, Ralph, it's supposed to take five minutes. Don't worry, we'll come to it.

We've got to go through the stages first. So the first two stages of mnemonic-induced lucid dream, we're talking about dream recall, which is the dream journal. Okay, we've got that. You're practicing that. And then we're also talking about reality checks. So before we even begin to master the art of lucid dreaming, you have to become aware of dream journaling and reality checks.

Now, what are reality checks? Reality checks are checks to see if you are dreaming or you are actually awake. Oh my gosh, are you dreaming or not? We don't know, right? So you test yourself to see if you are dreaming or not. How can you do this? Hold out your fingers and then count how many fingers you've got.

If you've got 17, you are definitely in la-la land. Another great reality check for lucid dreaming is the reading test, where you can actually look at a book, look at a word and then turn away and look back. If it's changed, then you are dreaming because remind yourself that many of our dreams are gonna be super exaggerated.

Okay, sometimes you might have eight legs. You might be like a spider or something, right? Might have wings, okay? Might have a hundred hands. Dreams are where anything is possible, but your dreams are real. And this is a dream world. Everything you see in existence came from someone's mind. Man-made that is.

Okay, the next step we have to look at is knowing how melatonin works. Melatonin is produced in high amounts in complete darkness. So what I love to do before I even begin to lucid dream, I'm closing my blinds, right? You can't see me. You can't see me, baby, right? Everywhere is total darkness. That's perfect.

That's what we need to have the most amazing lucid dream because if you have a lot of electronics, you see a lot of people sleeping with their mobile phone, you've got bright lights, it's gonna be very hard. It's gonna interfere with your melatonin levels. It's gonna drop them.

To increase them, you need pitch darkness. Now, serotonin, once again, during the day you can go out partying in the sun. That will charge your serotonin, get the levels up. And then at night you want total darkness. That brings melatonin levels up. Now you are ready to lucid dream.

Now we're close to the five minutes of how to lucid dream. What I want you to do, this is what's helped me along my journey. Set your alarm for six hours after you sleep. You're gonna wake up and be like, oh, what happened, Ralph? Don't worry about it. You are in the fifth stage of sleep, which is what we call the REM, which means rapid eye movement, right? You're like, what's happening? It means you are having intense dreams, right? That's the time where you're having really intense dreams. So that's the time to wake up.

And once you wake up, now this will only take five minutes. And this is where you really have the most powerful, lucid dream, amazing dream in the world. So you get up, you spend two minutes just gently massaging your forehead and then your head, giving it a little massage to really even relax yourself more. And then just make sure your body is relaxed.

Then you spend another three minutes in the last part, MILD, mnemonic-induced lucid dream. The last two stages are lucid affirmations and dream visualizations. So I repeat for three minutes, I am gonna have the best lucid dream in the world. I am going to lucid dream. I am going to have a lucid dream. I'm gonna fly to the pyramids, stuff a whole load of grapes in my mouth, right? I am gonna lucid dream. I am gonna become aware in this dream. I am going to become anything I want. So you're affirming to the universe, right? That will take three minutes, that's five minutes.

And then you just fall back to sleep. And then you'll find yourself having a lucid dream. Mnemonic-induced lucid dreaming works like this, that when you expect to lucid dream, you are more likely to have a lucid dream because you are willing it into existence. Remind yourself this, that you might think, oh my gosh, who cares, it's just a dream. No, it's not. Dreams are the language of your subconscious mind.

That table you see, that computer, all came from someone's mind, from their dreams. And then it materialized. You've got to visualize to materialize, right? And then tell me what happened in your lucid dream.

Like what weird, amazing stuff did you get up to, baby? And then lastly, just practice every single day. Realize that with lucid dreaming, what's helped me along my journey is the practice, practice, practice. The reason why I went through those stages is because it's so important. And then once you practice, you'll be finding that you'll be having a lot more frequent lucid dreams.

Chapter Sixty One

The Dark Side Of Being Highly Awake

A lot of people right now are waking up and sometimes you wake up when you're really young. Happened to me. When I was a teenager, I started to wake up. And there are so many benefits about being highly awake. But there's also a dark side. Oh, no. Yes, there is a dark side to being highly awake.

Now, you laugh at me because I'm different. I laugh at you because you're all the same. Now, there is a dark side of being highly awake. A lot of people say, Ralph, gosh, your life must be perfect. There's a dark side. And dark isn't always bad.

Why do we think dark is bad? It's a dark day. No, dark is good. Dark is illuminating. Without the darkness, you would not be able to see the stars. We become illuminated in the darkness. There's a dark side, a real dark side. To being highly awake. But this is actually liberating. And it's nothing, nothing to be afraid of.

The dark night of the soul happens. That is the rite of passage. That is the initiation to having an awakening. Going through the dark night of the soul. You see, it takes the breakdown to have the breakthrough. And that's why I said, religion is for people who are afraid of going to hell. Spirituality is for people who've already been there. Oh, you've been to hell, Ralph?

Absolutely. Absolutely. Let me tell you this. The dark side of being highly awake. It reminds me of a song and it goes a little something like this. You go through life being misunderstood. A lot of people who are waking up right now, they go through their life every single day being misunderstood. Family don't get you. Friends don't get you. It seems like you're the black sheep of your family. Seems like you're the fringe dweller.

It seems like you're the outcast. It seems like you're the outlaw. And because of this, a lot of people who are highly awake, they often find themselves alone. They often find themselves cut off from the rest of the mainstream because it's not that they aren't likable or they don't have a lot of friends. It's just that they don't have time to pretend.

Okay? They have a low tolerance for bullshit. And that's why when you are highly awake, a lot of the time you get a massive awakening. Sometimes when you're still in the system. It happened to me. And this is why you choose. It's a choice to say, actually, I don't want to follow the crowd. It's better to be alone than follow the crowd going in the wrong direction. So because of this, a lot of the time, people who are highly awake often spend a lot of time alone. And that's a blessing.

You see, I'm here to remind you that actually we are never alone because the universe always sends someone. But for those who find it hard sometimes just to be alone, I'm here to remind you. Remind yourself. You don't want to follow the crowd because the crowd is the matrix. So being highly awake, you've got a choice to make. To go with a crowd going in the wrong direction or to stand in your truth. And sometimes you might find yourself standing alone with a cat down the road. Well, we can do that. We can do that.

Okay? The dark side of being highly awake. I spoke of the dark night of the soul. You also have to confront your shadow. You see, most people in this society have not done their -shadow work. And when you are highly awake, you have to see things about yourself. You have to be honest, say, actually, I have a lot of unresolved issues. I've got a whole lot of work to do. We've got a whole lot to talk about. And therefore, you are faced with this reality that you aren't only good, you're bad and darn right ugly.

You see, authenticity includes both positive and negative. And you realize that actually I'm the positive, but also I'm the negative. And a lot of people right now are highly awake, because a lot of people I meet are very awake.

The dark side, though, comes when sometimes people say you're a conspiracy theorist because you're saying every single day, we ain't having it. They call you a conspiracy theorist because you don't want to wear a face mask. They call you a conspiracy theorist because you don't want to be in lockdown. They call you a conspiracy theorist because you don't want a vaccine passport. They call you a conspiracy theorist because you've got a mind of your own. They call you a conspiracy theorist because all you want to do is just breathe in that good-ass prana, baby.

And I want to remind you, conspiracy theorist, that this term was created by the CIA to stop people waking up. And I'm here to remind you, you're not crazy, you're just waking up. You see, most people don't think for themselves. They are only living a life that their parents want them to live, that society wants them to live. They're not free. They are living according to traditions, to traditions and cultures which actually enslave them. And a lot of people who are highly awake, they want to be free.

They're free spirits. Their soul is free. And because of this, because of this, sometimes they get in trouble because they forget that they're living in this 3D matrix and there are rigid rules. But as you are awakening, you realize the only laws are divine laws, divine order. Man-made laws aren't real. Look, they can change the time at any time. One hour backward, one hour forward. Therefore, it's an illusion.

Time, man-made time is an illusion. Shout out to everyone right now who is standing in their truth. When we talk of the dark side of being highly awake, we have to also talk about being the odd one out. Now, I actually see this as a blessing in disguise. Like I was always the odd one out. I'm left-handed, by the way.

Do you know my grandma? She was born in Sierra Leone. And if you were left-handed, they used to beat you because they thought you were like a chosen one, that you had special powers. Because everyone used to write with their right hand. Only a few people would write with their left hand. You see, as someone who is highly awake, you are sometimes singled out because you are unique. You are sometimes singled out because sometimes you are the odd one out.

Everyone in your classroom is just listening to the teacher. Press rewind back at school. You are looking out of the window because you're like, actually, I should be out there, not in here, getting programmed.

The dark side of being highly awake is actually when you realize, 7-Day Vegan Challenge, you're all around the table and they say, hey, stop being fussy. 7-Day Vegan Challenge, okay? What? You don't eat butter? What? You don't eat eggs? What? You don't eat meat? And sometimes it was hard for me. I've been plant-based. I've been a vegan for over 15 years, okay? I wake up every single day with a whole bunch of grapes in my mouth.

I remember, the first time when I went plant-based, I was at a wedding and I had people, even I know, family, certain family members, they're like, gosh, Ralph, you're losing weight. Gosh, that's a terrible thing to do. Don't you know you need to eat meat? You need to eat eggs? You need to eat processed foods? I'm like, no, I don't. I can just eat leafy greens and vegetables and I'm good to go. So you are often seen as fussy because you actually care about your health. Go figure.

Oh, you're the person who loves cold-pressed juice. That's because cold-pressed juice actually preserves the enzymes which actually help you digest food, okay? So continue being a fussy plant-based eater. I'm rooting for you, okay?

The dark side of being highly awake. Let me talk to you. Now, this happens to me all the time. People are like, Ralph, gosh, I can't believe you said that. You are supposed to be spiritual.

I told you. Spirituality means accepting the good, bad, and ugly about yourself, okay? So you are often sometimes seen as holier than thou, the Dalai Lama, okay? Because people think, oh, because you're highly awake, you must be meditating every single day and burning sage and being a perfect righteous being. And they forget that, hey, you're still human.

Like, I am a multi-dimensional being having a human experience. At the same time, I'll still put your ass in your place, okay? I can't believe you said that. Oh, I got more to say for you, okay? So a lot of people forget that just because you're highly awake, it doesn't mean that you're a softy. It means that you're also confident. It means you're also full of audacity. It means you can also speak up for yourself. And sometimes people might find you a bit hard. They might see, gosh, this person really can speak so much power. And I don't like that because spiritual people are just supposed to be passive and quiet and docile. No, you got the wrong one.

The dark side of being highly awake, it's actually a blessing. But many times we put pressure on ourselves to reach unattainable goals of Nirvana. And sometimes we give ourselves such a hard time in trying to meditate five hours a day and six hours a day. And there's a lot of competition. Spirituality, once again, is when you accept who you are.

You're not here to compete with Ralph Smart. I'm not here to compete with you. And you definitely aren't here to compete with the cat down the road, okay? So when we talk of us realizing we are enough, we don't have to try hard to be. We are already a magnificent creation. And this is why a lot of people who are highly awake, sometimes they've got to learn how to give themselves a break. You're doing better than you think. I'm proud of you. I'm proud of you. Like a proud dad, deep divers.

The dark side of being highly awake is that sometimes you forget many people are just blindly listening to what the media say, what the television says, and they can't think for themselves. And sometimes because of this, you realize that so many people have been programmed and because of this, you often get into arguments with people. Sometimes you get into disagreements because you're like, I just wish you would wake up, right? Happens to me all the time.

Actually, not anymore, but it used to. Because I now realize everybody wakes up at a different time. And as a highly awake being, you have to understand that the truth can't be told. It has to be realized.

Sometimes we can think we know so much, then life humbles us, okay? Enlightenment is knowing how much you don't know. So as a highly awake being, you realize, gosh, I thought I knew it. No, there's always more to learn. So you are faced with this reality that you don't know. Shit, you could have just read like 5,000 books, but that isn't the truth, right? Because the truth is something you can't read in a book. So you realize you are just the same as everyone else.

It's just that you are aware that there is more to life than meets the eye. So I want to remind you, it is a blessing, a gift to be highly awake. At the same time, being highly awake means that you have to take a look at your shadow. You have to integrate your shadow into yourself. You also have to realize you didn't come here to be perfect. You came here to be real.

Also, you have to realize everyone wakes up at a different time. Not everyone's going to make it. And a lot of us who are highly awake, we have to watch people close to us, family and friends be programmed in the matrix and still keep a straight face.

They tried to bury us. They forgot we were seeds. Remind yourself, stay as free as you can because that's our birthright after all.

Chapter Sixty Two
____

The Nine Types Of Chosen Ones

The nine types of chosen ones explained and their missions, which one are you? The universe works in my favour, why? Because I'm a chosen one, I'm a chosen one deep divers, born on March 3rd at 3.03, yes, I've always known I'm a chosen one, but I'm not the only one, a chosen one is a being who remembers who they truly are, a spiritual being having a human experience and the truth of the matter is we are all chosen ones, it's just that a lot of people have forgotten who they really are, but there are different types of chosen ones deep divers, because each one of us has a different role to play, so read this and find out which one you are.

1.   The oracle

Let's start with the first type of chosen one, it is the oracle, that's right, the oracle, the seer, the one who can see things before they happen. The oracle goes back to ancient times and the oracle was the one that generals would consult in ancient Rome to ask the oracle, would we win in war, would we win in war or would we lose? You're going to lose, okay, right, the oracle is the being who goes back to ancient Kemet or Egypt, who would remind people to know thyself, she is the medium, he is the mystic, it is a being who embodies the truth, their aura is wonderful, exuberant and beautiful, people come to them for counsel, for advice, because they possess tremendous gifts, what I call the triple C, the triple C's: clairvoyance, clear sight, they can see what most people cannot see, they can see deeper, clearer, so they have the gift of clear, they have the gift of clairvoyance, right.

Also clairaudience, they can hear what most people cannot hear, did you hear that? The cat down the road did, okay, they have clairsentience, clear feeling, they can touch someone and they can feel what this being is going through, this is the reason why the oracle, the chosen one, is an empath, an intuitive empath, but their gift of clairvoyance means that they have literally got a crystal ball in their hand, right, they can tell you what is going to happen to you in the next five minutes, tomorrow, in the next month, this is the reason why the oracle is the medium, the oracle is the prophet, the oracle is amongst us, and they are the chosen one, so shout out to all the oracles in the house, you are appreciated. Is that you?

2.   The free spirit

Okay, the free spirit, this is the being who is just a free spirit, are you a free spirit, like nobody can hold you down, like you know what you want in life, you know there's more to life, you're sometimes an outcast, an outlaw, because you don't fit into society, you realize that you didn't come here to fit in, you came here to stand out, you came here to stand out, you came here to stand out, and you realize that it's not about fitting in, it's about being custom-made.

You are awake and aware that this whole system is a big joke, this whole matrix is a big lie, and you're like, ain't nobody got time for that, I just want to be free, your parents are telling you to do this, your friends are telling you to do that, and you're like, all I want to do is be free, is that too much to ask, is that too much to ask, no it's not, right, so are you a free spirit, deep divers, are you a free spirit, because that's the second type of chosen one, a being who craves freedom more than anything, and their mission is to remind people that being free is your birthright, okay.

3.   The truth teller

Are you someone who is always telling the truth, the whole truth, and nothing but the truth, like you can't lie, you just have to keep it real all the time, exposing the matrix for what it is? Like you wear the truth on your sleeve, and you're not ashamed to talk your truth.

Are you someone deep divers who is speaking their truth, even if their voice is shaking, because you know it's the right thing to do, are you the one who's keeping it real in a whole room of fakes? That's the third type of chosen one, and we've seen it, like throughout time, we've seen people who have been brave enough to speak their truth, even though it's not popular. But they've made it popular, because now people are starting to listen, and this type of chosen one is extremely powerful, because the voice holds power.

So shout out to all of you, if you are speaking the truth, your truth, keep doing it, if you are in the mission to use your voice to awaken people, keep doing it, right, it's beautiful to see people really embodying the truth, and reminding people of the truth, of things, and who they really are.

4. Inspiring infiltrator

Now this is a being who is a very inspiring being, naturally, they inspire people, their mission is to inspire, and they are a powerful co-creator, and they hold the light in their hands to bring it back to the mainstream, and oftentimes this type of chosen one is a very beautiful woman, or very handsome man, you're so kind, yes, okay, this type of chosen one, their mission is to bring their message of truth to the mainstream, and they often use their beauty to do it, and oftentimes it's someone that you would least suspect is awake and aware, but they really are, right, they're really diving deep.

And they're aware that we are multi-dimensional beings having a human experience, they're aware that we're living in the maya, the illusion, and they're here to wake you up, but they have to do it in a very subtle way.

So they are the inspiring infiltrator, sometimes they are artists who are very awake, and they're like, you know what, I can't just tell people, wake up, I've got to put it in a song, you know, we've got to do it like how grandma did, we've got to put the goodness in the whole stew, mix it around, the vitamins and minerals, right, we can't just give it to you like that, we've got to do it in a very subtle way.

Sometimes these are influencers, entertainers, and they're giving you that message to wake up, but they're doing it in a very subtle way, and their message is being heard by millions of people, right.

5.   The confused chosen one

Like they can't make up their mind, right, they're like, I know I'm different, I know I came here for a higher purpose and reason and calling, but you see, the problem is, Ralph, I'm stuck in between, two worlds, it's like, I'm awake and aware, but at the same time, my ass is trapped in the matrix, my ass is trapped in the matrix, and I don't know what to do, Ralph.

So these are the kinds of chosen ones who have the knowledge, and they're aware that we are so much more, they're aware that the media is lying to them, they're aware that this system is corrupt, but still, they're still confused, because they're like, I don't know how to live free, and this is the reason why a lot of people who are in regular jobs, some of them are chosen ones who are very awake and aware, it's just that they haven't yet transitioned to really living the life that they're talking about, or thinking about, or reading about.

So this is what I call the confused chosen one, they are stuck between worlds, the true world and the illusion world, is that you?

6.   The hermit

Are you always spending time alone, this type of chosen one enjoys their own company, they love meditating, they love hugging trees, they love being connected to the elements, they love being in nature, breathing in that good ass prana baby, they love having inner body experiences, they love trying really weird stuff, like turning their phone off for a whole day, and just sitting with their emotions, mastering their emotions.

This type of chosen one, they would rather be with themselves than follow the crowd going in the wrong direction, they love exploring their emotions, their feelings, and they love having time for themselves, and this chosen one, you often see them by themselves, in that buddha pose, that lotus position, right, and their mission, their mission is to really be bold enough to live their truth, and this requires you being alone.

Have you noticed, like all the great masters, the sages, the gurus, and guru means teacher, right, when you see them in pictures, they're always alone, like buddha always alone, jesus christ all alone, cat down the road all alone meditating, oh my gosh, oh my gosh, right, is that you? But they realize they're never alone, because the universe will always send someone, and we are all connected.

7.   The warrior

The warrior queen, the warrior king, shout out to all the warrior kings going hard, shout out to all the warrior queens going hard, helping humanity wake up to the truth of who they really are. Helping people get right with themselves, reminding people that they aren't powerless, they are powerful.

Now the warrior queen and the warrior king, this is an individual, a being who is really not about turning the other cheek, right, they are on the battlefield, and they are fighting for the truth, they are fighting for your freedoms, they are fighting for your sovereignty, they are fighting the dark forces, and they are bringing the light.

So many times we come across these beings, this woman here holding a long sword, warrior queen right here, and these are beings who don't back down, they are always going to protect the truth, they're going to fight for the truth.

Sometimes it gets them in trouble, because sometimes they say stuff they shouldn't like, it gets them in trouble, they do things like, they don't care, because they're like being free is my birthright, we're going to expose the matrix for what it is.

Shout out to all the warrior queens and kings, right, these are the way showers, these beings are on the battlefield, fighting the illusions, fighting the lies, and they're no pushover. Are you a warrior king or queen? Are you a warrior goddess, warrior god? Congratulations.

Their mission is to fight for you, they fight for your freedoms, they fight for your truths, and they are so needed, so needed, the light workers, I love all of you, I love all of you, I'm getting emotional.

8.   The healer.

Now this is the individual, the being who is all about helping you eat to live, seven day vegan challenge, I wake up every single day with a whole bunch of grapes in my mouth, they are showing you that health is wealth, they're all about healing, body, mind, and soul, and they do this through showing you that there's another way to eat.

You can eat to live, many times these people are also not only showing you what to eat, they're showing you a lifestyle that is healthy, through fitness and health, you often find these chosen ones, they are fitness instructors, body gurus, they know how to get a six-pack in like six days.

They're going to help you get a better body, mind, and spirit, right, through eating to live and getting your body in shape, because it's all connected. Is that you? Are you someone who's like a health nut, right, you're always in the gym, you're always encouraging people to eat better, stuff a mango in your mouth, and you're like, hey let's run a marathon right now, right, and people are like, no, no, no, no, you can do that!

9.   The elder

The elders are so needed, and this type of chosen one is the shaman, this type of chosen one has been here for a long time, they are guiding humanity to a better path, because they are the guardians.

I call them the gatekeepers of the truth, the gatekeepers of the light, the guardians of the light, and because they've been here for a long time, they hold the secrets. They've seen a lot, they've been around for a long time, and until this day, many people go to Peru to meet the shamans. They do the ayahuasca retreats, those chosen ones are chosen to guide people, because they've been here for a long time, they are elders.

Respect your elders, right, also in Africa, you have the shamans there, the master teachers, the gurus, right, in India, the elders, so respect your elders. These beings are wonderful, because these chosen ones, their only mission is to spread love to all of humanity, through their wisdom of being here for a long time, and seeing the cycles of life.

So there you have it, the nine types of chosen ones explained, and their missions; which one were you?

Chapter Sixty Three

8 Messages From The Universe You Shouldn't Ignore

If someone sends you a message, a lot of the time it can wait, it's not that important, it's not that serious. But if the universe sends you a message, it's one that you don't want to miss. Because any time the universe sends you a message, you better recognize and realize that this could be a matter of life or death. Like the universe doesn't play around here.

Eight messages from the universe that you really need to start pondering upon. Like, oh my gosh, really universe? Yes, really. Are you ready to dive deep? It's all energy. That's all there is. And every single day, the universe is sending you a message that is helping you become your greatest version. The universe wants to see you win.

Do you want to see you win? Because I want to see you win as well. Let me share with you what's helped me along my journey.

Realize that all there is energy and that we are spiritual beings having a human experience. Because we are energy, and because all there is is energy, we are part of the universe. The universe is not something abstract. The universe is in everything and everyone. The universe is communicating with us every single day. The universe is sending us messages every single day.

Do you think the universe waited for human beings to create mobile phones before it sent you a message? No, the universe has been sending you messages since way before mobile phones, right? Everything is recorded. We can talk about the Akashic Records in this universe.

The universe is always communicating with us. If we learn how to read these messages and watch out for these signs, not only is your life going to improve, you're going to become wiser, happier, healthier, and more loving like the cat down the road. So let's look at messages from the universe you shouldn't ignore:

1.   Accidents and coincidences

I've realized this along my journey, that there are no accidents or coincidences. Everything is happening in divine order.

Like a lot of the times, we think we're so high and mighty, right? But when something happens to us, it humbles us. It humbled me. Like when I had an accident, when I was skating, I twisted my ankle. I'm like, oh, my gosh, why did that happen? That was a message from the universe to me. You see, the universe communicates to us through our accidents and coincidences. So what was the message from the universe when I twisted my ankle, when it was so bad I couldn't even walk? Ralph, you weren't paying attention.

That's right. I wasn't paying attention. If that didn't happen, it could have been a whole lot worse. Thank goodness I only twisted my ankle. I could have broken my leg. Universe forbid, right? And that was the message from the universe to me. Ralph, pay attention. Ralph, be vigilant. Ralph, make sure you're not taking your life for granted. Because a lot of the times when I would be skating, I wouldn't be really concentrating. My mind would be somewhere else. And the message from the universe, in any accident you have, many times it can be prevented.

My twisted ankle could have been prevented if I was more cautious, more careful, more diligent, more vigilant, okay?

Coincidences. There are no coincidences in this universe. Everything is in divine order. Check this out. I'm flying one time, and the person sitting next to me is also a Deep Diver. What are the chances of that? Over 7 billion people on planet Earth and we start talking. Ralph, I know you, right? And they were telling me stuff I didn't know about. I'm like, the universe has ordained this meeting for us to connect in this moment.

I could have sat three rows back. But this coincidence was a message from the universe that, hey, you need to meet this being today because both of you have something to talk about. You see, the people we are meeting now, we already planned to meet in a previous lifetime.

What a coincidence. There are no coincidences in this universe.

2.   Repeating numbers

Any time you are seeing 1111, 222, 333, 444, 555, 666, 777, 888, 999, and this is not a new song, but it could be.

Probably go number one, right? Considering most of the music right now goes number one. Repeating numbers. Why do I keep seeing 1111, Ralph? Because you are leaving the matrix and you are entering the new world.

Why am I seeing 22? Why am I seeing 33? These are master numbers. 1111, 22, 33. On a deeper level, when we come to realize that you have 11 organ systems inside of your body, when you realize you have 22 bones inside of your skull, that's why they talk about skull and bones.

It's a secret society because you don't know about it. 33. Why did Walt Disney talk about the 33 Club? He was in the know. Why does Ralph always say 33? I was born on March 3rd. That's 33 right there.

33 is the number of the master teacher, Christ consciousness. The most powerful number in the universe, 33. Did you know, you have 33 vertebrae in your spinal column? 33 is the number of divine alignment. That's the sign the whole universe is working in your favor. Deep Divers, every single day, the whole universe is working in my favor. That's the message from the universe to me.

Ralph, you were born on March 3rd at 3.03. What are the chances, once again, no coincidences, what are the chances of me being born at 3.03 on March 3rd? That's 3.3. A lot of threes, 33, divine alignment. So if you are seeing these repeating numbers, it's showing you, it's a message from the universe that, hey, you're waking up to a greater truth.

This Matrix illusion world where so many people are turning into robots, so many people are clones, so many people are just followers, copying, doing what everybody else is doing. Who don't have a mind of their own. When you are seeing these angel numbers, it's showing you that you are different. You are one of the chosen ones. You came here for a greater purpose. You are awake. Your third eye is opening. You are entering a whole new world. You are moving from the 3D into the 5D.

3.   Recurring dreams

Your dreams are real. That's what the ancients knew. They say life is but a dream. Everything is reversed, right? A dream is life. That's what the ancients knew. When you go to sleep, you are actually waking up to the real world. When you wake up, you're back in the dream world, the illusion matrix world of make-belief.

That's why the dream world is so powerful because you can do anything, be anything, go anywhere. You can travel to any place you want. You can become as powerful as you want. You can create anything in the dream world because that's the true world. You are limitless. No borders, no boundaries.

So if you are having these recurring dreams of you being in a certain location, this is a message from the universe. I used to dream a lot about being in ancient Egypt, and I still do. Now, that was part of my past life.

In fact, Ralph Smart, that's my matrix name, right? This channel used to be called Kemet Prince One. What is the name of Egypt? Kemet. I was the prince of Egypt. When I go back to my past life, I was a priest in ancient Egypt in the mystery schools. What am I doing right now? Inspiring millions with wisdom. Can you see us all connected?

If you are having recurring dreams, once again, the language of the subconscious mind is image. Images. That's why they say a picture is worth a thousand words. So if you are having these recurring dreams of being somewhere, something happening to you, that's a message from the universe because your subconscious mind communicates to you through your dreams.

No dream is random. Everything, happens for a reason. Everything you dream is significant. Grab a dream journal because your dreams are messages from the universe that you have to wake up to.

CHAPTER SIXTY THREE

4.   Roadblocks, dead ends, detours, delays, closed doors, missed appointments

There was a time whenI was supposed to be somewhere, a long time ago, I had to actually meet a career advisor. This was when I was in the matrix. Now, if I was driving on that route, there was actually an accident that happened, a very bad accident.

I actually missed that appointment, but that was the exact time when the accident happened, I would have been driving along that way. It could have been me in the accident. Thank goodness it wasn't. That was the message from the universe that, Ralph, hey, I saved your ass.

Detours, same thing. Many times, if you have to take a detour, the universe is protecting you from places not meant for you. If you're supposed to meet somebody and it gets delayed, and then you find out this person's a really nasty person, that's the universe protecting you from people who aren't meant for you.

Dead ends. In the matrix, I used to work 12-hour shifts, and when I would work, I would feel like a robot. I'm like, this is a trap. This is a dead end. I'm young. I'm supposed to be living my best life. That was a message from the universe, like, Ralph, your life ain't going anywhere. Get your ass into nature. Just breathe in that good-ass prana, baby, and you are going to manifest beyond belief. My, oh, my. That's what's happened.

5.   Synchronicity

Divine synchronicity. Synchronicity emanates from Greek, with sin meaning to-gether, and kronos, which is the word Greek for time, so together, time, happening at the same time. When things happen at the same time. How many times have you been in the car and you're thinking of something, you turn on the radio, and the lyrics are the exact same thing that you're thinking of? You're like, oh, my gosh, she's thinking about exactly what I'm just thinking of right now. Synchronicity.

Sometimes you're thinking of something, then it just pops up on the computer. Synchronicity. Sometimes you're thinking of something, and then you turn around, and then someone's wearing a t-shirt of the exact same thing you are thinking about.

What is synchronicity? Synchronicity is where your consistent thoughts, your most consistent thoughts, align with your life and become your most consistent reality. What? Synchronicity is where your most consistent thoughts align with your life and become your most consistent reality.

Every single day I'm having synchronicity. People are coming into my life for a reason, and I know it's because everything is aligning for me. Synchronicity. It's not random. It was meant to happen. So that's the message from the universe you shouldn't ignore.

Take a look at all the synchronicity in your life, even the people you are interacting with on social media. This is part of the synchronicity. You weren't meeting these people by accident. You weren't meeting these people like, hey, it's so random. No, it's happening because it's part of the synchronicity. Everything is reconnecting. Everything is coming back to the essence.

6.   Advice

You see, the universe sends us messages through other people. Let me repeat that. The universe sends us messages through other people. The universe is using me. I'm only a vessel. I'm only a divine messenger. The universe is using me to give you a message.

The universe is talking through me to give you a message. That's how the universe sends you a message every single day. One you shouldn't ignore. My grandma used to tell me stuff. She was a very religious woman. I'm more spiritual, but I used to listen to her anyway.

She used to be like, she used to give me the most profound wisdom. And I'm like, okay, I know the universe is talking through her to give me a message I shouldn't ignore. She's like, Ralph, just learn when you go through life, there are going to be ups and downs.

Make sure you stay positive. You keep a good heart of love. She used to give me advice. Where do you think I got my advice from? I got it from my mom and my grandma, right? The universe is sending you a message you shouldn't ignore in the form of advice from people closest to you that care about you.

That's the universe using them to give you a message and you shouldn't ignore it. Many times we think, hey, I know everything. Not me, I can learn from everybody because everybody you meet can teach you something.

7.   Seven day vegan challenge

What's your life like? What's your health like? Anytime you have great health, that's a message from the universe like, hey, those mangoes are doing you so much good. Full of vitamin A. Anytime you are in poor health, that's a message from the universe that, hey, we need to find a plan to get your cells back in working order.

It's a message from the universe. Once again, we are the universe in human form. The universe communicates to us through our cells, through our mind state, through our emotions and feelings. These are messages from the universe you shouldn't ignore. Never ignore how you feel because your emotions are valid. Your experiences are valid.

Everything you feel is a message from the universe you shouldn't ignore. Everything you experience is a message from the universe you shouldn't ignore because if you can learn from the past, you grow wiser. Many times we go through stuff and we're like, what was that about? But if you can learn from it, you grow wiser.

8.   Your gut

Did you know Deep Divers? Just like our brain, our gut is actually a mini brain full of neurons, okay? And that's why people say, I feel it in my stomach, right? Because our gut is our inner GPS. Our gut is our intuitive master inside of us. It knows everything before it happens.

It can sense stuff. And that's a message from the universe you shouldn't ignore. Never ignore your intuition.

If you have a feeling about somebody and something, trust it because that's the universe sending you a message you shouldn't ignore. How many times, have you gone to a party, a nightclub, but you're not feeling the vibes? You're like, oh my gosh, the energy is so heavy here. It's time to leave. And the moment you leave, a fight breaks out. You're like, whew, bottles flying everywhere. Even the cat down the road is involved.

You should see it. It's crazy, right? Thank goodness you got your ass out of there, though. That's a message from the universe you shouldn't ignore, right? Your gut instincts.

Thank you, universe. Everything happens for a reason. There are no accidents or coincidences in this universe.

Chapter Sixty Four

———————

10 Signs The Universe Is Trying To Tell You Something

So We Are Out Here Chillaxing In The Heart Of Nature. Can You Hear That Call From The Universe? Ring, Ring. Yes, The Universe Is Attempting To Contact You Right Now. Please Pick Up. Here Are 10 Signs The Universe Is Trying To Tell You Something.

Ever wake up one day and think someone's talking to you and it just might be the universe and we ain't even had breakfast yet. The universe is trying to warn you about something. The universe is a great messenger and we are the universe because we are made of stardust.

However, the universe works in mysterious ways. It works through people. It works through objects. It is all around us trying to help us every second, trying to send us messages every single second. And right now on the planet, there is a massive, beautiful awakening happening. So what are the signs?

1.　　Increased intuition

The first sign the universe is trying to tell you something is that you have this increased intuition. Intuition emanates from the Latin word 'intuary' which means to notice. You are noticing so many things, okay? And the universe is telling you right now that you are growing in awareness.

You are growing in consciousness. We are approaching the age of Aquarius. The hidden is coming to light. And you've got the eyes to see it. Thank goodness for that. Your eyes are opening. Your mind is expanding. And you are, uh-oh, you're feeling into things right now. You feel people's energies right now. You're like, actually, maybe I'm not going to go there right now because I'm trusting my intuition. My intuition is growing. Trust your vibes, okay?

You are having an increased amount of intuition right now. And the universe is telling you that your mind, your consciousness is expanding. And you should be proud of yourself, frankly.

2.   Triggers

That's right, you get triggered easily. You care way too much what people think about you. I don't like you. Are you trying to diss me? Are you trying to tell me something? I don't like that. You got triggered. You see, the universe works through other people.

Sometimes people tell me stuff and I'm like, who are you talking to? Don't you know who I am? Hold me back, cat down the road. I got triggered, okay? Because ultimately, you have to take responsibility for your internal condition. Nobody can make you feel a certain way without your permission.

So the universe is trying to tell you if you are getting triggered, if you're caring way too much what people think, okay? The universe is trying to tell you to take a look within yourself to say, okay, why am I externalizing my power to strangers? I don't even know, okay? Do whatever you want. Forget about society's expectations, okay?

So anytime I'm caring way too much about what people think, the universe is trying to tell me that, Ralph, it's because maybe they've got a little bit of a point. Oh my gosh. Don't worry about it, Ralph, okay? I've got to start taking a look within.

3.   Reckless accidents

Now, I was on my iPhone walking down the stairs and I'm like totally not concentrating. And I slip and I actually twist this baby finger. Ouch. And yeah, it pretty much snaps. It bends. Thank goodness I do yoga. So I just put it back into place. Like get back into place. Ouch.

It was painful. But the universe was trying to tell me that I had just caused a reckless accident to myself because I wasn't paying attention. So the lesson there for me was, Ralph, focus on going down the stairs, okay? Now, accidents can happen to any of us, the best of us, okay? And sometimes when we have these accidents, we think it's something personal.

For me, the universe was trying to tell me, and by the way, we are not separate from the universe, okay? The universe was trying to tell me, pay attention. Be in the present moment. Because so many times, let's face it, we're texting, then we're eating, then we're walking down the stairs and that's how accidents happen.

Sometimes you're even driving and you're not even concentrating, okay? You're watching an Infinite Waters video and you really should be paying attention to what's happening, okay? So the universe was telling me, just focus, Ralph. Focus, focus on the here and now. Then the rest will take care of itself, okay?

4.   Repeating numbers

I meet a lot of people who see 1111, 222, 333. Okay, the universe is trying to tell you that you are in alignment. The number one, meaning a new beginning. Meaning a new beginning. Many times, people who see 1111, it's at a time when they are going through a massive spiritual awakening. You are waking up from the deep sleep.

The world that has been pulled over your eyes to blind you from the truth. What truth? That you are an infinite being with unlimited power and potential. It's time to wake up from the matrix, okay? The universe is trying to tell you that hey, these repeating numbers, one, one, one, one.

What are the chances of you seeing 1111 every single day? Well, people write to me and they tell me about their experiences. And I see it too, these repeating numbers. And I'm like, okay, one and zero. This is the language of computers, binary. So we are starting to realize that reality is one massive simulation. It's just like a computer program.

That means if this is a video game, I can do what I want to. The universe is trying to tell you, you can create your own reality. That this universe is built on divine mathematics. The numbers don't lie. Keep seeing 1111, 222, 333. It's showing you that you are in alignment, baby and it's time to do a little Samba.

5.   Seven day vegan challenge.

Now, I wanna give a special shout out to Dr Sebi again. If you don't know who he is, this is a guy who cured AIDS, cancer, he was a phenomenal healer who really helped me along my early journey.

And he was talking about how mucus is the number one cause of all disease, okay? So when I was starting to listen to him, this was many, many years ago, okay? Over a decade ago, okay? I wasn't eating the best, okay? I was eating French fries, pork chops, drinking soda, okay? Potato chips, greasy foods, and I didn't feel good. In fact, I was constipated, yeah. And the cat down the road was taking a selfie of me.

Gosh, look, I was sick. And the universe was trying to tell me that if you don't change your life in terms of what you are eating, you won't be here for long. So thank goodness for people like Dr Sebi. And he really helped me realize that we have to be eating more electrical foods. Avocados, spinach, leafy greens, okay? Pumpkin seeds, butternut squash, okay? Hemp seeds, okay? We have to be eating life to get life, okay?

So when I was not really caring about what I was putting into my mouth, the universe was telling me, cause I was feeling sick, when you don't feel well, that's a message from the universe that, hey, you've got a choice. You can start stuffing a whole load of grapes in your mouth and be healthy, or you can stay constipated. You don't really want to stay constipated, do you? I thought not.

6.   Lyrics to songs

A song comes on the radio and the lyrics match exactly what you were just thinking about. Have you experienced this phenomenon? You're in the car, you turn on the radio, and the lyrics match exactly what you are thinking of. Like I was thinking of some beautiful red grapes, and I hear Adele singing I love grapes.

And I'm, oh my, what are the chances of that? Okay, beautiful synchronicity, where your dominant thoughts, synchronicity is where your dominant thoughts align with your life and become your dominant experiences. And it usually happens when we turn on the radio.

Try it today, think about something, and then be aware of the lyrics. And oftentimes, if it matches, the universe is trying to tell you that you are in alignment because the universe works through other people and your favorite song. Your favorite song, right?

7.   Dreams

I'm gonna do a whole video on dreams, but like if you are dreaming of your ex, the universe is trying to tell you that you've maybe got some unfinished business. I dreamt of my ex and I'm like, oh my gosh, I really loved her, right? Yes, if you are dreaming of winning the lottery, it's probably because you're broke. I'm just kidding.

Look, if you are dreaming about traveling the whole world, it's probably because that's what you should be doing. So the universe communicates to us in our dreams. The dreams we have are reflections of the life we live. If you just had a nightmare, the universe is trying to tell you, stop watching so many scary movies or maybe it's time to stop living at such a low frequency where undesirable entities exist.

Okay, there was a time when I wasn't in tune with myself. I wasn't in tune with myself and I would go to bed and dream of monsters and gremlins and it was all because the life I was living was very toxic, okay? Once I changed, I'm living a lot better now, got into nature, did a little samba and I started to dream of unicorns and grapes and I can live with that.

8.   The universe talks to us through animals

One day, before I was about to shoot a YouTube video, there was an ant on my microphone.

So the universe is trying to tell you something when you see tiny insects and animals, okay? And you're aware of what they're doing. I'm like seeing this ant crawl on the microphone and I'm like, it's so tiny, but it's showing me that all life is sacred. It's showing me that, Ralph, you don't know anything.

You think you know a lot, but Ralph, you don't know anything because I'm a tiny little ant. I'm a tiny little ant, okay? But in my eyes, everything is so massive, right? I was also in nature the other day and I saw a bird just hovering in the air and I'm like, it's so beautiful. It is so beautiful.

Now, growing up, my sister and I, we would see magpies, okay? And one magpie was good luck. Two magpies was something good is gonna happen and three magpies was bad luck, okay? So we always used to see like one magpie because sometimes three would be there, but we wouldn't focus on the other two, right? We wouldn't focus on three. We'd only focus on one.

Okay, that's good luck, right? So the universe is talking to us through animals. Do you love your dog? Yes, Ralph, of course I love my dog, okay? Your dog has a message for you from the universe that you better start taking it for a walk. Stop being lazy, okay?

Now, animals are sentient beings and that's why I've been a vegan for over 13 years because I realized that when I'm with a cat down the road, when I'm with a dog, when I'm with a lizard, when I'm with a snake, when I'm with an orangutan, a bat, whatever animal it is, I'm like, this is divine intelligence and I can learn from an elephant. I can learn from a leopard. I can learn from the black panther. This is Wakanda. Right, I can learn from all beautiful animals because I say animals are our teachers, right? Animals are our teachers. They are always in the present moment.

Look at your dog right now. It's in the present moment while you're thinking of something that hasn't even happened yet. So you can learn from animals. They are your greatest teachers, okay? And that's what the universe is trying to tell me.

9.   Unexpected delays

I was in Cape Verde Islands, okay? Cape Verde Islands, beautiful island, okay? And paradise, okay? I was with my partner and guess what? It was delayed. My ex-partner, yes.

You remember, if you're watching this, you remember what happened. The flight was delayed on the way back. So we had to stay on the island for an extra one week, which was fantastic.

The only thing though, I had to get back because I had to start working. This was when I used to work, okay? In a regular job. And I'm like, oh my gosh, I'm gonna probably lose my job even though I'm in paradise, okay? But these unexpected delays, and sometimes it happens, you miss your flight, you arrive at the airport late and you're really angry with yourself and whatever is happening to you, it doesn't look good right now, okay? And you're mad at the universe.

So the universe is telling me whenever these unexpected delays happen, road-blocks, you're stuck in traffic, okay? And the radio doesn't work and someone's yelling at you from the side and hooting at you from the back. Oh my gosh, Ralph, stop, okay. The universe is trying to tell you to be patient, right? Because you have to learn patience. And I had to learn patience, that sometimes life isn't gonna go your way because you need sometimes roadblocks, delays to really appreciate what you have right now. Be thankful for roadblocks and closed doors because they keep you away from places not meant for you. How about that?

10.   People change

Ever been around someone, they're really friendly and they grow really cold and are unreliable people, okay? The universe is trying to tell you that people will change.

They can love you one day and hate you the next. Hey, that's human beings for you, okay? But also, now I had to go to the post office before I was making a video to drop something off. And a woman told me, she said, if you park there, you're gonna get a ticket.

So, and she was homeless, all right? And I'm like, thank you so much. So I gave her a good contribution for helping me not get a ticket because I'm like, thank you so much. Like other people weren't even telling me stuff. So sometimes the people that you think won't help you because they've got problems of their own will actually be the ones that helped you in the end.

The people who say, oh, I love you so much. I love you so much. When things get a little bit hard, even in relationships, ever been with someone they're like, I love you. You're the only one for me. And then the next time, the next day when you break up, they don't even care anymore. I feel crushed, I love you, right? People change, right?

So I realized the universe is trying to tell me that don't just think because someone says they love you, they actually do. Talk is cheap. Don't tell me you love me, show me. How about that?

So those are the 10 signs the universe is trying to tell you something. Once again, we are the universe. We are made from the same fabric as the universe. However, the universe works through people, objects and things. And there are universal messages everywhere you look. There's one there, there's one there, and there's one there.

What the hell is that? That's another message the universe, it is trying to tell me to come to nature earlier. Thank you, universe.

Chapter Sixty Five

10 Signs The Universe Is Trying To Tell You Something

Are you on the wrong path? Can you feel it in your bones? You're going the wrong way. Here are ten warning signs from the universe that you're on the wrong path.

Recently, I made a video, how to find your purpose. And I've found my purpose. But many years ago, I was lost, confused, isolated, not knowing what I was doing, totally on the wrong path. And not even the cat down the road was there to comfort me. I know what it's like. This may be you right now.

So you've got a feeling you're on the wrong path. Well, let me go through some of the signs that you are definitely on the wrong path, and give you some solutions.

1.   You are always trying to escape from your life

The first sign, warning sign from the universe, you're on the wrong path is that you are always trying to escape from your life. Okay, you're like, I can't wait for this to be over. I can't wait to get away from here.

So this means you're on the wrong path. You know, you're on the wrong path... when you're on the run from yourself. Many years ago, I was living a lifestyle which wasn't serving me. It was hard. And to cope with the pain, the frustration, the boredom, I would go to nightclubs, I would distract myself. I was living a lifestyle which wasn't serving me.

This might be you right now, and you have to really pay attention to say actually, if I'm always trying to escape from the present moment, I'm on the wrong path. If I go to work and I check the time as soon as I go in and I'm like, oh my gosh, I've got another nine hours of this. You're on the wrong path.

Because you should be content and happy where you are right now. And that's how you know you're on the right path or left path. Because I'm left-handed, right? So once you stop running away, you are on the right path. And how do you stop running away? To be on the right path? Start actually loving what you're doing every single day.

2.   You are having anxiety attacks

So those red lights are flashing right now from the universe, showing you that you're on the wrong path. You are having anxiety attacks. All anxiety comes from the desire to escape the present moment.

Yikes! Okay, and that's how to know if you are on the wrong path. Do you have panic attacks? Do you have high levels of anxiety? You see, so many of us, we suppress how we feel. But you're looking a bit shaky, baby. We are so stressed out. And we lie to people. We're like, I'm actually okay. Or, I'm fine. That four-letter word. Fearful, insecure, neurotic, and emotional.

So, what actually helped me get back onto the right path was to be real with how I was truly feeling. And I'm like, actually, I'm not fine because I'm having all of this anxiety. And all anxiety emanates from the desire to escape the present moment. I was once again trying to escape the life I was living. Now, I'm actually content. I'm happy. I love being in nature, baby. And that's how I know I'm on the right path.

3.   You can't focus

It you can't concentrate, if you are highly distracted at all times, then you're on the wrong path. I was along my early journey.

You see, many times we're so distracted, not realizing we're living a lifestyle which is so detrimental. If we stay there any longer, there's going to be hell to pay. And that was me along my early journey. I could never focus, never concentrate. And I realized this lifestyle was not serving me, right? This lifestyle was not serving me.

Yes, this lifestyle was not serving me. And sometimes it comes in the form of friends. It comes in the form of addictions we have. And how I actually found my right path or left path was, I'm like, where can I really focus? Where don't I feel distracted? And you have to find an environment that really wants to see you win.

Most of us, we are going on the internet, WorldStar, all of these sites, all of these websites, which really keep us in a perpetual state of distraction. And that's why we get carried away. We lose focus. We lose our true calling, our true purpose. And that leads us astray on the wrong path. So to get back, stay focused and then say, okay, which environment helps me to stay focused? Like when I'm in nature, there are not many people around.

When I'm in the forest, I can really stay focused on creation. And that's how I know I'm on the right path.

4.   Crippling self-doubt.

If you're always doubting yourself, second-guessing yourself. If you go and work in a job and spend 12 hours there only to come home to have no energy for the life you're working for, you're on the wrong path.

You're on the wrong path, because many of us, we expend our energy, we waste our energy at pointless jobs only to come home to have no energy for the life we're working for. And that was me along my early journey. I used to actually work 12-hour days, okay? I was so tired. I would get home and be drained, and have no energy. And then I would tell myself that actually this is healthy.

Krishnamurti said it is no measure of health to be well-adjusted to a profoundly sick society. So how I actually got onto the right path and got my life back in order was to quit any activity which was draining my energy.

Any activity which makes me feel subhuman, less than human, that makes me feel weak, and I started embracing activities which actually uplift me, motivate me, help me go to the next level, okay?

5.   Your health is deteriorating

7-Day Vegan Challenge. A sign you're on the wrong path is that your health is deteriorating. If you're living a lifestyle which is encouraging you to eat hot dogs full of nitrates which cause cancer, then you're on the wrong path!

And that was me along my early, early journey. Been a vegan for over 13 years. Best choice I ever made. That's what helped me to get back onto the right path. Because you are what you eat. Every 35 days, your body makes new cells from the foods you are eating. Eat to live, eat to live, eat to live, okay?

6.   Accidents

Accidents happen, right? Accidents happen. Things break. Things go missing. And this is what I started to see along my journey. When I was on the wrong path, so many accidents were happening.

Then I realized the universe does not make mistakes. There are no accidents or coincidences in the universe. But you know you're on the wrong path if you are having so many accidents at the worst times, delays all the time.

The universe is trying to send you a message that actually maybe this path you're on is not the right one. Because the moment I started to become my greatest version, get on the right path, things were flowing a lot smoother. It doesn't mean that everything's going to be perfect. I still have my trials and tribulations, but definitely there were a lot less accidents. Thank goodness.

7.   You're playing a role.

You know you're wearing a mask every single day. You're pretending. You're acting, okay? That's when you know you're on the wrong path.

Like I would sometimes go into work and pretend to my boss, my manager, but that wasn't really me. Now, I'm my own boss, my own CEO, and I know I'm on the right path. If you are honest with yourself, you can say, actually, am I pretending? Does the world know who I truly am?

If you're always pretending, you're on the wrong path. The more authentic you are, you are on the right path. The more authentic you allow yourself to be, you are on the right path.

8.   You're always late.

Now, working in so many different jobs growing up, I used to work since I was 16, and there was this job I was working in, in retail. This was when I was like a teenager, okay? And I was going in late on purpose because I didn't really want to be there.

I didn't want to be there, right? And I was actually on the wrong path because I knew I deserved more. That wasn't my true purpose to start like just staying in retail, right? Now, I would arrive to work late on purpose, and I would get briefed and shouted at. What are you doing? Why are you arriving late? And I'm like, sorry, right? I was on the wrong path.

Now, every single day, I'm in nature on time. Thank goodness, okay? If you are on time, and yes, time is just an illusion, you catch my drift. If you are on time, you are on the right path. So, the way to start getting on time, being punctual, is to actually have a lot of love for what you are doing. Have a lot of passion for what you are doing because the moment your passion dries up, you are going to be late all the time. And the cat down the road is going to get really worried about you.

9.   You're always scared.

You fear everything. You fear the next moment. You fear the next day. I've been there, and that's how I knew I was on the wrong path.

I was living a lifestyle which wasn't serving me, but I wasn't looking forward to tomorrow. Now, I am looking forward to tomorrow because I absolutely love this lifestyle. And that's how I know I'm on the right path.

So, how do you move to the right path? Very simply, let go of anything that makes you feel afraid. Let go of anything that makes you doubt yourself. Let go of anything that makes you feel scared. Let go of anything that your soul disagrees with. Let go of anything that your soul disagrees with.

10.   Bad dreams and nightmares.

You wake up holding your bed sheets. Frightening. What were you dreaming of, by the way? Nobody knows. That's how I knew I was on the wrong path. Through our dreams, you see, the dreams we have are reflections of the life we live. If you're always dreaming of bad things, the worst case scenarios, bad situations, that's a universal sign that you're on the wrong path.

And right now, my dreams are truly reflections of my innermost thoughts. I love my life. So, when I dream, I'm dreaming of a beautiful beach. Nature. And that's how I know I'm on the right path. Your dreams don't lie.

So, pay attention to your dreams. Get a dream journal. And that's how to know you are slowly moving towards the right path.

Chapter Sixty Six

12 Signs You're Doing Better Than You Think

The moment you love yourself is the moment you allow other people to love you. Ever pay someone a compliment, saying you're amazing, and they say no, I hate myself. Well, if you love yourself, you're allowing other people to really show you how great you are.

Do you realize how well you are actually doing? Here are 12 signs you're doing better than you think.

Someone asked, Ralph, how does one know one is doing better than they actually are? Because sometimes I'm really hard on myself, but then sometimes I'm like, actually, I've come a long way.

That's a sign you're doing better than you think you are. It's time to start patting yourself on the back. It's time to start feeling yourself, baby. Start hugging yourself, baby. Because you are doing better than you think.

You see, so many times we're all so hard on ourselves, and I'm like, Ralph, relax. You've done enough. Be proud of yourself. You've come a long way, okay?

1.   Your spending more time in nature

What's helped me along my journey is that I work outside. Yay! I work outside.

I live my lifestyle in nature every single day. That's why I'm very healthy, because I'm not always indoors in front of the computer. This is my workplace. This is my office. I've got birds over there, kangaroos down there.

Nature is everywhere around me, okay? So I'm actually doing a lot better than I think, because someone right now is stuck in an office, and it's very stuffy.

Sorry about that. I didn't do it. So be proud of yourself. If you are spending more time in nature practicing ecotherapy, there's a reason why I do most of my videos in nature, because it feels so good, and that bird is like, I agree with you, Ralph. That's beautiful. It keeps you young. You feel healthier and happier.

2.   You're in a better place mentally.

Now, I've had the dark night of the soul. I've gone through my trials and tribulations where I thought, gosh, I'm not going to make it out of here alive, and I actually did. You are doing better than you think if you are in a whole new frame of mind. You are no longer being programmed in the matrix. You can actually think for yourself, open your mind to new information. You are doing better than you think. Can I just clap for you right now? Well done.

3.   You're eating well

7-Day Vegan Challenge. Eating healthily is a choice as soon as you wake up, it's a choice between avocados and pears, okay? It's a hard choice, right? Because you're doing the 7-Day Vegan Challenge, you're eating that plant-based diet, and it's hard to choose between dates or strawberries. You're doing better than you think, when you can actually have that choice to say, actually, do I want a chia seed porridge or a moringa powder smoothie with flax seeds and bananas and maca powder and cacao? It's a hard choice, isn't it? It's a hard life, right? When you have to choose between two delicious plant-based foods, you are doing better than you think.

Realize most of the world lives on less than $10 a day, and some people didn't actually have breakfast today, for real. So if you are eating good, you're doing better than you think.

4.   You woke up today

What's the fourth sign you're doing better than you think? You woke up today, you've got a roof over your head, you've actually got a mobile phone connection for the first time on this iPhone X, you have a signal.

Look, look, I've realized this, that the mere fact that you actually woke up healthy and someone loves you, I'm talking to my good friend on the beach, that he's just had a child, the whole family is elated, and I'm like, what has changed? And he's like, to know that everybody was loved the heck out of at one point.

So the mere fact that you woke up healthy, you can move your body, and even if you didn't, if you have a positive attitude, if you have a positive attitude, I guarantee you there is also someone out there that loves you, you are doing better than you think.

Anytime I don't feel loved, I'm like, actually, I woke up, I'm grateful, I'm doing better than I think, because the cat down the road loves me, my mom loves me, and you love me, don't you? Don't you love me? You do, right? Exactly. So I'm doing better than I think. You woke up, celebrate. Some people didn't even wake up today.

5.   You have a platform

If you have a platform, like any platform, you don't have to have a million subscribers or a hundred thousand subscribers, no, no, no. If you have a platform, like a website, a blog, even a small YouTube channel, that's good enough. If you are using that platform to positively influence people who watch your videos, read your articles, you're doing better than you think, because once again, you are realizing how much influence you have.

Like, I'm realizing, gosh, I can say something and potentially inspire millions of people in a few seconds, right? Potentially inspire millions of people on my website in a few seconds. I'm doing better than I think. I'm like, Ralph, relax. You're actually doing pretty cool.

So shout out to everybody on Instagram, Facebook, YouTube, Twitter, who is using their platforms to actually inspire people. You're doing better than you think.

Be proud, celebrate. Let's start the clapping again.

6.   You've traveled to a few countries and took a few selfies.

Now, I've traveled to a lot of different countries and I'm going to keep traveling to many different countries. And when I think about it, I'm like, oh my gosh, I actually took some pretty cool selfies in that place, in Egypt, in Sierra Leone, in Ethiopia, in Brazil, in Greece, in Turkey, right?

If you go to Turkey, go to a place called Elania. Beautiful place. I went there and the water is so warm. I'm like, gosh, this is amazing. I'm doing better than I think because it's nine o'clock at night and it's bloody hot in the water. Thank you, universe. It's like a jacuzzi in here, right? You're doing better than you think. Once again, some people have never even left their state.

I spend a lot of time in California. Some people are like, Ralph, I've never actually left California, right? So I'm like, wow. Some people have never even left America. Okay.

So be grateful that you've managed to step on a plane, that you've managed to move out of your comfort zone. That's the secret. If you are always craving new experiences, you are growing at an exponential rate. You're doing better than you think.

7.   You are not the same person as you were last year.

You've changed for the better over the last year. You've made a lot of mistakes in relationships and now you're correcting them with a new person, right? That's always what happens. Okay. But you've changed.

You have evolved to a better place emotionally and mentally. You're doing better than you think. If you are open to learn more about yourself, how your subconscious mind works, you're doing better than you think, right?

If you are reading great books that will help you become your greatest version, going to seminars, you're doing better than you think. If you're working on your dream right now and quitting a job you absolutely hate and you've done all of that, you're not the same person anymore. You're doing better than you think.

8.   Your dog loves you.

If your dog loves you when nobody else does, you're doing better than you think, right? If the cat down the road loves you, you're doing better than you think. The cat down the road absolutely adores me.

I realize I'm doing better than I think because some people's cats don't even like them. They don't even look at them. They just walk past them. The cat down the road actually is right there. Hi, hi. Yeah. It's peeing on me right now, right? So I'm doing better than I think.

If you have this amazing connection to animals who are these amazing sentient beings, 7 Day Vegan Challenge, if you are helping animals, opening up an animal sanctuary, spreading and promoting a healthier plant-based lifestyle to protect animals, you're doing better than you think. Plus, your dog loves you. Just feed it now, right?

9.   You love yourself.

I love myself. Kendrick Lamar said it. That's right in that song. I love myself. If you sing that as well when that song is playing on the radio, you're doing better than you think. Because for a long time, it was hard for me to love myself. I would look in the mirror and think, gosh, I'm not good enough.

Now, I absolutely, absolutely, absolutely love myself. And I'm doing better than I think. Because the moment you love yourself is the moment you allow other people to love you.

10.   You finally accept yourself.

That big toe of yours, okay? Those flaws, those imperfections that you have. Nobody is perfect. But if you can finally love all of those disowned aspects of yourself, you're doing better than you think.

Look, everybody has sides of themselves they are working on because we are work in progress. You're doing better than you think if you acknowledge it.

But you still, despite all of that, accept yourself. Like, I had to accept myself to say, actually, Ralph, accept yourself that you love coming to nature every single day and being around birds. That bird is singing to me right now. You're doing better than you think, okay? Accept yourself when no one else will.

11.   You've stopped judging.

You've stopped judging people for where they are because you're like, actually, at one point, I was also there.

Like, I don't judge people anymore. I see where people are coming from because who am I to judge people? If I'm going to judge you, I'm going to give you the best solutions and I'm still not going to judge you. I'm going to be an example. I'm going to be a lighthouse so when you see me, you get inspired.

If you've stopped judging people, bringing people down, you're doing better than you think. Like, I have never disliked a person's video on YouTube. I swear on the cat down the road. Cat down the road is like, don't swear on me. Okay. Okay. Then I remembered that, right? I have never disliked anybody's video on YouTube on any social media platform because I just don't give out that energy.

I'm giving out positive energy. You see, universal law states that the energy you give out is the energy you will attract. I only have time to uplift people. I only have time to take people to the next version, the next best version of themselves. So you're doing better than you think.

12.   You've actually somehow, someway managed to find a lot of calm in being alone, a lot of serenity in being alone.

You're doing better than you think when you actually enjoy your own company, right? Because what's worse than being alone?

Huh? I love being alone because it means I can reconnect back to the truth of who I am. I'm doing better than I think when I actually embrace who I truly am. When I'm actually like, I'm cool, enjoying my own company, strolling around nature.

Like, this is where I find tremendous harmony. If you are at peace with yourself, not blaming yourself for what you did in the past, what you didn't do, you screwed up, but you're actually absorbing yourself in the present moment, you're doing better than you think. And you should congratulate yourself.

CHAPTER SIXTY SIX

Chapter Sixty Seven

10 Smart Ways To Find Your True Purpose

A lot of people write to me. They're like, Ralph, I just want to know my true purpose and live my best life. Can I do that? Of course you can.

We're going to talk about 10 powerful ways to discover your true purpose today and become your greatest version. Now, let me share with you what's helped me find my true purpose and become my greatest version. We're going to go through the smart method, okay?

When I was lost a long time ago, I didn't have a purpose. I was like a loose leaf. And a lot of people are going through this right now. I had just graduated, had a degree in psychology, a degree in criminology, all of that stuff. But I was still without a purpose. Had a job, but I was still without a purpose.

Everyone knew what was best for me, but I was still without a purpose. And so many people find themselves in this predicament. They wake up to unfulfilled lives.

Well, this is where it ends, because this information, oh, it's going to blow your mind and change your life. I'm in my purpose. When I never had my purpose, I wasn't as animated as I am now.

The moment I found my purpose, I became rich. Wealth is linked to you being in your true purpose, okay? So what is the first way to find your true purpose and become your greatest version?

1.   Learn how to press pause

It is stop, stop, stop, right? Stop everything. Press pause on your life right now. You see, what if I told you, you might tell me you don't have a purpose, but you're doing something right now which is creating momentum. You're moving in a direction right now and you've got to stop because if you don't, it's going to be harder to find your true purpose.

Every activity, every activity creates momentum. A lot of people are working somewhere they absolutely hate. The more you do that, you're literally changing your brain and you're programming your brain to keep doing it. Even though you don't like doing it, you become addicted to a routine not serving you. So you have to learn how to press pause. That's what I had to do.

I said, okay, I'm going to quit my job and find out what I'm here to do. And it worked out because I had time to really be with myself, sit with myself and say, okay, what is it Ralph Smart really loves to do? And I've got to do more of what makes me happy because that's why we're here. Life is short.

You're going to be out of here in a few decades. Live life to the full. So stop what you're doing. Have time for introspection, reflection to say, okay, what does my soul want me to do? Because you see, you've got a voice inside of you and this voice has led you to do what you're doing right now, which may not be your purpose. And that voice is not your voice. It's your mom's voice.

It's your friend's voice. It's your teacher's voice. It's some guy on the television's voice, right? You've got influences internally and they encourage you to live a certain lifestyle, but that may not be your purpose.

So you've got to learn how to ignore everyone, stop everything and really re-connect back to yourself. Come out into nature, do a little Samba baby and just be still, be present. The more present you are, the more you can connect with your true purpose, okay? When you're always worried about the past or living up to other people's expectations or you're worried about the future, you become a little bit shaky baby and you're going to do something that's not actually your true purpose.

So learn how to stop everything, be still and reconnect with your true self, okay?

CHAPTER SIXTY SEVEN

2.   Identify your core needs and your wants.

You should have a balance between your needs and your wants. You need to have a good balance between your needs and your wants, okay? So if you haven't found your purpose yet, it's because you're not honoring your core needs. There are certain things that you need and once you start to honor and prioritize your core needs, you will be led to your true purpose.

Many people prioritize their wants. I want to make money. Cool, you need money, right? In this world to pay your rent, to pay your bills, to feed the cat down the road, I get it. However, if you're only prioritizing your wants, I want to make my family proud. Cool, fantastic. But if you are only prioritizing your wants, you will not find your true purpose.

So you have to have a balance of the wants with the core needs. I need to feel like this is what I've been called to do. I need to feel good about myself every single day and this will lead you back to your true purpose.

So once again, you have to have 50% wants and 50% needs and this is a smart method, okay? And this will lead you back to your purpose so you can become your greatest version.

3.   The 80/20 rule

Do you know deep divers that I follow the 80-20 rule that's led me to my true purpose? So the 80-20 rule goes like this. Every single day, Ralph's Smart should experience 80% of positive emotions and 20% of negative emotions, okay? Every day is not going to be perfect even when you're in your purpose. Sometimes things just don't work out, things go wrong.

It can be really crazy, really crazy, right? And that's cool. But 80% of the day is going to be positive. What happens when you're not in your true purpose? You have 80% of negative experiences and then 20% of positive experiences.

Some people, they go into work and they're like, I hate being here. They feel terrible and then maybe you might get a little bit of sunshine and they're like, oh, a bit of sunshine. No.

If you really want to find your purpose and you haven't a clue, pay attention to the energy in motion. Emotion means energy in motion. Your emotions are your inner GPS.

They're always guiding you to the place of your true purpose. So you want to realize that the universe is so intelligent, so smart that it realizes that positive emotions will always be showing you that you are in your true purpose, okay? So when you're feeling good internally, you're moving closer to your true purpose.

Stop doing something that's only bringing you pain and it's just making you feel terrible, tired, frustrated and stressed out. You can't live a life like that. It's not healthy and also it's going to lead you away from your true purpose. So once again, follow the smart method, the 80-20 rule. 80% positive emotions.

We came here to party. I'm having fun, only experiencing 20% negative emotions. And this will lead you to your true purpose.

4.   It feels natural

Look, make sure that when you do something, it's bringing you back to who you really are. It's making you more of who you really are. It's authentic. It feels natural. It doesn't feel forced. Look, when you are not in your purpose, it feels forced.

It feels like you've got to force yourself to wake up and go to that place, go to that job. You've got to force yourself to be here. You're waiting for the time to fly by so you can go home and watch Ralph Smart.

No, no. When you've found your purpose, you're enjoying the moment, okay? And it's also making you more of who you really are. It's bringing you back to your true authenticity.

And this is a clue to find your true purpose, okay? What makes me relax so I can be myself and express myself 100%? Your purpose is linked to your self-expression. I used to work in a school. And in the staff room, it's like, okay, I wanted to dive deep and I did, and all the teachers looked at me like, huh? Yeah, because I was breaking out of the matrix. You should have seen me. And I realized at that moment, I was in the wrong environment.

And I had to realize that for me to find my purpose, I had to honor my true authenticity, which is my true expression and place myself in the right environment, which is in the heart of nature, raising the frequency. I'm so myself here. Can't you see? And this has led me to my true purpose.

5.   What would you do if money wasn't important?

Alan Watts, a great mind said, what would you do if money was no object? Would you still be there doing that, working there, living that life? Would I? Absolutely, because I love being in the heart of nature, just breathing in that good ass prana, baby.

But a lot of people are only doing it for a check. They're only doing it for the gram. What would you do if money was no object? That thing there is your true purpose.

So always keep that in the back of your mind. What would I do if money was no object, if they weren't paying me to do it? Because that's always gonna bring you back to the pure true purpose of why you're here.

6.   Ask: what am I good at?

What are my talents and my gifts? Talent means some money. We're talking about something that should bring us something back in return.

We've got to remind ourselves, the universe is so smart that the things we enjoy to do, the things we're really good at are often linked to our purpose, okay? Ralph Smart is a great communicator. And I realized that ever since I was small, I just wanted to talk in front of people. And this is also linked to my purpose, okay? So remind yourself, find out what you're really good at and realize this is always gonna be linked to your true purpose.

What am I good at? Things you're not good at are usually a sign that's not your true purpose. So find out today, what am I good at and honor what you're good at and more so invest in what you're good at, okay? And this will lead you back to your true purpose.

7.   Ask: what is worth suffering for?

There are certain things which we want to suffer for, that we want to go through the grind for. We don't mind experiencing a bit of pain, some road bumps and all of that stuff.

That's your true purpose. When you're doing something that's worth suffering for because you've seen the bigger picture. Along my early days, diving deep, it was tough, it was hard but I realized this is worth suffering for and this is the smart method to lead you back to your true purpose.

If you're doing something right now and you're like, this is a waste of time, this is not worth suffering for, that's not your true purpose, okay? So your true purpose is always worth suffering for.

8.   What brings you peace of mind?

Your inner peace is the highest form of wealth. Your inner peace is linked to your purpose.

The greater the inner peace, the more you are in your true purpose. The more disharmony you feel every single day, you're irritated, annoyed, frustrated, always angry, mad, always a screwed up face, that's not your true purpose because once again, your true purpose breeds positive emotions and it breeds a state of gratitude. I'm so thankful to be here.

Look, it's good for my mental health. When you're doing something and your mental health is being improved, nourished, cared for, it's always gonna lead you to your true purpose. So pay attention to your mental state because if you always have a headache being there, that's not your true purpose. Your true purpose is always working on behalf of good mental health.

9.   What has a future?

Look, you've got two lives. One of them does not have a future and one of them does.

What led me back to my true purpose, the smart method was to realize what has a future and what doesn't have a future. Can I see myself doing this? Doing what? Breathing in that good ass prana, baby. Doing that in the next 10 years.

Absolutely. What about the next 20 years? Of course, the next 30 years. Obviously, the next 50 years. I'm here. The next 100 years, let's go. That's how I knew

I'd found my purpose because I always wanted to be here. And I realized that this has a future. I realized I can expand. Your purpose is always going to expand you.

When you're not in your purpose, it's always going to contract you. So what you're doing right now, if you haven't found your purpose, be honest with yourself and say, actually, can I see myself here in the next year? If the answer is no, start once again pressing pause to say, hey, where can I go that has a future? Where can I go so that I can see myself here in the next 10 years because it makes me more of who I really am? That's your true purpose. And that's a smart method.

10.   Your true purpose will always grow you as a human being.

If it's not helping you evolve, it's not your true purpose. Look, I found my purpose, helping people become their greatest versions. You know how? Because I said, actually, I'm growing in the process. I can grow here. I can evolve here. I've learned so much and I'm learning every single day so much about myself as a human being. It's beautiful. At the same time, I'm helping your ass and the cat down the road. Fantastic.

However, a lot of people find themselves in situations, in jobs, in lifestyles, which their growth is being stunted and they're literally, they've reached a dead end. That's not your true purpose. Your purpose will always give you wings. It will always grow you mentally, emotionally, physically, spiritually.

Chapter Sixty Eight

How To Let Go And Trust The Universe

A lot of people write to me saying that they don't trust anything at all. Not even the cat down the road. Do you have trust issues? Do you find it difficult to trust life and the universe?

Do you find it extremely hard to trust yourself? Oh boy, that's a lot of people. Let me share with you what helped me along my journey to let go and trust the universe. Now, I started to realize that we are made from the same fabric as the universe. We are all made of stardust. That is a scientific fact. And that's beautiful to know. So we are part of the universe.

I've learned this. Let go of control. That is the first thing to do. Accept that you can't control everything. That's how to let go and trust the universe, which in essence is really yourself. I want to control this, I want to control that. And then you realize you don't control anything. Let go. I'm not going to try and say, hey, I'm making a video right now. Be quiet.

So you've got to realize that you don't control everything. Once you know this, your life will become more harmonious, more stress-free and more relaxing. The reason why so many people find it hard to let go and trust the universe is because they're always trying to control everything around them.

Control, external control is an illusion. Yes, we have power over our internal condition, but you can't control how someone sees you. You can't control the weather. Maybe you can, you can do a little rain dance. Okay? Accept that situations will work themselves out. That's what I've discovered along my journey. Situations will work themselves out. Answers will come when you stop looking for them.

Once again, expectations create a lot of resistance. Resistance makes stronger. So I've learned that situations will work themselves out when you just let them be. When you let everything happen the way it's supposed to happen, you can finally let go.

You see what happens to so many of us. We're like, this situation is so hard right now. It will pass. Allow it to happen and realize that situations always work themselves out. I know what it's like. I've been there. Sometimes the future looks gloomy. Sometimes uncertain.

We're afraid of the unknown. I get it. If you can realize that no matter how bad you think your life is, how many worries you have, whatever you're going through, this too shall pass. And situations will always work themselves out once you let them. Stop trying to control them. Let them. Accept that whatever is meant to be with you will be with you. The right people who are supposed to be in your life will.

And the left people, because I'm a left-handed Pisces, right? Sometimes what happens? We find it hard to let go of certain people. We have unhealthy attachments to them. Sometimes we try to force people to be in our lives who aren't supposed to be there. That's why it feels incredibly uncomfortable. It doesn't feel good, does it? That's a sign. It's time to let go and trust yourself.

Trust the universe. You see, whoever is supposed to be in your life will appear. We don't meet people by accident. They are meant to be in our life for a reason, to help us grow, sometimes for blessings, sometimes for lessons.

I always say that the lessons are the blessings anyway. And the blessings are the lessons, right? So you don't have to stress about, hey, I want this person to be in my life. No, it was written. Maktub, right? Maktub, an Arabic word meaning it was written. And that's what I've realized along my journey. There are no accidents or coincidences in this universe. Everything is happening in divine order.

Accept that overthinking will only give you more problems. That's how to let go and trust the universe. Realize that the more I am thinking and overthinking and ruminating, I'm only gonna get more problems.

You see, thinking doesn't change things. Only actions do. And so many of us, we get caught up in thoughts, thinking, okay, if I'm living upstairs all the time, my life is gonna become magically fixed. No, it's not. Only radical action, getting up, moving your butt, or allowing, that magnificent word, allowing.

That's also an action. You see, I meet a lot of people who have a problem with overthinking. Thinking is fine, but anything in excess, anything in excess will be a problem for you. I overthink all the time, don't worry about it. But I realize that it only makes it harder for me to let go. Sometimes, so many of us, we get stuck in a comfort zone.

So many of us, we get stuck in thinking and thinking that, hey, this is all I'm good at. In thinking and thinking, hey, what else am I gonna do? So I've realized that you've gotta stop overthinking. And once again, allow. I do this through mindfulness meditation, where you tune into your senses, right? Every single sense. Okay, there's a plane flying above there. Woo, that good-ass prana smells good.

Smells pretty good today, right? Right, and that helps you, it puts your mind at rest. And that's how to really let go of the stresses you have, the worries, the anxiety, right? All of that disappears once you stop thinking so much and realizing that thoughts don't change anything. It's beautiful to ponder, but don't try and change the world through your thoughts.

That's a start, but it takes place through actions and allowing. Seven-day vegan challenge. Accept that if you are drinking a green juice smoothie, everything is gonna be okay. Oh yes, because there is spirulina in there. Spirulina is in there. E3 Live is in there. A complete source of protein. Like sometimes if I'm having an off day, I just make a green juice smoothie, put some E3 Live inside, some spirulina, and I feel like everything is okay. You see, food has a magical way of making everything feel okay.

Like while I'm drinking my green juice smoothie, everything is okay. And then once I stop, I'm like, oh my gosh, problems are back again. But hey, it went away while you were drinking that green juice smoothie.

Food can heal and food can hurt. Foods can help us to let go. If you are embracing a more plant-based diet, you're gonna be more confident. You're gonna be healthier. Health is wealth. You're gonna feel better about yourself. You're gonna help it. You're gonna help yourself to let go.

If you are eating a lot of toxic junk food, drinking a lot of soda, you're not gonna really love yourself. Therefore, you're gonna create a lot of resistance within yourself. Therefore, it's gonna be harder to let go. Plus, you're gonna be constipated. If you're constipated, you're definitely not gonna let go, right? So you just want a perfect flow. And that comes from healthy foods, a good digestion, right? And that's what's helped me along my journey.

Been a vegan for over 13 years, baby. And what do I say every day? Can I get a hello there? I've got tons of energy. Accept that if you do something today, your future self will thank you for, that's how to let go and trust the universe, which is really yourself.

So many of us, we don't realize if we were to start right now, learn a language, you wanna do that? Great. Travel, great. Work on your dream, great. Start a business, great. Research, great. Watch Infinite Waters, great. Do it right now. Because just imagine what will happen in a week's time, where you would be. In a month's time, where you would be. In one year's time, where you would be if you start right now.

Once again, if you start right now, everything will take care of itself. You see, there's a problem. There's a problem when this happens.

A lot of people, are you like this? Do you leave everything until the last minute? You see, that's why it's very hard to let go and trust the universe. Trust, which emanates from the Latin word confidere, which means to trust. So confidence is all about trusting.

Now check this out. When I first started making videos, when I had the massive Afro, and I was chilling in my backyard, right? With the cat down the road and stuff. I was sowing the seeds. Now I am reaping the benefits. Because I did something way back then, which has got me, it has got me to where I am right now. That's how to let go and trust the universe.

You've got to start where you are and start right now. Look at it like this. Accept, you don't need to know all the answers. You don't need to know everything. That's why so many people find it hard to let go. All you've got to do is listen to that small voice within you. What we call the higher voice of intuition. It knows more than you do. That's what's helped me to let go and trust the universe, right? Listen to that voice. It's not speaking to you for nothing. There's a message in that. It's just so many of us, we drown it out.

So how do I listen to this voice? Well, first of all, I accept that I've got to be alone sometimes and it's perfectly healthy to be alone. Find your solitude for even three minutes a day and then listen because that higher voice is really your subconscious mind talking to you. It's telling you the next step to take.

You see, to let go and trust the universe, you have to learn how to be fully grounded in the present moment. The future is nothing more than a continuation of present moments. I realized that along my early journey and I'm like, oh, I get it.

Are you afraid of the future? That is because you are not taking care of the present moment. That is because you are not in the present moment. So I realized, okay, all I've got to do is take care of the present moment and then the future will take care of itself because the future is nothing more than a continuation of present moments. And that totally helped me to let go. And trust. When we talk of really trusting life, you have to not only believe in yourself, you have to prove to yourself you know what you're doing.

Like when I'm making these videos, there is no script. I know what I'm doing because I've got the cat down the road for support and it feels fantastic. I've been doing it for so long, it's like, it's just natural for me.

So I trust myself when I'm making these videos and I trust the universe that everything will go great. Whoa, see what happened, right? Practice, practice, practice. That's how to let go and trust the universe.

If you aren't practicing your talent, your gift, you're gonna look a bit shaky, baby. You're gonna be very fearful. You learn how to let go and trust the universe when you really have that confidence within yourself to say, actually, I've been doing this for years. I know what I'm doing. Do you? Yes. Great.

Accept that there is a cycle to life, what we call the ebb and the flow. I've realized that you've really got to surrender to the ebb and the flow of life. When we talk of really letting go and trusting the universe, surrender, surrender, surrender.

CHAPTER SIXTY EIGHT

Chapter Sixty Nine

How To Receive Messages From The Universe

Have you checked your phone recently? Have you received any messages from the universe? A lot of people ask me, how do I know the universe is trying to communicate with me or send me mental messages? And that is a fantastic question. Look, all the time, I realize I am getting messages from the universe and it feels great. So let me share with you what's helped me along my journey.

1.   Your birthday

Okay, the first best way the universe sends someone messages is through their birthday.

When were you born? What day? What month? What year? More so, what time? You see, once you find out your sun sign, which is the normal zodiac sign, okay, Pisces, I'm a Pisces by the way, Leo, Sagittarius, Aquarius, but the time you were born, where was the moon? Find out your moon sign. That is going to be a key indicator to your shadow personality. Okay. Your shadow self. So I was born on March 3rd. That's why I always say three, three, but also at 3:03.

So the number 33 is very powerful to me. And I take that as a universal message for me. 33, meaning the illuminated one and there are 33 vertebrae in your spinal column. So when they say some spiritual masters died at age 33, it's a metaphor for being reborn into higher consciousness.

33 is a master number. Super powerful. So find out your sun sign, your moon sign, the time you were born, because through our birthday, you see men lie, women lie, numbers don't. And that's what's helped me along my journey.

2.   Synchronicity

A lot of people write to me saying, Ralph, I was thinking about something and then you started talking about it. Like what are the chances of that? That's synchronicity, baby. Has this ever happened to you? You're in the car and you're thinking about something and a song comes up and they're singing the exact same lyrics.

Like what are the chances of that? Like sometimes I'm just thinking about saying hello there. Then Lionel Richie comes on the radio saying, hello, is it me you're looking at? That's synchronicity. When your dominant thoughts align with your life and become your dominant experiences, number synchronicities, 1111, one, the number of new beginnings, number one, the number of beginning a new beginning, a fresh start. So you've got to become aware of the numbers you are seeing.

Are you seeing 222? That's the master builder. 333, that's the master teacher. So the universe is sending us messages through numbers, through synchronicity. Sometimes we're thinking about something and then we see it on someone's t-shirt. Sometimes you just meet someone and it feels like you've known them your entire life because you both say something at the exact same time. That's synchronicity.

Syn means together, chronos means time, so happening at the same time. And lots of stuff is happening at the same time right now. That is a universal message for you. You? Yes, you.

3.   Intuition

What's helped me along my journey is intuition. I've realized you have to follow your intuition. You see, the body never lies. Whatever you feel in your gut is telling you something. The gut is actually a mini brain. It has neurons inside. So that's why when people say, oh, I feel it in my gut.

Something feels off, right? I feel it in my heart too. So when you realize that you've got to trust your intuition, if the vibe feels off, chances are it is. If the vibe feels off, chances are it is, right? I am always using my intuition to guide me.

And I realized that's a message coming from the universe. Now the universe, you can call it the field, God, whatever name you have for it, we know what we're talking about. And I've seen along my journey that we are also made from the same fabric as the universe. The universe is not something separate from us. We are stardust. We are the universe experiencing itself. We are the universe experiencing itself in human form for a tiny bit of time. And we go back to the stardust. How awesome is that? Okay. So trust your intuition.

Sometimes you might meet someone and it looks good on paper, but you feel something is off. You've got to trust that that is a universal message for you. Okay.

4.   The people in your life

Now what's helped me along my journey is becoming very attentive and aware to the people that are coming in and out of my life. Through people, the universe will send you mental messages through people.

Sometimes I've been around someone who tells me something that I needed to hear. A lot of times people say, Ralph, your videos, they talk to me. I needed to hear this at this time, at this moment.

That's the universe sending you a mental message through other people. You see the universe talks through other people. The messages you need to know sometimes are coming to you through the voices of other people.

That's why you need to listen. Sometimes I didn't really want to take advice, but when you listen to certain people you see that maybe you can actually learn something from them right? Because sometimes people come into our lives and they really bless us. They teach us something we didn't know before. That is a universal message for you. Okay.

I've met people and they've just told me, Ralph, thanks a lot. Your videos are helping me so much. That's the universe congratulating me. Thank you universe, right? Through other people, we are vessels. We are channels which pass on this primordial life force energy, which permeates everything in existence.

If you have a beautiful person in your life right now, that's a gift from the universe. Oh, lift them up high right now. Okay. Sometimes we get warnings. I got warnings as well along my journey. Some people would say, Ralph, slow down. You're working too hard, that was when I was in the matrix caught up in so many different jobs.

Now they say, Ralph, you look different. Now I look a lot younger, right? But back then I was rushing and people were like, Ralph, you need to slow down, relax. That was the universe talking through them to give me a message I needed to hear. So become aware of what people are saying to you. There is a message inside that will help you become your greatest version.

5. Your health

Now, this someone could be you and it could be a mental message. Seven day vegan challenge, health.

Health. What is my body saying? You see, the reason why I say the body never lies is because the body is the subconscious mind. Our words might lie. I'm healthy, but our body could say otherwise. Cause if we don't take a look at what we're eating, are we exercising enough? The body communicates to us all the time. It tells us how it feels.

That is the universe sending you a message you need to hear. So I used to have a lot of anxiety and I used to have sharp pains in my chest. That was the universe talking to me to say: hey, you need to sort this anxiety problem out right now.

Okay. So listen to your body. How is your body? Do you feel healthy? Are you eating a plant-based diet that serves you with a seven day vegan challenge? Cause if you're not, sometimes you might have these ailments, unnecessary ailments. That's the universe sending you a message that if you don't change your diet, you may not be here for a long time. And we don't want that. We don't want that.

We want you to be here for a long time. Right? So through your health, you get to know yourself more. You get to know what your body is going through. Your body is alive and it's talking to you all the time based on how you feel through your emotions. So optimum health, the body's cool, it's chilling.

When you are in dis-ease, the body is in dis-ease and we have to sort that out. And we do this by the fruit, the veg, the leafy greens, the beautiful papaya. Okay. There is an abundance of food on the planet, which is going to be eaten by the cat down the road.

6.   Alignment

Alignment. Okay. This is what's helped me along my journey. You see, I've learned this. Once you change your vibrational frequency, everything aligns to that same frequency.

You see, I've been to university, got degrees, studied. I was working. Things look good on paper, but I wasn't in true alignment with my higher calling with my true purpose.

The universe was sending me a message to say, look, you can stay in that job, but it's not your purpose. So you're not going to be truly happy there because you're not in alignment. And guess what? When I was in crummy jobs, not serving me, my relationship was the exact same way.

How I felt about myself was the exact same way. Could you see how everything was lining up? Okay. So what happened? I realized I had to change one area of my life and then all the other areas would change.

So I started to become more in alignment with my higher calling, which was to inspire millions of people to become their greatest version. That's what I did. Well, my love life, well, it was so amazing. I got on better with my neighbors. That's good. They actually lent me the sugar cane, right? Alignment.

When you are in alignment, the universe is sending you a message, like keep going. You're doing great. When you are out of alignment, the message is, if you don't get back into alignment, you are going to have big problems.

When you aren't doing what you know you came here to do, you can fool the world, but honey, you can't fool yourself. Right?

7.   When you are still

My grandma, she's now passed away, but she would have these visions and she was super psychic. I think that's where I got it from. Okay. What happened? She was very calm, a very calm woman, very meditative. And when you are still, the universe can send you a mental message.

Why? Because you are in that alpha brainwave state, which is the most receptive brainwave state, the most creative brainwave state. Okay. And a lot of us are always in the beta, which is the normal erratic brainwave state. Okay. But once you drop down and you can do that by listening to 432Hz music, you become incredibly still. That is the essence of meditation, which is being in the present moment, that's called mindfulness meditation and it's super powerful.

So I realized the more still I am, the more I can receive. I can actually hear myself. I can hear my inner voice. I know my needs. I know my desires. That is the universe sending me a mental message. I can actually read it. I can see it and I can feel it.

However, when we are not still, when we are rushing around on this planet, like a crazy lab rat, you might get the messages from the universe you need to see in here, but you don't have time to read them. You don't have time to see the hidden messages that you need to see because you don't have time to be still. So I had to learn to stop doing so much stuff and just chill.

Do you know when I'm in nature, what happens? I am so still sometimes just lying on the beach, lying on the grass. What happens? I get downloads. Streams of information just floods through my body. Those are universal messages. They come to you when you are incredibly still. That's why there is so much noise on the planet because it's there to distract you from your higher calling. So you need to get still if you really want to get those universal messages you need to hear.

8.   Accidents.

A lot of people say, Ralph, yes, I saw your video by accident, but thanks. What if I told you there were no accidents? There are no accidents. Everything is happening for a reason. You see, I used to feel life was random. Life was random. Okay. There are accidents. Then I realized cause and effect. That is one of the seven principles.

Everything is based around cause and effect. For every action, there is a re-action. Whatever you do now, like Marcus Aurelius said, echoes on into eternity. Okay? There are no accidents.

I remind myself time and time again, I used to go to a barber shop and this barber was super, super, super duper awake, enlightened. And I would just be sitting, waiting, and he would be talking about really deep stuff. And I'm like, okay, I just heard this at the right time when I needed to hear it. That's not an accident. Okay. There are no accidents when you hear something.

Oh, I shouldn't have heard it. I don't know what I was doing there, but I heard it anyway. Or I met this person, like, there are no accidents. Getting into a relationship with someone, that's not an accident. Them leaving you, that's not an accident. Them coming back because you're so beautiful, that's not an accident either. There are no accidents. Everything I've realized is happening for a reason. You have to find it. And that is the universal message. That everything is connected.

In the Indus Valley, in ancient Egypt, they talked of the thousand petaled lotus. The symbol of how everything is connected. The Native Americans said humanity, humans you didn't weave the web of creation; you are part of the web of creation. So humble yourself with your massive ego. Right? It's an ecosystem, not an ego system. Right? There are no accidents.

9.   Coincidences.

Oh, it's just a coincidence. What if I told you there were no coincidences? It's not a coincidence that you saw my video when you needed to see it. It's not a coincidence that you met this person who's helped you or who's given you a lesson or a blessing. There are no coincidences. Right?

Sometimes you get saved by the nick of time. That's not a coincidence. That's the universe sending you a message that look, there is something going on far beyond your comprehension that is governing your whole existence. And that's the message that came to me.

I started to realize my life is not a coincidence. It's not an accident. I was born for a reason and everything happening to me is part of the divine order. I accept it 100%. We have free will. We are architects of our reality.

At the same time, there are no coincidences. I've seen there are patterns. You see this whole world we are living in, scientists now are realizing is a kind of simulation. Like a computer, zeros and ones. There are no coincidences or accidents.

CHAPTER SIXTY NINE

It's all about numbers. It's all about divine order.

So I've realized that you have to let go to really receive these messages and realize if you're meeting someone, oh, I just met them in a supermarket, Ralph, like of all the places, and we just clicked. That's not a coincidence. You were supposed to meet them because they left late. You left late. Like what are the chances of you meeting someone who you just clicked with at a random place? There are no coincidences.

10.   Detours

Now what's helped me along my journey is detours. Be thankful for detours, blocked roads, blocked pathways, because they prevent you from places not meant for you.

Sometimes you might meet someone who you're really not supposed to meet because they don't have any good intentions for you. And guess what? You end up, the car breaks down so you don't meet them. And guess what? Down the road, they were supposed to do something very bad to you.

So be grateful for detours. That is the universe's way of sending you messages. You see, I always say you never have to force anything. Allow things to flow. Whatever will be, will be. It happens to me all the time. I'm driving and there's a lot of traffic. I get stuck only to realize that in my destination, something bad was happening, right? It's a good thing. I was stuck in traffic.

Sometimes I needed to hear a beautiful piece of classical music on the radio while I'm stuck in traffic. I'm like, oh my gosh, I've never heard this before. Be thankful for detours. Okay. Sometimes what happens, there are delays and all of these things. And we think, oh, it's a bad thing. That's also a universal message. Sometimes you need to learn how to be still.

You need to learn patience. Okay. And what's helped me along my journey is to not get so mad at the detours like I used to be because sometimes not getting what you want is a stroke of luck. Oh yes. Oh yes. Oh yes!

11.   Dreams

Now dreams are the language of the subconscious mind, which works through imagery only. No words, no, just imagery pictures.

Okay. That's why they say a picture is worth a thousand words. So what are you seeing in your dreams right now? Dream interpretation is super powerful because the universe is communicating to you in your sleep. Whatever you are dreaming off, there is a message in it. Whatever you are dreaming off, there is a message in it. A hidden meaning you need to decipher. You need to decode.

Okay. Sometimes people dream of flying and it's just a sign their whole life is taking off in a beautiful way. Sometimes people dream of being chased by someone all the time. Does that ever happen to you? That could be a sign that you're always under stress. You need to slow down because there's too much anxiety in your life.

You need to relax, de-stress, right? So dreams are the universe's way of communicating to us. A lot of the time people who are being chased have a lot of fear sometimes about confronting people. And I realized I was always sometimes dreaming of being chased. And I'm like, okay, I'm going to face my demons, my inner demons. Right. And it always lies within us.

You see, there's an African proverb, which says when there is no enemy within us, the enemy outside cannot hurt you.

So I've learned that dreams are super powerful. I'm always getting a dream journal, writing down my dreams to find out the hidden meanings because I realized that's how the universe is communicating with me to tell me what I need to know, where I need to be and where I need to go.

12.	Glitches

Now I advise you to see the film, The Matrix. Okay. And sometimes I realized that we are kind of living in a matrix, which means a kind of artificial reality, right? There is a true organic world, but also there is an artificial inorganic man-made illusion, which so many of us are stuck in called the matrix. And we have to get out of it. We have to get out of it.

We have to be free. And I've realized that the only way to do it is to start seeing the glitch in the matrix. So the film, The Wizard of Oz, okay. Dorothy finds out who is behind the curtain. And she's like, oh my gosh, it's just an old man. Oh my gosh. Oh my gosh. Right. And it's kind of like how our life is. Sometimes we think, oh, it's the powers that be. You find out it's just normal people.

So when you see the glitch in the matrix, sometimes you see numbers. Once again, that's the glitch in the matrix showing you the binary nature of our reality, zeros and ones, like we're almost in a kind of computer simulation. Another kind of glitch is deja vus. You see two cat down the roads. Okay. Glitches in the matrix. The emperor has no clothes. Oh my gosh. He's naked. Yes.

Glitches in the matrix. Sometimes there was a film called they live and the guy put on his shades. He would see advertisements around and it would be like, have a good life or something. And then he put the glasses on and it would be like, obey. And he would put glasses on and see news reporters and they would just have like skulls, right? Saying how you can't even trust people who you think are in power, who are going to help your life. Okay.

Because once you put those glasses on, you start to see the true nature of reality that we have to get free for so long. We've been lied to. You've got to break the chains of the matrix. That's how you know the universe is sending you a mental message. Okay. Philip K. Digg talked about it saying that reality is kind of like a simulation. He wrote Blade Runner, fantastic writer, check his stuff out. Okay.

So I've started to realize that you've got to look for glitches. Glitches are where you realize the news is pretty fake. Even our money is fake. That's another glitch in the matrix, right? So the universe is sending you messages through glitches. Sometimes you go into a shop. If you ever worked in retail, you look in the warehouse and it's a flipping mess, right? But on the surface, it looks wonderful. Okay. That's a glitch in the matrix. So the glitch in the matrix is where you realize things aren't always what they seem.

And if you keep seeing that, that's a way the universe is communicating to you because now you are becoming more empowered through greater wisdom of knowing that there is so much I don't know about. And there are things I don't know that I don't know about. Oh my gosh. And that's so empowering, right?

So those are the 12 best ways the universe sends someone mental messages or even you. Oh, I see you're checking your phone for a message; did you get a message from the universe? That's pretty special. What did it say by the way? Oh, it said that you need to say: can I get a hello there?

Chapter Seventy

Shadow Work 101

There are many wolves in sheep's clothing all around us. There is a Japanese folktale, Deep Divers, which goes like this. Each one of us has three faces.

The first face is the face we show to the world. The second face is the face we show to our close friends and family. And the third face is the face that nobody sees.

And that is the truest reflection of who you really are. Now I say this, we all have three versions of ourselves, including the cat down the road. The first version is who we show to the world.

The side of ourselves we show to the world every single day. The second version is how we see ourselves in our minds. And the third version is who we actually are.

And sometimes we don't even know who we really are. We don't even know all the sides of ourselves. We don't even know that we have a shadow side.

Each one of us has a shadow side. And until you face it, you are never going to activate your true potential. Deep Divers, we have a whole lot to talk about.

Peace, infinite waters, diving deep once again. Beautiful Deep Divers, we are out here in the heart of nature, baby. We have the sun shining.

We have butterflies all over the place. We have the cat down the road. I'm in a zen state, Deep Divers, just breathing in that good-ass prana, baby.

Sending you tons of light and darkness. Yes, take those shadows, take those shadows, and take those shadows. Shadow Work 101 Explained.

Now, are you aware that you might be repressing your shadow side? We all are to some extent. And the whole of life is actually about no longer suppressing that shadow side. No longer being afraid of the darkness.

Were you afraid of the dark as a child? Many people in this matrix are wolves in sheep's clothing. On the outside, it looks fantastic. I'll buy it.

But on the inside, there's a monster lurking. Each one of us has an angel and demon within us. Each one of us has dark and light within us.

But in this society, you have been told to be ashamed of the darker side of yourself. You have been told to be ashamed and to feel guilty about the undesirable aspects of yourself. So throughout life, a lot of people suppress their shadow side until one day, it comes out at the most unexpected time.

And people are like, "Oh my gosh, I can't believe she said that." " "Oh my gosh, I can't believe he said that." You see, if you don't learn about your shadow side and do shadow work, it's going to come out.

And it might come out at a very inconvenient time. And we haven't even had breakfast yet. Can I get a hello there? So wonderful deep divers, let me share with you what's helped me along my journey.

Shadow work 101. What is shadow work? Simply put, it's when you learn that we all have unconscious personality disorders. We all have a dark side to us.

We all have things which society calls unacceptable, not allowed, undesirable. We are all deeply flawed. We all have a hidden dark side to us, not just peace, love, and light and kumbaya.

No, a lot of us, we have a monster inside of us. And it's not a bad thing. In fact, it's natural.

Your shadow side is natural. When you turn your back to the sun, a shadow forms. Shadows are natural.

If you are a photographer, you know that you need shadows, mid-tones, and highlights to get the perfect exposure. But in our society, we call dark things bad and light things good. That is why growing up, a lot of people have suppressed their emotions.

And there is a lot of repression going on with so many people. We only want to be seen as living a perfect life, but that's not reality. The truth of the matter is a lot of us, we have a whole lot of skeletons in our closets.

Now, Ralph, what's your shadow? Because you always seem to be smiling. Deep divers, I'm telling you my shadows. I'm expressing my shadow side every single day.

I'm talking about COVID-19. We aren't having it. I'm talking about, "Hey, I think that nobody should be wearing a face mask 24-7 because it causes hypoxia."

People can't breathe. I feel that the whole world is a stage. I feel that we have to stand up for what we believe in.

I feel that this whole thing is planned. This whole pandemic is total nonsense. Oh my gosh, Ralph, I can't believe you said it.

Yeah, I said it. And what? That's my shadow side coming out, deep divers. I've made videos that most people would be afraid to talk about in their whole existence.

Because for a long time, I had thoughts in my mind, deep divers, like actually I feel a certain way about this, but I was afraid to talk about it. So I would repress my feelings and emotions and suppress them as well. Then one day I said, hey, I can no longer hold this in.

Then I just said, this whole thing is a joke. This whole matrix is so fake. And I started to allow my shadow side to come out and it freed me.

It liberated me. You see, once you learn to own your shadow side 100%, it will actually be the gateway to your freedom, the gateway to your self-healing. When you realize that actually, there are so many different sides to yourself that you have to learn about.

A lot of us in this matrix, a lot of us in this matrix, we wear a happy mask or we just wear a mask. It's not who we really are. You at your job just overbroke.

Sometimes you have to be a certain way. Otherwise you're going to get fired. Right? Right.

So a lot of us, we realize that certain behaviors are rewarded in society and certain behaviors are shunned upon. Now, a lot of us, we have a tendency to always be liked by other people. That's why the like button is huge, right? In social media and in society.

A lot of people don't like to be an outcast. A lot of people do not like to be unpopular. A lot of people don't like to be a well, in actuality, that is your shadow side.

It is the undesirable aspects of yourself. It is the flawed you. It is the you nobody knows about.

It is the darker side of you, not just the peace, love, and light. It's also the anger, the frustration, the madness. You want to pull out your hair.

It's the screaming side of you. Now, how do we access that? We have to learn how to lose this persona, which is this social mask. And talking of face masks, we ain't having it.

We've got to learn to speak our heart and mind. We've got to learn how to speak our heart and mind every single day without sugarcoating it. We've got to learn how to embrace a bit of truth instead of a sweet lie.

What? Slow motion this side. We've got to get real with ourselves. Stop putting on a front.

A lot of us hide our shadows and we replace them with lights, flashing lights. Hey, look at me. My life is perfect on social media or in real life.

It's perfect. No, it's not. When we can learn how to be honest, our shadow springs forth.

When we can learn how to be vulnerable, our shadow springs forth. I've been making a lot of videos exposing this whole pandemic, and a lot of people have been watching them. A lot of those videos have gone viral, but I'm like, wait a minute.

Why aren't other people making videos as well about how they feel? You see, they are, that could be you, repressing your shadow side. They feel what I'm saying, but they're afraid to say it because they don't want their shadow to come out. Because everybody knows them to be this goody-goody two-shoes.

Me, I don't care what you think. I am that I am. Shadow Work 101.

You have to realize this. Life is not just about kumbaya, meditation under a tree. Life is not just about Nirvana.

Life is not just about seeing the positive in everything. It's also seeing the in everything. You see, if you look at a battery, you've got negative and positive, but it's the one force.

So what happens if you disregard the negative? What happens if you disregard the shadows? There is no power. Your true power comes from owning your shadow side to make sure you realize that your shadow side is not negative. In fact, it can become your best friend because it can help you work on areas of yourself you didn't know you had to work on.

Like shadow work begins when you become conscious of your shadow. Now I'll expose myself right now. You see, that's how B Rabbit won the battle in 8 Mile.

He exposed himself so nobody can use his past against him. He exposed himself. That's what I do every single day.

I say, actually, my life's been rough. Actually, I'm not perfect. Actually, I was hospitalized.

Actually, sometimes I can be pretty rude to people, deep divers, because people always say, Ralph, you're so compassionate. But sometimes I can be a total asshole, but I own it. That's the shadow side.

Awareness. To say, actually, sometimes I've got a monster lurking inside of me, and that's okay. Sometimes I can be really annoying, and that's okay.

Sometimes I can get really angry, and that's okay. Sometimes I can get really frustrated about what's happening. I can get really frustrated about what's happening on this planet.

I feel like lockdowns are totally out of order. I feel like mandatory face masks are totally out of order. I feel it's like a form of child abuse.

When you start to say how you really feel, that's embracing your shadow side. When you stop worrying about what other people think of you, that's embracing your shadow side. So I had to learn that, actually, I wasn't just this saint.

I was also the sinner at the same time. What? Slow motion this side. When we talk of shadow work 101 explained, you have to realize a lot of us, we have unresolved issues.

We have childhood trauma. Unresolved issues, childhood trauma. A childhood trauma I had when I was actually doing the work, the shadow work, was actually because I was always traveling as a child.

I was born in London, but I've lived in West Africa, Sierra Leone. I've lived in Sudan. I've lived in Ethiopia.

I've been all around the world. And because I was always moving around, I never had a home. And that was an unresolved issue I had.

I could never actually be in one place. And it was sometimes hard for me to connect with other people because I'm like, " I've got to move soon." So it's when you realize all of these unresolved issues that you have within yourself and you learn how to make peace with them, this is how to uncover your shadow side.

When you recognize the unresolved issues within yourself, a lot of people have issues of attachment because maybe they were abandoned as children and they feel everyone is going to abandon them. So they really hold on, right? So we have to learn who we are today is a result of who we were yesterday, the traumas we endured. And this is what shadow work is.

It's when you actually go back to your childhood and say, "Okay, that really screwed me up back then, and it's still screwing me up right now, but now I can do something about it." You see, this is how you learn how to integrate your shadow. Every single day, I want you to realize in our society, we think that everything that is dark is negative.

The dark night of the soul. That's so negative, Ralph. No, because in our darkest moments, we become illuminated.

What? Slow motion this side. Like, be honest, deep divers, how many times have you gone through a really dark experience, a really dark day? But afterwards, you're like, "Oh my gosh, I learned so much, Ralph. Oh my gosh, it made me a stronger person."

Oh my gosh, it taught me the biggest lesson of my life. You see, it takes the darkness for us to become illuminated. It takes the darkness for us to become wise.

So we have to form a better relationship to the dark side and realize it's not negative. In fact, it's our biggest friend, our best friend, our biggest helper, because it makes us see things we couldn't see before. If you look at the English language, just poke your nose into a dictionary.

Everything white is good. Everything black is bad. Blackmail, black market.

So, whitelisting. So you have been conditioned and programmed to believe that darkness is something negative, when in actuality, that is your freedom ticket. Because I told you, everything in this matrix is in reverse.

The dark night, only in the dark night can you see the stars shining. I want you to always remind yourself of that. Now, when we talk of shadow work and how we go about it, it's about realizing you have to say the stuff that's scary.

Because suppression is depression. And that's why a lot of people, oh, they're going to be in for a rude awakening once that shadow is let outside of the bag. Because it's going to come out.

It's inevitable. You might have to tell your parents something, but you're afraid. You might have to tell your friends something, but you're afraid to speak up.

Now, this creates an even bigger shadow because they don't really know who you are or how you feel. You see, shadow work begins when you really learn how to open your throat chakra and say what you mean and mean what you say. I do that in every one of my videos.

I regret nothing. What you're seeing, I'm bearing my soul out here and I'm speaking my heart and mind. I don't care what anybody thinks.

Oh my gosh. Yeah. That's the shadow.

And that's why we find the empowerment there. So stop suppressing your emotions, stop biting your tongue. And if you feel a certain way about this whole pandemic, start speaking up and start staying true.

Because it's actually when you realize your shadow side can actually lead to a more authentic life, a life of self-healing. Your shadow side in actuality is your authenticity. Mmm.

What? Slow motion this side. Mmm. And do you know what, Deep Divers? What? I had to leave a fake life to embrace this real life, where I could actually express my shadow side.

Because in that fake life in the matrix, I had to suppress it. Now people know who I really am. Do you know how many friends I have out of the blue? Oh my gosh, Ralph, I've seen your videos.

I didn't know. I didn't know you were like this. You're so inspiring.

You really make me think. Now they know me. I don't know them.

Because they're hiding who they really are. I'm exposing it. Shadow Work 101.

Have a shadow work journal and write in it every single day. Have a shadow work journal and write in it every single day. I want you to write.

I want you to check yourself. Like, because we often feel that we are all angels and saints, when in actuality, we're no different sometimes than other people down the road. Right? Write about all of your flaws.

Write about all of these undesirable aspects of yourself every single day that you notice. You see, once again, once you realize that shadow work begins when you are more mindful of your everyday actions without keyword, without judgment, it's more about acceptance. It's more about being an observer of your daily attitudes and actions.

And the more you observe who you really are, the more you will stumble across who you really are. The more you will begin to know thyself. Know thyself.

And you have to learn never to judge how you feel. Never to judge how you act. Just observe it.

Never to judge how you feel about someone else. It could be really negative. Don't judge it.

Just observe it. And then you'll start to find out, okay, maybe there's some work I need to work on. Like, why am I envious of someone else? That's your shadow side.

Maybe because I'm coming to the realization that I don't have what they have. Okay. Now we're getting somewhere.

Right? So that's what shadow work is. Learn to question. Questioning.

Learn to question why you feel the way you do. Learn to question your actions. Learn to question your beliefs.

Learn to question your motives. I want you to remind yourself every single day. It's not about running from the darkness.

It's about integrating the darkness into yourself. To say, actually, I am the light and I am the darkness. I am the good and I am the bad.

I am the positive and I am the negative. Now we become more authentic, more real. And that's what shadow work is.

It's total integration. Total integration without judgment, guilt, or shame. And to do that, you have to be willing to expose yourself.

You have to be willing to ruin your reputation. You have to be willing to throw yourself into the lion's den and then become the lion. And roar, roar, roar, deep divers.

And then just say, feels so good to be alive, baby. Can I get a hello there? Seven-day vegan challenge. Shout out to everybody who is not only eating leafy greens and fruits and vegetables, but also taking a day off just to stuff their face with vegan junk food.

That's your shadow side. And that's okay. Deep divers, I'm just breathing in that good-ass Prana, baby.

I love all of you deep divers. Shout out to everybody who's been getting the wonderful good-ass Prana shirts at ralphsmartt.com slash clothes and spreadshirt.com. And if you are a sexy-ass model with a whole lot of heart who wants to model the clothing, show me what you got. Deep divers and go and buy some.

Got a question for me, add me on the verified Instagram page at official Ralph Smartt at Infinite Waters and Facebook at Ralph Smartt at Infinite Waters. Check out the bestselling book, Deep Divers for more powerful information like this. Feel alive by Ralph Smartt on Amazon and at ralphsmartt.com slash the book.

It's okay to smile. It's okay to be sad. It's okay to show the world the real you.

Oh my gosh. Yeah. Kind of shocked me too, but that's okay.

Have a beautiful day, deep divers. Peace. Infinite Waters, diving deep.

Once again, stay well, stay healthy. Peace. There's who we show the world.

There's how we see ourselves and there's who we really are. When it comes to shadow work, we must begin to realize that we are sometimes not even who we think we are and we have to allow ourselves to reveal our truth, our true selves to ourselves. And that may not be pretty, could be very ugly, but at least it's the truth.

Have a beautiful day, deep divers. Peace.

Chapter Seventy One

How To Stop Thinking About Someone (Forget Someone You Love)

Peace, infinite waters diving deep once again. We're out here in nature, baby. We've got the birds all around us.

We're in Jurassic Park. We're in a beautiful, tropical, lush rainforest right now. This is sexology.

Water, fire, hot, cold, yin, yang. Daddy's home, we're back. Someone wrote to me saying that they want to stop thinking about someone they love, huh? They're like, Ralph, yes.

I want to forget someone I love, huh? Let's just, woo, breathing in that good-ass prana, baby. And I receive a lot of messages like that. So we're really going to dive into it today.

Is that you out there? They were like, I love this person, but this person has a lot of issues. And we ain't even had breakfast yet. Can I get a hello? So let me share with you what helped me along my early journey, because I was in a similar position when I was in my teenage years.

I wanted to stop thinking about someone. I wanted to forget someone I loved. I was so deeply in love with this person.

And when we weren't together any longer, it's like I couldn't function properly. I would always keep thinking about them. And I wanted to stop it.

I wanted to forget someone I actually cared about, I actually loved. Thank goodness I'm not in that situation any longer, but I learned a lot from the experience and you might be going through it. I'm going to share with you what helped me along my journey.

You see, you don't want to admit it, do you? You don't want to admit how much you miss them. That's why you can't stop thinking about this person, because you are in resistance. Resistance makes stronger.

So you're like, I'll be just fine. I'll be just fine. No, you won't, because you can't stop thinking about them.

So what helped me along my early journey was to admit how much you miss this person, right? Admit how much you miss this person. Say, I miss you so much. Allow yourself to miss this person by saying, I miss you so much.

Don't try to have what I call foolish pride and say, I don't miss this person, but I can't stop thinking about them. I want to forget about someone I love, right? Admit that you miss them and realize it is okay to miss them, right? It is okay to miss people. Look, if you think about someone, really think about them, eventually you'll get bored.

It's just that a lot of us, we don't really think about people. They just pop into our minds. So maybe it's time to start really thinking about this person, right? And that actually helped me along my journey.

Many of us don't even realize it is a privilege to meet someone, a privilege to be in their presence, even if it didn't go the way we want. It's a privilege because out of 7 billion people on planet Earth, you had the privilege to meet me. Are you proud right now? No? Yes? Good.

Right? So along my journey, I always say that I'm grateful that it even happened. It didn't have to happen, but it did. Slow motion this side.

When you learn how to put everything in perspective, you'll say, okay, I can go on to the next chapter of my life knowing that I had the privilege of meeting this wonderful person. And that's actually how to stop thinking about someone and forget someone you love. If you wanna do that, okay? Be grateful for the experience itself.

Now, every single day, we have people around us who actually love us, who actually care for us, yet we spend, have you ever noticed this? We spend our time thinking about people who don't serve us, who don't bring us anything. So what helped me along my journey was to say, okay, right now I'm gonna actually think about people who are serving me, who are helping me become my greatest version. I'm gonna replace those thoughts, right? Of thinking about someone, okay, who isn't serving me with someone who actually is.

Everyone has issues. Everyone is dealing with their own baggage and we have to accept that. We have to accept people as they are and realize nobody is perfect.

Love doesn't have to be perfect. It only has to be real, okay? Now, if we are missing someone, have you ever noticed this, that when you are so engrossed in doing something you love, all thoughts cease, right? Maybe you're dancing around and you actually, for one moment, stop thinking about that person you love, right? And then once that stops, you start thinking about them again. What happened? You became present.

And what's helped me along my journey just in general to stop thinking, in general, right, overthinking, ruminating, right? Harvard studies have shown that overthinking kills productivity. So what's helped me along my journey is to become present. Seven-day vegan challenge alert.

Much love to the beautiful deep divers out there, by the way, right? Making me really hungry, by the way. Okay. Food presence.

Many of us, we're not even eating our food. We are thinking about various other things, therefore allowing ourselves to become disturbed. Now, when we talk of getting rid of someone from your mind that you even love, but you're like, well, they've got way too many issues, ask yourself, are you becoming present when you are eating that beautiful acai bowl, that beautiful quinoa, right? Are you present to your food right now? Because if you're not, of course you're gonna be thinking about someone and thinking about a job and thinking about the future, of course.

But ground yourself in the present moment. And that's what's helped me along my early journey, right? It starts like this. Many of us, we have to become honest and say, would I be any happier with this person? A lot of us, we are in love with the memory.

We are not actually in love with the person. Because if we were, we would still be with them or we would try to make it work. When it comes to forgetting about someone, even though you love them, because you're like, well, Ralph, they've got issues, ask yourself, would you be happier with them? It's what I call the love assumption.

We can never truly know unless we are with them, right? But a lot of the times we might start thinking, actually, I would be a lot happier with them, right? Well, we don't know that, that's an assumption. They could make you more happy or less happy, we don't know. We have to see where we are right now and realize the greatest relationship you can have is with yourself.

Slow motion this side. Other people can enhance our happiness, but it starts with us. You have to really ask yourself, what do I miss about this person? Why do I miss them so much? Well, Ralph, yes, it's because I know, even though they have a lot of issues, okay, they are a great person.

I get it. They are so fantastic, Ralph. Okay, that I can't stop thinking about them.

I get it. But I wanna forget someone I love right now, Ralph. I get it.

Why do you miss them so much? It's the great moments, Ralph. Okay, there are so many great moments all of us have and they are to be cherished. We don't have to forget that.

We don't have to forget that, right? But also realize it wasn't just the good times, it was also, there were also a lot of bad times. So for every beautiful moment you have of yourself with them, also think of a really terrible one. Create balance when you think of them to give you more perspective, more clarity when dealing with the situation, right? So when I was really young, a teenager, I was always just thinking about this person just like the really good things and the highs.

And then I wasn't actually thinking about why it started to fall apart in the first place. You gotta put the spotlight on that to say, okay, I've gotta remember the good times, the highs, but I've also gotta remember the lows, right? And then be proud that you can actually feel. Be proud that you actually miss them because it shows and it speaks a lot about your character that you can actually feel for a, that you could actually feel, that you could actually feel for a person.

There are a lot of people on the planet right now, on planet Earth, who don't feel anything. But because you feel, it shows that you have a great capacity to love someone. So they always say just, if you could love the wrong person this much, imagine how much you can love the right person.

But what if I told you there was no right or wrong person? Just people helping us along our journey to become our greatest versions, right? There are no bad people. It's just that the shoe didn't fit. That's okay.

We are all about finding our complimentary part. Right? So realize that you should be proud that you miss them so much, right? And the prouder you are, the prouder you are, the more easier it is to let go and go on to the next chapter of your life if that's what you wanna do. Many times we don't realize that time heals everything.

Time heals everything. Time heals everything. They are not kidding when they say that.

Just wait a few years and everything would have changed. Can you remember when you were like, I'm never gonna get over this person? Like two years ago and then two years passed, then you're like dancing all over the place. You've moved on.

They've moved on and it's okay, right? So remind yourself that time heals everything and that's the beauty of life. Meet them up. Meet up with them.

See them eye to eye because maybe there is still something more. That's why you can't stop thinking about them. Maybe that's a sign from the universe like maybe you should get together, make some babies, just maybe, right? Maybe you don't have to forget about someone you love.

Maybe you both have to see each other, meet each other, feel each other again to see if there's anything there worth fighting for. Can I get a hello? Okay, and that's what I realized along my journey that like people on planet Earth are so final because we are living in an age of instant gratification. If it doesn't work out, then I'm over.

It's over, I'm bye. What, whatever happened to fixing stuff, to working through stuff? That's what real relationships are about. It's not just peaches and cream.

This ain't a breakfast club. So, what I've realized also along my journey is that not everyone you lose is a loss and more so, it is never a loss when you learn something. Slow motion this side.

So, remind yourself to take from the experience. Be grateful for the experience and learn from the experience. That is how to stop thinking of someone.

That is how to forget someone you love if that's what you wanna do. Learn from this amazing experience that has changed your life forever. Honor it, that is how to move forward.

Right now on the planet, it is a beautiful time. Why? Because many of us are finding ourselves in relationships. Once we see we attract what we are, as we change, the types of people we meet also changes.

And that is a beautiful thing to remind ourselves of. Okay? You begin to let go of someone when you are not in resistance to them. Have a beautiful day.

We just, woo, breathing in that good ass prana, baby. Feels so good to be alive, baby. Can I get a hello? Infinite waters.

Dive in deep once again. Stay well. Stay healthy.

Acknowledgements

A Special Note of Gratitude

A big thank you to all the deep divers who are on this beautiful journey with me on Infinite Waters on the YouTube channel. Your support means everything and I love to inspire you everyday and I will always continue to do so, This is just the beginning and let us remind ourselves anything is possible. Thank you to everyone who has taken the time to read the pages of this book. Continue to remember the world is yours, you can create your own reality and become your greatest versions. Thank you to my family and soul trible. As we all move through this life let us remind we are all connected and it is one humanity. Let us all continue to spread love, because only love is eternal. One love to you all!

"Feel Alive II" by Ralph Smart is a captivating journey to becoming your greatest version and triumphing over any obstacles in your way. Over ten years in the making, this masterpiece explores the hardships of life; love, better habits, overcoming fear, knowing thyself, and becoming the master you came here to be. Ralph delves deep into the human experience, weaving a tapestry of resilience, courage, and the enduring power of hope. From moments of profound darkness to glimmers of radiant light, this evocative narrative invites readers to embark on a journey of self-discovery and transformation. Ralph invites readers to become the heroes and masters of their destinies.

Armed with a wonderful personality, a wealth of empowering experiences and a head full of higher-level knowledge, Ralph Smart has been changing people's lives for the better. His knowledge is backed by years of deep research along with a Bachelor's Degree in Psychology and Criminology. It is amazing to think of how one man can trigger such a big change in the lives of so many people.

Ralph explores the issues that affect people the most. He is tuned in to the needs of the modern human being and offers solutions to the problems that plague mankind. This is the type of guidance that many people seek today. People who grapple with internal conflicts and feelings of low self-worth will find a way out of the doldrums through his words. People who need that extra push to attain their goals will find exactly that in his discussions and those who seek serenity will find it in its purest form. Read this book and find all the tools to live your best life, one without limits; go from the broken you to the limitless you.

MEET THE AUTHOR

Born with a passion for being of service to humanity, Raph has spent the last two decades helping millions to become their greatest version. This inspirational man wears numerous hats including relationship mentor, alchemist, psychologist, criminologist, life coach, author and counsellor.